STANLEY® COMPLETE TILING

Meredith® Books
Des Moines, Iowa

Stanley Complete Tiling
Editor: Ken Sidey
Contributing Writer: Marty Miller
Senior Associate Design Director: Tom Wegner
Photo Researcher: Harijs Priekulis
Copy Chief: Terri Fredrickson
Publishing Operations Manager: Karen Schirm
Edit and Design Production Coordinator: Mary Lee Gavin
Book Production Managers: Pam Kvitne, Marjorie J. Schenkelberg, Rick von Holdt, Mark Weaver
Contributing Copy Editor: Kim Catanzarite
Technical Editor: Pete Bird
Technical Editor, The Stanley Works: Mike Maznio
Contributing Proofreaders: David Craft, David Krause, Courtenay Wolf
Indexer: Donald Glassman
Editorial Assistant: Renee E. McAtee

Additional Editorial Contributions from Art Rep Services
Director: Chip Nadeau
Design: Ik Design
Illustrator: Dave Brandon
Photography: Inside Out Studios
Technical Direction: Dave Morse

Meredith® Books
Editor in Chief: Linda Raglan Cunningham
Design Director: Matt Strelecki
Managing Editor: Gregory H. Kayko
Executive Editor: Benjamin W. Allen

Publisher: James D. Blume
Executive Director, Marketing: Jeffrey Myers
Executive Director, New Business Development: Todd M. Davis
Executive Director, Sales: Ken Zagor
Director, Operations: George A. Susral
Director, Production: Douglas M. Johnston
Business Director: Jim Leonard

Vice President and General Manager: Douglas J. Guendel

Meredith Publishing Group
President, Publishing Group: Stephen M. Lacy
Vice President-Publishing Director: Bob Mate

Meredith Corporation
Chairman and Chief Executive Officer: William T. Kerr

In Memoriam: E.T. Meredith III (1933-2003)

Note to the Readers: Due to differing conditions, tools, and individual skills, Meredith Corporation assumes no responsibility for any damages, injuries suffered, or losses incurred as a result of following the information published in this book. Before beginning any project, review the instructions carefully, and if any doubts or questions remain, consult local experts or authorities. Because codes and regulations vary greatly, you always should check with authorities to ensure that your project complies with all applicable local codes and regulations. Always read and observe all of the safety precautions provided by manufacturers of any tools, equipment, or supplies, and follow all accepted safety procedures.

Acknowledgments
Ceramic Tile Works
Westminster Ceramics
Provenza
Monocibec / Naxos
Stone Design Chicago
Laticrete
SunTouch
Dens-Shield
Durock
Aqua-Mix Sealers
Rubi Cutters
Delta
First Quality Supply
A-1 Minnetonka Rental
Emtek
Nob Hill Decorative Hardware Minnesota
Floors of Distinction
Cutting Edge Tile / North Prairie Tile
RBC Tile
Carpet Mill Connection, Bloomington MN
Wirsbo
Kozy Heat
McCormick Cabinetry
Sunderland Brothers Company

Photography
(Photographers credited may retain copyright © to the listed photographs.
L = Left, R = Right, C = Center, B = Bottom, T = Top
Ron Blakely: 10, 11 (TL), 13 (TL), 32 (B)
Holtorf Photography: Cover, 1
Robert Perron Photography: 9 (TL), 11 (TR), 12 (TL), 12 (TR), 33 (TL), 33 (TC)
Kenneth Rice Photography: 9 (TR), 9 (BL), 9 (BR), 33 (TR)

All of us at Meredith® Books are dedicated to providing you with the information and ideas you need to enhance your home and garden. We welcome your comments and suggestions about this book. Write to us at:
Meredith Corporation
Stanley Books
1716 Locust St.
Des Moines, IA 50309–3023

If you would like more information on other Stanley products, call 1-800-STANLEY or visit us at: www.stanleyworks.com

Library of Congress Control Number: 2004102133
ISBN: 0-696-22113-6

CONTENTS

CONTENTS

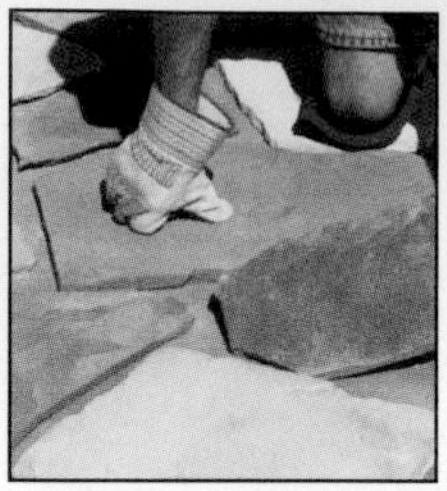

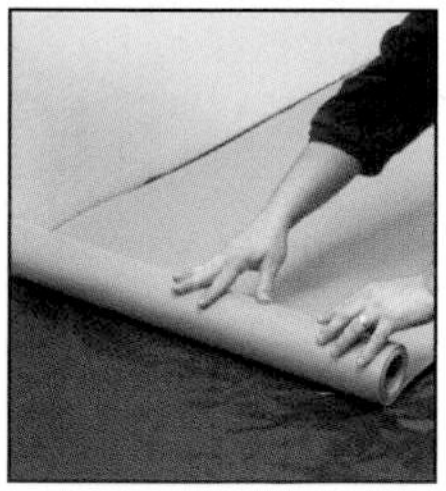

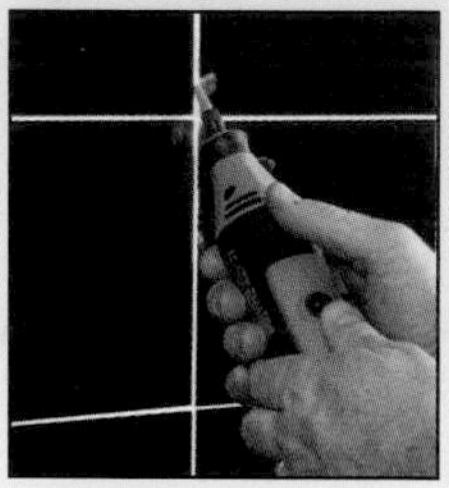

How to Use This Book

Because your success with any tiling project will depend on how familiar you are with all of its aspects, it goes without saying that you should start your project with the first chapter of this book and read at least the first six chapters.

The first two chapters concentrate on design tips and methods for selecting materials—information that will help you choose the right materials for the practical aspects of your project and its style. In fact, a number of illustrated examples are included to get your creativity "cooking," in case you're having a little trouble deciding which kinds of stylistic elements to employ.

The next three chapters contain information that will help you plan your project, carry out essential preparation tasks, and become familiar with basic installation techniques. After that, you're ready to apply your new knowledge to a specific space. "Tiling Floors, Walls, and Countertops" demonstrates installation techniques with photos and descriptions of each step.

Practice makes perfect

If you are a little unsure of your skills, you can take a "practice run" and develop both skills and confidence in any of the projects in "Tiling Special Places"—projects smaller in scope than tiling a full-size room. You'll find similar opportunities in the decorative accents illustrated in the following chapter, "Tiling Decorative Accents," along with step-by-step instructions specific to applications for bathrooms and for outdoor projects.

In general, the first part of this book is devoted to techniques associated with the installation of ceramic tile. Because resilient tile and all of its nonmortared counterparts require specific techniques, separate chapters are devoted to them.

Each project comes with a general introduction and a "Prestart Checklist" that will give you an idea of how much time the project will take and what tools, skills, and materials you need to get started.

What if…?

Because no two projects are alike, you may encounter conditions that depart from the norm. So if the steps shown for any task don't conform to your situation, check the lower half of the page for boxes that provide additional information.

Those labeled "What if… ?" help you apply techniques to specific needs. You'll also find "Stanley Pro Tips," "Refresher Courses," and "Safety First" boxes. These items contain tricks of the trade, quick reviews of methods found elsewhere in the book, and information you need to keep in mind so that your work proceeds safely.

Know your limits

Understanding your limits and the constraints on your time will go a long way toward making your work enjoyable and safe.

Plan your time carefully—make a list of the stages of your work, if necessary. Check the "Prestart Checklist" at the beginning of each project to get an idea of how much time it will take, and allow a little extra if you're new to the business of do-it-yourself home maintenance.

Prepare yourself with contingency plans, especially if you're working on a kitchen or bath. Those rooms might be out of commission while you work on them. Rescheduling showers in the spare bathroom or a family night out at everyone's favorite restaurant might be just the thing to relieve some of the pressure caused by the inconvenience and disruption of the family routine.

Safety First
Plan for safety from the start

Installing tile is a relatively safe home improvement activity. Depending on your project, however, you may be using power tools and working with materials that can pose safety hazards. Keep yourself safe with the following steps:

- Set goals, allow enough time to complete them, and take breaks. Nothing detracts from safety more quickly than fatigue and frustration.
- Make the workplace comfortable. Keep tools spread out but close at hand. Invest in a good tool belt or bucket belt and put each tool back in the same place after using it. Not having to look for a tool saves time and reduces frustration.
- Wear a respirator or high-quality dust mask when sawing wood or tile, or when engaging in any activity that produces airborne dust.
- Eye protection is a must when sawing or chiseling any material. Get the kind of safety glasses with protection on the sides.
- When working with mastics and other fume-producing chemicals, provide plenty of ventilation. Wear a respirator if necessary.
- Save your knees—wear knee pads. Get in the habit of wearing gloves when working. They will not only protect your hands from abrasions and cuts, they'll give you a better grip on tools and materials.
- Make sure you have all the materials and tools you need on hand before you start a project. Running to the home center or hardware store in the middle of a project interrupts the work and can increase your frustration.

DESIGNING YOUR TILE PROJECT

The word "tile" brings to mind a variety of materials and installations—from the hard, durable finish of ceramic tile found in kitchens and bathrooms to the soft, versatile surfaces of carpet and cork tile used on living room and playroom floors.

The word, in fact, has a long history, originating from an old European word for "covering," and perhaps first applied to hard-bodied, fired clay products—ceramics. As new materials have been developed, people constantly find new applications for the word, using it most often to describe any material manufactured for covering surfaces, made and applied in individual, modular units.

For many homeowners "tile" also means a material that requires installation by a professional, someone with years of practice and on-the-job experience. Although that may have been true in the past, new materials and techniques make tile installation well within the reach of any homeowner with moderate skills. Installing any kind of tile does take patience, but armed with the right information, most homeowners can install a professional-looking project they will be proud of.

That's where this book comes in. *Complete Tiling* contains all the information you'll need for virtually any kind of tile project: ceramic, parquet, resilient, or even cork and carpet tile. You'll find tips for designing your project, as well as inspirational examples you can use in your own home. You'll learn about the different kinds of materials and what each is best suited for. You'll discover methods for making specific plans. Perhaps most important, you'll find everything you need to know about installing and maintaining the material of your choice so your project yields years of service.

You may think of tile primarily as a covering for kitchen floors and baths, but you can use almost any kind of tile in any room of the house. It functions just as well in family rooms, dining rooms, bedrooms, and home offices. Installing tile is cost-efficient; its initial expense is paid back in the form of reduced maintenance and replacement costs. Large floor installations can add to the resale value of a home.

Tile can dramatically change the look of any room, and when properly installed, it will last a lifetime.

CHAPTER PREVIEW

Start compiling a folder of information as you're planning your tiling project. Save clippings from home decorating magazines, brochures with photos of installations in designer homes, and color charts from home centers. All of this material will help you make informed design decisions.

Basic Principles Of Design

In its simplest terms, design is a mood or look that is both visually appealing and physically comfortable. Design, however, does not start with aesthetics. It begins with decisions about how you want to use a room. After that, you employ a style that corresponds to that use.

For example, bedrooms are usually restful; dining rooms are comfortable and inviting; children's playrooms are colorful and active; and kitchens are functional and organized. No matter what surface you will be tiling, make sure your choice of style is consistent with your intended uses for that room. A family room, for example, may call for a boldly stated tile design. In a formal dining or living room, you may want the tiled surface to blend into the surroundings.

Definitions of style

Style is categorized under two broad terms—formal and informal. Formal styles are characterized by symmetrical patterns, straight lines, right angles, and strictly geometric figures. Informal styles rely on curved lines, irregular edges, and random or asymmetrical patterns of decorative accents. A formal design conveys organization and order. An informal design is casual and free.

Within these broad categories are variations based on nationality, geography, and historical period. French, Art Deco, Southwestern, and contemporary are examples. Don't be overly concerned with terms or formulas—they may influence you to choose a style with which you might not feel comfortable.

Trust your intuition

Use your intuition as a guide when designing your tile project. Although modern trends in interior design, especially for floors, tend to favor muted or neutral colors, there's nothing that says you can't bend or break the rules to create a room with the right character and individuality.

Stick with your own ideas and incorporate the principles outlined in this chapter—color, form, pattern, texture, and scale—to achieve the look you want.

Formal tile installations, although characterized by regular geometric shapes and symmetrical arrangement of their elements, can still look lively and exciting. By carefully offsetting the tones of the wall tile with the sides of the tub surround, the homeowners have created an alternating pattern of light and dark vertical tile lines. The rectangular pattern is tastefully interrupted by the inset borders, complementing the classical look and creating a visual highlight that makes the room appear comfortable and stately at the same time.

STANLEY Pro Tip

Choose a style that suits you

Discovering a style that best expresses your personality can be a confusing process. Here are some steps that will help you:

- Read home decorating magazines and books. Gather photos of tile installations that appeal to you. Put your clippings in a folder.
- When you visit friends' homes, pay close attention to locations where they have used tile. Make mental notes of colors and other decorative aspects—both things you like and those you don't like. Ask your friends about the advantages and disadvantages of the materials. When you get home, jot down your impressions and put your notes in the folder too.
- Visit tile suppliers, home furnishings stores, decorating showrooms, and home improvement outlets. File material samples, brochures, and paint chips in your folders.
- When you're ready to plan your tiling project, go through your collection of design ideas. As you study them, you'll notice that certain themes emerge—colors, textures, and patterns that appeal to you. Make notes about these features and select those you think will look best on the surface you plan to tile.
- Design the installation around these themes, modifying colors, patterns, and textures to suit the room and its uses.

Informal layouts, with curved outlines and irregular contours, can be difficult to design, but tile can prove especially helpful in solving such problems. In this shower area, the broken tile pattern and random colors create a contemporary Southwestern background in which the large showerhead is a perfect accent.

Period design doesn't have to slavishly follow a formula. This updated Arts and Crafts kitchen incorporates light slate-colored tile as a contrast to the period lighting and the simple but contemporary lines of the cabinetry. Notice how the orientation of the tile changes from the countertop to the wall. Such subtle alterations and the thin linear accent on the wall help personalize the kitchen.

A country design scheme is a variation of an informal style that often combines warm and bright textures. Glazed terra-cotta floor tile and wide grout lines create a contrast that highlights the painted cabinets and refinished antique table. Area or throw rugs make a tile floor feel warmer underfoot.

A contemporary design scheme will include many of the elements of a formal design style, as this kitchen demonstrates with its simplicity and straightforward, uncluttered lines. Contrasts are evident here, especially in the multicolored backsplash, which energizes the uniform natural finish on the cabinets.

DESIGNING WITH COLOR

Color is the most noticeable design element in a room; therefore it's the one that must be used with the most care. Review the photographs on these pages to see how the attributes of color work together to help create a particular mood. Keep these guidelines in mind to make your color selection easier.

■ Ignore color names. They can influence you more than you think. Take sample tiles of several colors home with you.

■ Trust your impulses. They indicate a preference for a certain color.

■ Samples will look different on the surface than in your hand. Set them on the floor or countertop, or tape them to the wall.

■ Check colors at different times of the day and under different lighting. Sunlight will give the truest hue. Incandescent light adds a pinkish tone. Fluorescents may change the hue completely.

Experiment with color combinations, but remember that restraint is a good tool to use when mixing colors. Too much harmony turns bland, and a combination that's too dynamic becomes jarring.

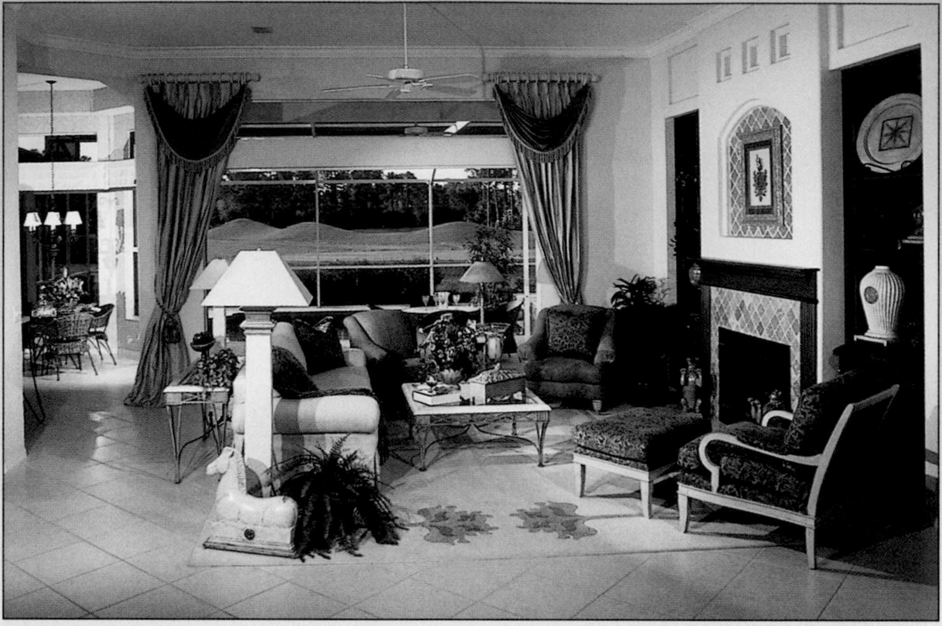

Neutral colors or color schemes with low contrasts create a subtle background for other design elements in the room. In this eclectic blend of several styles, the light floor tile allows the furnishings to take center stage, highlighting the subtle differences in the tones of the curtains and the overstuffed chairs. At the same time, the floor complements the light tones in the rest of the room: the walls, lamps, comfortable couch, and coffee table. The whole interplay of similar colors and subtle contrasts opens up the room, adding to the spaciousness of the view through the divided picture window.

The vocabulary of color

HUE

WARM TONES

COOL TONES

EARTH TONES

Here are some terms you might hear when discussing the color of your tile with suppliers or decorators.

■ Hue is a pure color. Hue refers to a primary color by its name—red, blue, yellow.

■ Value defines the relative brightness of a hue. Colors of lower value (a murky red, for example) usually recede and make a room seem smaller. Those with high values (a bright green, for example) tend to stand out and can make a room appear airy and larger.

■ Tone describes whether the color is darkened (a shade) or lightened (a tint).

All of these aspects of color will work together to create a surface that either dominates a room or acts as a backdrop. A pattern with high contrasts (a checkerboard white on black tile, for example) calls attention to itself and not to the other elements in the room. Pastel tiles or tiles with earth tones allow other features of the room to stand out.

Certain colors tend to evoke certain moods.

■ Reds and oranges create excitement; darker shades of both colors create warmth.

■ Yellows and whites are cheery—use them to brighten up a dark room. Too much of either, however, may be overpowering or sterile.

■ Greens and blues create calm; deep tones evoke associations with wealth, strength, and status.

■ Black is the universal contrast. It makes large rooms appear smaller.

Contrasts create interest. Tiling a surface with colors that contrast sharply, either within the tile pattern itself or with other colors in the room, will tend to call attention to the tiled surface. Here the blue glazed tiles and wide grout lines call attention to themselves, making the two-tiered countertop the focal point of the entire kitchen.

Borders can create contrasts in a design scheme, either with contrasting colors or with geometric patterns that accentuate or depart from the pattern of the field tile. Both elements come into play in this bathroom design. This black and white border both frames the large mirror and accents the square edges of the room.

Low, dense colors tend to make a room seem smaller. Although the predominant blue tones in this kitchen offer a cool contrast to the wood flooring and tiled wall, they also make the room seem dark, confined, and uninviting. When designing a room with little window light, use low-value colors sparingly or not at all.

High, bright color values help make a room appear larger. Here the yellow wall tile and neutral white cabinets not only open up the appearance of the room, they also unify the pattern of tones and architecture of shapes in the room—the rectangular cabinets, the rounded island, and the triangular range hood.

DESIGNING WITH SCALE, PATTERN, AND TEXTURE

After you have chosen the color scheme for your tiling project, turn your attention to the size of the tile (its scale relative to the room size), the pattern in which you will set it, and the textures. All will affect the atmosphere you create.

Scale your project to the size of the surface so the tiles will seem balanced. Tile size and pattern can dramatically alter the appearance of a room.

Choose patterns consistent with your style and textures that will enhance it. The rough, uneven surface of handmade pavers, for example, can impart a rustic feel to a Southwestern or colonial design. For a more formal effect, set machine-made pavers with a smooth surface and precise edges. Use glazed tiles on your countertop and walls to brighten the area. Vary the texture within wall designs with embossed floral accent tiles interspersed in the field. Or cap the layout behind a formal cabinet with engraved border tiles.

Squares create a formal appearance, but that doesn't mean your design has to be stiff. The lemon-tree insert on the back wall of this range hood breaks up the uniformity of the glazed wall tile with color and texture. Do-it-yourself accent patterns like this are available in kits.

Patterns can define the mood of a room as effectively as color. Like color, they require careful application. To avoid being overly repetitive, alternate rows with tile of a slightly varied pattern and tone. Patterns soften hard corners and make decorating nooks and crannies easier.

ALTER THE APPEARANCE OF A ROOM
The effect of scale and pattern

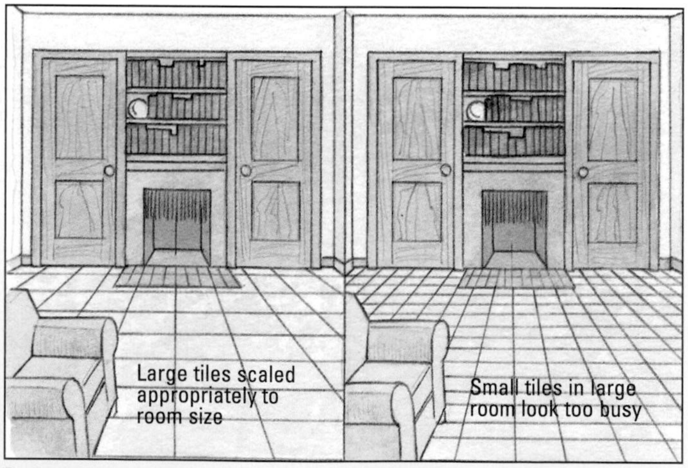
Large tiles scaled appropriately to room size
Small tiles in large room look too busy

Both scale and pattern can have dramatic effects on the perceived size of the room and on its ambience. Large tiles tend to call attention to themselves and can make a room look smaller. They look best in large rooms. Small tiles tend to get lost in a large room. They look more appropriate in a small area.

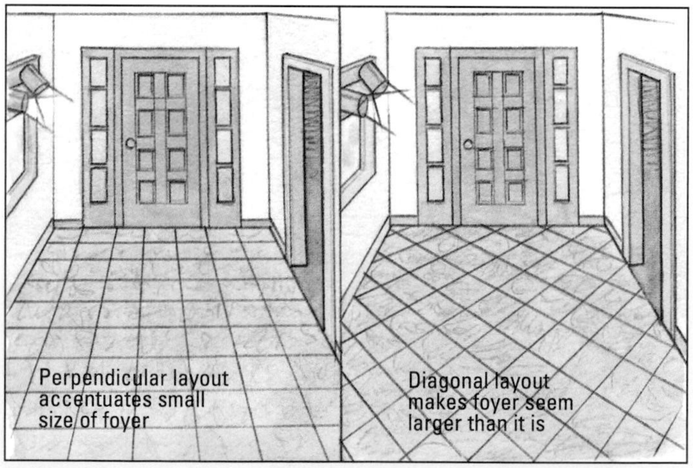
Perpendicular layout accentuates small size of foyer
Diagonal layout makes foyer seem larger than it is

A diagonal pattern distracts the eye from the perimeter of the room and works wonders in making a small area seem larger than it is. Small patterns can add an air of informality. Large formal and informal patterns can function as decorative accents.

Texture helps make a room feel relaxed. The rough textures of this floor tile are complemented by the rough herringbone pattern and enhanced by careful placement of different color tones. Such textures soak up light, enhancing the informal mood of this family room and home office.

Glazes present a smooth texture that brightens up a room, regardless of the color of the tile. Rectangular wall tiles set in a horizontal running bond pattern lend elegance to this bathroom. The period feeling is enhanced by the embossed border tile capped off with a curved trim.

Slate makes an excellent floor for all rooms, especially entryways. Its neutral surface acts as a background for any design scheme, and its naturally rough surface provides a built-in nonslip safety feature. Slate is also durable. Hard slates are easy to maintain; softer Indian slates require sealer

SAFETY FIRST
Texture and safety

Texture contributes to the design of your tiled surface and is an important safety feature as well.

Make sure that tiles laid on bathroom and kitchen floors—areas that are likely to get wet and slippery—have a nonslip surface to reduce the risk of falling. Avoid high-gloss glazed tile in these areas. If glazed tile is necessary, select one whose surface contains carbide chips or is otherwise designated as a nonslip tile. For stair treads, install a tile with a built-in tread.

Help with design
Don't be afraid to ask questions. Many home centers retain professional designers on staff.

STANLEY PRO TIP: Evenly spaced tiles save money

Save money on your tile project by installing tile whose dimensions fit as evenly as possible on the surface you are designing. An evenly spaced layout means fewer cut tiles, less waste, and less installation time. Measure the room and divide both its length and width by the combined width of the tile and grout joint. A slightly larger or smaller pattern that still meets your design requirements may be a better choice than a tile size that requires many cut edges. Changing the width of the grout joint also affects how the tile fits in the room.

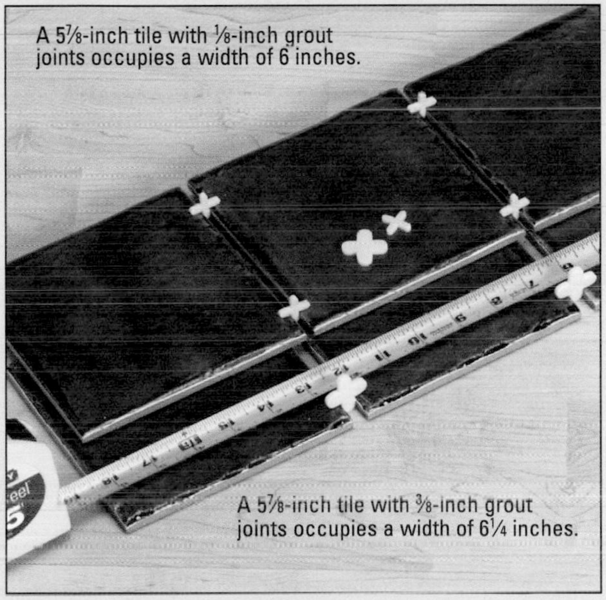

A $5\frac{7}{8}$-inch tile with $\frac{1}{8}$-inch grout joints occupies a width of 6 inches.

A $5\frac{7}{8}$-inch tile with $\frac{3}{8}$-inch grout joints occupies a width of $6\frac{1}{4}$ inches.

A GALLERY OF STYLE

Mixing sizes of tiles, especially within the same color family, creates a pleasing overall effect in a small bathroom such as this. The larger limestone tile squares on the floor counterbalance the mosaic tiles used on the walls. Listellos (page 29) and liner tiles create a chair-rail effect that provides a divider between the tile wainscoting on the lower walls and paper on the upper portion of the walls.

Glass tiles in 12 colors create a colorful, fun shower enclosure in this children's bathroom. Confining the tiles to the shower area keeps the splash of color from overwhelming the room. Glass tile is generally translucent and available in myriad colors, so it provides almost endless design possibilities.

A random pattern of square tiles in three colors lends punch to a field of cream-color tiles in this small bathroom. The floor tiles are laid in a diagonal pattern that echoes the angle of the sloping ceiling, and that visually expands the space. Using colorful tiles in a field of neutral tiles, as shown here, is a simple and inexpensive way to prevent a room from looking bland.

Marble-like tiles make a striking statement in this master bathroom. Natural stone tile such as marble, granite, and slate that has been dimensioned—cut to a uniform size—can be installed much like ceramic tile. Porcelain tile is an alternative to stone tile and is available in finishes that are difficult to distinguish from natural stone.

Travertine tiles cover this shower enclosure and bathroom floor. The wall tiles are set on a diagonal, while the floor tiles feature a herringbone pattern. Varying the size, shape, and pattern of the tiles, yet keeping the tile material and color family consistent, as in this bathroom, produces visual interest without making the space look busy or visually distracting.

Terra-cotta-color saltillo floor tiles cover this outdoor patio room. Smaller, 4×4-inch cobalt blue tiles arranged throughout the floor offer spots of color. To protect the tiles, they were coated with a penetrating water sealer and then finished with another penetrating sealer that brings out the color and adds a low sheen.

Tile is a natural choice for an attractive and durable pool surround. To minimize the danger of a slippery surface, select tiles that have a low-gloss finish and that are slip-resistant, especially in an application that will frequently be wet. For a poolside or other application in which tiles will be subject to almost constant moisture, it is also important to select impervious or vitreous tile that will absorb very little water.

A GALLERY OF STYLE *(continued)*

Hand-painted tiles form a suitable mural above the range in this French country-inspired kitchen. As a more affordable alternative, ready-made tile murals are available in a variety of designs and sizes at many home improvement centers and tile suppliers.

Decorative tiles accent the off-white field tiles in this kitchen backsplash and form a border both for the backsplash and island countertop. Wall and countertop tiles are generally available with coordinating trim tiles to neatly turn corners and provide a smooth countertop edge.

Blue and white hexagonal tiles on the countertop and backsplash give this vintage kitchen much of its charm and style. Though this pattern is generally reserved for floor tiles, the floor-grade quality of the tile makes it a tough, durable work surface. In general, floor-grade tiles can be used in wall and countertop installations, but wall-grade tile will not withstand the wear of a floor application.

Colorful glass tiles create a whimsical backsplash that contrasts with the dark concrete countertops in this kitchen. The backsplash features 1- and 2-inch squares of recycled glass tiles in a mix of opaque, translucent, and iridescent finishes in a random pattern that forms part of a larger modular design.

Vinyl tile installed in a classic black-and-white checkerboard pattern is an affordable, durable, and easy-care option for this dining area. If you've overlooked vinyl flooring in the past, now is the time to consider it as a viable flooring option. Vinyl tiles are available in many styles, patterns, and even custom designs. Vinyl can also mimic the look of much more expensive flooring options, such as stone or wood, at a fraction of the cost.

Here blue and white tiles are grouped in blocks of four and set on a diagonal to create a cheery backdrop to the crisp white cabinets. Before beginning any tile installation, plot your design on graph paper and do a dry run to avoid unnecessary cuts and small pieces of tile.

Create additional space for guests by converting an unused garage or basement into an inviting room. Brick tiles in this former garage provide a durable flooring surface. Before installing brick tile over an existing concrete pad, patch any small cracks with a concrete patching compound. Use a self-leveling or patching compound to even out low spots.

Parquet wood tile offers a warm backdrop for this dining area filled with country charm. Parquet tile is available in numerous geometric patterns and sizes and can be composed of a variety of woods, offering almost endless design opportunities. Because it is moisture-sensitive, parquet does not work well in bathrooms. To preserve its natural beauty, this type of floor tile should be properly sealed and finished.

CHOOSING THE RIGHT MATERIALS

Ceramic, vinyl, or parquet? Cork or carpet? What substrate? Which adhesive? The more you know about the various kinds of tile, the easier it will be for you to answer these questions and design and install a practical and durable surface.

In this chapter, you'll find information about different kinds of tile and learn which material works best in different settings. You'll read about membranes, mortars, and mastics, which, along with substrates, provide the foundation for the tile.

How to shop for tile

When you begin to look for tile, don't start with a list of materials. First, ask yourself, "How do I want to use this space?" The answer to that question will help determine what kind of tile and other materials to use.

Make a list of the characteristics needed for the area. Does it have to be waterproof? Will it need to stand up to a lot of heavy traffic? Do you want it to feel comfortable and cozy?

Then consider your budget. High-traffic areas, such as a foyer, call for the durability of ceramic tile. But if your bank account won't accommodate a ceramic floor, solid vinyl tile is a tough and affordable alternative. In the kids' room, carpet tile can help quiet the noise of children's play, and stained or damaged sections can be easily replaced.

After considering the uses of a room, make some general decisions about how you want the space to look. Then go shopping at several suppliers. Compare prices and take samples home. Fit them in a trial layout; if they don't work, go back and borrow other samples.

Ask plenty of questions and choose a supplier who can provide answers about the permeability, durability, and maintenance of any tile you choose.

Look for an outlet that will lend or rent tools. A store that offers how-to seminars will likely provide good service after a sale. Purchase all the tiles and materials you need from the same supplier. That way you will be assured of consistent information and compatibility among the products you choose.

Tile terms

The terminology used to describe tiles and materials may vary among suppliers and from region to region. Porcelain tile, for example, may mean large, modern floor tile to one supplier and small, hexagonal mosaics to another. What one dealer calls an "isolation membrane" may be a "slip sheet" to another. Clarify specifics as you go, so you know what you're buying.

Many tile sizes are listed as nominal, not actual measurements. The actual size of a 6×6 tile, for example, may be 5⅞×5⅞ inches, which allows for the width of the grout joint.

A little study and planning will provide all the know-how you need to select tile for any project.

CHAPTER PREVIEW

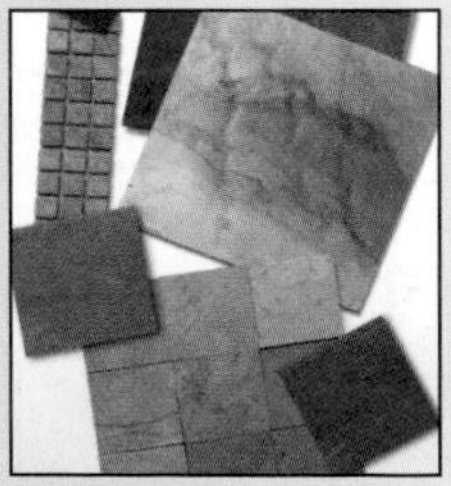

Selecting materials for a new tiling installation can be an adventure. Visit as many general and specialty stores as time permits. This will give you a broad base of information and may provide you with additional options and ideas for your projects.

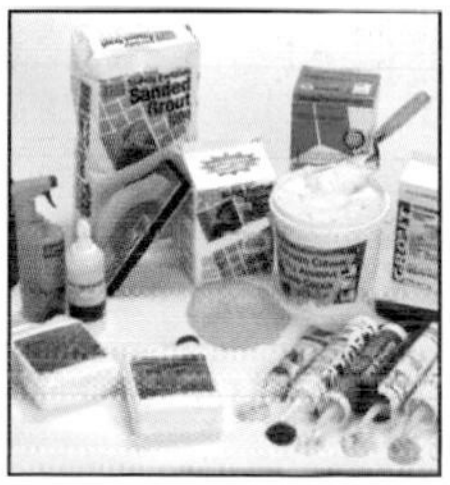

CERAMIC AND CEMENT-BODIED TILE

Ceramic and cement-bodied tiles are the hardest and most durable members of the tile family.

Ceramic tile

The term ceramic refers to any hard-bodied material made chiefly from clay and hardened by firing at high temperatures. Most modern ceramic tiles contain a mixture of refined clay, ground shale or gypsum, and other ingredients that reduce the shrinkage of the tile as it's fired.

Once mixed with water, the clay body of the tile (or its *bisque*) gets its shape by being squeezed into a mold, pressed into a die, or cut like cookies from sheets. From there, temperatures from 900°F to 2,500°F harden the bisque. Most ceramic tiles are fired at about 2,000°F. In general, higher temperatures produce a denser tile. Most unglazed tiles are fired only once, but some are fired twice. Those with decorative glazes are fired up to five times. The more firings, the higher the cost.

Other hard-bodied tile

In addition to high-fired clay products, you'll find a host of other hard-bodied tiles. Some, such as *brick veneer,* originate from clay mixtures fired at lower temperatures than ceramic tiles. Others, such as *saltillo* tiles, are handmade from unrefined clay and bonding agents and don't get fired at all—they are sun-dried or allowed to dry in low-temperature kilns. *Cement-bodied tiles* are made from a mortar-and-sand mix that cures in a chemical reaction.

Some of these nonceramic varieties have specific uses and come with a few restrictions. For example, most imitation brick veneer is too soft for floors but is a great choice for walls. Handmade tiles, such as saltillo, have a rough texture. Their natural imperfections can add rustic charm, but they also absorb water readily. That relegates them to indoor use, and they still require sealing. Cement-bodied tiles are a less expensive, long-lasting look-alike for ceramics that work well in many kinds of applications.

Quarry tile, extruded and fired at high temperatures, is semivitreous or vitreous. Made in $\frac{1}{2}$- to $\frac{3}{4}$-inch thicknesses, it is fired unglazed with bisques in many colors, sizes, and shapes: 4- to 12-inch squares and hexagons, and 3×6-inch or 4×8-inch rectangles.

Porcelain tile, made of highly refined clay and fired at extremely high temperatures, absorbs virtually no moisture. Porcelain tiles may be glazed or unglazed. Sizes range from 1×1-inch mosaics to large 24×24-inch pieces, some with stone-look patterns.

Choosing tile for different locations

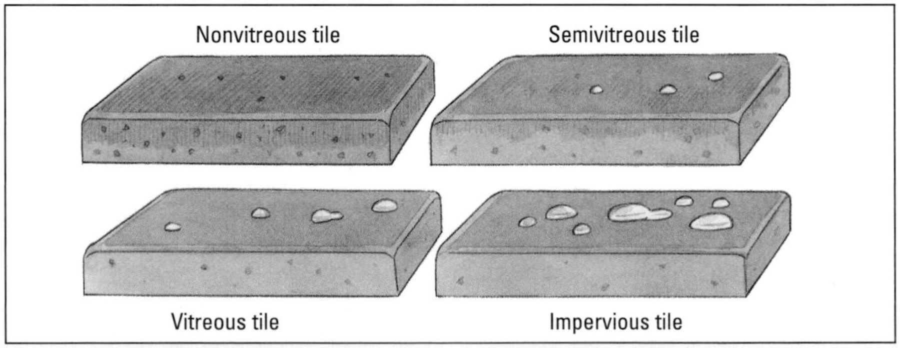

Tile varies in its ability to absorb water, and its vitreosity should be a factor in choosing tile for different locations.

Nonvitreous tile can absorb more than 7 percent of its weight in water and is not suitable for areas that will get wet.

Semivitreous tile has an absorption rate of 3 to 7 percent—good for family rooms but not desirable for outdoor use.

Vitreous tile is dense; it absorbs only 0.5 to 3 percent of its weight in water. You can install it in almost any location.

Impervious tile is almost completely water-resistant. It is more commonly found in hospitals, restaurants, and other commercial installations rather than residential settings.

Terra-cotta tile, though technically not a ceramic because it is fired at low temperatures, is a low-density, nonvitreous tile suitable for dry areas. Its surface defects add to its charm. Available sealed or unsealed, it comes in squares from 3 to 12 inches and in other geometric shapes.

Cement-bodied tile, a cured sand-and-mortar mix, is a nonvitreous tile with excellent durability. Some look rough-hewn, others sport smooth finishes. Available in squares or rectangles from about 6 to 9 inches and in mesh-backed paver sheets (up to 36 inches) that mimic cleft stone.

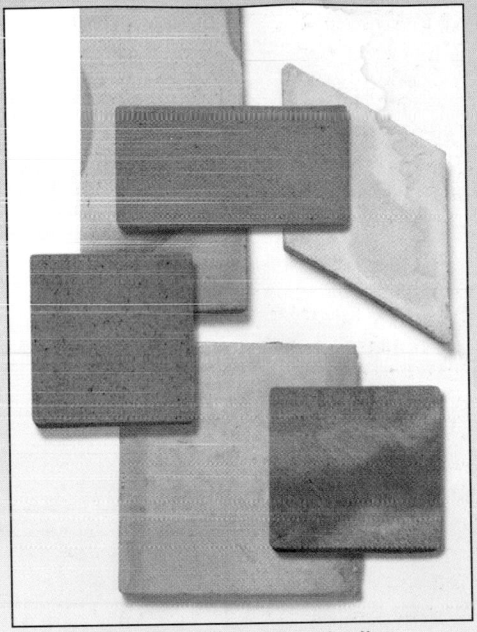

Saltillo tile is not a true ceramic tile because it is dried, not fired. Nevertheless it is treated as a ceramic tile and enjoys wide use in rustic and Southwestern designs. Available in squares, rectangles, octagons, and hexagons, from 4 to 12 inches, it is a low-density, nonvitreous product.

Tile technical terms

As you make decisions about tile purchases, you may encounter the following terms associated with tile manufacturing:
Bisque: The clay body of the tile. Bisque that is "green" has not yet been fired.
Cured: Describes bisque dried naturally or in low-temperature kilns.
Extruded: A process in which wet clay is squeezed under pressure into a mold
Fired: Bisque hardened in high temperatures.
Glaze: A hard, thin layer of pigment applied to the tile to give it color and protection.
Vitreosity: The resistance of a tile to water absorption, ranging from nonvitreous (very absorbent) to impervious (almost completely water-resistant).

Glazes

Glazes made of lead silicates and pigments brushed or sprayed onto the surface of the tile add both color and protection. Some glazes are applied to the bisque before it's fired. Others go on after the first firing and are fired again. Single-fired tiles exhibit greater strength and durability. Additives introduced to the glaze will provide the surface of the tile with a texture.

Glazed tiles are water-resistant, but the grout joints between them are not. Even when grouting tiles with a latex- or polymer-modified grout *(page 38)*, you should seal the joints.

Unglazed tiles soak up water and always need sealing to prevent water from penetrating them and damaging the adhesive or surface below.

STONE TILE

Stone cut from local quarries was likely the first tile used in ancient construction, and the qualities that made it desirable then—an unending variety of colors, patterns, and textures—are the same ones people admire now. Today stone tile is cut with diamond blades from slabs and polished (gauged stone) or split by hand from large sections of rock (cleft).

Gauged stone is fairly uniform in size and thickness. Cleft stone is irregular. You'll find highly polished, matte, and flamed finishes (which gives the surface a coarse texture), as well as roughed-up tumbled stone.

Not all stone is tough enough for floors, and it's not rated by density like ceramics. Four grades, however, indicate its tendency to break *(page 33)*. Exercise caution when cutting stone tile.

Most varieties are sold as 3- to 12-inch squares, but 4×2-inch rectangles and 2×2-foot squares are becoming increasingly popular. Oversize tiles make striking design elements and also make installation go more quickly.

Marble, granite, and slate are the most popular stone tiles, and like anything natural they're prone to damage and color changes. Buy extra tiles, and when you get the boxes home, examine each tile for damage and consistency of color. Don't be afraid to return a tile that detracts from the beauty of your installation.

Substrates for stone tile

All tile must be set on a surface that's smooth and free of deflection. A substrate of ½-inch backerboard laid over ¾-inch plywood will provide sufficient stability to keep stone tile and its grout joints from cracking.

Installation of such a substrate, however, increases the height of the floor and is often impractical in existing construction. In addition, the combined weight of substrate, mortar, and stone tile may exceed the structural limitations of the subfloor. Stone tile weighs considerably more than ceramic tile, so before you commit yourself to a stone floor, engage the services of a structural engineer or architect. An inexpensive deflection test will tell you quickly if your subfloor is up to the job.

Marble colors range from almost pure white to nearly black, with shades of pink, gray, and green in between. Some varieties are dense and vitreous; others are soft and absorbent. Be sure to consider how much wear your marble tile will be subject to before making a purchase.

Granite is the hardiest of the stone tile family. Its density is the same as vitreous ceramic tile, so it can withstand freezing conditions, resist staining, and stand up to heavy use. These qualities make it extremely versatile; it's well suited for floors, walls, and countertops.

Tumbled stone is marble or slate that has been roughened by abrasives and acids. The result is a dimensioned tile with a rough-hewn texture, accentuated veining, and rounded edges. It can add classic or rustic character. Tumbled stone must be sealed to prevent staining.

Agglomerates are formed from a mixture of stone dust and epoxy resin. The mix is molded, hardened, and then polished to a high gloss. It is a manufactured stone, and not as durable as the natural material from which it came. It is, however, less expensive than natural stone tile.

Slate originates from petrified mud, and although some varieties are as soft as marble, others are as hard as granite. It comes in a surprising variety of greens, grays, and blues, which are often installed in quiltlike patterns. Its slightly ridged surface makes harder species ideal for floors.

Limestone and sandstone come in a wide variety of muted colors and offer a rustic look. As sedimentary rocks, both are porous and vary in hardness, so make sure you're purchasing a stone suitable for long wear when planning to install it on a floor.

Quartzite is sandstone that has been buried deep in the earth, where pressure and high temperatures have fused its minerals into an extremely hard and weather-resistant rock. Like marble, quartzite comes in many colors, but in pure form is a light neutral color.

Cutting stone tile

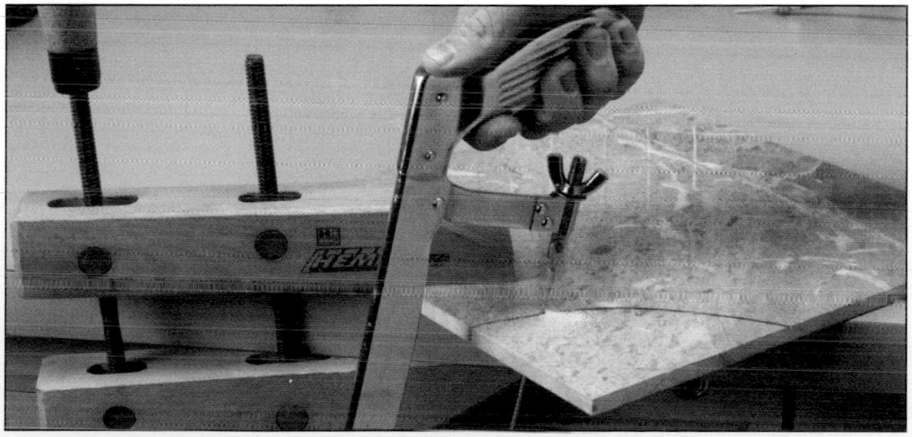

Unlike ceramic tile, stone fractures unpredictably, so you can't cut it with a snap cutter or trim it with a tile nippers. Make straight cuts in stone tile with a wet saw or a small stone saw equipped with a diamond blade *(page 108)*. Cut curves with a rod saw and carbide blade. To make curved cuts, mark the cut line on the tile with a china marker (felt-tip markers may bleed into the surface). Support the tile on a firm surface and cut along the line with the rod blade. Go slowly to avoid splitting the cutout. Smooth exposed edges with a rubbing stone.

STANLEY PRO TIP

Choose grouts and sealers that match the materials

Because granite and marble look best with thin joints or no joints at all, and slates can tolerate both wide and narrow grouting, your choice of grout depends on the material you use.

Fill thin joints with an epoxy adhesive or grout (use unsanded grouts to avoid scratches). Epoxy fillers are good for countertops because they create waterproof joints.

Sealers enhance the looks of stone tile and protect tiles from stains. Marble, slate, limestone, and sandstone generally require sealing. Granite does not. Some sealers produce mirror-like glosses; others leave low-luster mattes. Ask a tile dealer to recommend a sealer compatible with your tile and its uses. Better yet, apply a penetrating sealer or an impregnator, which doesn't leave a coating on the surface and lasts longer.

NONMORTARED TILE

Ceramic and stone tile are mortared to their supporting surfaces, but the remaining members of the tile family—vinyl, parquet, laminate, cork, carpet, and metal tiles—adhere to substrates with mastics. Mastics are chemical compounds—generally liquids. Depending on how they're made, they are applied with a trowel, roller, or brush.

Nonmortared tiles offer increased design options at various prices. Resilient tile, generally the least expensive, can give you a floor that looks like wood, stone, or ceramic tile at a fraction of the cost of the natural materials. Parquet brings the warmth of wood into a room and adds patterns not offered by solid wood flooring. Laminates, slightly more expensive than resilient tile, wear like iron and can mimic everything from wood to abstract designs. Cork is the most environmentally friendly of all materials, and its natural variations guarantee a one-of-a-kind design. Carpet tiles add comfort underfoot, and although their pile is not as deep as broadloom carpet, they wear extremely well.

Choosing the right tile

Most nonmortared tiles are useful in several rooms. Make sure your tile choice matches the room you'll install it in.

Resilient—playrooms, family rooms, bathrooms, kitchens, almost any room where durability and affordability matter.

Parquet—living rooms, dining rooms, kitchens (if properly sealed), any room in which durability and style are paramount. Cannot be used below grade.

Laminate—any room in which durability is required at an affordable cost. Can be used in rooms below grade.

Cork—living rooms, dining rooms, bedrooms; any room that requires a unique floor style, where sound insulation is preferred, or where cost is not an impediment. Not for rooms below grade, bathrooms, or kitchens.

Carpet—living rooms, playrooms, dining rooms, bedrooms, any room in which comfort is primary. Not as many design choices as other materials. Cannot be used below grade.

Resilient tile comes in many forms, which vary in the amount of vinyl they contain and in their durability. Solid vinyl is more resilient, boasts more patterns, and costs more than composites. Vinyl composition tiles usually come with self-stick backings. Patterns are plentiful. Cushioned vinyl dents easily.

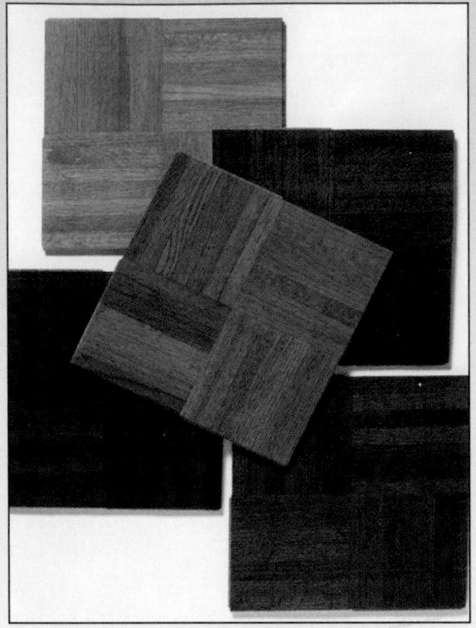

Parquet is an assembly of wood strips (called fillets) laminated into tiles. It comes in both unfinished and prefinished units, usually in 12-inch squares, though other geometric shapes are available. Flat edges result in a smooth surface. Beveled edges add texture to the floor design.

Metal tiles of stainless steel, aluminum, copper, brass, bronze, and even titanium are finding their way into design styles for kitchens, family rooms, and entryways, often as accents. Metal tiles come at a premium cost, but no other material can duplicate their contemporary appearance. Some metal tiles are made for mastic installation, others must be installed in thinset mortar, making them excellent companions for ceramic tile.

Interlocking tiles are the answer if you want a tiled surface in the garage or basement and you don't have the time or the resources for a permanent installation. Made of a flexible version of the same PVC used to make plumbing pipes, these tiles snap together with tabs molded on the sides of each piece. They are available in a variety of solid bright colors and embossed patterns.

Laminate tile, composed of layers of wood topped off with an extremely hard melamine coating, combines numerous design options with durability and moderate cost. Its patterns—stone, ceramic tile, and wood—are printed with a photographic process below the wear layer so they won't wear off.

Cork tile brings rich textures, numerous patterns, and a soft feel underfoot to floor installations. It resists dents and adds both thermal and acoustic insulation. Cut from the bark of the cork oak, which regrows in about nine years, cork is primarily used for floors but makes an excellent wall covering.

Carpet tile takes the effort out of laying carpet and comes with a bonus—you can replace damaged or worn pieces without replacing the entire room. Normally manufactured in 18-inch squares, it comes in various thicknesses and hundreds of weaves and patterns.

ANATOMY OF VINYL, PARQUET, AND LAMINATE TILE

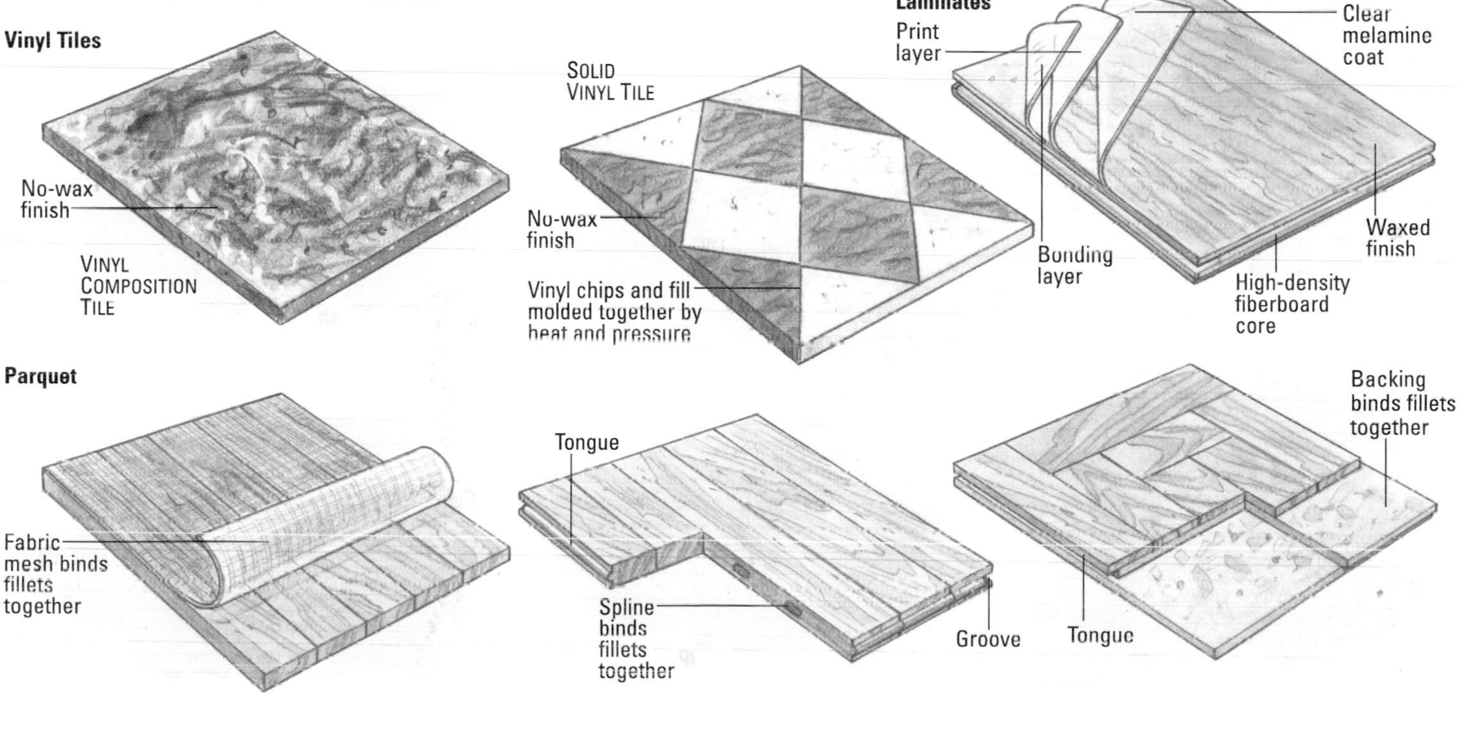

CERAMIC TRIM TILE, BORDERS, AND EDGINGS

Trim tiles finish the installation and hide the edges of the field tiles. Borders and edgings are also classified as trim tile whose shapes, colors, designs, and patterns add accents to your layout.

Trim tile falls into two categories. *Surface trim* is used when the setting bed is on the same plane as the surrounding surface. *Radius trim* is used when the setting bed sits above the surrounding surface (see below).

Buying trim tiles, borders, and edgings
Make sure you can get trim tiles from the same manufacturer as the field tiles. If you can't find trim to match, consider wood, metal, or PVC edging. Be sure to budget for trim tiles—they can cost twice as much as field tiles. Borders define edges dramatically. When you plan the layout, be sure to include these tiles so you have a good idea of its final appearance.

SURFACE TRIM

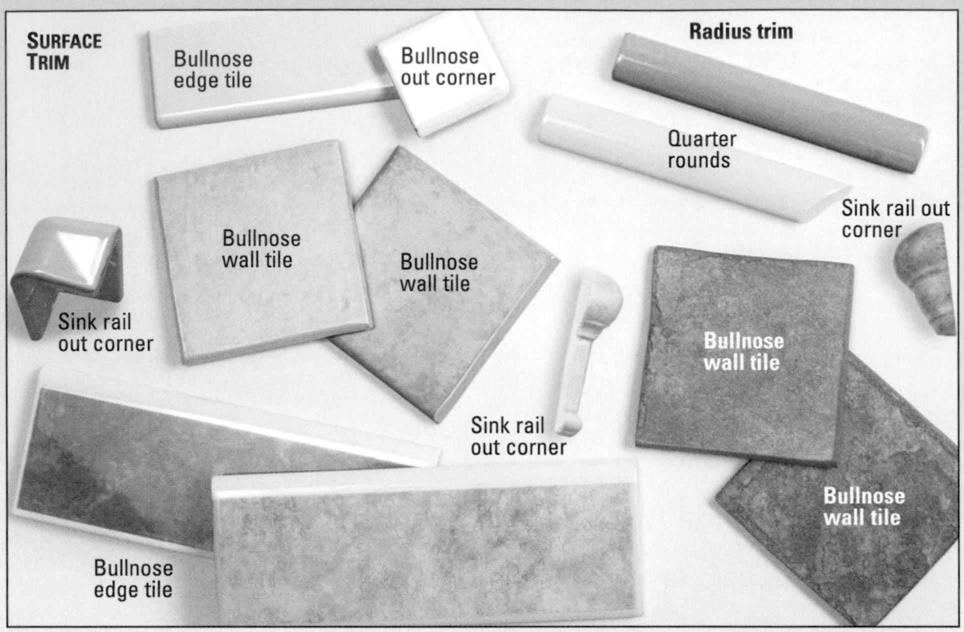

Trim tiles come in a variety of configurations to satisfy the design requirements of almost any installation. Edge trim has one or two rounded edges for use along the perimeter of walls and countertops. You can also install it as base tile for a floor. Wall trim is similar—use it where you want a full-size tile and don't need a special edge treatment. Some trim tiles are made especially for countertops. Quarter round and out corners provide a smooth and stylish transition between the countertop surface and the front edges.

RADIUS TRIM

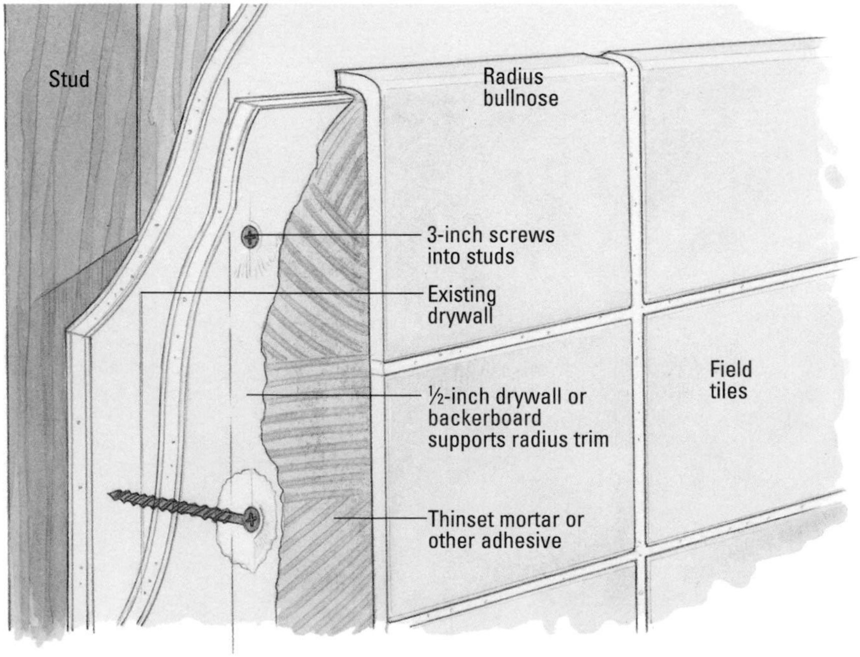

Radius trim is made so its rounded lip turns a right-angled corner at the edge of the tile. In installations in which the setting bed is raised over the existing wall surface, the turned edge covers the thickness of the setting bed. Use it on the perimeters where you have installed backerboard over drywall.

Install a wood edge

Install a wood-trim edge if you cannot find V-caps or bullnose tiles to finish your countertop.

Because wood expands at a different rate than tile and adhesive, separate it from the tile with a bead of caulk. Use a caulk that matches the color and consistency (sanded or unsanded) of the grout.

You can fasten the wood edge to the countertop with finishing nails, or screws and plugs *(page 129)*.

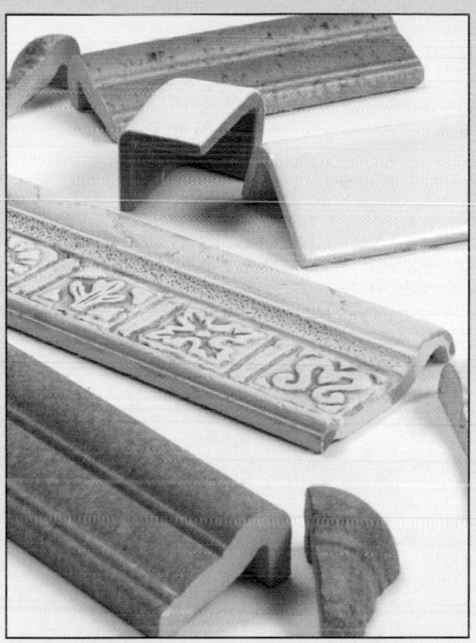

V-cap edging allows you to finish off almost any tile installation with professional-looking results. The lower leg of the cap takes the place of a separate cut tile to face the front edge of the countertop base. Both legs of the cap require back-buttering with adhesive *(page 129)*.

Base tiles finish off a floor installation. Those specifically made for this purpose have a coved foot at their base. Bullnose floor tiles are sometimes available. If base tiles are not available in the same style as your field tile, you may be able to cut field tile and use it as trim.

Borders and accent tiles spice up an installation. A border tile is usually a narrow length that is used to finish off an edge. Accent tiles, some made of glass, can take almost any form but usually have a contrasting color, size, shape, or texture.

Types of thresholds

Tiled floors are generally higher than the adjacent floors, and thresholds bridge the floors to make the transitions easy, safe, and attractive.

- Flush thresholds are used when there is no height difference between the surfaces.
- Metal thresholds are the easiest to install and come in a variety of types and profiles. Z-bar is a form of metal threshold used where tiled floor meets carpet.
- Many hardwood thresholds are beveled on two planes and fastened to the lower wood subfloor with finishing nails or screws.
- Stone or synthetic materials also provide safe and attractive transitions. Ask your supplier for suggestions that will match your installation.

For more information on thresholds and transitions, see *page 113.*

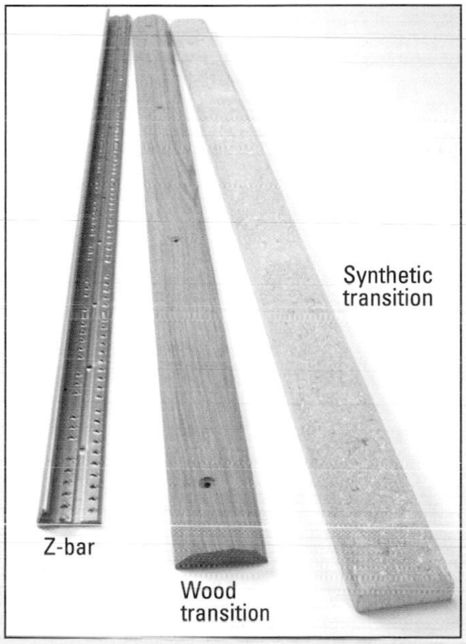

STANLEY PRO TIP

Round the edges

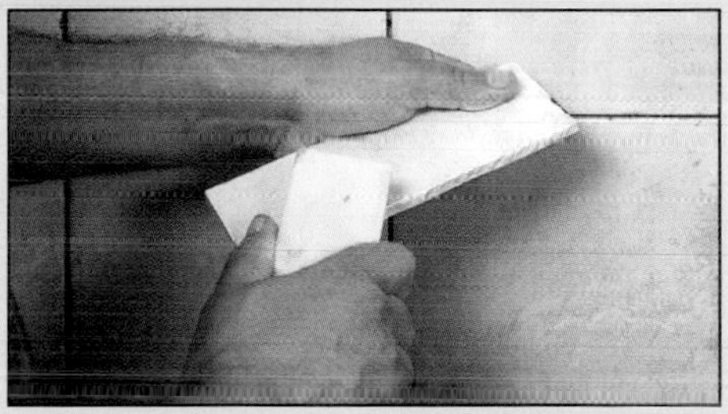

Some manufacturers do not make trim tile in the same style or colors as their field tile. If the tile is a soft-bodied variety, you may be able to fashion the trim tile yourself by rounding the edges with a masonry stone.

Making your own trim demands accuracy and effort. Pull the stone toward you, keeping the pressure even and the angle consistent on the edge of the tile. Make frequent comparisons to tiles you have already shaped.

DECORATIVE TILES

All tiles add personality and character to a wall or floor, but nothing does it quite like decorative tiles.

Decorative tiles turn ordinary projects into works of art. You can use them to call attention to an architectural feature of a room (a range hood or alcove, for example), create a focal point on a floor or wall (a mural on a backsplash), or separate one area visually from another (glass tiles at the top of a wall design or listellos mounted as a chair rail).

Before you use decorative tiles, inventory the light patterns in the room. Pay special attention to areas where the light falls off into darker spaces. Strategically placed decorative accents can make these spots seem brighter.

Visit a tile specialty showroom and study sample boards or vignettes that designers have created. This will help you formulate the combination of color, texture, and style that is just right for your setting.

Pick the grout carefully. Light colors tend to disappear; dark grouts make the design stand out. To cut costs, accent the accent—surround one or two decorative tiles with field tiles of a contrasting color.

Relief tiles, with their recessed or raised patterns, add striking accents to a tile design. Keep maintenance in mind when using these tiles—their textures make them more difficult to clean. They are generally better suited to embellishing a wall design than ornamenting a pattern of floor tiles.

Hand-painted tiles display the work of craftspeople who paint the bisque before firing the tile. The paint doesn't scratch easily, but most hand-painted tiles won't stand up to the rigors required of floors or countertops. Use them to spice up a tiled wall. They're great for random accents.

Murals are tiled or stone pictures in which each tile displays a section of the scene. Although they're often used to embellish wall designs, they also make stunning floor accents. Murals can come with as many as 50 or more tiles; be sure you have enough time to set an elaborate pattern. If you can't find a commercial design that fits your decor, consider contracting with an artisan who can create a custom design from a sketch or photograph.

Do-it-yourself designs, featured by many ceramic specialty outlets and design boutiques, have been bisque fired so they're already shaped and sized. All you have to do is apply any number of glazes and colors freehand or with precut stencils. You may have to order tiles of the size to fit your pattern. Once you've applied your design to the tile, the shop's staff will fire it.

Listellos are border tiles made to embellish both floors and walls. Floor pieces usually come as a mesh-backed mosaic, which makes for easy installation. Listellos designed for walls are perfect for chair rails, mural frames, and cornice moldings. Use them to separate a tiled wall into decorative sections. Some are high-fired ceramics. Others are molded limestone, a product that is several times softer than ceramic tile.

Antique tiles—found at flea markets, antique stores, and auctions—bring an aged charm to your tile installation. You're not likely to find enough for an entire wall or floor, but they go a long way as accents. Buy the old styles first, then choose modern field tiles that provide a complementary background. Quality control was not so important 50 to 100 years ago, so you may have to cut some tiles or employ wider grout lines to fit your design.

Glass tiles date back thousands of years, but new manufacturing methods have thrust this age-old product into modern design. Glass tiles nonporous so they're easy to clean, but glossy units scratch easily so they're not good choices for floors or countertops. Use them as accents, setting them in rows or bands on backsplashes, walls, or stair risers. A wide selection of colors and patterns includes heat-molded varieties with three-dimensional textures.

STANLEY PRO TIP

Where to find decorative tiles

You probably won't find many decorative tile selections at a home center or commercial tile outlet. Look for retailers that specialize in decorative tile. They have access to a wider variety of suppliers. Look in the phone book for "Specialty Tile" or browse the Internet. Many artists who work in tile have their own websites that display their work.

SAFETY FIRST

Check local building codes

Communities establish building codes to ensure that materials and construction techniques are safe and meet minimum quality standards. Although most tiling projects are not likely to require building permits, check with the local building department to make sure your installation is not subject to local codes. Adding stone tile to an existing interior floor or building a patio are projects that building codes may cover.

CERAMIC TILE FORMATS

In addition to differences in materials and methods of manufacture, tile (especially ceramic and other hard-bodied varieties) comes in many formats. Format can affect where you choose to use tile and how you install it. Tile formats fall into two broad categories: loose tiles and sheet-mounted tiles, with different subcategories of each.

Loose tiles

Much of the tile you are likely to lay will be loose tile; that is, each piece requires that you set it individually and space it consistently to keep it straight. The term loose tile has broad applications. Every type of tile comes in loose formats, but some have limited application. You can set most loose tiles in both organic mastic or thinset mortar—some, however, require thinset mortar *(page 37)*.

Sheet-mounted tiles

Sheet-mounted tiles come prespaced and mounted on various kinds of backings. Sheets translate into reduced time and effort required to properly space small tiles. Sheet-mounted tiles are usually vitreous and almost always smaller than 4 inches.

Face-mounted tiles are held together with a removable sheet of paper that remains in place until you set the sheet of tiles and the mortar cures. Moistening the paper allows for easy removal.

Back-mounted tiles are joined with paper or a plastic mesh that stays in place when you set the tile.

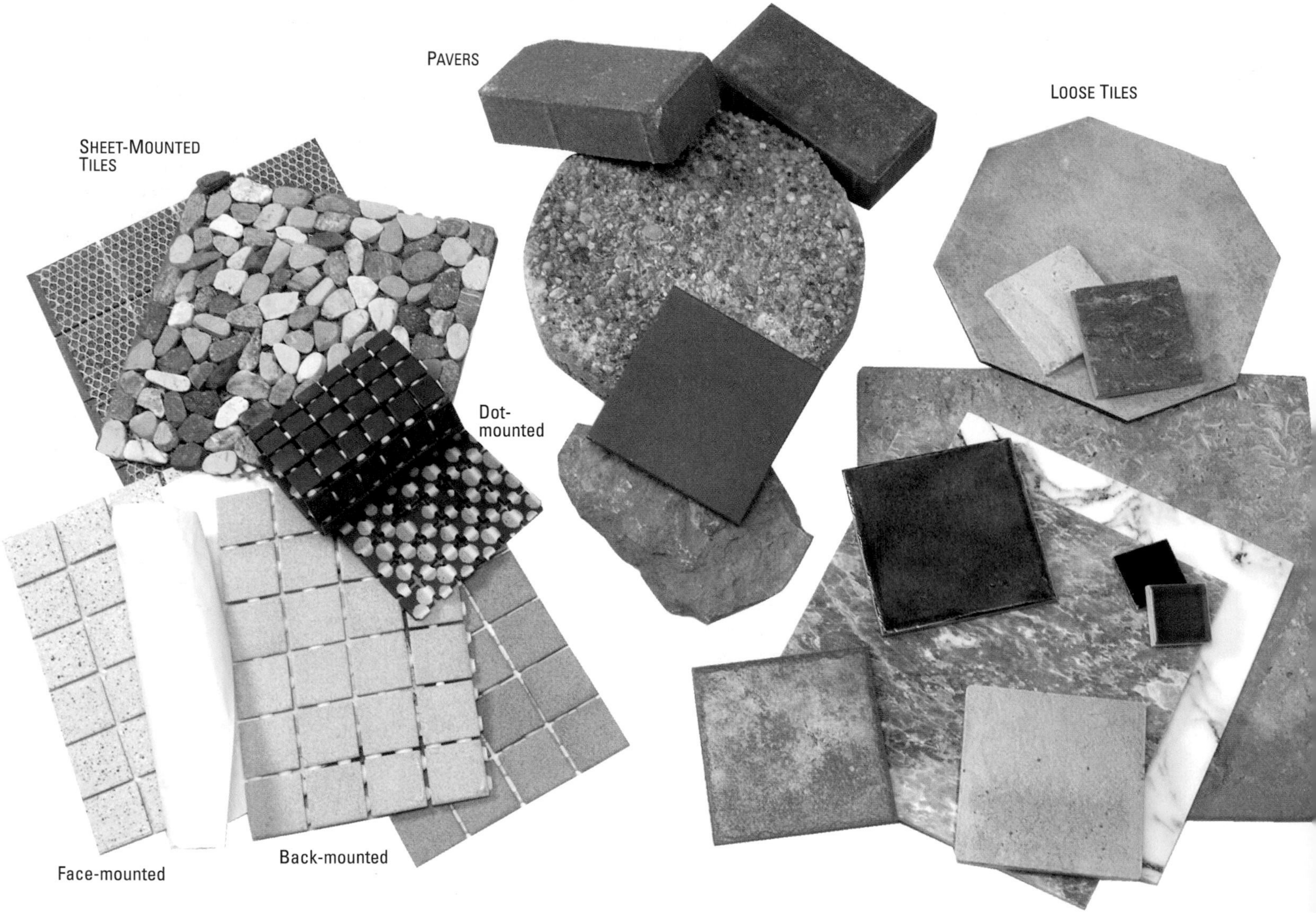

Dot-mounted tiles are fastened to each other with plastic or rubber dots on the sides of the tile. The dots remain in place when the tile is installed.

All mounting materials cut easily with a utility knife, but they display a potential for weakening the bond of the adhesive. Most sheet-mounted tiles are set in thinset mortar *(page 37)*.

Mosaic tile
Any tile less than 2 inches wide falls into the mosaic category. Once set by hand and now almost always sheet-mounted, mosaics are made as porcelain, clay, or glass tiles. Individual tiles are manufactured in ¼- to 2-inch squares, rectangles, or hexagons that range from 3⁄32 to ¼ inch thick. Glass tile mosaics are usually limited to 1-inch squares. Mosaics are sold in a variety of colors and patterns. Most are unglazed, but glazed varieties are available.

Pavers
The term *pavers* defines a category of loose clay, shale, or porcelain tile at least ½ inch thick and designed primarily for floors. Certain types also make suitable wall or countertop surfaces.

Machine-made pavers are generally fired as semivitreous or vitreous tile, both glazed and unglazed, in 4×6-inch and up to 12-inch squares. Vitreous pavers work well on walls and countertops.

Handmade pavers, both glazed and unglazed, are nonvitreous. Some are as much as 2 inches thick; most come in 4- to 24-inch squares. You can set handmade pavers on walls, but their porosity prohibits use in shower enclosures and on countertops. Both machine-made and handmade pavers are set in thinset mortar. Rough-textured tile requires additional mortar on the back (a process called back-buttering) so it will adhere more securely *(page 101)*. All unglazed tiles should be sealed.

Brick-veneer tile
Brick-veneer tile is manufactured with several different methods. Some are real brick cut in thin cross sections. Other coarsely textured varieties are made from clays similar to those used in tile production, but they are fired at lower temperatures. Others are actually a cement-bodied tile.

You can set brick veneer in both outdoor and indoor locations, whether they are wet or dry. Brick veneer in shower walls and tub surrounds, however, will prove almost impossible to clean, and the low durability of imitation brick generally limits its use to wall installations. Brick veneer is set in either organic mastic or thinset; the latter is required for outdoor use.

Glazed wall tile
Although you can use many floor tiles successfully on walls, glazed wall tiles—usually nonvitreous with a soft glaze—are made specifically for walls.

Wall tiles are usually ¼ inch thick and fired in 4¼- and 6-inch squares; larger sizes are also available. When installed with a waterproofing membrane, they are suitable for wet locations such as shower and tub surrounds. They are set in either organic mastic or thinset *(page 37)*.

What's on the back?

On the back of most pieces of tile you'll find various configurations such as raised ridges, dots, or squares. Some of the configurations—dots or buttons, for example—are built into the tile so manufacturers can stack them and heat in the kiln will pass evenly over all surfaces.

Regardless of the manufacturer's purpose, all patterns increase the rear surface area of the tile. The more surface with which the adhesive comes into contact, the stronger the adhesive bond. Ridges on a tile can actually increase its surface area up to three times.

Some tiles are engraved or embossed with information that records a specific run of tile, manufacturing process, or location. These marks can help you match tiles in historic restoration or remodeling.

Spacers and lugs

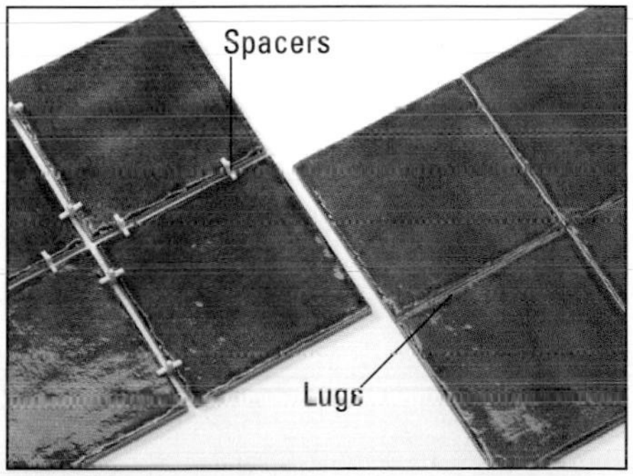

Many tiles, most commonly those made for walls, have lugs molded into their edges to help you space them accurately. Nonlugged tiles require the use of spacers.

Small plastic spacers are made in various shapes and sizes and in 1⁄16- to ½-inch widths. You may find rectangular spacers better than X-shape spacers for holding wall tiles firmly in place.

USING CERAMIC TILE

When it comes to choosing tiles for a particular room or setting, there is perhaps only one unbending rule—you can use many floor tiles on walls and countertops, but you can almost never set wall tiles on such horizontal surfaces. Your choice needs to account for durability, maintenance requirements, and safety. Many manufacturers will specify how their tile can be used.

Floor tiles

Floor tiles are generally ⅜ to ¾ inch thick (although pavers are thicker). In general, porcelain, quarry, and terra-cotta tiles, both glazed and unglazed, and cement-bodied tiles are suitable for floors. However, even within these categories, tile quality varies. Check the tile's rating to make sure it will stand up to the requirements of your room. Terra-cotta floor tile, for example, is not as durable as porcelain, so it's not the best candidate for use in an entryway. Choose glazed tiles that are slip-resistant. Seal soft-bodied tile against moisture and stains.

Wall tiles

Most wall tile is made from a white-bodied clay in thicknesses not much more than ¼ inch. Their thin profile keeps them light enough for wall structures to support them. Since wall tiles are not subject to the abuse of floor tiles, your main considerations in most rooms will be color and style. In shower enclosures and tub surrounds, however, choose a vitreous wall tile that will not absorb water. Avoid porous tile such as brick veneer—even dense varieties. Porous tile attracts bacteria and is impossible to clean. If using a heavy floor tile, make sure the structure and setting materials are strong enough to support it.

On the countertop

Install vitreous or impervious tile on your countertop, preferably glazed for easy cleanup. Scratch a sample with a kitchen knife to make sure the glaze will stand up to countertop use.

Family rooms receive constant use and heavy traffic, but their atmosphere is informal. Choose a high-quality, dense floor tile, such as this large porcelain tile, that can take the abuse and not show wear. Irregularly shaped tiles add a touch of informality.

Countertops take a beating from chopping, mixing, dropped utensils, spills, and frequent cleanup. Some vitreous floor tiles, such as this porcelain marble look-alike, make excellent countertops. So do stone and glazed tiles, if the glaze is impervious. Hard, dense tiles make cleanup easy.

Choosing the right tile

Foyers and entryways receive heavy use in all kinds of weather. Foot traffic brings in moisture and grit that will quickly wear away a soft tile surface. Take durability and maintenance into consideration when choosing entryway tile. Consider hard, vitreous tile among your choices, and glazed tile that comes with a nonslip surface.

Foyers and entryways are good places to make a style statement. They are the first element that visitors or friends see in a home and therefore contribute to that important first impression. They are well-suited to formal designs. To enhance a formal tiled entryway, consider a geometric mosaic border or an arrangement that features angular elements laid out symmetrically.

Wall tile doesn't have to stand up to the wear and tear that floor tile does, so it will play a decorative role in most rooms. Let design guide your choices and use borders to vary the pattern. Pregrouted tile panels install easily and require less maintenance than grouted tile.

Kitchen floors benefit from the traditional choice of tile because tile cleans easily. Choose vitreous tile and seal the grout. Use throw rugs to soften the floor's hard surface underfoot and in-floor radiant heating or an electric heat mesh to warm it in colder climates.

Bathrooms and sheet-mounted ceramic mosaics, which are vitreous and highly resistant to water, belong together. On walls that won't get wet, you can use standard wall tile with a soft glaze. For floors, shower enclosures, and tub surrounds, use a vitreous tile.

Tile wear ratings

Manufacturing associations grade ceramic and stone tile according to its wearability.

Ceramic tile grades:

- Group 1: Suitable for walls only
- Group 2: Suitable for residential floor use, but not in heavy traffic areas, such as kitchens or entries
- Group 3: Suitable for all residential areas
- Group 4 and 5: Suitable for commercial applications

Dimensioned stone grading:

- Group A: Uniform and consistent; not subject to breakage
- Group B: Similar to Group A, but more subject to breakage and surface damage
- Group C: Natural variations may increase risk of breakage
- Group D: Often the most beautiful, but the most subject to damage and repair

STANLEY PRO TIP: Match outdoor tile to the climate

Tiling an outside patio will provide you with a durable and easy-to-maintain surface that's ideal for relaxation and for entertaining family and friends.

Since patios are subject to outdoor weather conditions, choose tile that will withstand the climate in your area. Porous, nonvitreous tile will absorb moisture and may be fine for warm, dry climates, but it will likely crack in cold, freezing weather.

Patio tile requires a concrete slab as a base. If one doesn't already exist, the job will require excavation and pouring concrete. With the slab in place, tiling proceeds as it would indoors. Use a mortar mix that will withstand the outdoor elements.

Patio tile often continues from outdoors to inside the entryway floor. Make sure your selection meets the needs of both installations.

SUBSTRATES AND SETTING BEDS

All tile requires a flat and stable surface, especially ceramic and stone tile. You can tile over properly prepared concrete, drywall, and plaster, but other installations call for a substrate (see chart on *page 51).* Plywood is not suitable for mortared tiles. It pulls water out of mortar, and its faster expansion increases the potential of cracked joints. Here are the common substrates used with ceramic and stone tile.

Drywall

Drywall, a core of gypsum compressed between two layers of heavy paper, provides an appropriate substrate for wall installations that won't get wet. Drywall is not suitable in wet areas. It is manufactured in different size sheets (4×8 feet is standard) and thicknesses (½ inch is common on walls). In wet areas, remove existing drywall to the studs and install a waterproofed backerboard or a waterproofing membrane and cement backerboard.

Greenboard

Greenboard is a drywall product whose paper layers are treated for water resistance. It is available in different thicknesses, but ½ inch and ⅝ inch are used on walls. You can install it in locations that will receive infrequent moisture, but it won't stand up to repeated wetting. In any wet location, it's better to use backerboard.

Cement backerboard

Cement backerboard is a cement-based material formed in one of two methods. A cement core is sandwiched between layers of fiberglass mesh, or the fibers are impregnated in the core. Cement board is the most prevalent substrate for both wet and dry installations. It is made in 32- or 36-inch widths, up to 60-inch lengths, and in ¼- and ½-inch thicknesses.

Another backerboard made of cement, ground sand, cellulose fiber, and additives does not contain fiberglass mesh. It is lighter than cement board, cuts easily, and includes an imprint to guide fastener placement. It comes in 4×8-foot sheets and ¼- and ½-inch thicknesses.

Glass-mat gypsum backerboard

Not to be confused with gypsum drywall, this material is made of a compressed gypsum core with embedded fiberglass and a water-resistant coating. It is lighter and easier to cut than cement backerboard but not as strong. It is available in 4×8-foot sheets and ¼- and ½-inch thicknesses.

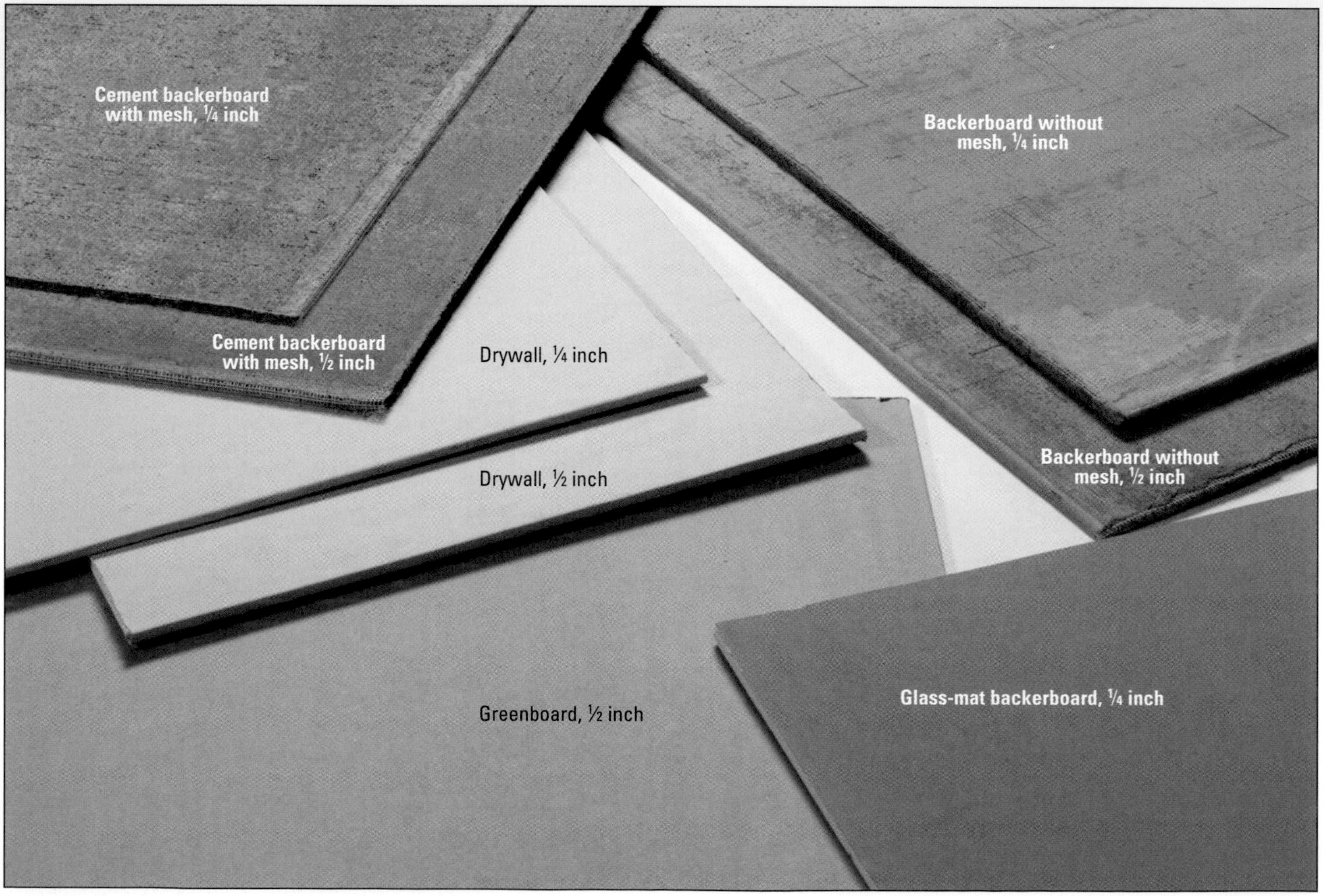

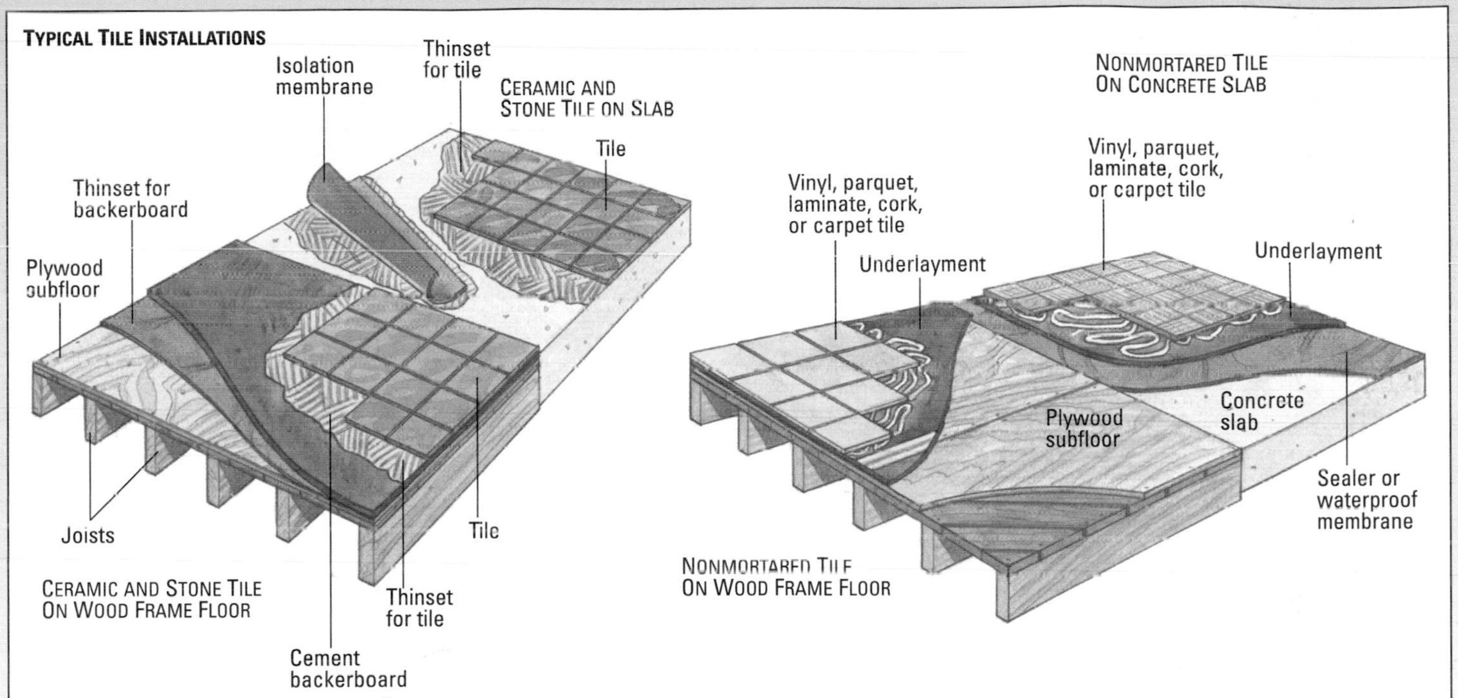

In a typical tile installation, a plywood subfloor provides a stable foundation and supports the weight of the tile. Cement backerboard laid on the subfloor in a bed of thinset mortar is screwed to the plywood and joists. Tile is set in a mortar bed and grouted.

Installations over a concrete slab may require an isolation membrane to keep cracks from telegraphing to the tile. Wet locations such as shower enclosures need a waterproof membrane under the backerboard.

Self-leveling compounds

Self-leveling compounds, technically not a substrate, are used to level depressions in slabs and subfloors. Most call for only light mixing with water and level themselves when poured. Quick-setting brands allow tiling within hours.

Self-leveling compounds work best when applied in thicknesses of less than 1 inch. If using a compound to fill a deeper depression, make more than one pour, but check the manufacturer's directions first.

Pour the compound after completing all other repair work. Doing so ensures that the compound stays clean and ready for tiling.

Commercially applied gypsum-based compounds are excellent for leveling floors on which surface radiant heating systems have been installed *(pages 82–88)*.

STANLEY PRO TIP

Don't substitute drywall screws

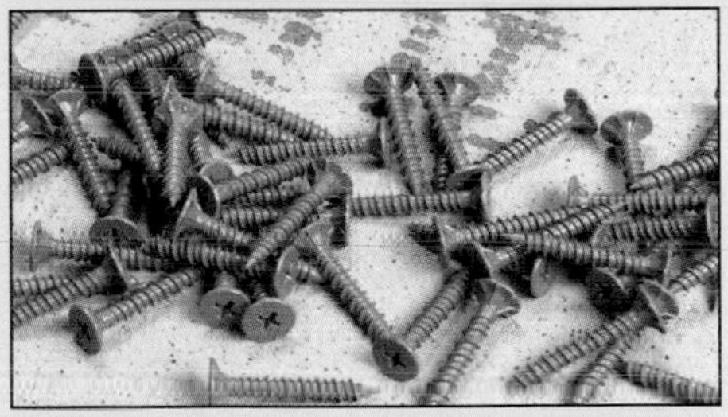

Screws made for backerboard installation are treated with a corrosion-resistant coating and are formed with self-countersinking heads. Drywall screws are not a good substitute—their heads may snap off and moisture may cause them to rust.

Purchase 1¼-inch fasteners when installing backerboard directly to studs and 2-inch screws when fastening backerboard over ½-inch drywall.

MEMBRANES

Wherever a floor exhibits the potential of cracking tile or allowing water to penetrate, you need to install a membrane. Isolation and waterproofing membranes are appropriate for hard-bodied tiles and are also necessary for certain vinyl and laminate installations.

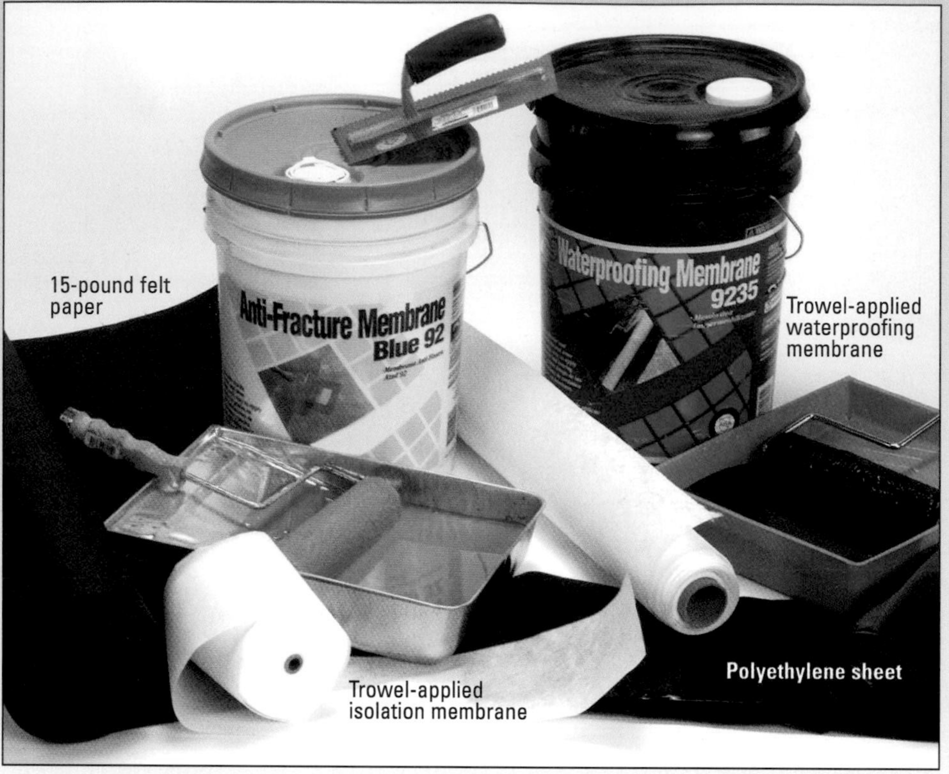

Isolation membranes

These materials allow substrates to expand and contract without telegraphing the movement to the tile. Two-part membranes, adhesive and mesh or chlorinated polyethylene (CPE), are applied directly to the surface to be tiled. The easiest materials to use employ a roller-applied adhesive. On old, stable concrete, cover each crack separately. On new concrete that you suspect will crack with age, apply the membrane to the entire floor.

Waterproofing membranes

Use a waterproofing membrane in shower enclosures and any area that will get wet. Felt paper, polyurethane sheets, and two-part products work well. Many products function as both a waterproofing and isolation membrane.

STANLEY PRO TIP: Use an isolation membrane

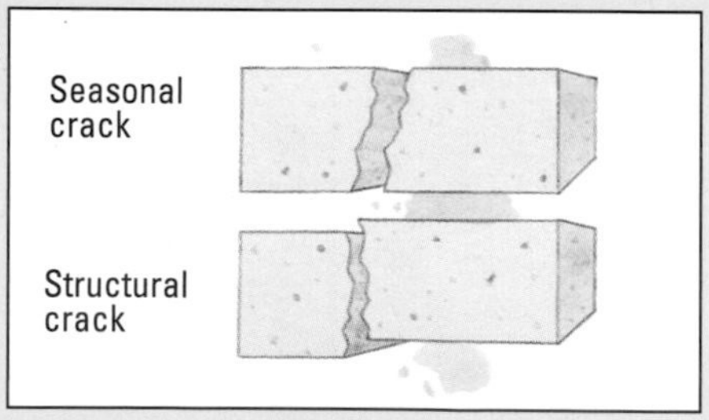

Look closely at a slab floor and you may discover that it contains two different types of cracks.

Seasonal cracking occurs when temperature changes cause the material to expand. At a seasonal crack, the concrete moves laterally, leaving the separated surfaces of the material at the same height.

Structural cracks, caused by vertical shifts in the slab, leave one edge of the crack at a different height than the other.

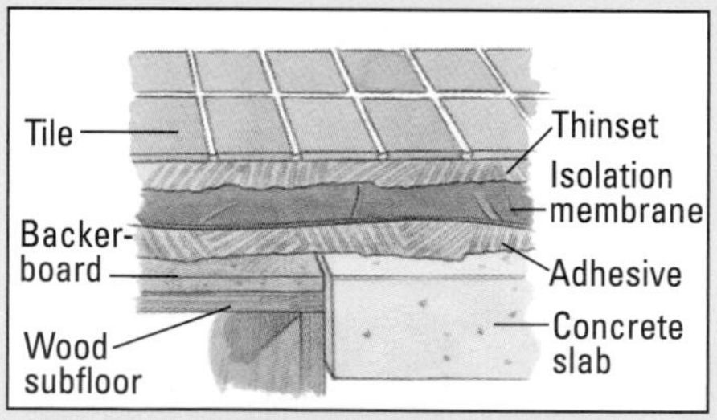

Isolate seasonal cracks less than ⅛-inch wide with a membrane to prevent them from being transmitted to the tile surface. Isolation membranes will not keep structural cracks out of your tile surface, however. Fix the cause of a structural crack before setting the tile.

Because different materials expand at different rates, tile applied continuously over slab and wood floors may crack where the two floors join. Use an isolation membrane at these junctures *(page 71)*.

Sound-control membranes

Modern home building methods have reduced the size of the structural members without sacrificing their strength. While these practices reduce costs, they also result in thinner walls that transmit sound more easily from room to room.

If your planned tile project contains a wall or floor that separates a noisy area from a quiet one—for example, a family room over or next to an office—ask your supplier about a sound-control membrane.

Sound-control membranes come in different forms and are applied in the same fashion as membranes used for waterproofing and crack isolation. Some products are multipurpose.

ADHESIVES

Adhesives hold the tile in place; they are generally divided into three categories.

Thinset mortar

Thinset mortar is the most commonly used adhesive in tile installations. It is almost always the best product for floors and has wide applications in wall tiling installations. It offers great flexibility in placing tiles when wet, and when cured it provides greater strength than organic mastic.

Epoxy thinset

Epoxy thinset sets up quickly. Its hard, almost impermeable consistency makes it useful in settings requiring chemical resistance. This thinset is more expensive and harder to apply than water-based or latex thinsets.

Organic mastic

Organic mastic is made with either a latex or petroleum base and a carrier that evaporates and leaves a bonding agent stuck to the tile. This adhesive is not as strong or flexible as thinset. It is good for flat walls in prime condition. Make sure it's compatible with your materials.

THINSET MORTAR
Additives and mixing

Although not impervious to water, thinset exhibits highly water-resistant properties. Thinset mixed with water, however, may crack when cured. To improve its flexibility, mix it with a latex additive, following the manufacturer's directions. (Latex-modified thinset is also available.) In addition, latex improves the bond strength of the thinset, which is essential with vitreous or impervious tile such as porcelain.

Thinset comes in premixed or mix-it-yourself varieties—a choice that comes down to preference and cost.

Premixed brands cost more, but mixing your own allows you to adjust the mixture to weather conditions, making it wetter in hot and dry climates or stiffer in cold and humid conditions. You can also alter its consistency to provide optimal adhesion over many kinds of substrates and tiles.

Mastics for nonmortared tile

When choosing mastics for nonmortared tile, you'll find many all-purpose pressure-sensitive adhesives made from latex. Although these products may work just fine for your installation, many types of nonmortared tile require different mastics for different installations.

For example, vinyl tile laid on a basement floor requires a different mastic than the same tile set on plywood. Carpet tile can be laid with a permanent adhesive or with a "release" mastic, which allows you to remove damaged units. Adhesives for cork are formulated specifically for its natural characteristics, and parquet will last longer with a rubber-based or similar adhesive that allows for the expansion and contraction of its wood fibers.

When working with mastics, stir the mastic if necessary, but do not thin it. If it has begun to harden, do not use it. Apply only enough to an area you can set within its "open" time (the time it takes the product to skim over). Clean tools and tile immediately with the proper solvent.

SAFETY FIRST
Handling adhesives

Thinset and other adhesives contain caustic ingredients. Solvent-based adhesives are potentially explosive and harmful when inhaled. Wear gloves and a respirator when mixing all adhesives and keep the area well ventilated.

GROUTS, CAULKS, AND SEALERS

Grouts, caulks, and sealers complete a tile installation. The use of each product will vary with the kind of tile installed.

Grouts

Grout fills the joints between ceramic and stone tiles, but it does more than take up space. It strengthens the entire surface, increases flexibility, helps prevent water damage to the subsurface, and contributes to the design of the installation.

You can buy grout premixed or you can mix your own. Premix offers increased convenience but is slightly weaker. If the powdered grout you purchase does not contain a dry polymer, mix it with a latex additive instead of water for increased flexibility, strength, color retention, and mildew and stain resistance. Sanded and unsanded grouts come in colors to match any tile.

Caulks

Caulks are flexible materials used to fill joints that require maximum flexibility—expansion joints, those around sinks and plumbing fixtures, and inside corners.

Caulk comes in two kinds of dispensers—in tubes for use with a caulk gun or in squeezable tubes. Both sanded and unsanded mixtures are available in many colors. Always use silicone caulk; latex caulk is not as durable and changes color over time.

Sealers

Sealers prevent liquid and stains from penetrating tiles and joints.

Penetrating sealers work their way into the surface of the material. Topical sealers remain on the surface of the tile in a thin layer and, depending on the product, can alter the appearance of the surface *(page 105)*.

To seal joints, use an applicator designed specifically for this purpose. Use a mop or sealer applicator to seal the surface of unglazed tiles, a roller or brush for parquet.

Sizing the joints

Certain kinds of tile generally look best with grout joints of a specific width.

- Glazed tiles: $\frac{3}{16}$ to $\frac{3}{8}$ inch
- Porcelain tiles: $\frac{1}{8}$ to $\frac{1}{4}$ inch
- Terra-cotta tiles: $\frac{3}{4}$ inch
- Cement-bodied tiles: $\frac{3}{8}$ to $\frac{1}{2}$ inch
- Granite, marble stone tiles: $\frac{1}{16}$ inch
- Slate tiles: $\frac{3}{8}$ to $\frac{1}{2}$ inch

Use these dimensions as a guide. You can vary the size to suit the aesthetics of your installation and to make tiles fit evenly across the room, but larger joints are more likely to crack. Irregular tiles such as saltillo and other handmade pavers usually need large joints to make their edges look even and aligned with one another.

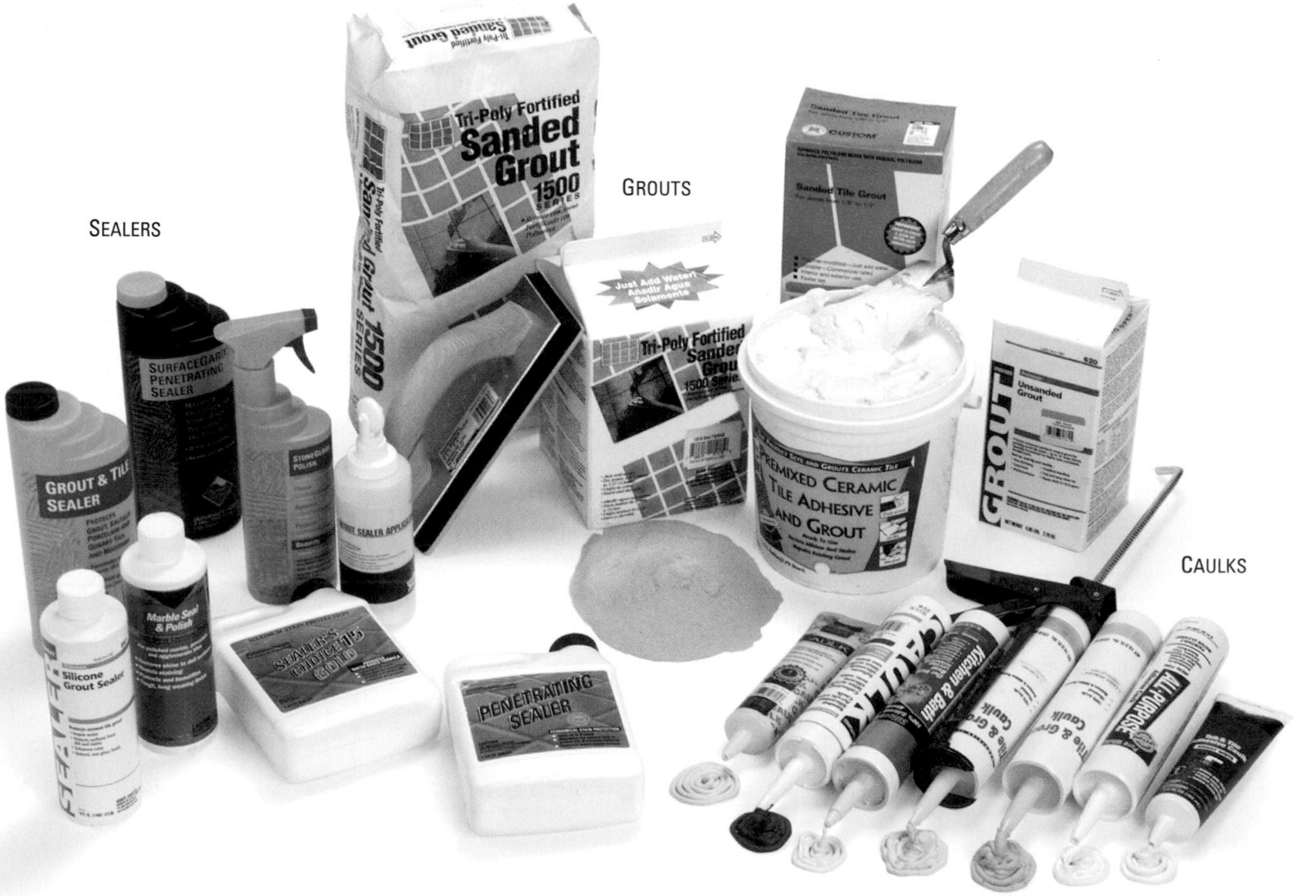

What type of grout to use

Type	Description and Uses
Unsanded grout	Portland cement and additives. Used for grout joints of ¹⁄₁₆ inch or less in ceramic, marble, granite, and other stone tile installations.
Sanded grout	Portland cement, sand (for strength), and additives. Used for grout joints wider than ¹⁄₁₆ inch. As the joint width increases, use grout with larger sand particles.
Epoxy grout	Epoxy resins and hardeners. Used for high chemical and stain resistance, and in installations exposed to high temperatures. Also used with epoxy thinset to grout mosaics. More difficult to work with than other grouts.
Colored grout	Unsanded or sanded grout with color additives. Premixed packages in hundreds of colors. Colors that contrast with the tile emphasize the geometry of the pattern. Grouts similar to the color of the tile will de-emphasize the pattern.
Mortar	Portland cement, sand, and additives mixed in proportions suitable for masonry installations. Used to set brick pavers, slate, or rough stone.

Don't forget to use expansion joints

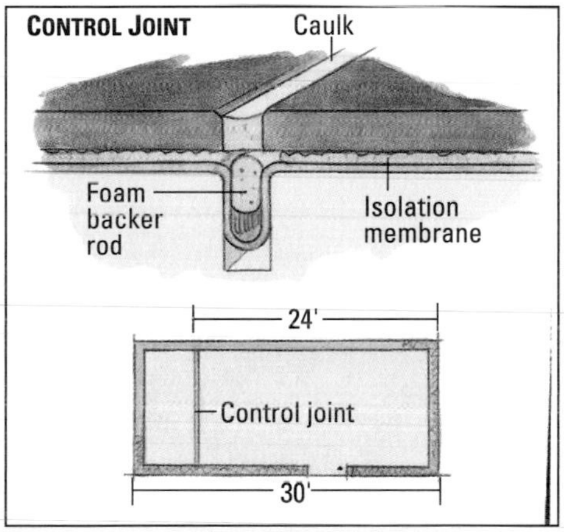

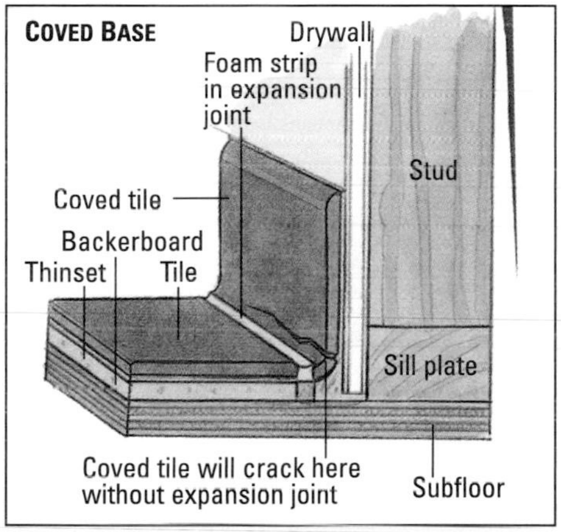

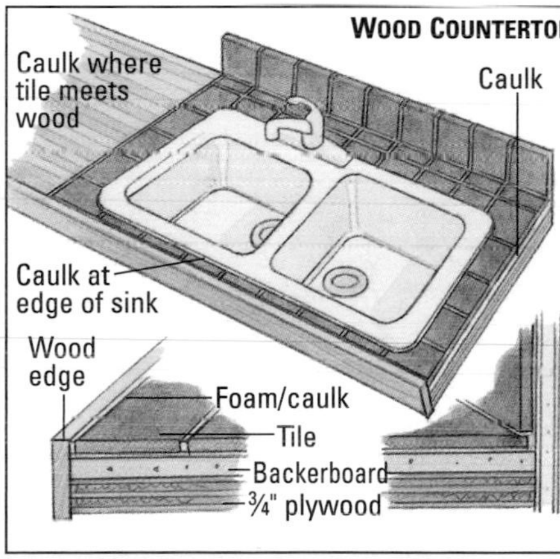

When tile or a masonry surface covers a large expanse or where any of those materials meet a different material, their expansion will subject them to cracking. These locations require a cushion called an expansion joint.

Expansion joints are filled with a foam backer rod and topped off with caulk. Include the foam strip on your shopping list if you're tiling any of the surfaces or situations shown above.

Control joints (above left) are separations in sections of a concrete slab. They are built in on the perimeter and every 24 feet within the slab when it's poured. Tile laid on a concrete slab will need an expansion joint over these points. Without the foam backer rod, the movement of the slab will be telegraphed to the tile, causing it to crack.

Also allow for an expansion joint at the perimeter of tiled floors (above center). Leave a ¼-inch gap between the edge tile and the wall or the base of a coved tile base. Fill this gap with foam backer rod and cover it with caulk of the same color as your grout.

Countertop tiles move, too, so allow for an expansion joint where the countertop tiles meet the backsplash (above right).

Fill the gaps with backer rod to the base of the tile and caulk the tile joint with colored caulk.

Planning Your Tile Installation

Nothing contributes more to the success of your tiling project than careful planning. Planning helps you produce attractive, professional-looking results, and it organizes the job. A well-drawn, detailed layout plan will help you create a more accurate cost estimate than sketches or generalized notes.

One aspect of remodeling, however, can't be solved with graph paper and a ruler—the disruption and mess. To minimize the stress, anticipate debris disposal. Collect sturdy cartons for hauling out old flooring, drywall, or plaster. Order your materials early and get all the preparation out of the way by the delivery date. If you won't be done by the time the materials arrive, plan where to store them away from the project site. Have all the right tools before you begin the job. Nothing stalls a project—or your enthusiasm—more than running back and forth to the hardware store.

If the kitchen will be shut down, make alternate arrangements for meals. Coordinate the removal of bathroom fixtures with your family's daily schedule.

Use this list to keep your tiling project organized from start to finish:

- Measure all rooms carefully and calculate their areas.
- Create a scaled drawing and layout plan of the surface you'll be tiling.
- Estimate material quantities, starting with underlayment and other preparation materials: adhesives, grouts, and fasteners. Be sure to include the trim tile.
- Make a list of the tools you'll need. Purchase or rent them. Plan your work so you can return rented tools within 24 hours to minimize costs.
- Estimate your total costs, including any for alternate living arrangements if needed. When shopping for tile, visit several suppliers to get the best deal.
- Plan for temporary storage of furniture and other objects. Store furniture in little-used rooms to keep disruptions in your life to a minimum.
- Prepare a construction calendar to keep yourself on schedule.

Careful planning is the key to every successful tile installation.

Chapter Preview

Making a dimensional layout drawing
page 42

Making a dimensional floor plan
page 44

Making a dimensional wall plan
page 46

Measure tile samples to transfer accurate tile pattern to scaled drawing.
KITCHEN
Arrange planning materials on large flat work surface with all materials at hand.
Scaled drawing on graph paper helps iron out design and layout problems in advance.

STANLEY PRO TIP

Principles of layout

When you are experimenting with various layouts on paper, these few guidelines will help you design an attractive installation:

- Use as many full tiles and as few cut tiles as possible.
- Avoid cut tiles that are less than one-half of a tile.
- Balance the edges of the installation so the cut tiles are the same width on opposite walls.
- If you have to taper the tiles on an edge, place them away from visual centers, along a far wall, or behind furniture.

MAKING A DIMENSIONAL LAYOUT DRAWING

A dimensional layout drawing puts on paper all the details of the surface you'll be tiling. It reflects the outline of tiled surfaces and the layout of the tile.

A dimensional layout drawing helps you plan precisely, assists a supplier in helping you make estimates, and acts as the basis for answering other questions about your project.

The making of a drawing is a fairly straightforward procedure. The process begins with a rough sketch on which you post the measurements of the room. Then you make a scaled drawing based on the sketch and measurements. In the final stage, you use tracing paper to draw in the tile pattern or to experiment with options.

Although tile is sold in cartons whose contents cover a specified number of square feet, you should count the tiles on your layout drawing to give you a more accurate estimate, especially if the project contains several cut tiles.

Before you measure the room, make a rough sketch of its contours. Start in a corner and measure to the nearest ⅛ inch the length of every surface where it changes direction. Post the measurements on the sketch as you go. A floor sketch will note the dimensions of appliance recesses, cabinets, and built-in furnishings. A sketch of a wall or countertop will account for anything on the surface that interrupts a line of tile, such as windows or electrical outlets.

PRESTART CHECKLIST

- ☐ **TIME**
  About an hour to sketch and measure a medium-size kitchen. Time for making a dimensional layout plan will vary with the complexity of the design and the number of alternative layouts drawn.
- ☐ **TOOLS**
  Sharp pencils, measuring tape, ruler, architect's scale, plastic drawing square
- ☐ **SKILLS**
  Measuring and drawing accurately
- ☐ **PREP**
  Selection of tile
- ☐ **MATERIALS**
  Large sheets of graph paper and tracing paper, masking or drafting tape

TYPICAL DIMENSIONAL DRAWING

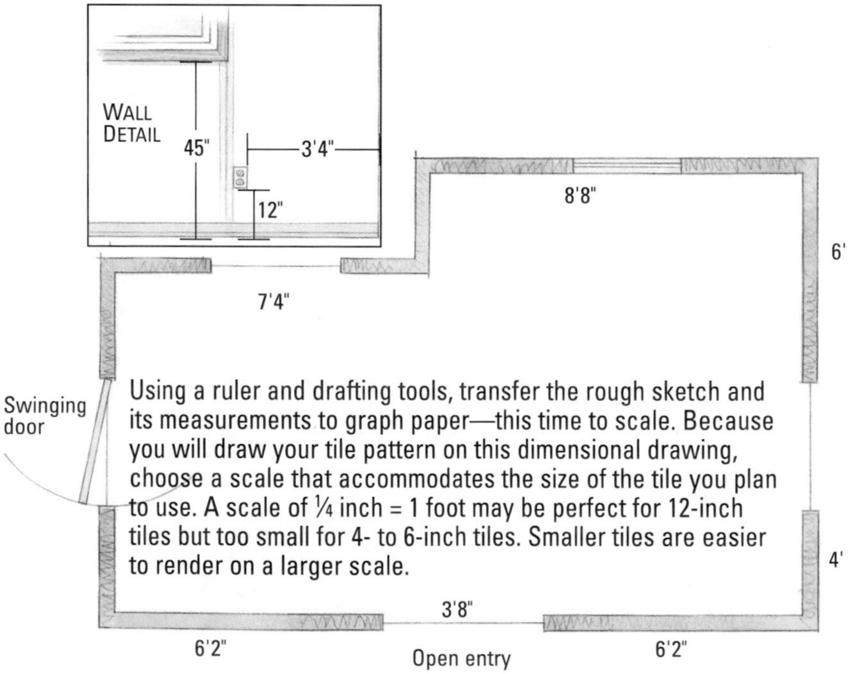

Using a ruler and drafting tools, transfer the rough sketch and its measurements to graph paper—this time to scale. Because you will draw your tile pattern on this dimensional drawing, choose a scale that accommodates the size of the tile you plan to use. A scale of ¼ inch = 1 foot may be perfect for 12-inch tiles but too small for 4- to 6-inch tiles. Smaller tiles are easier to render on a larger scale.

GETTING THE LAYOUT RIGHT

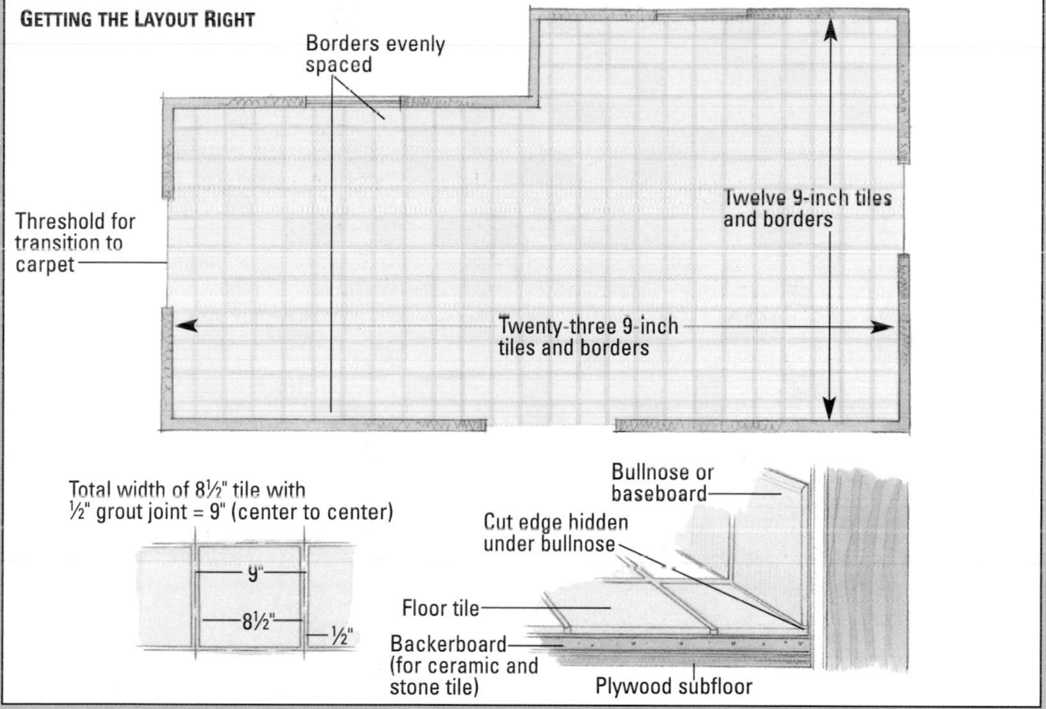

Tape your dimensional drawing securely to your work surface; then tape a piece of tracing paper over it. Carefully draw your tile layout on the tracing paper. Experiment with various designs, using new sheets of tracing paper until you arrive at the layout that looks best in the room. Use the total of the tile width plus the width of the grout joint in determining the layout. You can hide the edges of cut tiles under toe-kicks, along an inconspicuous wall, or under a countertop backsplash. Doorways should start with a full tile and edges should end in at least a half-tile border, if possible.

STANLEY PRO TIP

Estimate materials

To estimate the materials needed, first compute the area of the surface by multiplying its length by its width. For complicated surfaces, compute the overall area and subtract the space in the nooks and crannies.

Estimate tile quantities by dividing the coverage-per-carton into the total area and adding 10 percent for breakage, cut tiles, and mistakes. Count the tiles on your layout drawing for a more precise estimate. Save unused tile for future repairs.

For ceramic and stone projects, figure backerboard quantities by dividing the sheet area into the surface area. Grout and adhesive coverage will vary among manufacturers. Consult your supplier and don't forget tape, screws, and other materials.

HALF-TILE BORDER

Revise the layout

If your first layout results in unevenly spaced half-tile borders, try adjusting the grout lines. If things don't come out evenly, revise your layout. Remove the partial tiles and the full tiles on each axis. Redraw the layout with the remaining section of full tiles centered in the room. This will leave enough space for wider tiles at the borders. Measure to the edge and divide by 2. In this example, seventeen 2-inch border tiles and fifteen 12-inch full tiles were removed, leaving a space of 14 inches ÷ 2 = 7 inches, or more than a half-tile at each border.

This method also allows you to make more accurate material estimates. If you count the tiles in the first layout, you'll find there are 55 full tiles and 17 cut tiles. Counting the tiles in the final layout results in an estimate of 40 full and 32 cut tiles.

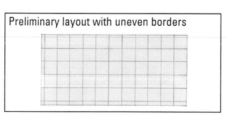

Preliminary layout with uneven borders

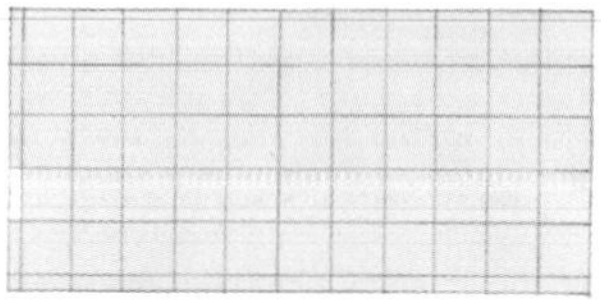

Layout with tiles removed

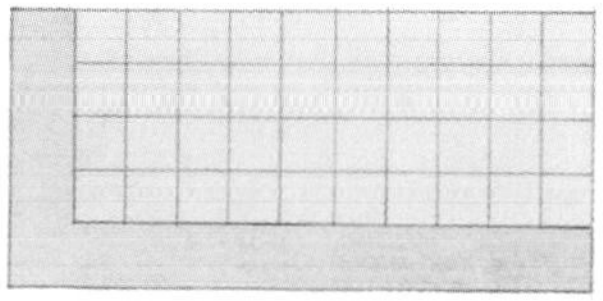

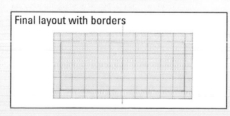

Final layout with borders

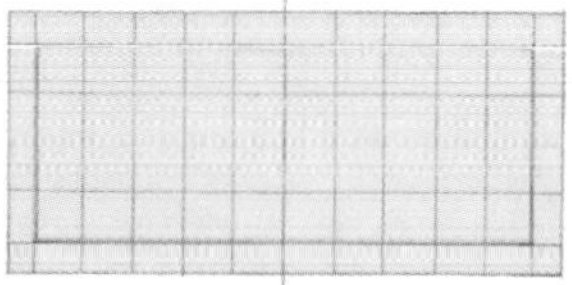

Laying out irregular ceramic tiles

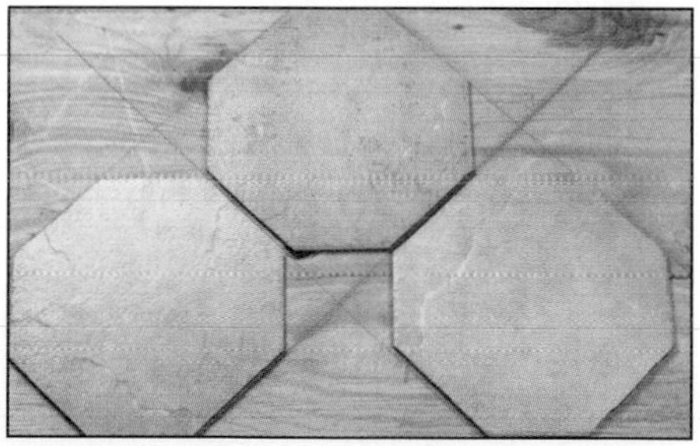

Almost all irregularly shaped tiles have a reference point you can rely on when making your dimensional layout. Use a ruler to lightly draw in layout lines and space them to conform to the tile-grout dimension. Cut a thin cardboard template scaled to the overall configuration of a square of the tile and use the template to draw trial layouts.

Most irregular tiles are sold by the square foot. To make material estimates, divide the total area by the coverage per carton.

MAKING A DIMENSIONAL FLOOR PLAN

One of the most common problems in planning a floor installation is out-of-square walls. Walls seldom define a room squarely, but you can make paper-and-pencil adjustments much more easily than you can rebuild a wall.

To determine if the area is square, use the 3-4-5 triangle method (illustrated below). Snap a chalkline on the floor, or tack a mason's line at the midpoints of each pair of opposite walls. From the intersection, measure out on one line a distance of 3 feet. Tape the line at that point and measure and tape a distance of 4 feet on the other line. Now measure the distance between the tapes. If it's 5 feet exactly, the floor is square. Adjust the lines, if necessary, until they are perpendicular. Now measure from the lines to the out-of-square walls at each end and post this measurement on your drawing.

Wavy walls may also affect your drawing. Check them with a 4-foot level and represent the condition on your drawing as accurately as possible.

CHECKING FOR SQUARE WITH 3-4-5 TRIANGLE METHOD

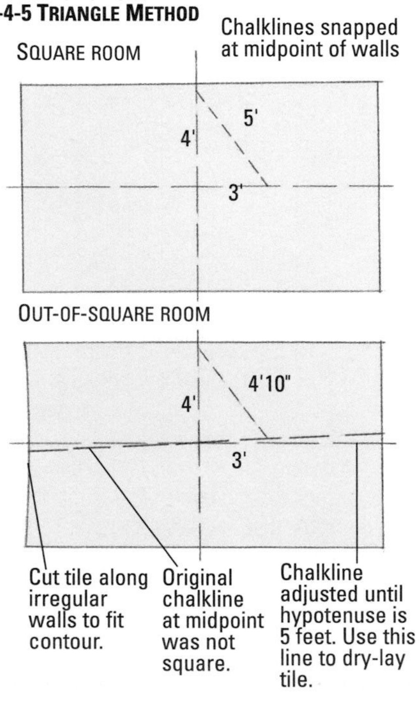

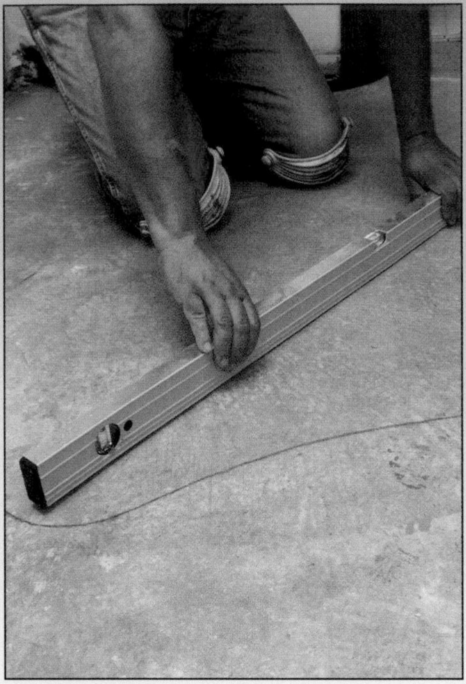

Chalklines snapped at midpoint of walls

Cut tile along irregular walls to fit contour.
Original chalkline at midpoint was not square.
Chalkline adjusted until hypotenuse is 5 feet. Use this line to dry-lay tile.

Check the floor to determine if it is level and flat. If the floor is not level, it won't affect the final look unless you are also tiling a wall. But floors must be reasonably flat (within ⅛ inch in 10 feet) to keep the tile from cracking. For more on leveling floors, see *pages 70–71.*

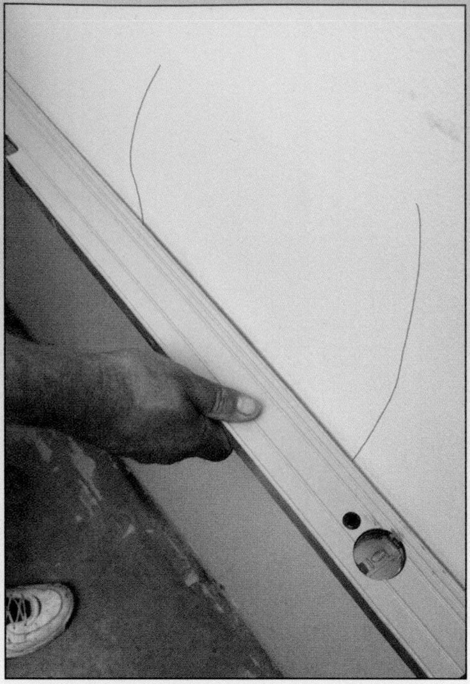

Wavy walls will affect the contour of the edge tiles on floors. Use a 4-foot level to check the lower surface of the wall near the floor. It's possible to remedy minor variations in the surface in many ways.

WHAT IF...
The floor is not square?

Hide tapered cuts under baseboard, behind furniture, or on inconspicuous walls

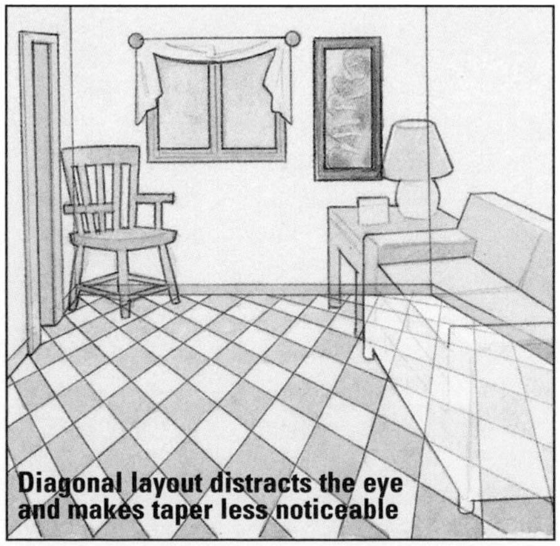

Diagonal layout distracts the eye and makes taper less noticeable

An out-of-square floor surface will result in tapered tiles on at least one edge. Draw the tiles on your layout plan to minimize the visibility of the tapered tiles. Modify the grout width, hide cut edges under toe-kicks, or arrange your layout so the tapered edges fall behind furniture (left). Try a diagonal layout (right) or a larger, irregular tile to hide the tapered edges. In extreme cases, you can shim out the wall and rebuild it.

Laying out different configurations

RECTANGULAR ROOM

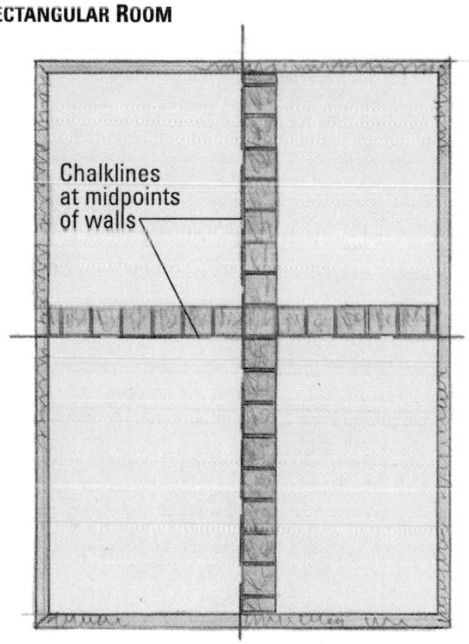

In a rectangular or square room, pencil in reference lines at the midpoints of the walls and draw in tiles on both axes. If you have the tiles, lay them out on the floor to make your drawing more accurate. Adjust the placement of the lines so the pattern ends in even borders, if possible.

L-SHAPE ROOM

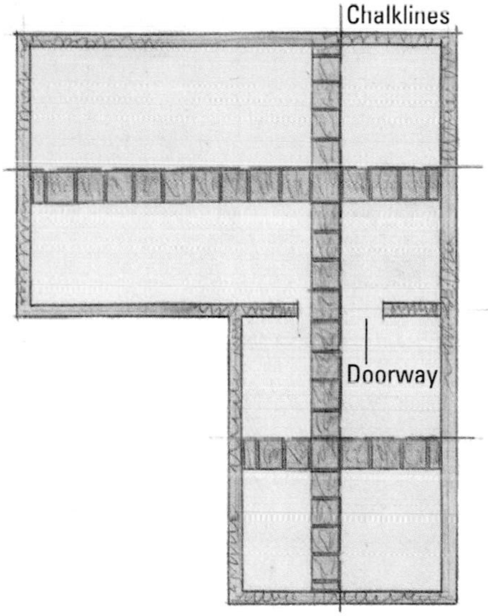

When laying out an L-shape room, position the lines so they carry from one room to the other. Adjust them so the layout results in even borders, if necessary.

DIAGONAL LAYOUT

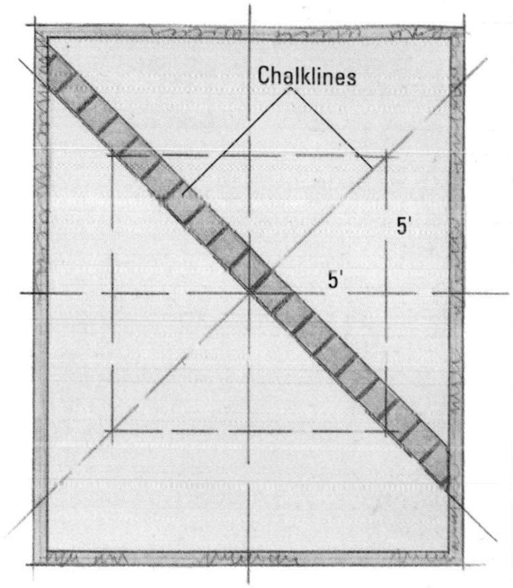

To establish lines for a diagonal layout, first pencil in lines at the midpoints of the room. Then on each axis, mark an equal distance from the intersection. Extend these points until the extensions intersect. Draw diagonal lines from the intersections through the midpoint.

WAVY WALLS

Hide or fix the problem

Wavy walls can result in edge tiles with uneven cuts. If the problem is not severe, the cuts may not be noticeable.

When drawing a layout plan, try the following solutions. Minor variations in a wall surface may actually "disappear" if hidden under a baseboard.

More severe depressions in a wall can be leveled with a skim coat of thinset prior to tiling the floor *(page 75)*. Feather the edges of the skim coat to blend in with the level surface. Skim-coating, however, requires proper preparation of the wall so the mortar will stick *(pages 72–77)*. You will also have to tile the wall, paint it, or cover it with another material.

STANLEY PRO TIP

Plan full tiles in doorways

When you are preparing a dimensional layout plan, draw the tiles in so a full tile will fall with its edge in the center of a doorway. If you can't set a full tile in the doorway because your plan already incorporates wide border tiles, you may be able to minimize the effect of a cut tile with a threshold in the doorway *(page 113)*.

If the tile continues into an adjoining room, center a tile at the doorway, if possible, so an even portion falls in each room.

WHAT IF…

The floor is not level?

An out-of-level floor creates tapered wall tiles at the floor. A diagonal wall layout may hide a minor condition. For severe problems, install a wallcovering other than tile or level the floor.

MAKING A DIMENSIONAL WALL PLAN

Walls can exhibit the same out-of-square conditions as floors. Walls might also be out of plumb (their surface may not run true to vertical) and their surfaces might be wavy. You need to perform some routine checks and identify any problems on your layout drawing.

Any of these conditions on one wall may not be noticeable if it is not severe and if you are not tiling an adjacent wall or the floor. These problems become noticeable when tiling a neighboring surface.

Use a 4-foot level to check the walls, as shown on this page. Make note on your plan how the condition will affect your layout. Adjust the pattern of the tiles as necessary to deal with the problem. For example, measure the amount by which the edge of the wall is not square and draw the edge on your layout plan to reflect its angle. Draw cut tiles on this line. Making the tiles as wide as possible will improve the appearance of the edge.

Check for plumb: Before drawing in the pattern of your wall tile, check the wall to see if it is plumb. Hold a 4-foot level vertically at the corner of the wall. If the spirit bubble centers in the glass, the wall is plumb. Repeat the process on the adjacent wall if you are tiling it as well. An out-of-plumb wall will not be as distracting if you are not tiling the neighboring wall.

OUT-OF-PLUMB WALL

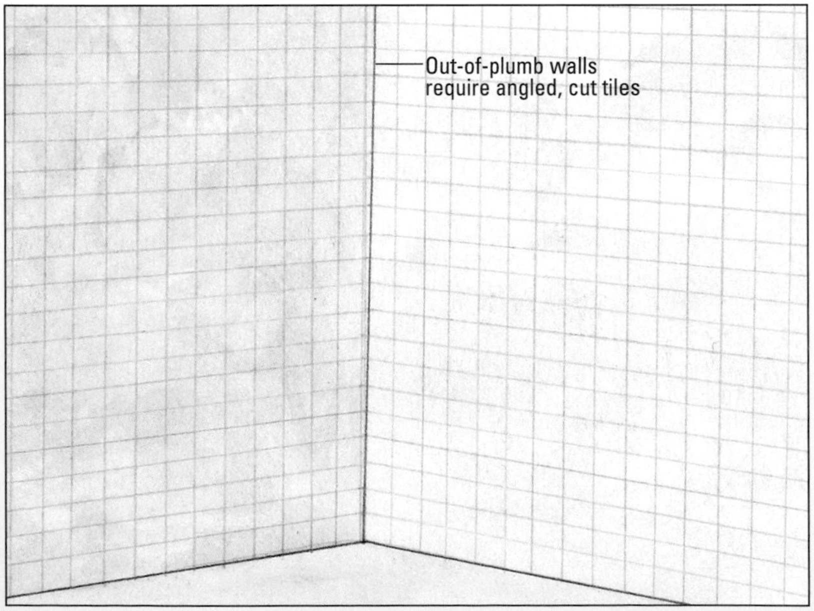
Out-of-plumb walls require angled, cut tiles

If your plans call for tiling adjacent walls and if one or both of them is not plumb, now is the time—when the plans are still on paper—to consider possible solutions.

For minor discrepancies and no matter what tile you plan to install, apply a skim coat of thinset mortar *(page 75)* at the corner of the out-of-plumb wall. Apply the mortar in the corner, building up one wall to create a square corner. Spread the mortar out on the wall's surface 2 to 3 feet, so when you sight down the wall, it appears plumb to the other wall. Check your work with a 4-foot level.

You can also plumb the wall by nailing or screwing vertical shims to the wall from floor to ceiling. Then screw drywall or backerboard to the wall and tape it *(pages 92–95)*. Use backerboard if you're installing ceramic tile in a wet location. If the condition is extreme, you can remove the wall surface to the framing and recover it with backerboard or drywall, shimming it out on the studs. Don't tile adjacent walls that are out of plumb.

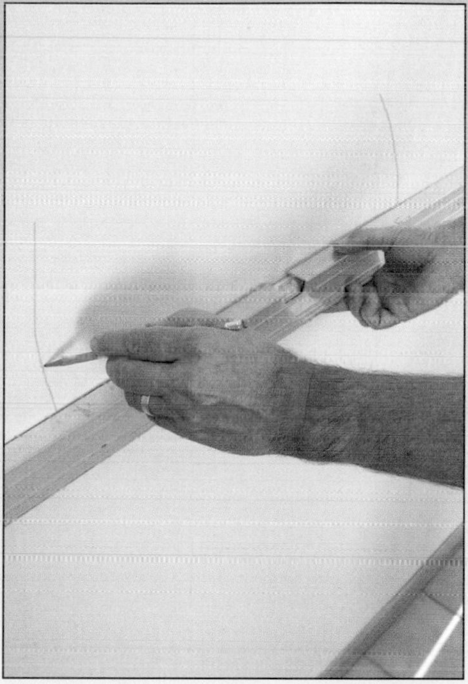

Uneven surface: Like floors, walls to be tiled must be reasonably flat. Wall tiles installed on an irregular wall surface are not as likely to crack as floor tiles, but an uneven surface is much more noticeable on a wall than a floor.

HIDING OUT-OF-SQUARE WALLS

Rigidly uniform tiles accentuate tapered cuts

Rough, irregular tiles diminish effect of tapered cuts

Walls that are out-of-square will require that you cut tapered tiles in the corners. If the condition is not severe, you may be able to make it less noticeable by arranging your layout so you have at least one-half to three-fourths of a tile at the edges. Slightly adjusting the grout width across the entire surface of the wall may help you space the edge tiles more evenly. Rigidly uniform tile will accentuate tapered cuts. Consider using a larger, irregular tile and/or an accent pattern to diminish the effect of tapered cuts. Set the cut tiles in the back corner of side walls where they will be less noticeable.

WHAT IF...
Walls are not flat?

When tiled, wavy walls will go unnoticed if the variations in the surface are broad and not severe.

Correct minor depressions by skim-coating them to level with thinset *(page 75)*. Feather the edges of the skim coat. Check your results by sighting down the surface of the wall with a 4-foot level.

For severe problems you may need to resurface the wall with backerboard, shimming it to level.

STANLEY PRO TIP: Lay out walls with windows

How you lay out a wall with a window depends somewhat on the width of the wall. On long walls with a centered window, pencil a line through its midpoint and draw in an evenly spaced tile pattern on either side of it. If the window is not centered, draw a line midway between the edges of the window and the corners.

Walls shorter than 8 feet will show uneven edges more dramatically. Try to position a full tile at the window with even cut tiles at the edges. Bullnose tile at the window may also help even out the placement.

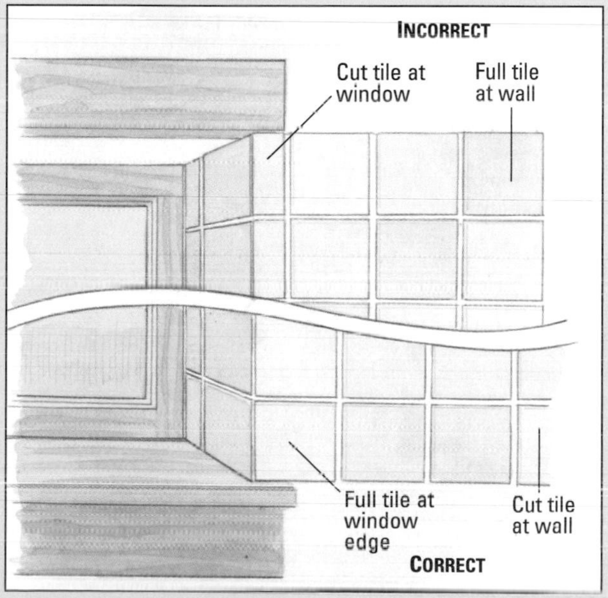

PREPARING SURFACES FOR TILING

Preparing a floor, wall, or countertop for tiling may account for more than half of the work your project entails. Careful preparation pays off—the installation will go more quickly and the results will look better.

Different surfaces and different kinds of tile require different steps of preparation. The chart on *page 51* provides a quick overview of the steps required for ceramic tile. Look for instructions for other kinds of tile in later chapters.

Structural requirements

If you are setting tile in new construction, it's easy to ensure the surface is ready for tile. If you're renovating an existing room, you may have to retrofit the surfaces to make them plumb, flat, and level. Such corrections generally require only basic tools and skills, and a bit of patience.

Ceramic and stone tile add substantial weight to a floor. Some methods to strengthen floor structures are included in this chapter. Other floors may require more extensive work better left to a professional contractor. Consult an architect or contractor if in doubt.

Organize your work

Plan the work in sections. When possible, do the easier tasks first and work your way up to more difficult chores. Most projects begin with removing trim or moldings or moving major appliances. The topics in this chapter are presented in the general order in which they should occur. Read through the chapter in its entirety, then make a list of the tasks that apply to your installation.

Take your time and work carefully. It's difficult and expensive to undo mistakes.

Tools and materials

For each project, make a list of the tools and materials you need and bring all of them to the work area before starting. Nothing will slow you down more than repeated trips to the basement, garage, or hardware store.

Tile requires strong and stable surfaces. Proper preparation is essential and saves time and money.

CHAPTER PREVIEW

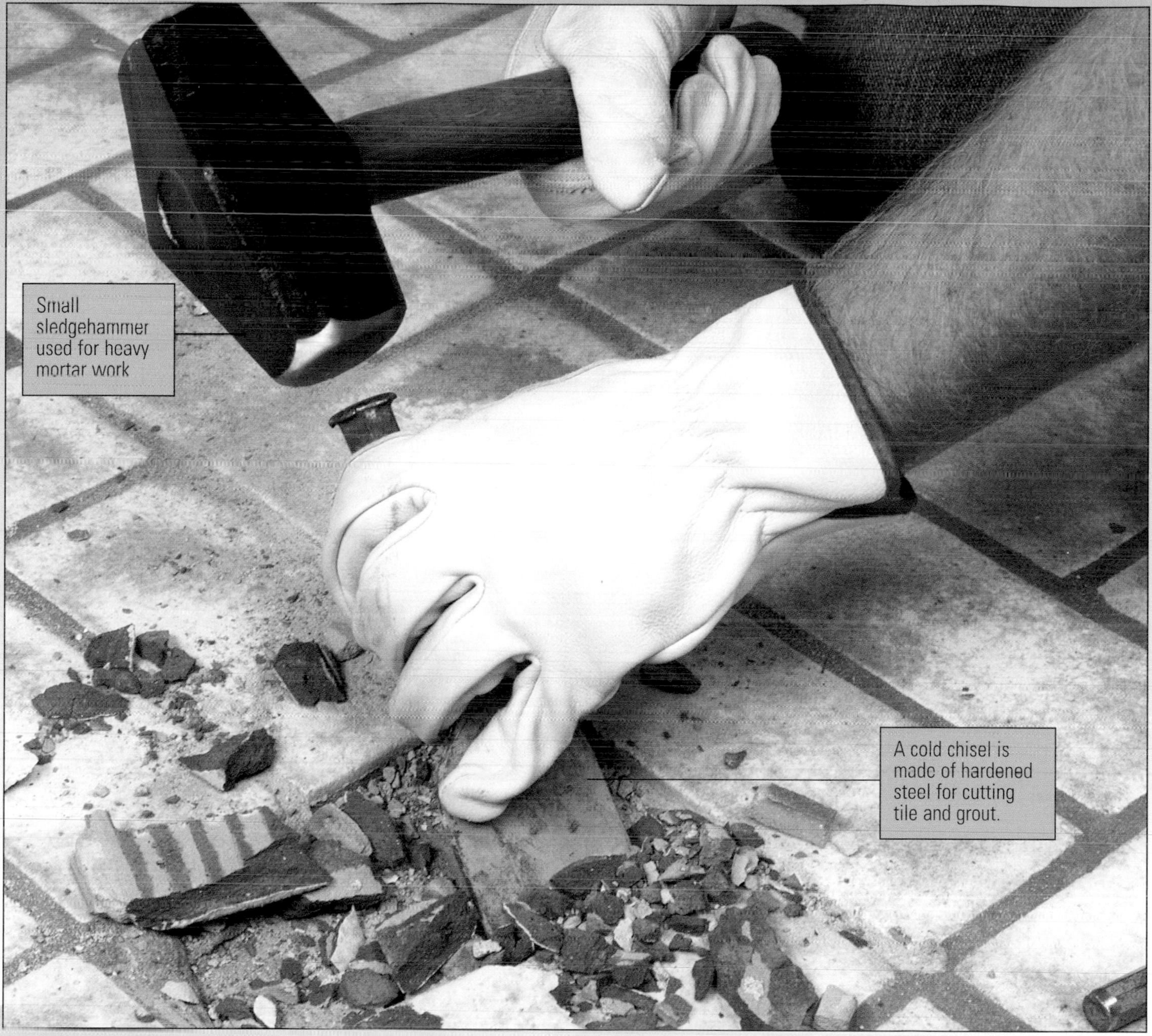
Small sledgehammer used for heavy mortar work
A cold chisel is made of hardened steel for cutting tile and grout.

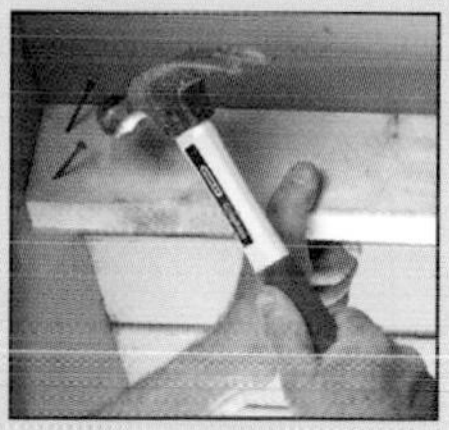
Preparing a wood subfloor
page 68

Preparing a slab floor
page 70

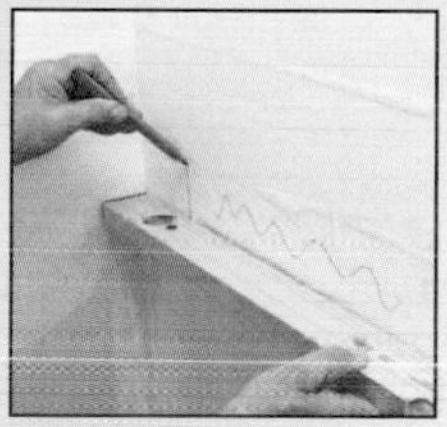
Preparing walls for tile
page 72

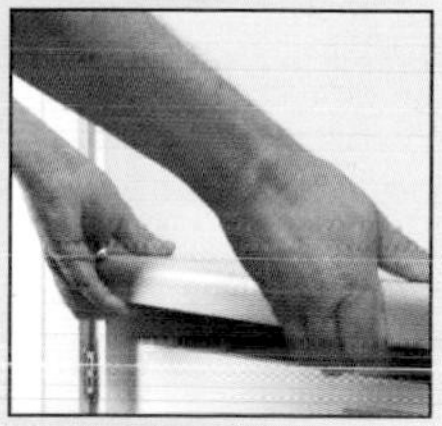
Removing countertops
page 70

Installing a new countertop base
page 80

Installing radiant heating
page 82

GENERAL ROOM PREPARATION

Before you begin any demolition or preparation, take steps to keep dust and debris localized to the room in which you're working.

Protect the surfaces

If you're not tiling the floor, protect it with a tarp or heavy-duty drop cloth. Tape the drop cloth if necessary to keep it from moving and exposing the existing floor as you work. Heavy rosin paper is an option, but mesh reinforced plastic tarps are inexpensive and reusable.

Lay tarps on hallways outside the work area to keep floors from being scratched by tracked-in dust. A small rug (a carpet sample works well) placed just outside the door of the work area will remove debris from your shoes.

Remove any furniture and use old bedsheets to protect built-in cabinets, bookshelves, and other fixtures. Cabinets and vanities generally don't require removal unless the subfloor needs repairing.

Keep dust from migrating into other rooms. Tape cardboard over heat and return-air ducts (remove the floor registers if tiling the floor). Tape plastic sheets over open entries or tack up an old bedsheet to allow access to another room. Put an exhaust fan in a window to increase ventilation.

What to do with the doors?

Leave the doors hanging, unless you need to remove them to take up the old flooring. A closed door helps protect other areas of the house from dust. You can trim doors just before installing the tile or after you have laid it.

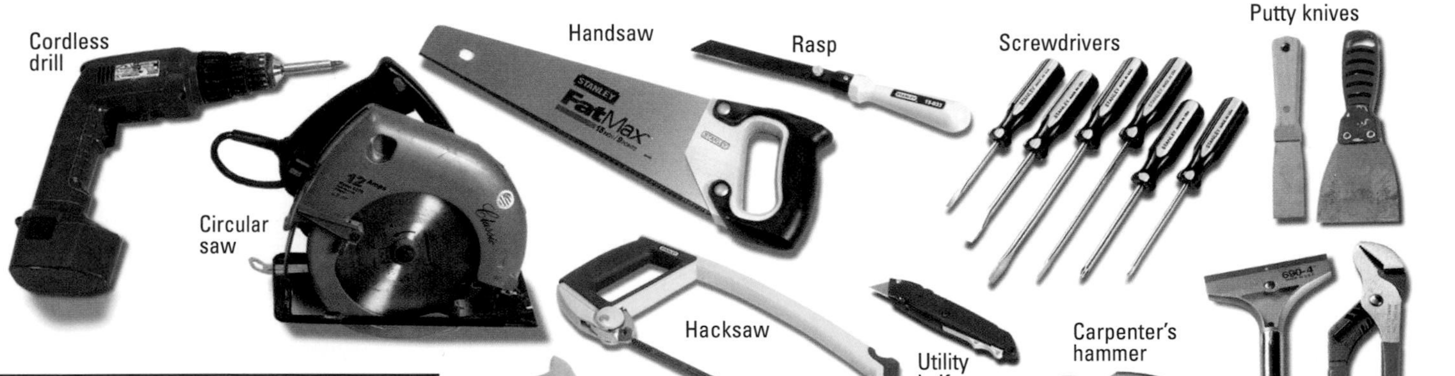
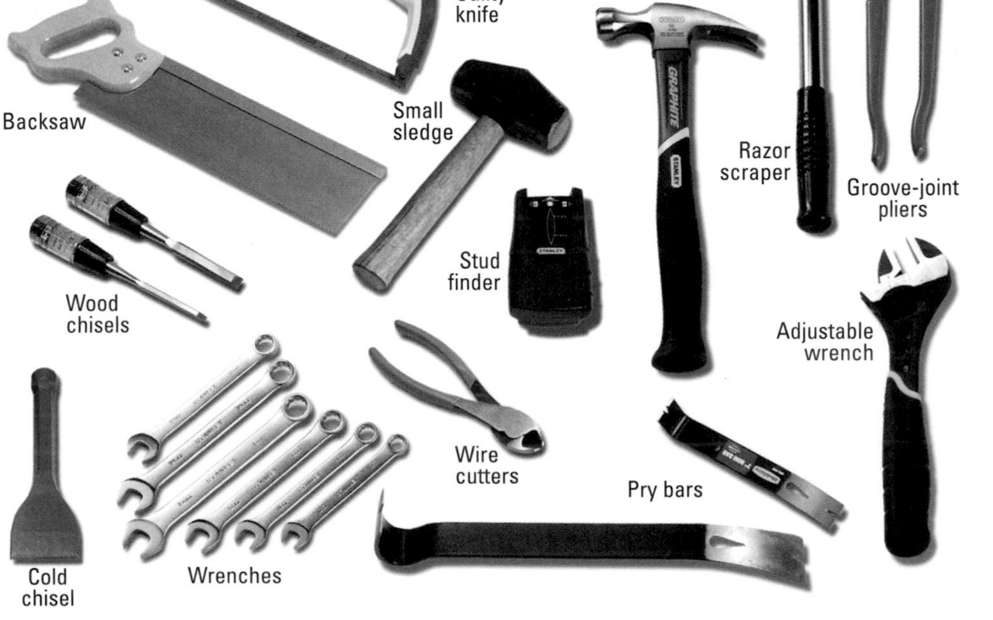

Although certain preparation tasks may require special tools such as a reciprocating saw or right-angled grinder, these tools will accomplish most of the work. Rent special tools at a local rental supply store and plan the work so you can return them in a day.

SAFETY FIRST
Tools for safety and comfort

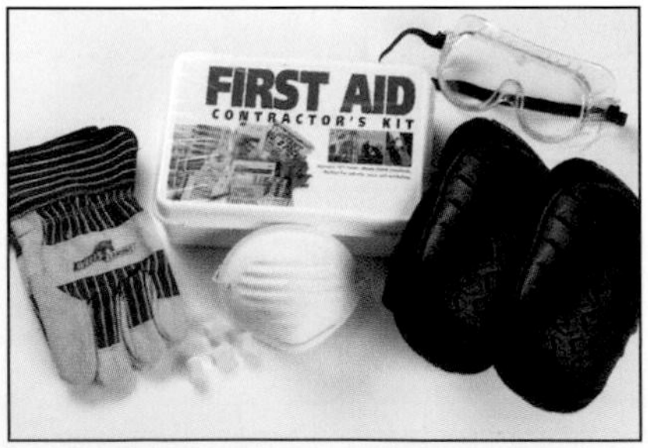

Demolition and preparation are hard work and not without certain dangers. Keep the work space safe and dress for safety. Plan the work in stages and bring only the tools you need into the work area. Remove clutter and tools as you complete each task.

Wear boots and gloves, a dust mask or respirator, knee pads, and safety glasses. Keep a well-stocked first-aid kit handy in case of mishaps.

PREPARING SURFACES FOR CERAMIC/STONE TILE

Existing surface types	Demolition	Preparation	Type of setting bed
FLOORS			
Hardwood strip or planks			
Strips/planks on wood frame	Remove if in poor repair, install new subfloor	If in good repair, stabilize and repair surface	Thinset
Strips/planks on slab	Remove flooring	Repair and roughen surface	Thinset
Carpet			
Padded carpet on slab	Remove carpet, pad, tack strip	Scrape off pad, glue; slip sheet over cracks	Thinset
Glued-down carpet on slab	Remove carpet	Scrape off adhesive; slip sheet over cracks	Thinset
Padded carpet on wood	Remove carpet, pad, tack strip	Glue and screw backerboard	Thinset
Resilient materials			
Vinyl on slab	Remove vinyl	Scrape off adhesives; slip sheet over cracks	Thinset
Vinyl on wood	Remove vinyl that comes off easily	Glue and screw backerboard	Thinset
Ceramic tile			
Ceramic tile on slab	If loose or damaged, chip out tile	Scrape off all old setting materials; slip sheet over all cracks	Thinset
Ceramic tile, mortar bed	If solid and resulting floor will not be too high, leave in	Remove loose tile and fill voids; clean and etch tile	Thinset
Ceramic tile on wood	Remove tile	Glue and screw down backerboard	Thinset
WALLS			
Drywall/plaster			
Painted	None	Degloss high sheen; scrape loose paint	Mastic/thinset
Wallpapered	Remove paper	Scrape off adhesive; clean surface	Mastic/thinset
Ceramic tile	Chip off tile	Scrape off adhesives; repair	Mastic/thinset
Ceramic tile (shower area)	Remove tile and drywall to studs	Install backerboard	Thinset
Cultured marble	Remove marble and drywall	Install backerboard	Thinset
Paneling			
Hardwood wainscoting	Remove hardwood	Repair surface	Mastic/thinset
Plywood/hardboard paneling	Remove paneling	Repair surface	Mastic/thinset

COUNTERTOPS

Removal of existing material and rebuilding new countertop base is generally preferred to installing tile over existing surface.

REMOVING MOLDING AND BASEBOARDS

In rooms without appliances, preparation of a floor for tiling begins by removing moldings and baseboards. (For kitchens and any room with appliances, see *pages 54–55*).

Most rooms with wooden baseboards also have a shoe molding (often called quarter round) that covers the gap at the floor. Shoe moldings come off first, then the baseboards—but take the baseboard off only if you plan to finish the room with a vinyl or ceramic tile base. A reinstalled or new wood baseboard will produce voids where it meets the tile. Those gaps are unsightly and difficult to clean, especially in kitchens and baths. So leave the baseboard in place if it is in good repair or if you're not adding a new one. When you lay the new tile, install it up to the baseboard.

If you plan to reuse the shoe molding, number the pieces as you remove them and mark the corner where you started. Shoe molding sections must go back in their original order.

PRESTART CHECKLIST

☐ **TIME**
About 10 minutes per lineal foot to remove shoe molding and wood baseboard, slightly more for cove molding and tile removal. Nail removal and adhesive cleanup can be time-consuming and varies with the length of nails and type of adhesive used.

☐ **TOOLS**
Utility knife, wide putty knife, pry bar, hammer, scrap wood (optional), nippers or side cutters, handsaw or backsaw—tools vary with type of molding removed

☐ **SKILLS**
Cutting precisely with utility knife, using a hammer and pry bar; threshold removal requires using a handsaw

Removing wood shoe molding and baseboards

1 Starting at a corner, slide a small pry bar behind the shoe. Loosen the shoe until you can insert the pry bar next to a nail. Pry the nail out a little at a time. To avoid splits, loosen at least two nails before pulling the molding completely off the wall.

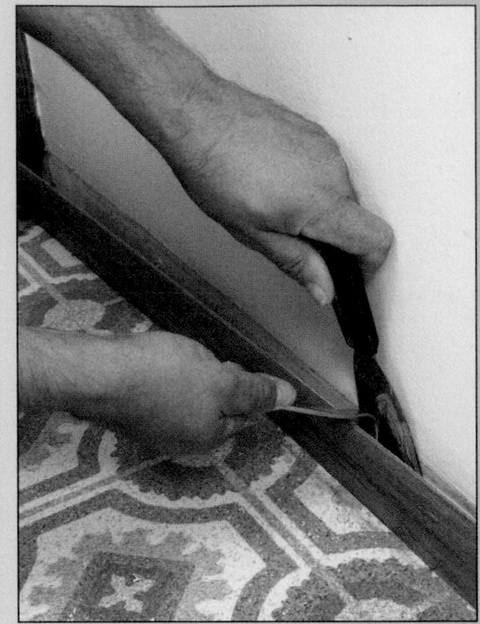

2 Begin at a corner or at a mitered joint, working a wide putty knife behind the baseboard. Loosen each nail with a pry bar. Keep the putty knife behind the bar or use a thin piece of scrap as a shim to avoid marring the surface of the wall. Loosen all nails before removing a baseboard section.

STANLEY PRO TIP: **Score the paint line**

Paint that has adhered to the wall and a wood baseboard, vinyl cove molding, or ceramic tile base may pull off the wall when you remove the molding, leaving unsightly chips that require repainting. Repainting is time-consuming, and new paint often doesn't match the old.

To avoid pulling the paint off the wall when removing a base molding, score the paint line with a sharp utility knife.

Insert the knife in the joint between the wall and the molding, and draw the knife toward you at an angle that follows the joint. Use enough pressure to cut through the paint. Paint can be stubborn—use two hands if necessary to cut through several coats. Make several repeated passes; the job will actually go faster, and you'll avoid broken blades and skinned knuckles.

3 If you plan to reuse the shoe molding or baseboard, pull out the nails from the back. Use nippers to grab the nail at its base and lever it partly out. Repeat the process until the nail pops loose.

Removing vinyl cove molding

1 Insert a wide-blade putty knife at the top corner of a joint in the molding. Push down on the knife and lift the molding off the surface of the wall. Slide the full width of the blade under the molding and strip it off, keeping the knife handle parallel to the floor as much as possible.

2 When you have removed all the molding strips, use your putty knife to scrape off the remaining adhesive. Keep the knife at an angle that will remove the adhesive without gouging the wall surface. Light pressure and repeated passes work better than trying to remove the adhesive all at once.

Removing ceramic tile

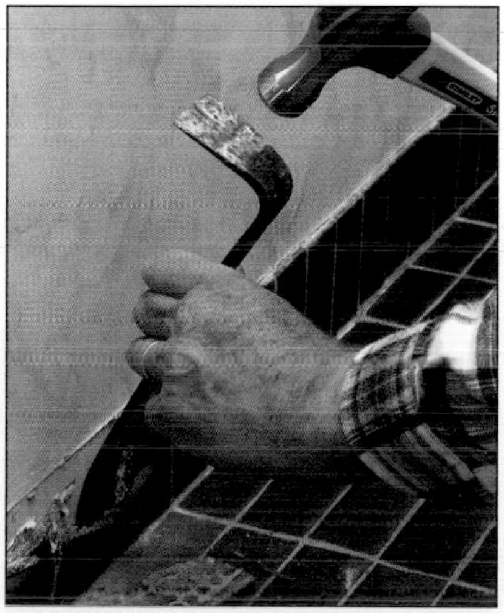

Tap the pry bar into the joint. Pop each tile loose. If necessary, protect the wall with scrap behind the bar. Scrape off adhesive.

Removing thresholds

1 Use a handsaw or backsaw to cut the threshold in half all the way to the surface of the floor. Cut carefully to avoid damaging other surfaces.

2 Pry each piece up with a pry bar and remove it. If the threshold is screwed down, remove the screws and slide it out from under the door trim.

REMOVING APPLIANCES

Tile must extend under appliances, such as dishwashers, compactors, and stoves, so cleaning liquids or spills and leaks won't drain over the tile edge and damage the floor below.

Remove appliances early in the preparation stage of your project so they won't be in the way when you perform the rest of the demolition, preparation, and repair work.

The space under appliances provides an excellent opportunity to use large pieces of cut tile, tiles cut inaccurately, or tiles whose glaze is flawed or whose color doesn't match the dye lot of the rest.

Before moving appliances, check to see if they will fit their enclosures after you've laid the new tile. Remember, new tile may increase the height of the floor, so measure each appliance and add the thickness of the tile and adhesive. To make room, you may have to cut the cabinet frame above a refrigerator or shim up a countertop to accommodate a dishwasher *(page 81)*.

Plan ahead for proper reconnection of water, gas, or electrical lines.

PRESTART CHECKLIST

☐ **TIME**
About 15 minutes to remove a refrigerator, 15 to 20 minutes for gas appliances and plug-in electric units, more for direct-wired appliances

☐ **TOOLS**
Groove-joint pliers, adjustable wrench, straight and phillips screwdrivers, cordless drill and bits, appliance dolly

☐ **SKILLS**
Removing screws with screwdrivers or cordless drill, removing nuts with wrenches, moving large appliances

☐ **PREP**
Shut off water-supply valves

☐ **MATERIALS**
Duct tape and wire nuts

Removing a dishwasher

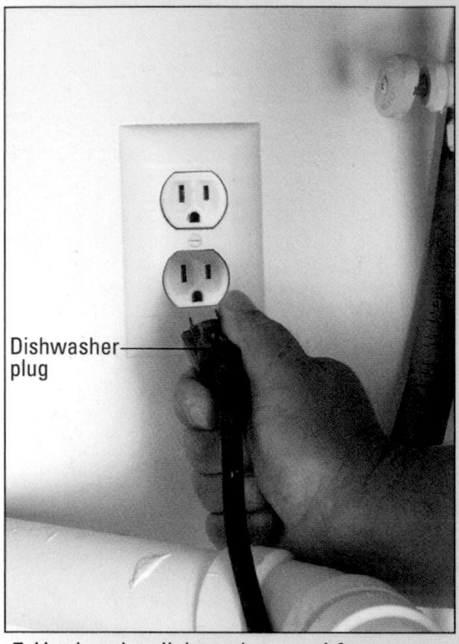

1 Unplug the dishwasher cord from the receptacle under the sink. If you don't see a power plug on the cord, the dishwasher is wired directly into the circuit and the wiring itself must be disconnected. In such installations, **shut off the power before proceeding.**

2 Turn off the supply valve. Disconnect the supply line and drain hose with a wrench. Remove the bottom dishwasher panel for access, tug on the lines to locate their connections, and disconnect them.

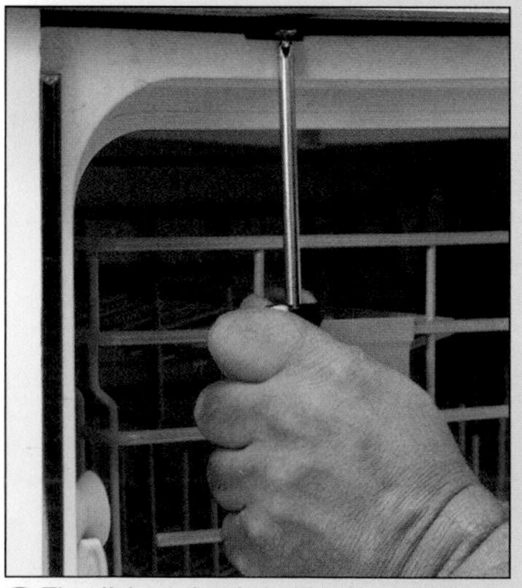

3 The dishwasher is held in the cabinet with screws fastened in the side (and on some models the top and bottom) flanges. Open the dishwasher door for access to the screws and remove them with the appropriate screwdriver or cordless drill.

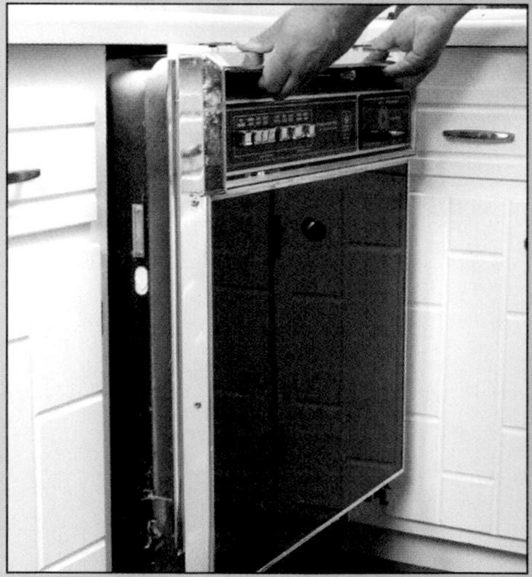

4 Close the door of the dishwasher and lock it. Grasp the dishwasher by the sides of the door and/or the door handle and slide it forward. Lift up slightly and rock the unit from side to side if it sticks. If necessary have a helper thread supply and drain lines back through the cabinet holes as you pull.

Removing a countertop range

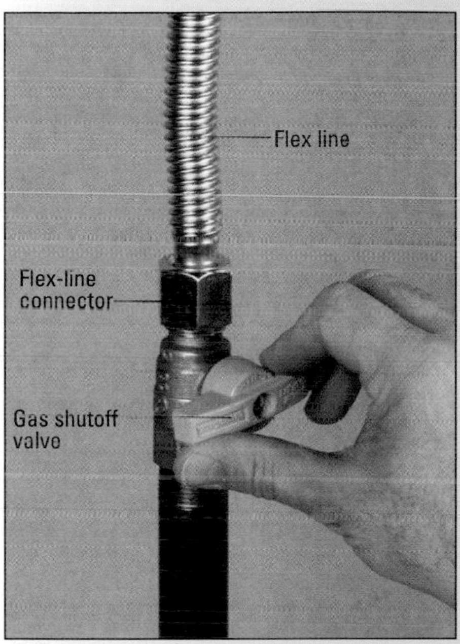

1 For a gas unit, **shut off the gas** by turning the handle on the shutoff valve. Using groove-joint pliers, loosen the flex-line connector (or pipe) and disconnect the line from the valve. For an electric range, **unplug the 220-volt power plug** under the cabinet.

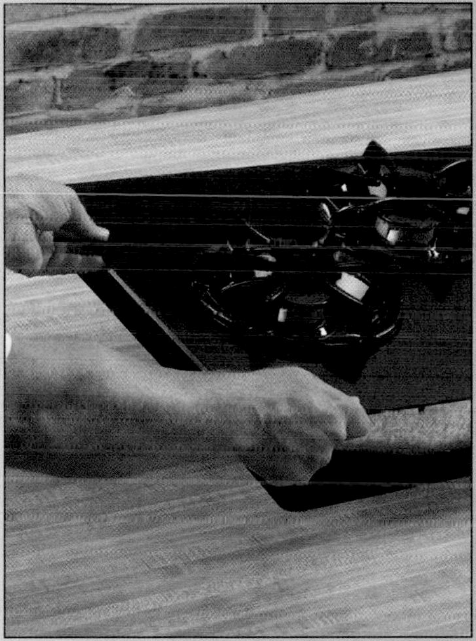

2 Your range may be anchored by clips or retainers similar to those used to anchor a countertop sink *(page 79)*. Remove any clips or retainers, push up on the unit from below with one hand to create a space for lifting, then lift the unit up and out. Do not kink the flex line; kinking may put holes in it.

Removing a stove

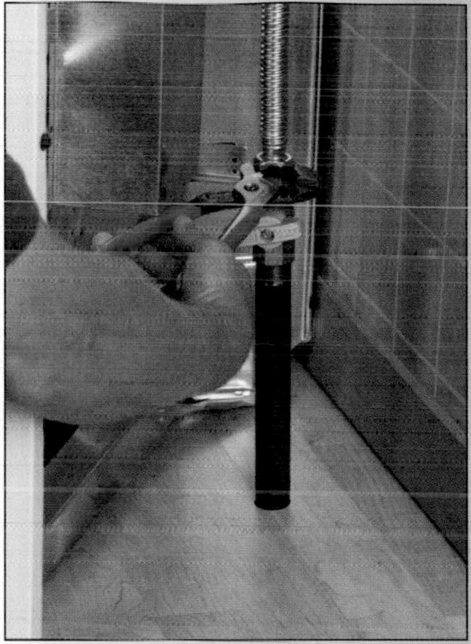

Pull the stove away from the wall enough to reach the power plug or gas valve. **Unplug the power cord or turn off the gas valve.** Using groove-joint pliers, loosen the flex-line connector. Bend the flex line gently and tape it out of the way. Dolly the stove to a different room.

WHAT IF...
An electric appliance is wired directly to the circuit?

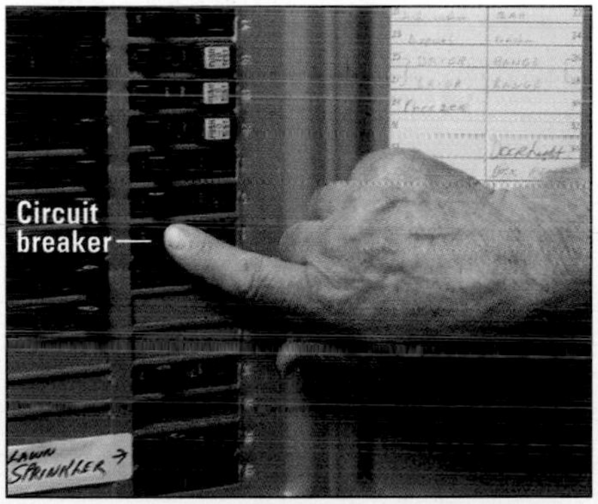

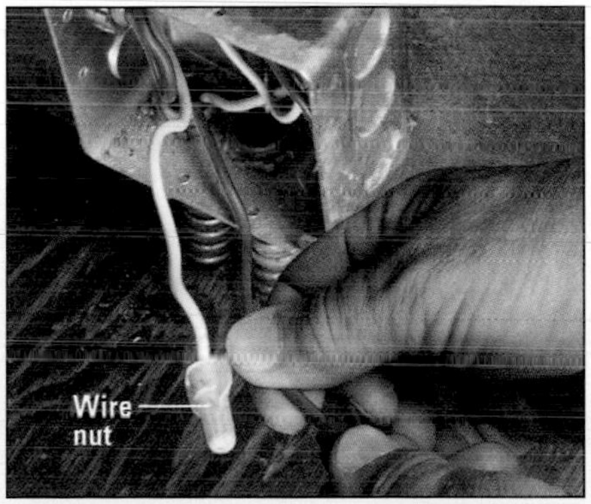

If you don't see a plug on the power cord of an appliance, the unit is wired directly to a circuit. **Turn off the circuit breaker** and tape a note to it so someone doesn't turn it on accidentally. Find the junction box to which the appliance is connected; remove the cover plate. **Use a voltage tester to check the wires for power.** If they are dead, disconnect the wires, noting how they are attached. Loosen the cord clamp on the side of the box and pull out the appliance cord. Screw wire nuts tightly onto the circuit wires and tuck them into the box. Attach the cover plate. **If in doubt, call a professional electrician.**

SAFETY FIRST
Use an appliance dolly

An appliance dolly moves heavy items safely. Slide the dolly plate under the unit, tighten the strap, tip the unit back slightly, and roll it away. Enlist a helper to move large appliances.

REMOVING FIXTURES

Although you can leave toilets and sinks in place and tile around them, removing them makes the job easier. With the fixtures out of the way, you'll have more working room, substantially fewer cut tiles to install, and fewer exposed joints to maintain. You'll spend less time removing fixtures than cutting tiles, and the result will be much more attractive and professional looking.

For tub and shower fixtures, removal is not an option. These fixtures must come off before you tile the wall around them.

Over time, fixture anchor bolts often rust, bend, and otherwise undergo alterations that make their removal a stubborn chore. A few special techniques *(page 57)* will quickly solve these problems.

PRESTART CHECKLIST

☐ **TIME**
About 30 to 45 minutes each for toilet, wall-mounted sink, and pedestal sink (more if anchor bolts prove stubborn); about 15 minutes for tub and shower fixture set

☐ **TOOLS**
Plumber's plunger, groove-joint pliers, locking pliers (optional), adjustable wrench, straight and phillips screwdrivers, allen wrenches, narrow putty knife, hacksaw, mini hacksaw (optional), pipe wrench, tape measure, bucket

☐ **SKILLS**
Removing screws with screwdrivers, removing fasteners with wrenches

☐ **PREP**
Turn off water supply valve(s) for each fixture removed

☐ **MATERIALS**
Bleach, rags, plastic bag, penetrating oil, wood shims, flange extension, new closet flange and bolts, duct tape, pipe nipples and caps

Removing a toilet

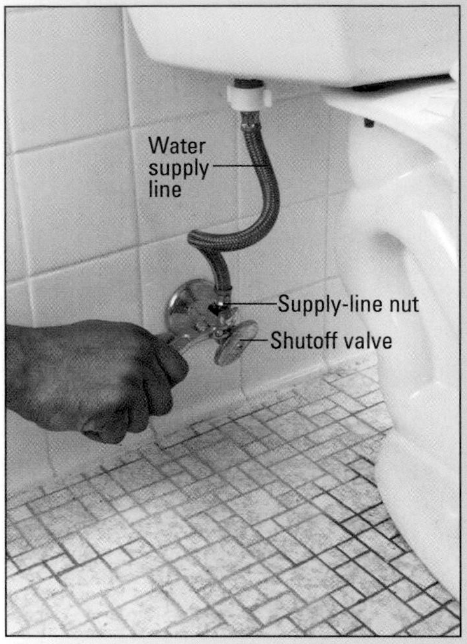

1 Pour a quart of bleach into the tank, flush, and let it refill. Close the supply valve and reflush, holding the handle down until the tank empties. Push the water out of the trap with a plunger and stuff the bowl with rags. Disconnect the supply line with a wrench or groove-joint pliers.

2 Pry off the anchor bolt caps. Remove the anchor bolts with an adjustable wrench or groove-joint pliers. If the bolts spin, snap, or won't come off, try one of the solutions below. Even if you have to cut the bolts, you can still remove the toilet and replace the bolts when you reinstall it.

TYPICAL TOILET INSTALLATION

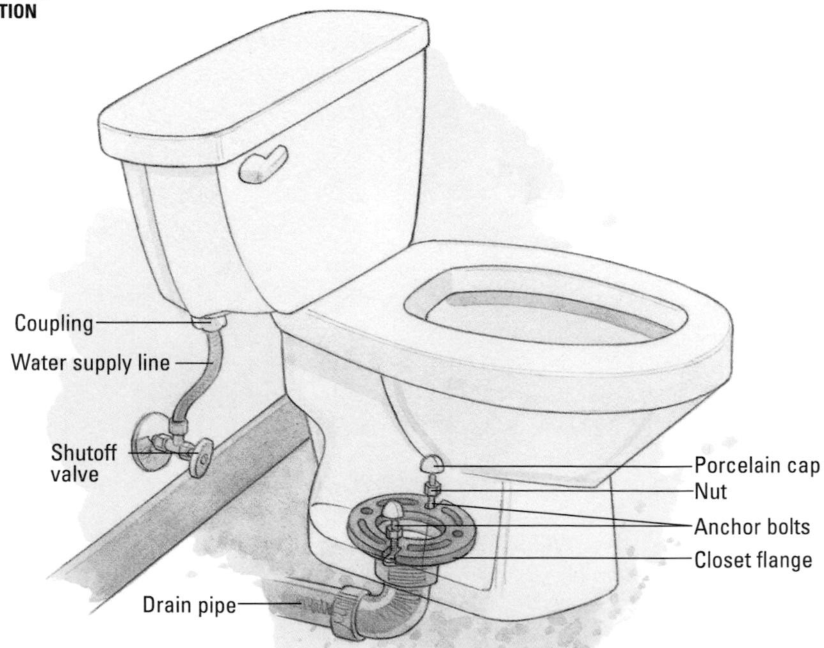

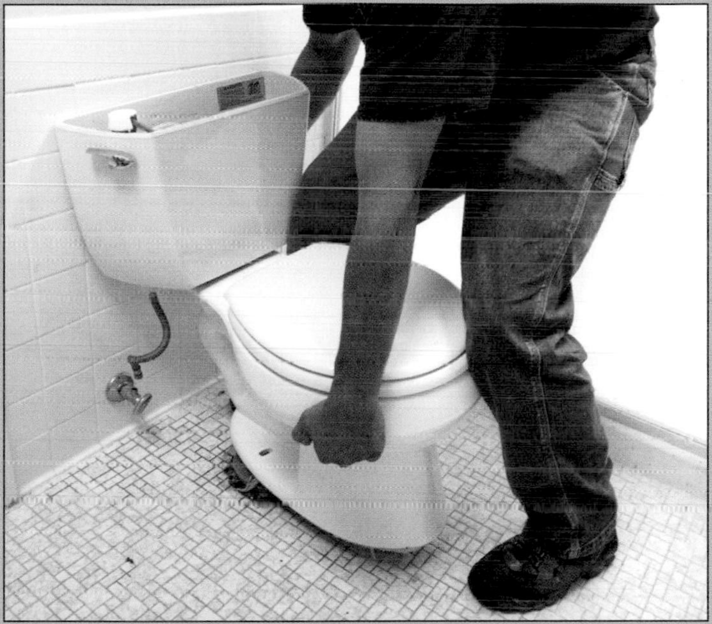

3 The bottom of the toilet trap fits snugly over a wax ring that seals it against the closet flange in the floor (see *page 56*). To break the seal of the wax ring, rock the toilet gently back and forth as you lift it off the floor. Newer, low-capacity toilets may be light enough for you to lift by yourself, but older toilets can weigh up to 60 pounds. Get help to avoid risk of injury. Lift the toilet off the floor and carry it to another room.

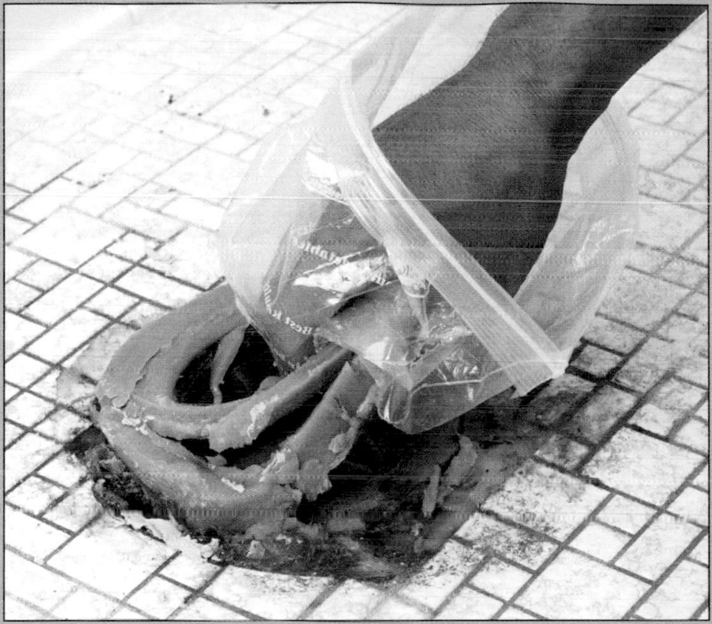

4 With one hand in a plastic bag, grab the inside bottom edge of the ring. Pull it out, pulling the bag over the ring with your other hand. Dispose of the ring. With a putty knife scrape residue from the flange. Stuff a large rag into the drain to keep out debris. Measure from the flange to the height of the new tile (the combined thickness of new tile and backerboard). Purchase a flange extension, if necessary, to bring the flange about ¼ inch above the new floor.

Toilet bolts spin, snap, or won't come off?

If the bolts snap when you try to remove the nut, pull out the broken piece, remove the toilet, and see if the pieces remaining in the flange will come loose with locking pliers. If they won't, you can install a repair flange before you begin tiling the floor.

If a bolt spins, drive a wood shim under the toilet on both sides of the bolt. The resulting upward pressure may keep it from spinning so you can unscrew the nut.

Stubborn nuts may loosen with a squirt of penetrating oil. Let the oil set for about 10 minutes before trying to loosen the nuts again.

If a nut still won't budge, or if the wood shims didn't stop the bolt from spinning, saw the bolt with a hacksaw. Insert the hacksaw blade under the nut and cut through the bolt. If there isn't enough working room for a full-size saw, use a mini hacksaw (as shown).

STANLEY PRO TIP

Install a flange extension

The combined thickness of new flooring materials—cement backerboard, thinset, and tile—may raise the floor by as much as 1 inch. Raise the height of the flange with an extender.

Available at most hardware stores, an extender consists of rings that are stacked over the floor flange and sealed with silicone caulk. Add enough rings to bring the flange at least flush with and preferably about ¼ inch higher than the new floor.

Removing a showerhead

1 If you are replacing the plumbing or valves to a shower, you must first turn off the water supply. Remove the showerhead with an adjustable or open-end wrench. If the showerhead is not machined for a wrench, use groove-joint pliers, protecting the collar with duct tape or rags.

2 Wrap the gooseneck with several layers of duct tape about 1 inch from the wall to protect it. Adjust a pipe wrench so it just fits over the gooseneck and position the jaws so the wrench will pull counterclockwise. Pull the wrench firmly, keeping it perpendicular to the pipe.

TYPICAL SHOWER INSTALLATION

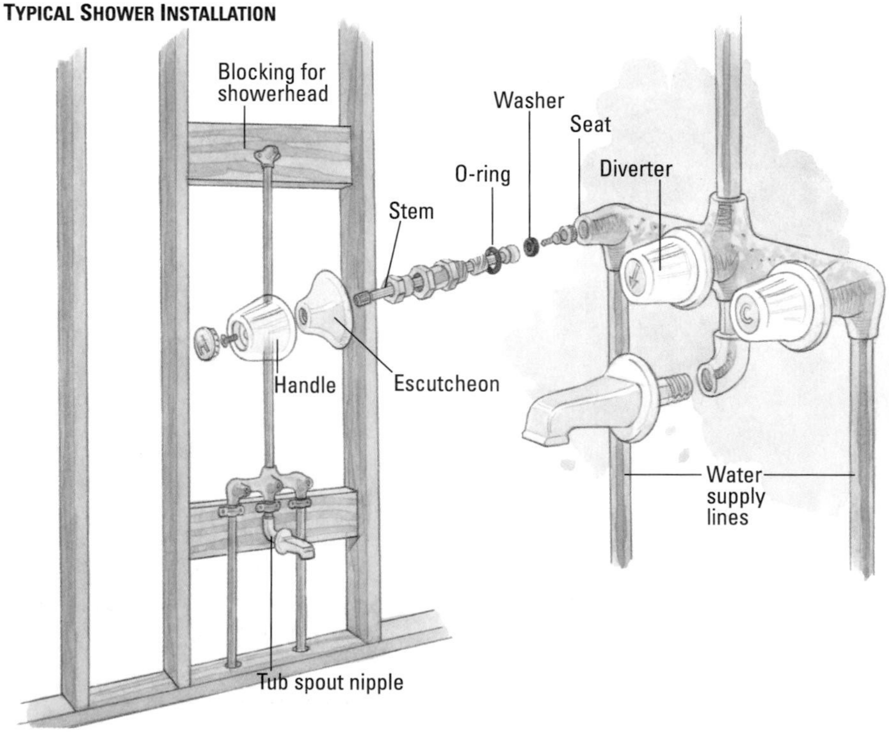

Removing a tub spout

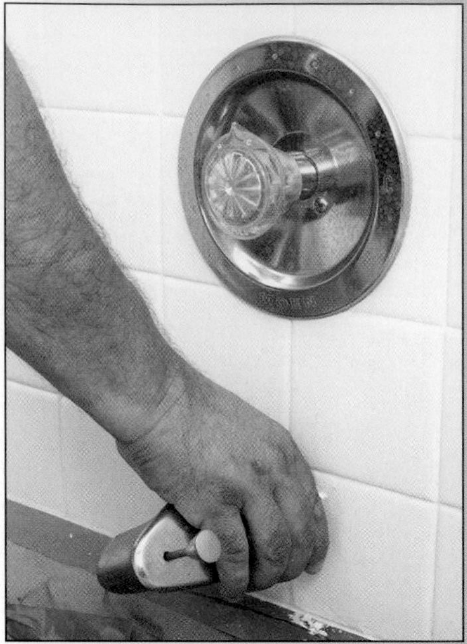

Grasp the spout firmly with both hands and unscrew it from the fitting. If the spout is fastened to the pipe with a clamp, loosen the clamp screw—usually accessible from the plumbing access door on the other side of the wall behind the shower. Pull off the spout.

SHOWER AND TUB FITTINGS
Cap the pipe

Once you have removed a shower gooseneck or tub spout, screw a pipe nipple into the fitting. A nipple is a 5- to 6-inch length of water pipe threaded on one end and capped on the other. It temporarily replaces the fixture and allows you to cut the backerboard in the exact location for the pipe. It also protects the fitting threads from becoming clogged with adhesive. Take the gooseneck or tub spout to the hardware store so you find the right nipple size.

Removing shower faucet handles

1 Most faucets fit on a valve stem and are held in place with setscrews. If the screw is not visible, you'll find it under a cover plate. Insert a thin screwdriver blade under the edge of the cover plate and use slight pressure to pop it off. Cover the drain to make sure you don't lose the screw.

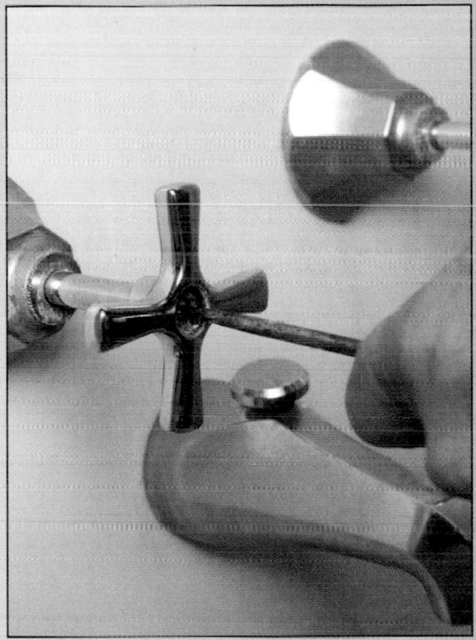

2 Select the proper size screwdriver (usually a phillips head) and remove the screws from each faucet.

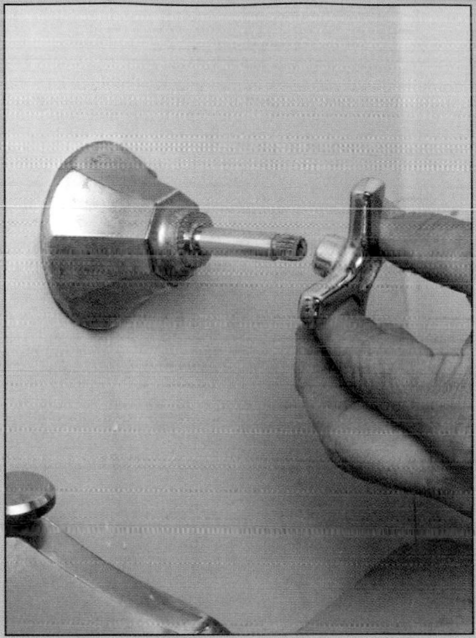

3 Grasp the handle from the back—with both hands if necessary—and pull it toward you. Wiggling the handle sometimes helps. Penetrating oil also helps. If the handle is especially stubborn, rent a special tool called a handle puller. Tape all the parts together and store them out of the way.

STANLEY PRO TIP

Measure the thread length

If you are tiling over existing wall tile or installing new tile with backerboard, the combined thickness of the new materials may exceed the length of the threads on the faucet valves. The threads of the valves need to extend beyond the new wall.

Measure the depth of the threads. If they are less than the thickness of the new materials, you'll have to install new faucets—a job best left to a plumber.

WHAT IF...

A faucet has only one handle?

1 Remove the setscrew (on the underside of the handle or under a plastic cap) with a screwdriver or allen wrench. If you can't find a setscrew, try unscrewing the handle itself.

2 Pull the handle off the stem and remove the escutcheon-plate screws. Pull off the escutcheon plate and any other plates under it, tape the parts together, and store them.

Removing a pedestal sink

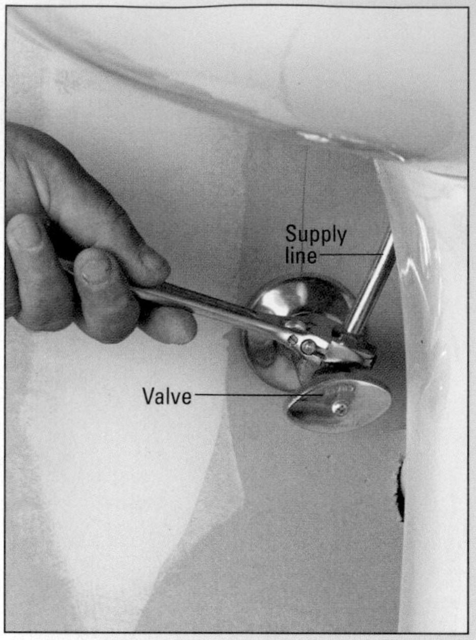

1 Shut off both the hot and cold water valves and loosen the compression nuts on both supply lines with a wrench or groove-joint pliers. Pull the supply line out of the valve. If the sink has fixed-length supply lines, remove the nut and push the lines gently out of the way.

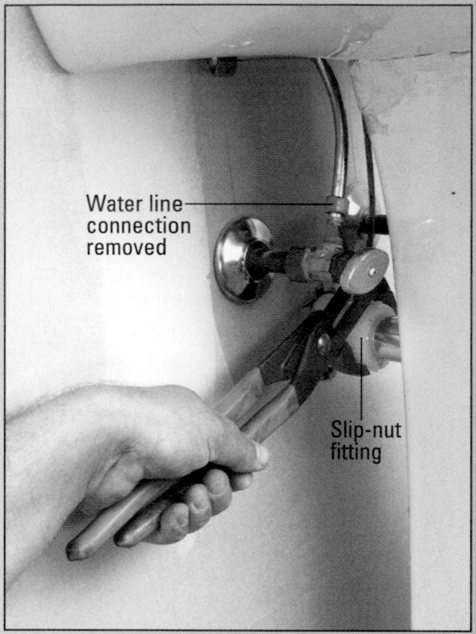

2 Place a pile of rags under the trap to catch any water released as you remove the pipe. Loosen the slip-nut fitting (on both ends of the trap, if possible) with groove-joint pliers or a pipe wrench and pull the trap off. Pour the trap water in a bucket.

3 Remove any bolts attaching the top to the pedestal. Lift the top off. If the sink is hung on wall brackets, grasp it near the wall and pull up. Unbolt the pedestal from the floor and lift it off. If the sink is a one-piece unit, unbolt it from the wall and floor. Remove the wall brackets if tiling the wall.

TYPICAL PEDESTAL SINK INSTALLATION

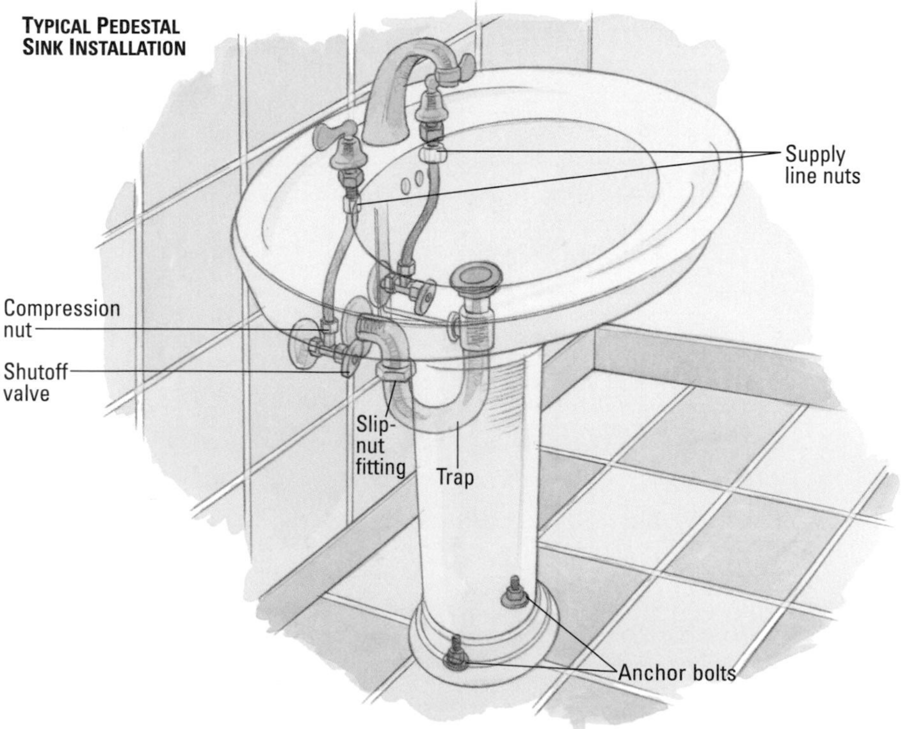

Tiling around floor pipes

Many steam and hot water heating systems that use baseboard elements and floor-standing radiators have delivery pipes that come up through the floor. When you lay the floor tile around these pipes, tile to within ¼ inch of them and fill the gap with silicone caulk instead of grout. The caulk will let the pipes move in the hole without making noise.

Remove floor radiators for floor tile installations and when tiling a wall behind them. You can leave wall-mounted heating elements in place when tiling a wall, but the job will look neater if you remove them.

In either case, shut off the heat supply and disconnect the unit at the outflow side of the valve. Steam and hot water system fittings can be stubborn. Use a pipe wrench or enlist the services of a professional.

Removing a wall-mounted sink

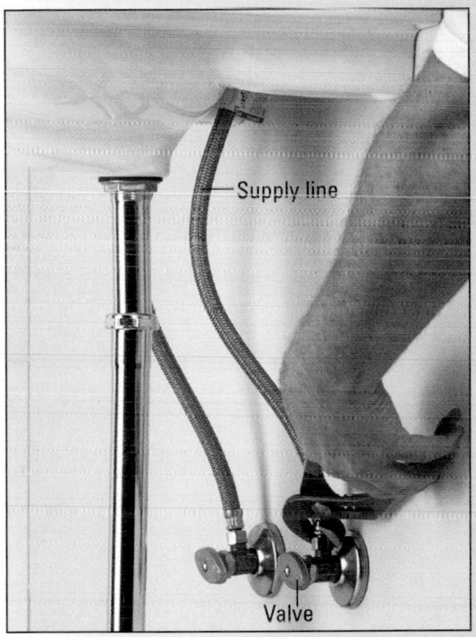

1 Shut off both the hot and cold water valves and loosen the compression nuts on both supply lines with groove-joint pliers or a wrench. Pull the supply line out of the valve. If you have fixed-length supply lines, remove the compression nut and move the lines out of the way.

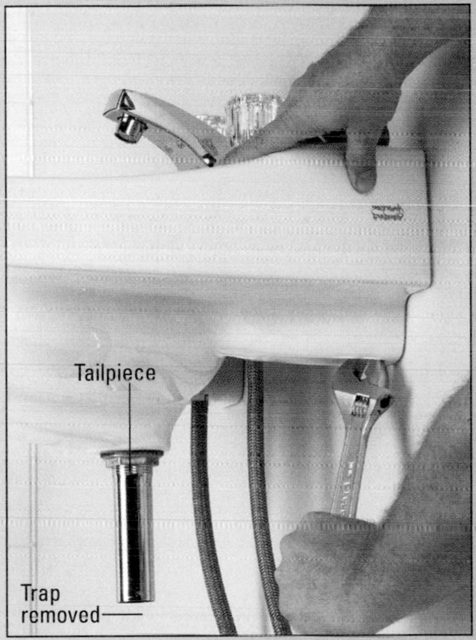

2 Set a bucket under the trap to catch any water released as you remove the pipe. Loosen the slip-nut fittings on both ends of the trap with groove-joint pliers or a pipe wrench and pull the trap off the tailpiece. Dump the trap water in the bucket and remove the sink mounting bolts.

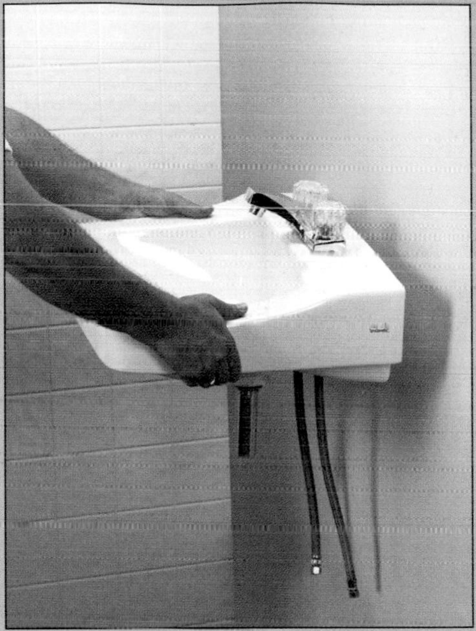

3 Remove any legs that support the front of the sink. Grasp the sink with both hands near the wall and pull it up and off the brackets. If the sink won't come loose, try loosening the wall-bracket bolts a couple of turns, then pull the sink off the brackets. Remove the brackets if tiling the wall.

Tiling around electrical boxes

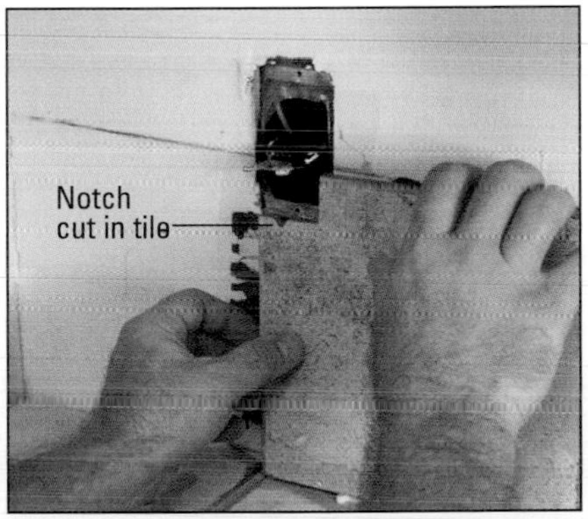

Turn off the power to the box, remove its cover plate, and push the receptacle or switch into the box. When you tile the wall, notch the tiles around the box and use longer screws to reattach the receptacle or switch. Reattach the cover plate. Turn on the power when the job is done.

TYPICAL WALL-MOUNTED SINK INSTALLATION

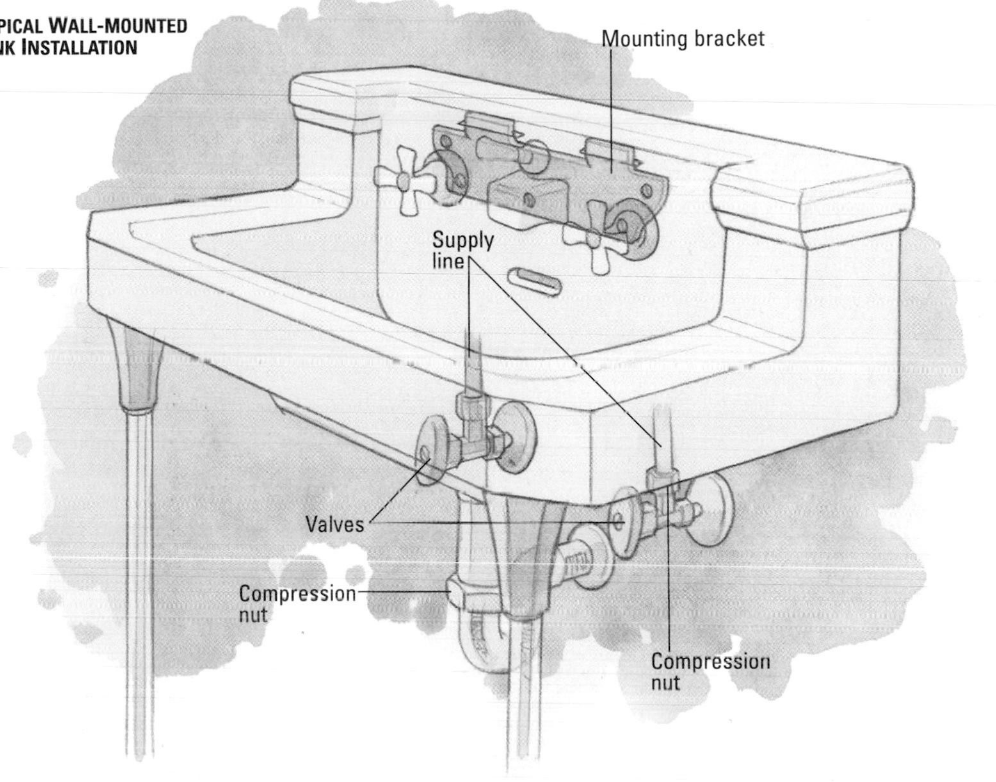

REPAIRING OR REMOVING THE EXISTING FLOOR

When preparing your floor for tile, first decide whether to remove the existing flooring or repair it and tile over it.

Carpet, of course, must be removed, but you can lay any tile over hardwood and ceramic floors—if the surface and subfloor are stable and in good condition, and if the new tile and materials won't raise the floor by more than ¾ inch. The same is true for uncushioned resilient tile or sheet materials on a wood frame floor. Remove cushioned resilients; ceramics can crack and new resilients will dent. Don't lay ceramic tile directly on resilients. Lay backerboard first *(page 34)*. Always remove resilients from a concrete slab before installing tile.

Removing the existing floor will minimize any change in floor levels and reveal any hidden faults that need repair.

PRESTART CHECKLIST

☐ **TIME**
From 30 to 45 minutes per square yard to repair or remove flooring

☐ **TOOLS**
Wood floors: framing square, circular saw, chisels, pry bar, hammer, cordless drill, plug cutter (optional)
Resilient floors: heat gun, wide putty knife, floor scraper, utility knife
Carpet: utility knife, pry bar, hammer, utility knife, screwdriver, floor scraper
Ceramic tile: grout knife, cold chisels, hammer, margin trowel, sanding block

☐ **SKILLS**
Removing and driving fasteners with screwdrivers and cordless drill, cutting with circular saw, using prybar

☐ **MATERIALS**
Wood flooring: ¾-inch exterior plywood, coated screws, ring or spiral shank nails
Resilient flooring: adhesive remover, thinset mortar
Ceramic tile: thinset mortar, extra tile

Repairing damaged hardwood flooring

1 Use a framing square and carpenter's pencil to outline the edge of the damaged area. Set a circular saw to the depth of the hardwood flooring, start the saw with only the front edge of the saw plate resting on the floor, and lower the blade into the cut. Repeat along each line.

2 Chisel out enough flooring to let you insert a pry bar under the flooring. Tap the pry bar under the strips or planks at a nail and pry up. Repeat the process at each nail location within the damaged area. Dispose of the flooring you have removed.

Removing a hardwood floor

1 Using the techniques shown above for repairing damaged flooring, make several plunge cuts in one or two strips or planks. Chisel out the cut area.

2 Tap a pry bar under the flooring at each nail and pry the material up, working along the length of each board. Insert the bar fully under the strip or plank, not the tongue. Otherwise you will split the tongue off the flooring and not remove the strip.

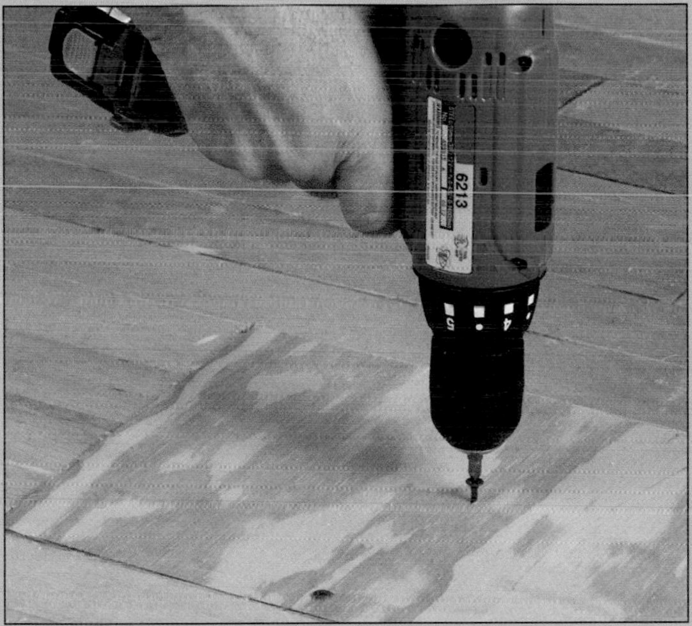

3 Measure the area you have removed and cut a piece of $\frac{3}{4}$-inch exterior-grade plywood to the same dimensions. Fit the plywood into the recess, and using a cordless drill, drive $1\frac{3}{8}$-inch coated screws at 3- to 4-inch intervals through the plywood and into the subfloor. Countersink the screws slightly. If your hardwood floor has been refinished, the patch might be thicker than the floor. Use a belt sander to sand the patch until it's level with the flooring.

Securing loose planks or strips

Floor tile requires a level, firm surface. Anchor any loose hardwood flooring securely. Walk the floor and mark areas that feel spongy or loose. Fasten loose boards at their edges with ringshank or spiral shank nails, or use a cordless drill and drive $1\frac{3}{8}$-inch coated screws through the hardwood and into the subfloor. Predrill the holes to avoid splitting the material.

WHAT IF...

Flooring is plugged plank or parquet?

Use an oversize plug cutter bit in a drill to remove one plug. If no screw is present, the plugs are decorative and don't need removal. Take up the flooring as shown on *page 62*.

If you find screws under the plug, cut out all plugs and remove the screws using a cordless drill. Then take up the flooring using the techniques shown on *page 62*.

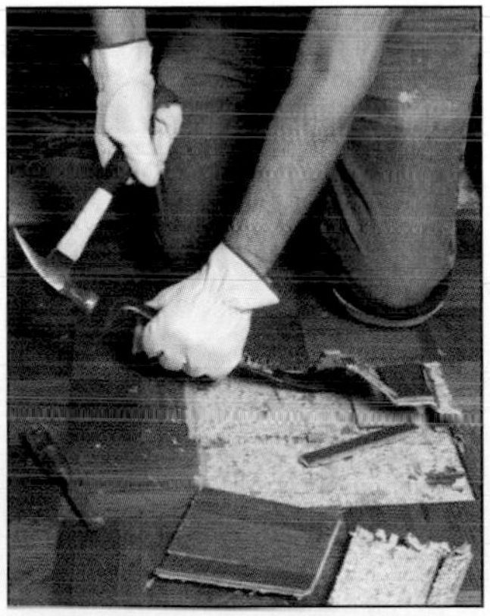

Tap the blade of a wide chisel under the edge of one parquet tile and pry the tile loose. Repeat for each tile and scrape up the adhesive with a wide putty knife.

STANLEY PRO TIP

Reduce the elevation

The combined thickness of new tile and adhesive installed on an existing hardwood floor can raise the height of the floor by more than $\frac{3}{4}$ inch. Such an elevation causes awkward or unsafe transitions between the new floor and the adjoining surface.

When laying tile over hardwood flooring, you can ease such abrupt transitions by using $\frac{1}{4}$-inch cement backerboard instead of the usual $\frac{1}{2}$-inch thickness. The stability of the hardwood when properly prepared and the subfloor underneath will provide sufficient strength and stiffness for any floor, tile or stone.

Removing resilient tile

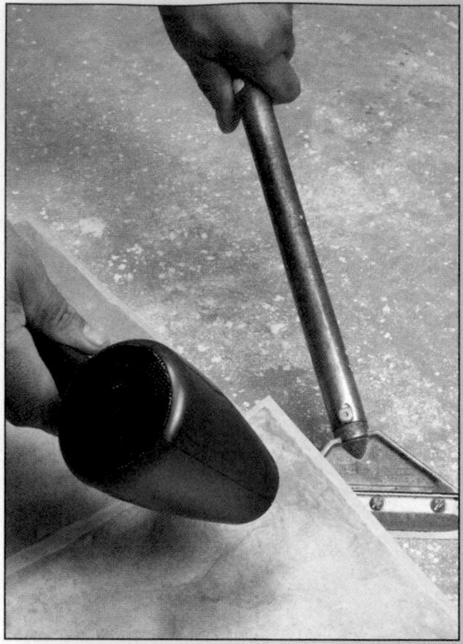

Warm the adhesive with a heat gun. If you don't have a heat gun, use a hair dryer set on high heat. Warm a corner first, insert a floor scraper or wide putty knife, and with the heat on, lift up the tile. Scrape the adhesive from the floor with a floor scraper.

Removing resilient sheet flooring

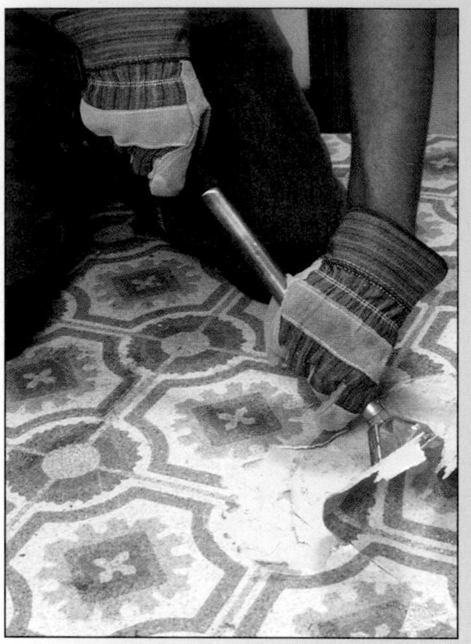

1 Start at a corner or at a bubbled seam. Insert a floor scraper or wide putty knife under the sheet flooring and pry it up. Work down each strip of the material, rolling the strip as you go. If the material is unbacked, use a hair dryer or heat gun to soften the adhesive as you go.

2 Once you have removed the sheet flooring, spray the surface in sections with adhesive remover. Let the remover work according to the manufacturer's instructions, then use a wide scraper or putty knife to peel the residue from the floor.

Repairing resilient surfaces

If you are tiling over a resilient surface on a wood subfloor, and the resilient material is damaged in only a few sections, you can repair it rather than remove it completely.

Using a utility knife, cut through the damaged area to the subfloor. Remove the damaged tile(s) or section(s) of sheet material with a wide putty knife or scraper. Scrape the remaining adhesive from the floor within the area.

Using a mason's trowel or a margin trowel, smear the recess with thinset mortar and level it. Let this thinset dry before applying backerboard.

Use this patching method only on resilient material installed over a wood frame floor. Always remove resilients from a concrete slab before tiling.

STANLEY PRO TIP

Cut flooring into strips

Stripping and removing room-size sections of resilient sheet flooring or carpet is time-consuming and heavy work. To make the job easier, cut resilient sheet flooring or carpet into 12-inch strips before you pull or scrape it up.

SAFETY FIRST
Asbestos warning

Before you remove any resilient material, check with a professional to determine if it contains asbestos.

Asbestos was used as a binder in most resilient flooring materials prior to 1985 and its fibers have since been found to be a carcinogen, especially dangerous when inhaled. Virtually no material installed prior to 1985 is guaranteed asbestos-free. Asbestos was used in asphalt tile, linoleum, vinyl-asbestos tile and sheet flooring, and asphalt adhesives.

If possible, leave asbestos flooring in place and install underlayment or backerboard over it. Never sand, dry-scrape, or dry-sweep any materials with asbestos content. Contact a professional for removal of asbestos flooring. Look in the phone directory under "Asbestos Removal."

Removing conventional carpet

1 Pry up all metal edgings at doorways. If the carpet is not tacked or glued to the floor, work a straight screwdriver under a corner or grab the corner with groove-joint pliers and pull each strip of carpet off the tack strip. Once you get started, the carpet should tear up easily.

2 If you didn't cut through the pad when you cut the carpet in strips, recut the pad with a utility knife. Then grab each section of pad with both hands and pull it from the floor. Roll the pad as you go and dispose of the rolls. Remove pad tacks or staples.

3 Starting at a joint in the tack strip, work the end of a pry bar under the strip at a nail, and pry the nail loose. Use care and wear gloves when carrying the strips to a refuse pile or garbage bin—the points of the tacks are sharp.

WHAT IF...
The carpet or pad is tacked or stapled?

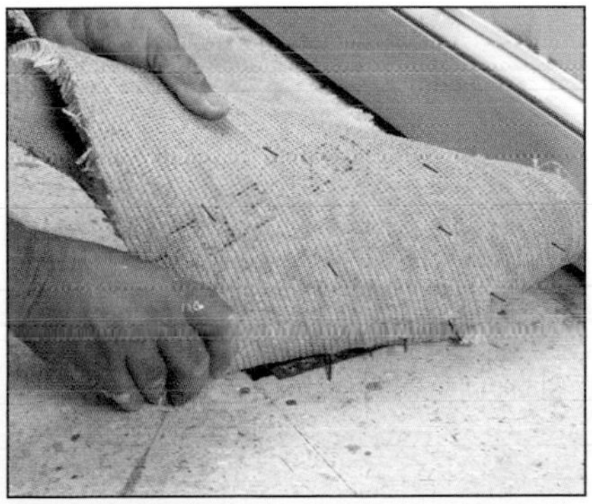

To remove tacked carpet, pry up a few tacks with a screwdriver or cat's paw and try to pull the carpet up. If that doesn't work, pull up each tack or staple separately.

Remove pad staples and any remaining tufts of pad with a screwdriver or cat's paw.

WHAT IF...
The carpet is glued down?

1 Starting at a corner or along one edge of a cut strip, drive a wide putty knife or scraper between the backing and the floor to break the adhesive bond. Roll up the carpet as you go.

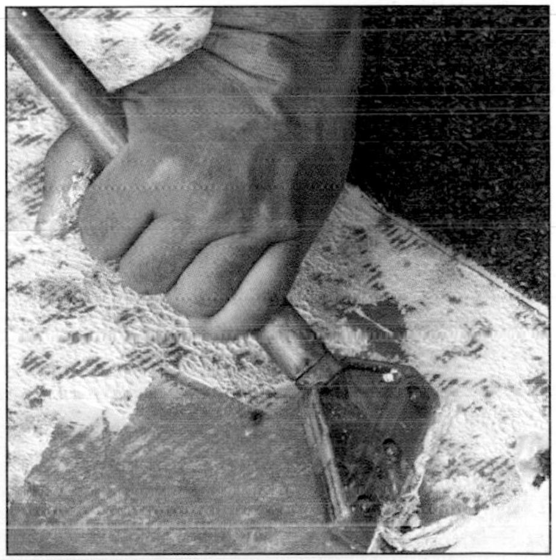

2 Once you have removed and disposed of the carpet, go back and scrape up the remaining tufts of pad and adhesive residue with a floor scraper.

Using existing floor tile as substrate

1 Existing tile works well as a substrate, but you'll need to repair any damaged sections. Remove the grout from the damaged tile with a grout knife. With a high-quality hammer or small sledge and cold chisel, break the tile, working from the center to the edges. **Wear eye protection.**

2 Pull out the chips of broken tile. Scrape up the fine pieces with a margin trowel or putty knife. Using the same tool, scrape off any adhesive remaining in the recess. Dust out or vacuum the area so the thinset can bond securely with the floor.

3 Using a margin trowel or wide putty knife, apply adhesive in the recess. If possible, use the same general type of adhesive as the original mastic or thinset.

Removing floor tile set in thinset

1 Create a starting point in a central area of the floor by cracking one tile with a small sledge and cold chisel. Grip the chisel firmly and strike it with a sharp blow of the hammer. **Wear eye protection.**

2 Break out the remaining area of the tile with the sledge and brush the loose pieces out of the recess. Chip out the grout along the edge of an adjacent tile.

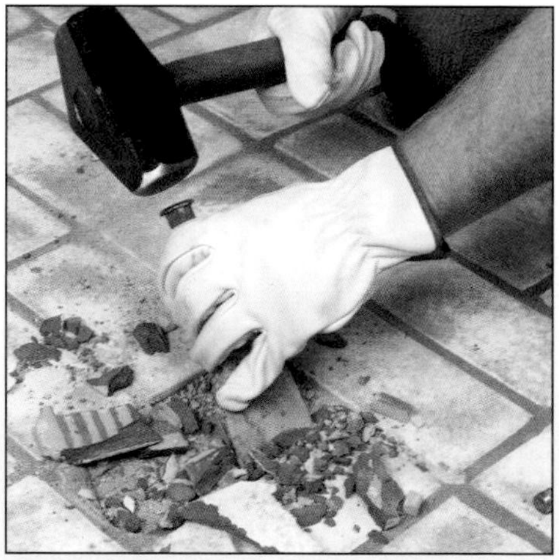

3 Tap a wide chisel at an angle under the edge of the adjoining tile and pop off the tile. Repeat the process for each tile until you have removed the entire floor. Dispose of the tile and scrape off any remaining adhesive.

4 Back-butter a replacement tile using a margin trowel or putty knife and push the tile into the recess until the adhesive oozes up from the grout joints. Make sure the tile is level with the rest of the floor, wipe off the excess thinset, and let it cure.

5 Use a sanding block and a coarse grit of abrasive paper to roughen the entire surface of the tile. This will give the tile a "tooth" for the adhesive and strengthen its bond with the floor.

6 With a margin trowel or mason's trowel, spread a thin layer of thinset across the entire surface of the floor. Make sure the grout joints are level with the surface of the tile.

WHAT IF...
Tile is set in a mortar bed?

For centuries, craftspeople set tile in a bed of mortar, which resulted in an extremely durable installation. Mortar-bed tile consequently proves more difficult to remove than tile set in thinset adhesive. If your mortar-bed floor is essentially stable and sound with all or most of the tiles securely adhered—and if the new tile surface won't extend above the adjacent floors to an unsafe height—you can install new tile over the old.

If the existing surface is cracked or in disrepair, or if the resulting floor will be too high, chip off the tile using the techniques shown for a thinset installation. You can also break the bed with a sledgehammer or saw it into sections with a diamond masonry saw and pry the sections out with a crowbar.

In either case, you will have to remove the mortar bed and prepare the floor for thinset.

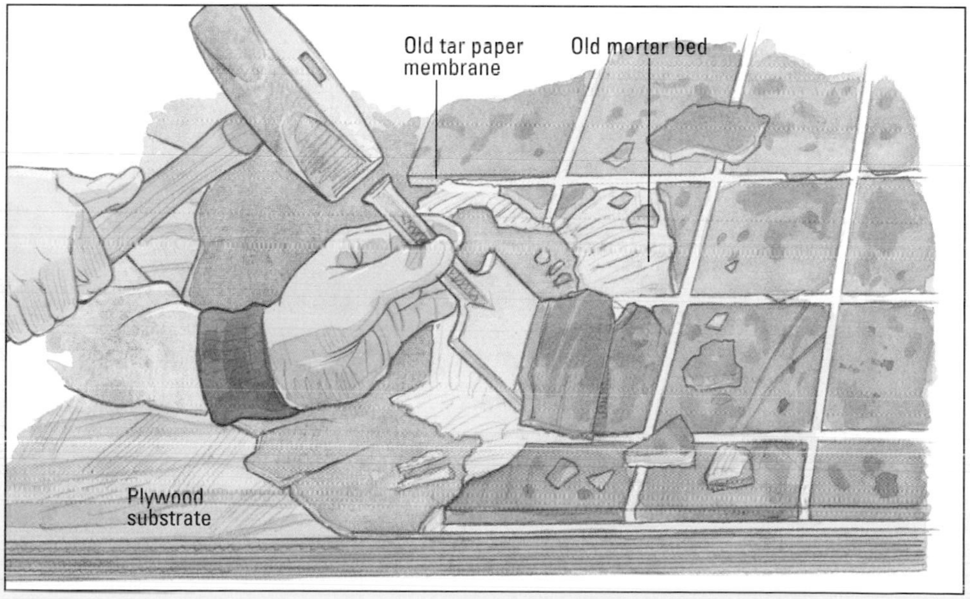

PREPARING A WOOD SUBFLOOR

After you have removed or repaired the existing surface of the floor, turn your attention to the subfloor. Ceramics and stone must be kept from cracking and all subfloors must not squeak or sag. Inspect the subfloor and make repairs that will assure it provides a solid, stable bed.

Dimensional lumber—1×4 or 2×6 planking—is not suitable as a bed for any tile. Planks expand and contract with changes in temperature and humidity, as does tile, but at different rates. The result is cracked tile, broken grout joints, or split seams. Install plywood or backerboard on plank *(pages 92–95).* If the resulting floor will be too high for smooth transitions to adjacent floors, tear up the planking and install ¾-inch exterior-grade plywood, followed by backerboard for ceramics.

PRESTART CHECKLIST

☐ **TIME**
About 30 minutes to check defects in an average-size room. Repair time will vary with size and condition of floor; could average 45 minutes per square yard.

☐ **TOOLS**
Repair subfloor: 4-foot level, cordless drill/bits, hammer, circular saw
Repair surface: mason's trowel, belt sander, nail set
Installing membrane: roller, trowel

☐ **SKILLS**
Driving nails with hammer, removing fasteners with cordless drill, sawing with circular saw, troweling, using a belt sander

☐ **PREP**
Remove or repair finished flooring

☐ **MATERIALS**
Subfloor: 2×4 lumber, 2½-inch coated screws, 8d nails, wood shims
Surface: thinset mortar
Installing membrane: membrane and adhesive

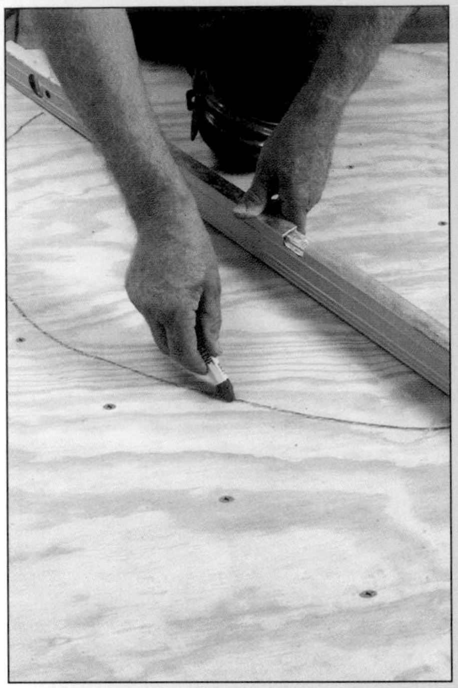

1 Divide the floor into imaginary 6-foot sections and within each section rotate a 4-foot level. Use a carpenter's pencil or chalk marker to outline sags, low spots, high spots, and other defects. Then walk the floor to test it for squeaks and weak spots. Mark these areas.

2 If the entire subfloor is weak, cut 2×4 bridges to fit between the floor joists. Measure the joist spacing across the floor and if the dimensions are equal cut all the bridges at one time. If the spacing varies, cut the pieces to fit. Nail the bridges in place, offsetting each one by 24 inches.

LOW SPOTS, HIGH SPOTS
Level the subfloor

Vacuum the floor thoroughly. Trowel thinset into depressions and chips with a mason's trowel or margin trowel. Feather the edges of the repair so it is level with the floor. After it dries, sand the edges of the repair if necessary.

Before you level any high spots on the floor, make sure the heads of all nails and fasteners are set below the surface. Level high spots on the floor with a belt sander. Keep the sander moving when it is in contact with the floor.

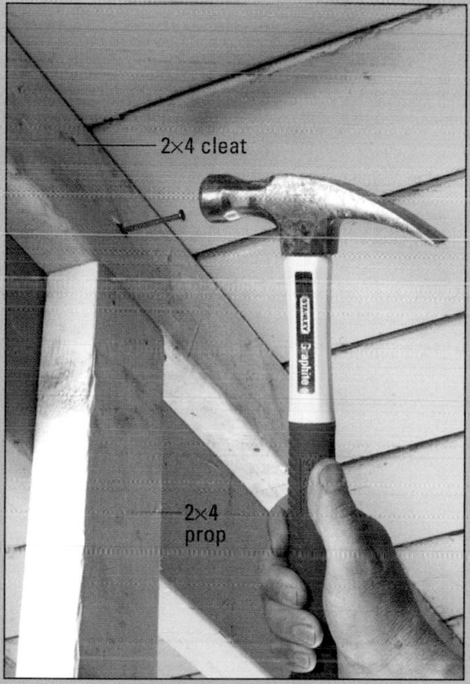

3 Shore up broken or sagging joists by nailing a 2×4 cleat up against the subfloor. Force the cleat snugly against the subfloor with a 2×4 prop, nail the cleat in place with 8d nails, and knock the prop out to remove it.

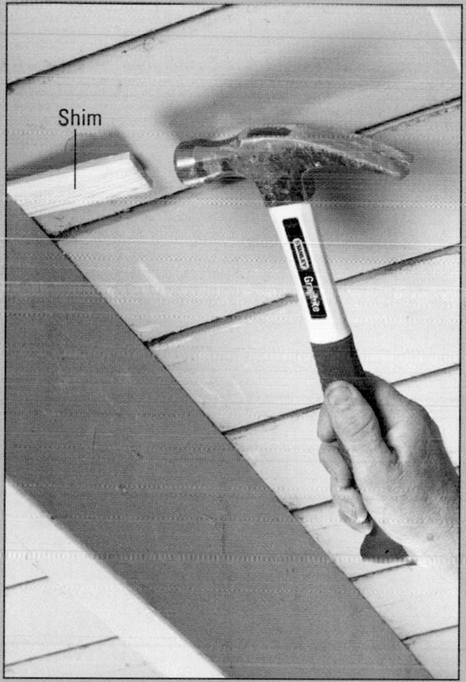

4 Fill minor sags and separations between the subfloor and joists by driving shims or shingles into the gap. Tap the shim gently until it's snug—forcing it may cause the flooring above to bow.

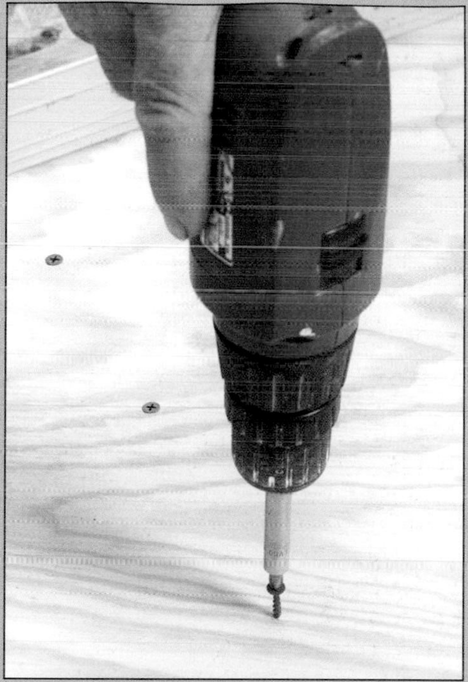

5 Fasten loose subflooring material securely by screwing it to the joists. Drive screws into any repairs you have made with shims. You can use ringshank or spiral shank nails as an alternative, setting the nailhead below the surface with a hammer and nail set.

STANLEY PRO TIP

Support the stone

Because stone tiles are more brittle than ceramic tile, they won't forgive unstable subfloors or surfaces that are not flat. Stone installations require subfloor support that is solid and free from deflection. Substrates also must be smooth and level.

When preparing a subfloor for stone tile, be thorough and precise when marking defects such as high spots or depressions. Finish the edges of thinset repairs with care and make sure you have removed all structural defects in the joists and subfloor.

Stone is substantially heavier than tile, and current flooring, especially in large rooms, may not be strong enough to support it. Check with a structural engineer if you are in doubt.

Waterproofing membrane

Although many tiles and setting materials are impervious to water, virtually no tile installation is completely waterproof without a waterproofing membrane.

Water that penetrates a tile bed weakens the adhesive, promotes rot, and nourishes organisms destructive to the wood subfloor. Bathrooms, kitchens, and surfaces that require frequent cleaning are especially vulnerable.

One of the easiest membranes to apply utilizes an adhesive that spreads with a roller. To install it, start at a wall opposite a doorway and apply the adhesive in sections with a roller (top). Let the adhesive cure, spread the fiber membrane over it (middle), and trowel the membrane into the adhesive (bottom).

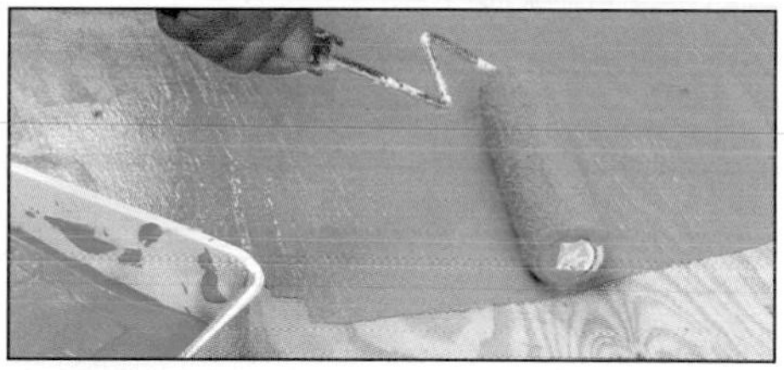

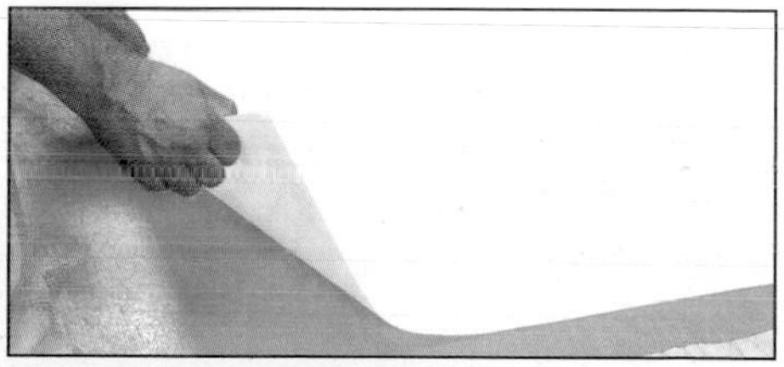

PREPARING A SLAB FLOOR

Water is the chief enemy of all building materials. Concrete floors, particularly those at or below grade, are especially vulnerable. Don't install any kind of tile on a slab until you fix water problems.

Condensation on water pipes and walls occurs in hot weather and is not technically a water problem. Increase ventilation to relieve condensation.

Install or fix gutters and slope soil away from the foundation so water runs away from it. If this doesn't fix the problem, consult a drainage specialist.

Cover isolated, inactive cracks with an isolation membrane "bandage." Completely cover new concrete and any floors suspected of developing cracks. Fix active cracks before tiling—don't cover them up.

PRESTART CHECKLIST

☐ **TIME**
From 30 to 45 minutes per square yard

☐ **TOOLS**
Repair or degloss surface: 4-foot level, hammer, cold chisel, margin and mason's trowels, grinder, sanding block, vacuum, brush, mop
Repair structural defect: sledge, crowbar, wheelbarrow
Install membrane: roller, mason's trowel

☐ **SKILLS**
Using a level, troweling, grinding with power grinder

☐ **PREP**
Remove or repair finished flooring

☐ **MATERIALS**
Repair/degloss surface: hydraulic cement or thinset, muriatic acid, rubber gloves
Repair structural defect: gravel, reinforcing wire, concrete mix, 2×4 screed
Install membrane: membrane, adhesive

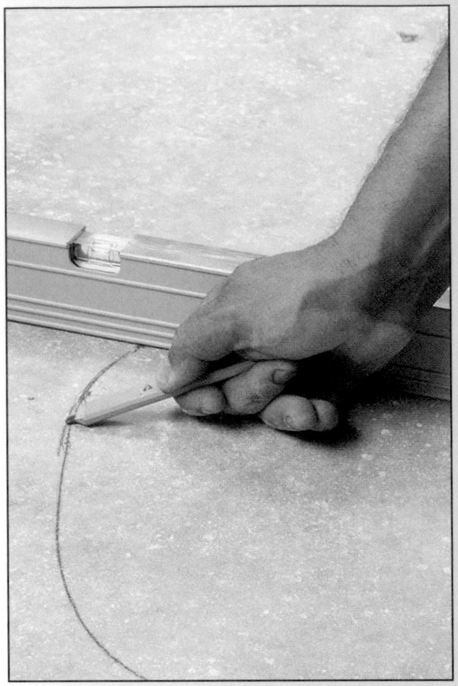

1 Divide the slab into imaginary 6-foot sections and check each section with a 4-foot level. Mark cracks, high spots, and other defects with a carpenter's pencil.

Cracks may be a sign of a structural defect. Some may be repairable. Others may require professional help.

2 Use a high-quality hammer or small sledge and a cold chisel to open small cracks so you can fill them. If possible, angle the chisel into each side of the crack to create a recess wider at the bottom of the crack than on top. This will help hold the patching cement more securely.

WHAT IF...
A slab is waxed, sealed, or smooth-finished?

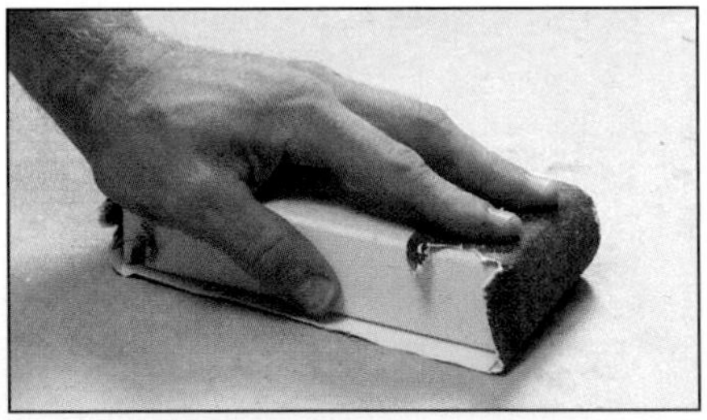

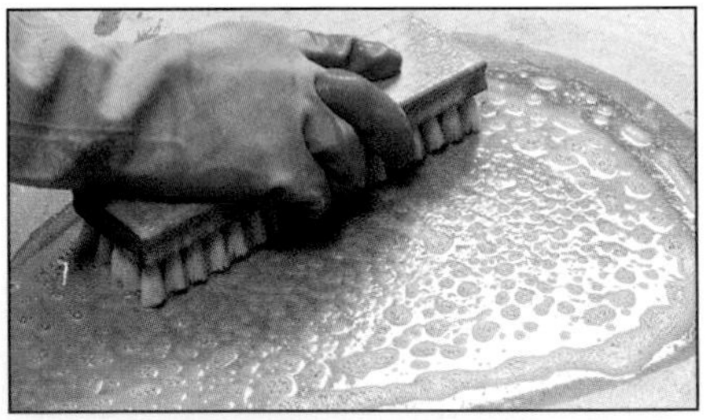

Thinset and other adhesives will not bind to surfaces that are waxed, sealed, painted, or finished to a gloss with a steel trowel. You can tell if your slab is waxed or sealed if spilled water beads up on it. If water soaks in and the surface is otherwise slick and smooth, it is likely to have been finished with a steel trowel.

Roughen slick or painted finishes with a sanding block or rented floor sander. Make your own sanding block by tacking a sheet of coarse abrasive on an 8-inch 2×4. Use light pressure and scuff the entire floor. Vacuum the floor when finished.

Remove wax and sealers with a solution of 4 parts water to 1 part muriatic acid. Scour the floor with the acid wash and a scrub brush. Rinse the slab with clear water and let it dry thoroughly.

Muriatic acid is highly caustic. Follow the manufacturer's directions and wear eye protection, rubber gloves, and old clothing. Ventilate the area.

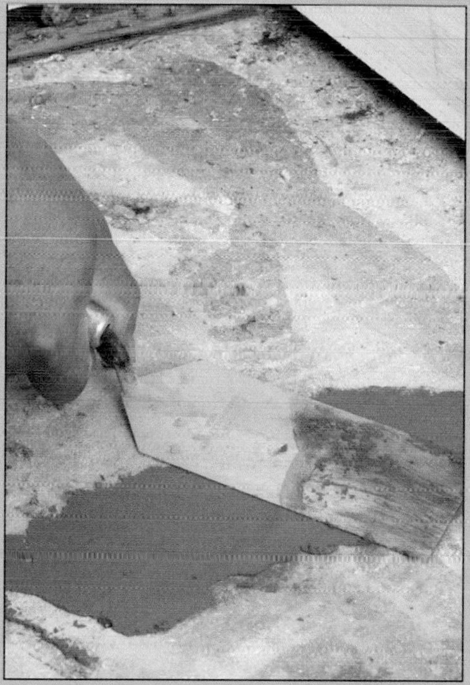

3 Wash out the crack with water and fill it with quick-setting hydraulic cement or thinset. Use a margin trowel or mason's trowel and feather out the edges until the patch is level with the surrounding surface.

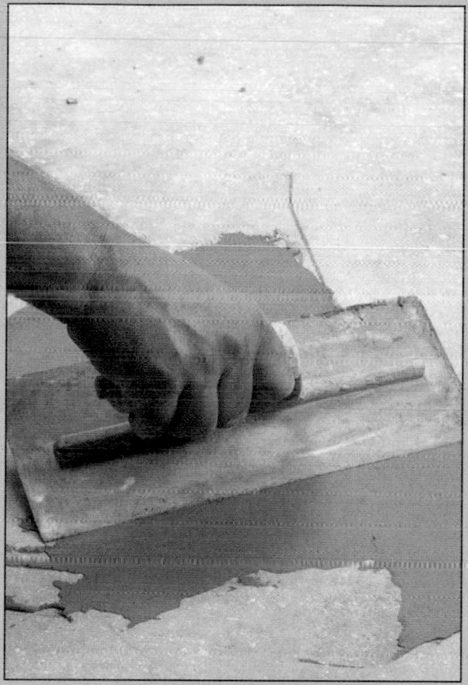

4 To fill depressions in the slab, pour a small amount of thinset or self-leveling compound into the depression and trowel it level. Add thinset or compound until the surface is level and feather the edges of thinset even with the floor.

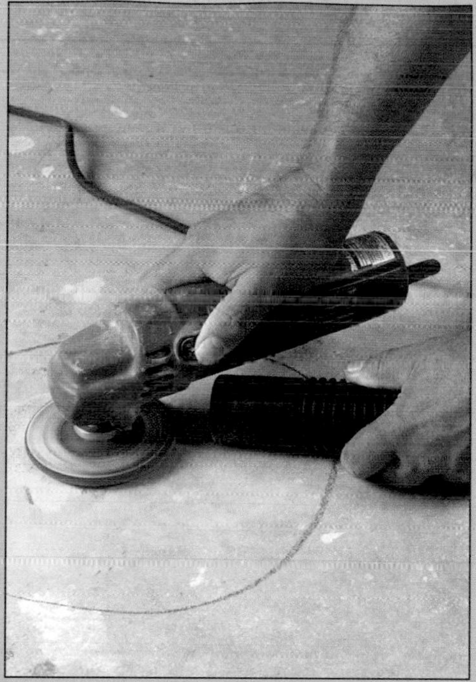

5 Grind down any high spots you have marked using a grinder equipped with a masonry-grit abrasive wheel. A right-angle grinder makes this job go quickly. Hold a vacuum hose near the grinder to remove the dust as you work. Vacuum and damp-mop the surface thoroughly.

Structural defects in concrete

Large holes, cracks with uneven surfaces, and sunken areas are signs of structural defects in a slab. You must repair these defects before tiling.

For most repairs, the concrete will have to be broken into manageable pieces and removed. The remaining hole must be excavated by an additional 4 inches and filled with a 4-inch gravel layer. New concrete calls for reinforcing wire and screeding (leveling) with a long 2×4. The patch must cure for three to seven days.

Fixing structural defects in a slab is a formidable job. Consult with a specialist before tackling it yourself. Contracting the work is often more cost-effective.

Apply an isolation membrane (slip sheet) over cracks

1 Apply the membrane adhesive equally on both sides of a crack or expansion joint. Use a roller to apply the adhesive and spread on a light but even coat.

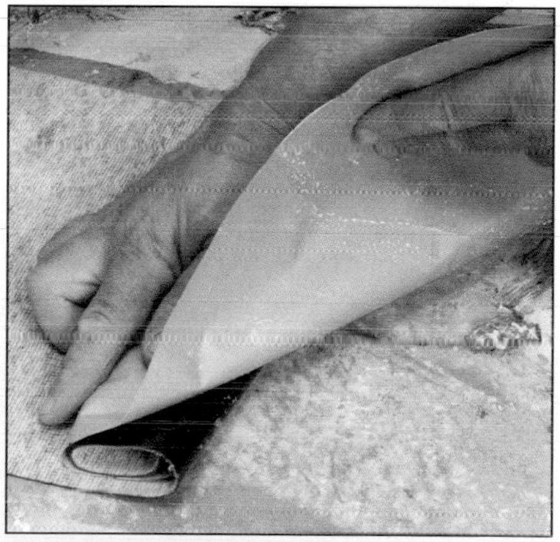

2 Follow the manufacturer's instructions to apply the membrane to cured or wet adhesive. Apply the membrane over the adhesive, following the contour of the crack across the surface.

PREPARING WALLS FOR TILE

Before you tile a wall, it must be straight, flat, and plumb. Remove any wallpaper or covering and degloss paint before you check for and repair other structural or surface defects. Do not strip paint with chemical removers. Paint stripping is unnecessary and may leave a residue that interferes with the tile adhesive.

Check the structural integrity of the wall by pushing between the studs. Drive screws into the studs to anchor soft spots where plaster or drywall has come loose.

Look for bows in the walls and crumbling surfaces. Fill in depressions, remove loose material, and repair holes. Although you can tile over a tiled wall, it is safer to remove it. Always remove tile from walls in wet locations, such as baths. Vacuum and damp-sponge the surface thoroughly.

PRESTART CHECKLIST

- ☐ **TIME**
  About 20 to 30 minutes per square yard, longer to remove wallpaper
- ☐ **TOOLS**
  Repairing and removing drywall and plaster: level, hammer, cold chisel, framing square, margin and mason's trowels, dry-cutting saw (for plaster)
  Preparing covered walls: wide putty knife, sanding block
  Removing tile: grout knife, wide cold chisel, hammer
- ☐ **SKILLS**
  Cutting with utility knife, driving fasteners with cordless drill, troweling patching compound
- ☐ **MATERIALS**
  Repairing/removing drywall/plaster: ¾-inch drywall, 3× lumber, 1-inch drywall screws, drywall tape, thinset, 2×4 lumber
  Preparing covered walls: deglossing agent, adhesive release agent, TSP

Repairing damaged drywall

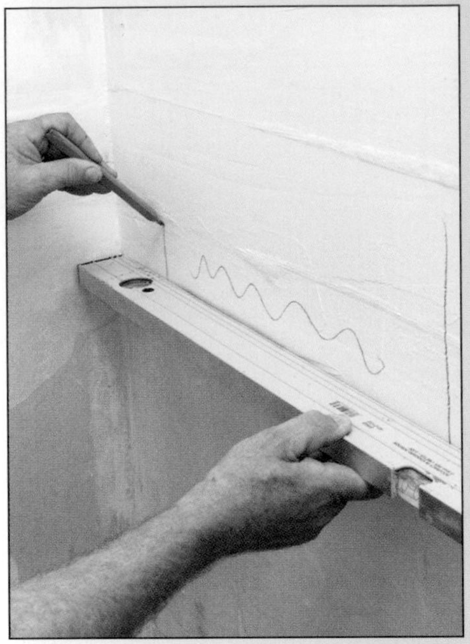

1 Push on the wall at various places to make sure it is firmly anchored to the studs. Mark places that give when you push on them. Using a 4-foot level, mark major depressions, high spots, and corners that are not plumb.

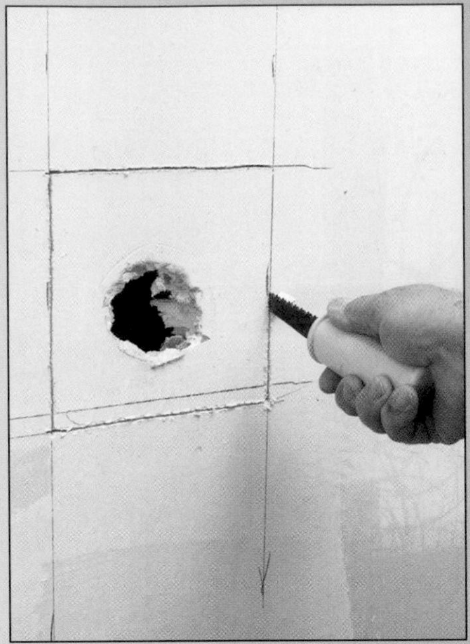

2 Use a framing square to mark a rectangular area around a hole. Score the drywall on the lines, then cut through it with a drywall saw or utility knife. Pry out the damaged area or knock it into the wall recess.

WHAT IF...
Walls are painted, papered, or tiled?

Scrape loose paint and roughen with 80-grit sandpaper. You can also degloss paint with a deglossing agent compatible with thinset.

To remove wallpaper, spray on a release agent. Scrape the wall with a wide putty knife. Wash the surface with a solution of trisodium-phosphate (TSP) and water.

To remove wall tiles, start at the top and remove the grout around one tile with a grout knife or saw. Tap a chisel under the tile and pop it off. Repeat for the remaining tiles, working down the wall. In wet areas, remove drywall or damaged greenboard to the studs. In dry areas, repair the wall surface.

3 Cut 1×3 boards about 6 inches longer than the area to be patched. Insert the boards into the recess on one side of the patch area and cinch them to the rear of the drywall with 1-inch screws. Repeat for the other side. These cleats will keep the drywall patch from falling into the wall.

4 Cut a drywall patch of the same thickness as the rest of the wall and to the dimensions of the repair area. Place it in the recess against the cleats. Use 1-inch screws to fasten the patch to the cleats. Tape the joint around the patch with fiberglass-mesh drywall tape.

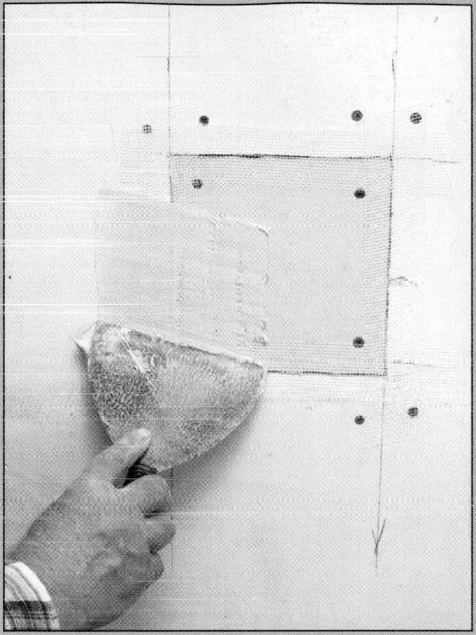

5 Finish the joints by applying a thin coat of drywall compound or thinset. Although the edges do not have to be perfectly smooth because you will be covering them with tile adhesive, do not leave any prominent high spots of drywall compound or thinset. Sand smooth if necessary.

STANLEY PRO TIP

Find studs in the wall

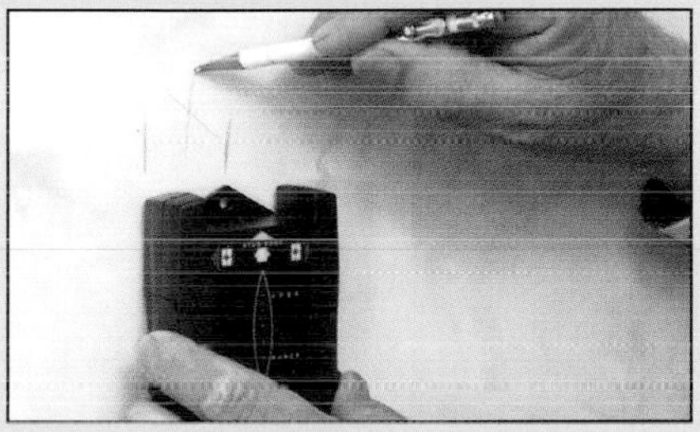

Certain repairs or installations require finding studs behind a finished wall. Electronic stud finders make the job easy. Be sure to mark both edges of each stud.

If you don't have a stud finder, probe the wall by tapping a long finishing nail through the wallboard until you find both edges of one stud. Mark its center. The remaining studs should be found at 16- or 24-inch intervals.

DRYWALL PATCH

Cutting drywall

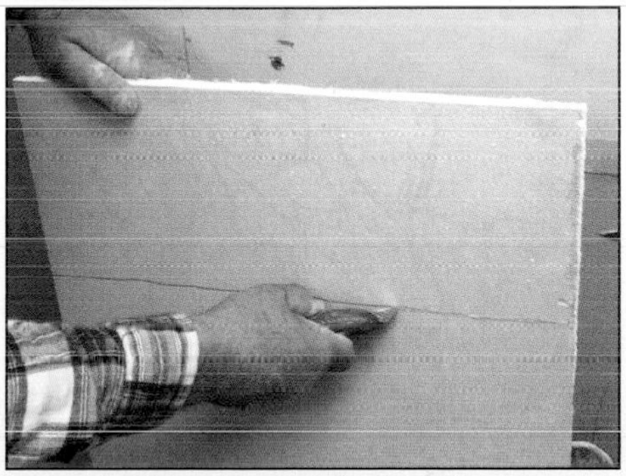

1 Mark a line at the length or width of the cut. Using a utility knife and a straightedge on long cuts, score one side of the drywall through the paper surface and slightly into the gypsum core. You do not need to cut all the way through or even deeply into the core.

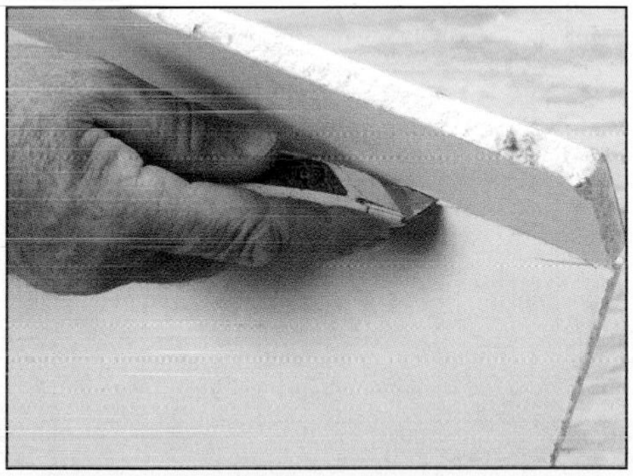

2 Turn the drywall piece over and support it, if necessary, either on the floor or on a flat surface. Break the piece along the scored line with a sharp blow of your palm. This will leave the paper backing intact on one side. Working from the unscored side, insert a utility knife through the paper backing and cut the two pieces free.

Repairing holes in plaster

1 Cut damaged pieces from the hole with a wide cold chisel. Plaster is held together with a fibrous binder, so there may be small pieces clinging to the edge of the hole. Remove them and, if possible, angle the edges of the hole so they are wider next to the lath than at the surface.

2 Brush out the area or vacuum it. Using a spray bottle, moisten the edges of the hole and the lath with water. Don't soak the area; a moderate misting is sufficient.

3 Apply patching plaster or thinset to the damaged area with a wide putty knife, forcing the material slightly into the lath. If the thickness of the plaster is more than ½ inch, apply a thin coat first, let it dry, and apply another coat. Thick patches tend to dry with cracks if applied all at once.

Repairing an outside corner

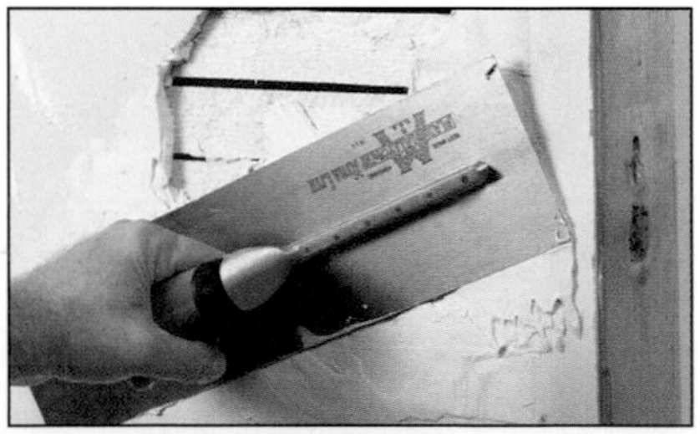

Using a wide cold chisel, pry out the loose plaster. Clean the edges thoroughly, making sure to remove small pieces still attached with the binding material. Tack a 2×4 batten on one wall flush with the corner. Moisten the damaged area with water and apply patching plaster or thinset in two applications, allowing one coat to dry before applying the other. Let the compound dry, move the batten to the other wall, and repeat the process. Sand smooth when dry.

Repairing cracked plaster

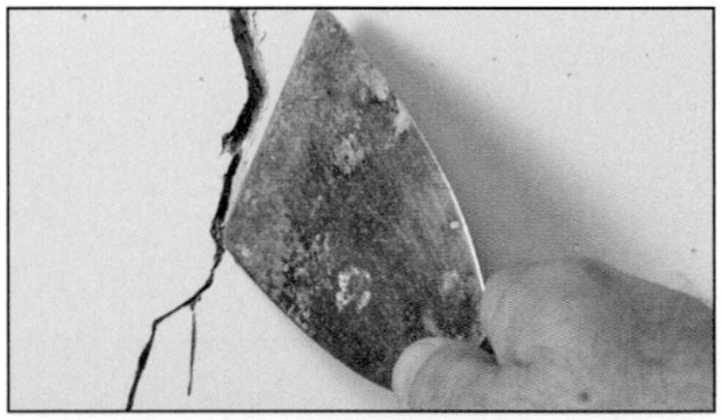

1 If the crack is a hairline crack, clean it out with the edge of a putty knife or can opener and dust out the crack with an old paintbrush. Moisten the crack and apply spackling compound.

For wide cracks, use a can opener to scrape plaster from the rear of the edge, making it wider at its bottom than on the surface. This will help hold the patching compound more securely. Clean out the crack and vacuum or dust it with an old paintbrush.

2 Use a spray bottle to moisten the interior of the crack and pack joint compound or thinset into the recess with a wide putty knife or drywall knife. Press the compound into the recessed edges. When you have filled the crack, draw the putty knife across the surface to smooth it. Allow the compound to dry and reapply if necessary. Sand any rough or high spots smooth with medium-grit sandpaper.

Repairing large damaged areas in plaster

1 Outline a rectangle larger than the damaged area and score the line with a utility knife. Use a wide cold chisel to remove the plaster, working from the scored line to the center. Work in small sections; tap gently to avoid cracking the remaining wall. Measure the thickness of the plaster at the edge of the cutout area and, if necessary, attach ¼-inch plywood strips to the lath so a ¼-inch drywall patch will be flush with the surface.

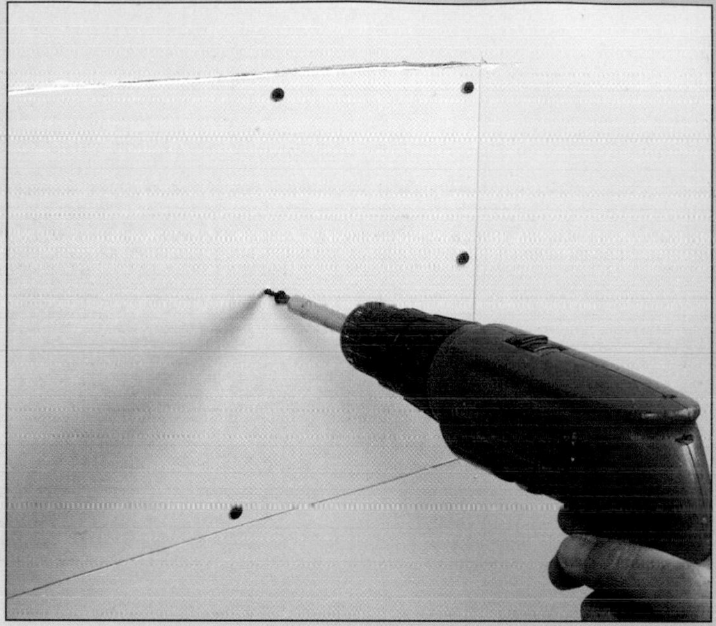

2 Cut a drywall patch to the dimensions of the cutout and apply a ¼-inch bead of construction adhesive to the shims or lath. Press the patch into the area. Starting at the corners, drive 1-inch drywall screws around the perimeter of the patch. Space the remaining screws about 6 inches apart. Tape the joints with fiber mesh drywall tape and spread a thin, level coat of drywall compound or thinset over the tape. Sand level when dry if needed.

WHAT IF...
The wall is sound but not flat or plumb?

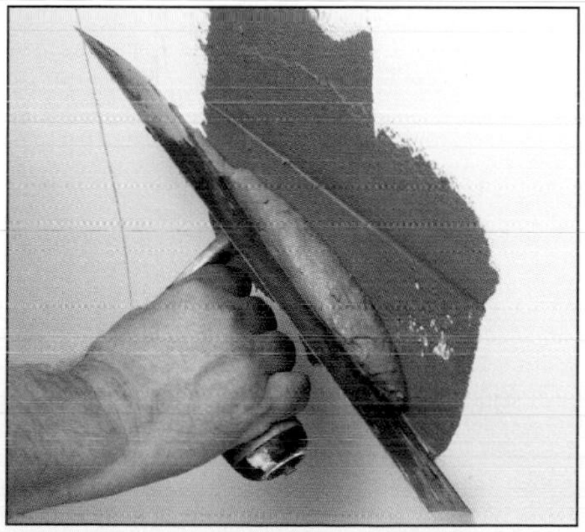

Fill minor depressions with thinset. Mark the perimeter of the depression carefully with a carpenter's pencil and apply the thinset with a mason's trowel. When dry, recheck the area with a level or straightedge.

Out-of-plumb walls are most noticeable at corners. Apply a skim coat of thinset along the corner to bring adjacent surfaces plumb.

If depressions or out-of-plumb conditions are severe, remove and replace the wall before tiling or don't install tile *(page 46)*.

STANLEY PRO TIP

Level the countertop

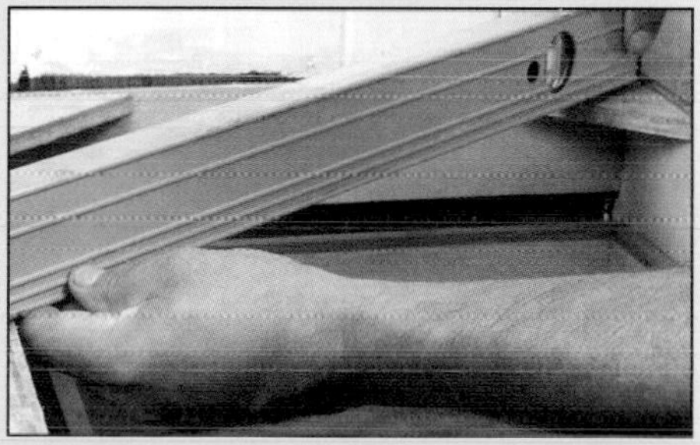

Even if you're tiling a wall and not retiling the countertop, now is a good time to check that the countertop is level where it meets the wall. If not, you'll have tapered cut tiles in your wall layout.

Check the countertop with a 4-foot level. If needed, remove the countertop and bring it to level by shimming it along the cabinet top. Severe problems may require you to reset the cabinets.

Removing water-damaged drywall

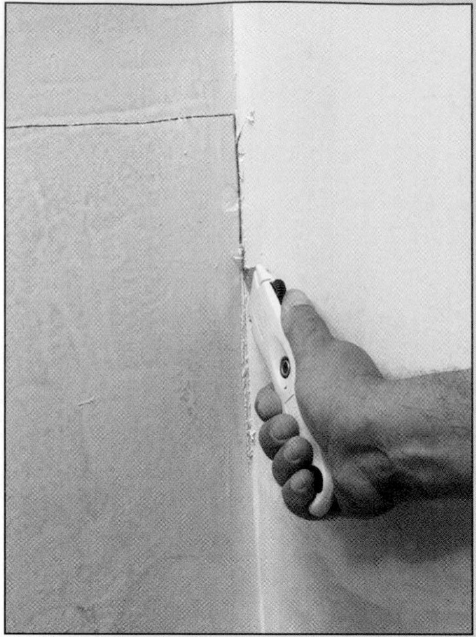

1 Mark the perimeter of the area to be removed. (If the surface is tiled, remove tiles along the edges.) To avoid damaging the surface that will remain, use a utility knife to score the cut line. Cut through the drywall with the knife or drywall saw. Protect the area below with heavy paper.

2 Use a hammer to punch a hole in the drywall between the studs. (If the surface is tiled, it may help to shatter one or two tiles in the center of the wall first.) Enlarge the hole until you can get your hand or a pry bar in it.

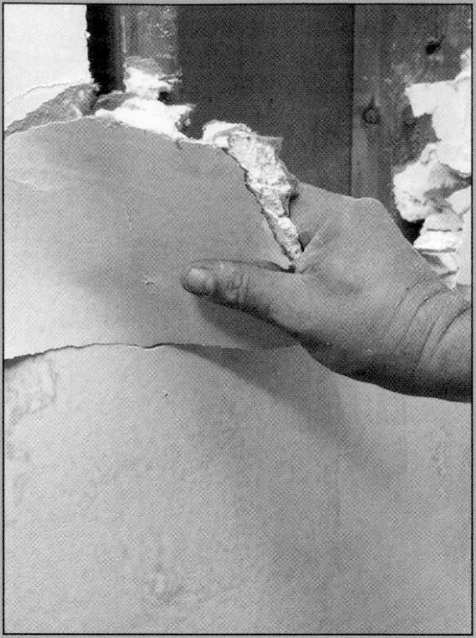

3 Grab an edge of the hole you have made and pull off the drywall. To remove large sections, space your hands as far apart as possible. Use a pry bar if necessary. To avoid puncturing the waterproofing membrane when it is installed, pull remaining nails. Check for rot and mold.

STANLEY PRO TIP: **Shore up rotted studs**

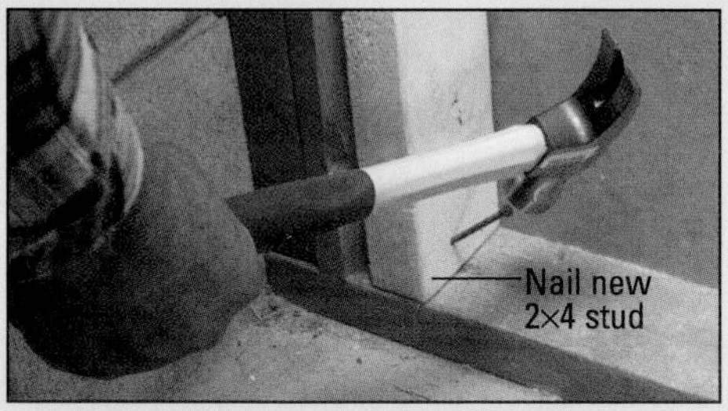

Rot decomposes materials through the action of bacteria, and these organisms thrive in wet conditions. Materials that get wet and don't receive enough air to dry them—especially materials behind kitchen and bathroom walls around sinks, tubs, and showers—are especially prone to rot. Rotted wood will not properly support the wall, tiled or otherwise.

Once you have removed the wall covering down to the studs, look for wood with dark blemishes, especially where the stud meets the bottom plate. Use a screwdriver to probe these joints and those where the stud is fastened to the top plate (left).

If the screwdriver penetrates the wood without much pressure or if the wood feels soft and spongy, the wood has rot. Dark or splotched areas that are firm are probably not rotted but may be infested with mold *(page 77)*.

First scrape out the rotted areas with a putty knife (center). Then cut a new 2×4 stud to the same length as the existing stud and toenail it (drive the nails at an angle through the face) to the top and bottom plate next to the rotted stud (right). Start with a corner stud and work your way along the wall, cutting and adding new boards one at a time.

Extensive rot in the bottom plate or in walls located behind bathtubs may require more complicated repair. Consult a professional carpenter or contractor before proceeding with a tiling project.

Removing water-damaged plaster

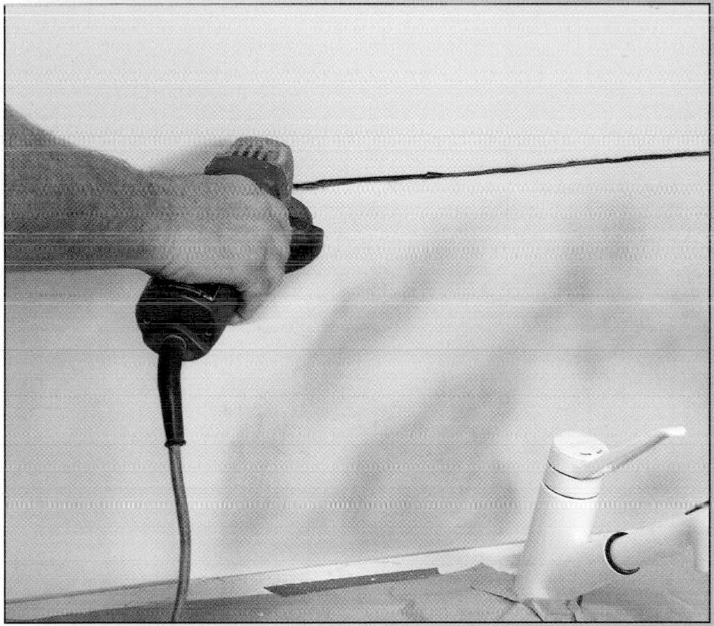

1 Outline the perimeter of the area to be removed. To avoid damaging the surface that will remain, use a dry-cutting saw equipped with a diamond or masonry cutting blade to cut through the plaster on the outline. Protect the area below with heavy paper.

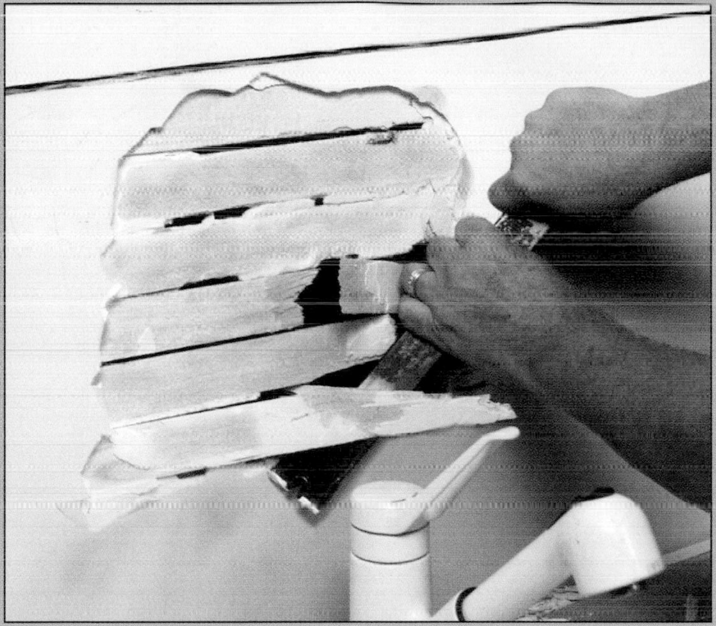

2 With a hammer and cold chisel, chip out a hole in the plaster large enough to allow insertion of a pry bar. Push a pry bar as far as you can between the plaster and lath and pry off the plaster in chunks. Remove any remaining nails to avoid puncturing the waterproofing membrane and check for rot and mold.

Stopping mold

Mold is a fungus that lives on the surface of damp materials. Mold does not present much of a threat to the integrity of building materials, but it has an offensive odor and its spores may present a health hazard.

Wear a respirator and clean off moldy surfaces. Then spray liberally with a 50/50 mixture of household bleach and water.

WATERPROOFING MEMBRANE

Installing membranes

Walls behind a shower enclosure and along a tub need protection from water that can migrate and damage the materials behind it. Such walls need waterproofing membranes.

If the condition of the wall has required removal, staple 15-pound felt paper to the studs. Overlap top pieces on lower pieces. Seal the overlaps and staples with asphalt mastic.

If the greenboard has not deteriorated, spread asphalt mastic over it with a ⅛-inch V-notched trowel. Embed the membrane in the mastic and staple it. Always remove drywall in wet areas.

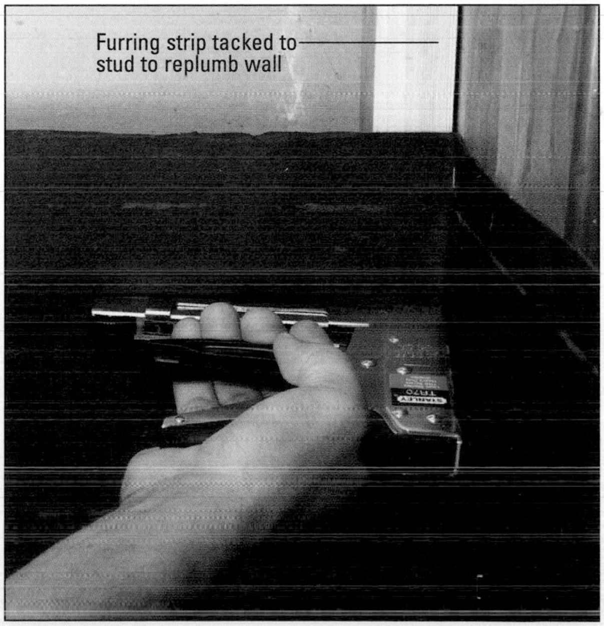

Backerboard is better
Replace drywall in wet areas with backerboard, even if the wall is in good repair.

REMOVING COUNTERTOPS

Although you may find many reasons for tiling over an existing laminate, wood, or ceramic tile countertop, removing the existing countertop and building a new base is generally the wiser option.

Removing a laminate or wood countertop is not difficult or time-consuming. Removing existing ceramic tile can add time to your project, but making a new base provides you with the assurance that the job will be done correctly.

One of the main advantages of this option is that you will not raise the height of the countertop. That may not sound important, but the addition of even the thickness of a new tile surface can disrupt the efficient and comfortable use of the kitchen. In addition, making a new base eliminates the necessity of piecing in numerous cut tiles over the existing backsplash.

Whether you leave the sink in or out of the counter when removing it is a matter of personal choice. Removing the sink reduces the weight.

PRESTART CHECKLIST

☐ **TIME**
From 45 minutes to one hour after appliances are removed, two to three times as long if removing tile. Total time will vary with the length and configuration of the countertop.

☐ **TOOLS**
Removing countertop: wrenches, groove-joint pliers, cordless drill and bits, utility knife, pry bar, hammer
Removing tile: hammer, cold chisel

☐ **SKILLS**
Removing nuts with wrench, scoring with utility knife, prying, breaking tile with cold chisel, driving screws

☐ **PREP**
Remove appliances

Removing a laminate countertop

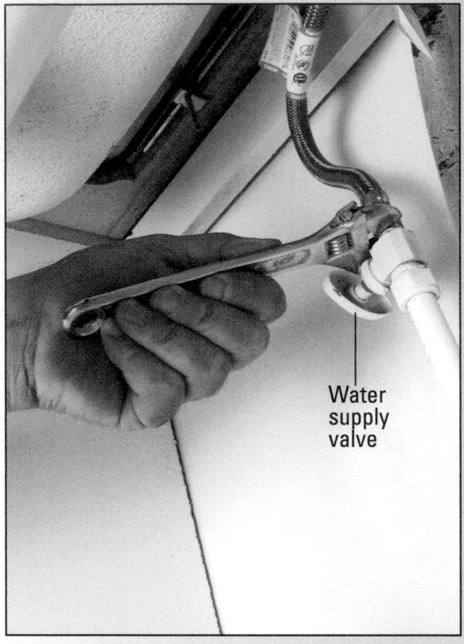

1 Turn off the supply valves to the sink and dishwasher and disconnect the lines. Remove the dishwasher *(page 54)*. Remove other appliances; **shut off the gas and power** as needed. You can remove the sink or leave it in.

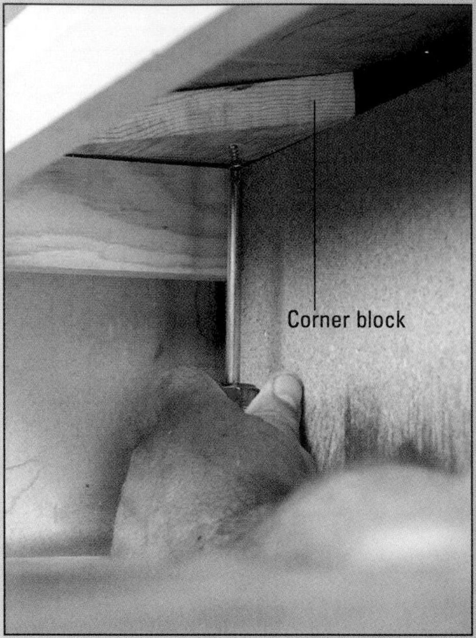

2 Locate corner blocks or cleats that fasten the countertop to the cabinet. Using a screwdriver or cordless drill, unscrew the fasteners. Do not unscrew the fasteners that attach corner blocks to the cabinet frame.

Removing a synthetic resin countertop

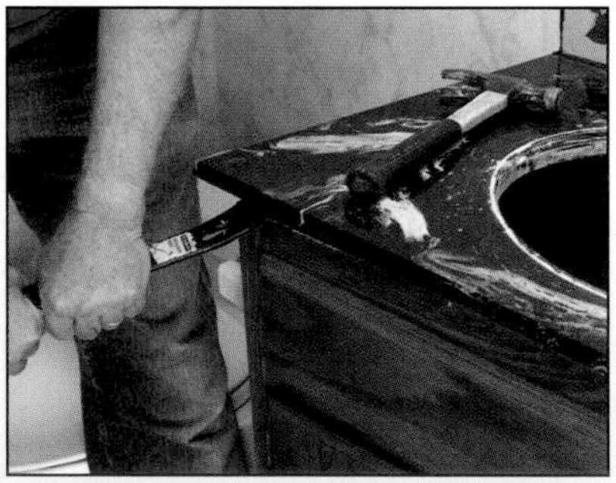

Synthetic resin countertops are fastened to the cabinet frame with glue. To remove them, use a sharp utility knife to cut the glue line at the joint between the countertop and the cabinet. Tap a pry bar into the joint and pop the countertop free. If you experience difficulty in inserting the pry bar, tap a thin putty knife along the joint to further loosen the glue bond.

WHAT IF... The existing countertop is tiled?

With a cold chisel and hammer, break the center of one tile. Tap the tile with a quick, sharp blow to break it. Chip out the pieces until you have access to a joint. Tap the blade of a wide cold chisel under the adjoining tiles and pop them loose. After removing one or two tiles, you can tell whether the countertop is set on backerboard or in a mortar bed. If the tile is set on backerboard, remove the tile and backerboard on the entire countertop. Hire a pro to saw out a mortar-bed installation.

3 To avoid pulling the paint off the wall when you remove the countertop, score the joint between the backsplash and the wall with a sharp utility knife. If the joint is caulked, cut completely through the caulk, if possible.

4 Using a utility knife, score the joint between the countertop and cabinet to break the bond of any glue or caulk. Keep the blade of the knife as perpendicular to the cabinet frame as possible to avoid cutting the wood.

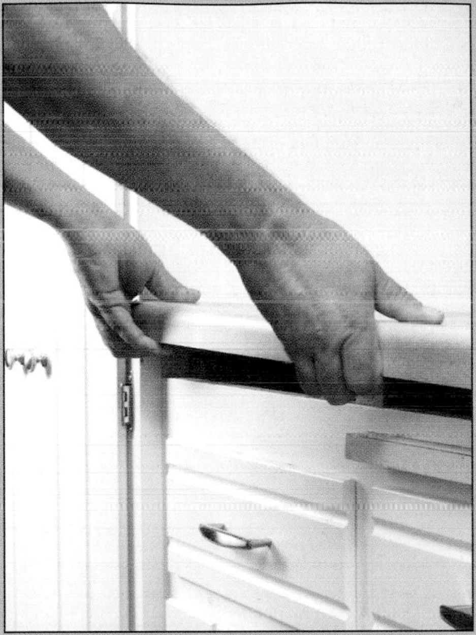

5 Pry off any trim at the countertop edge. Force a pry bar between the countertop and cabinet and pry up the countertop. If the countertop is too heavy to lift, cut it into sections with a reciprocating saw. Saw carefully to avoid cutting the cabinet frame.

REMOVE THE SINK

Removing a drop-in sink

1 If the weight of a sink makes removing the countertop difficult, remove the sink first. Shut off the water; disconnect the supply lines and drain pipe. Loosen any retaining screws and remove the clips.

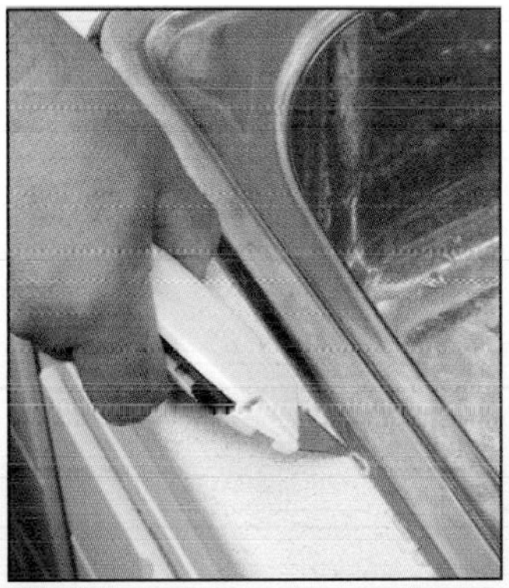

2 Cut any caulk along the edge of the sink with a utility knife.

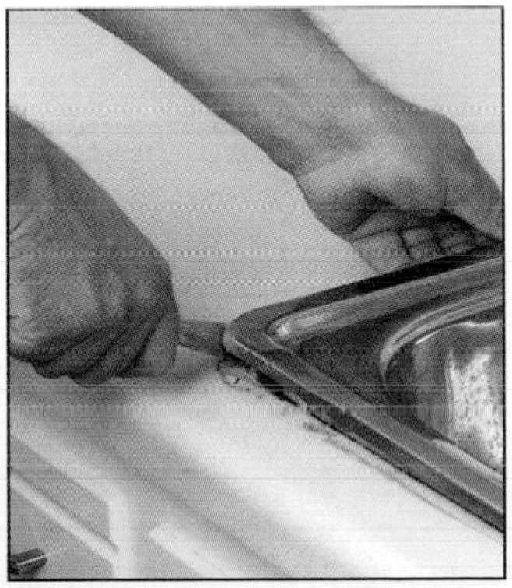

3 Either push up on the sink from below so you can lift it out, or insert a wide putty knife under the edge of the sink and pry it up until you can grasp it with your hands. Lift the sink up and out of the countertop.

Removing faucets from the countertop

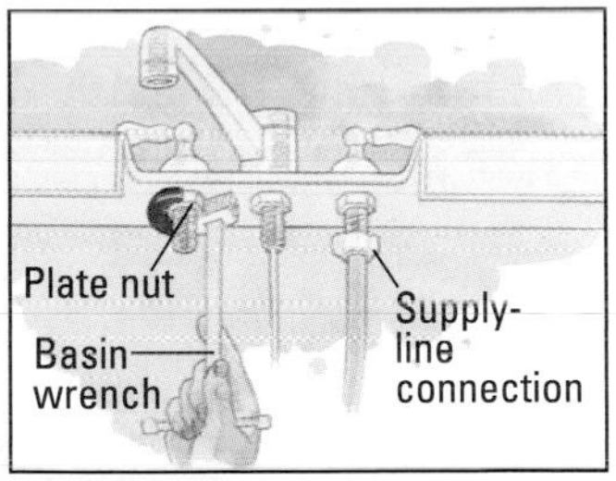

Almost all faucets have some style of plate fastened from below with nuts. In most installations, you will not have enough room to maneuver a wrench to loosen the nuts. A basin wrench is specially designed to work in the narrow space between the cabinet and the sink. Remove the supply-line connections first, then remove the plate nuts.

INSTALLING A NEW COUNTERTOP BASE

Ceramic tile requires a rigid base—use ¾-inch exterior-grade plywood. This grade is constructed with moisture-resistant glues. Most lumber outlets will stock 4×8-foot sheets. Larger sheets may be available by special order.

If your countertop spans an open area of more than 3 feet, screw 1× cleats into the front and back frame and attach 1×3 braces. Add bracing under any joints, for example, where two sheets meet in an L-shape countertop.

Cut the plywood precisely—a 24-inch depth is standard, plus enough to overhang the door fronts by ½ to ¾ inch. If the back wall is not perfectly flat, cut the sheet wide enough to allow you to contour it to the wall. If you're installing a drop-in range, cut the hole for it as you would a sink.

PRESTART CHECKLIST

☐ **TIME**
About 30 minutes to measure and cut countertop base; one to two hours to install it, depending on its size and configuration

☐ **TOOLS**
Carpenter's level, table saw, hammer, cordless drill and bit, jigsaw and plywood-cutting blade, holesaw

☐ **SKILLS**
Measuring and leveling, driving fasteners, sawing with jigsaw and table saw (optional)

☐ **PREP**
Remove old countertop, order new sink and faucets

☐ **MATERIALS**
Wood shims, ¾-inch exterior-grade plywood, 2-inch coated screws, sink and faucet template or stiff cardboard for making template

Checking cabinets for level

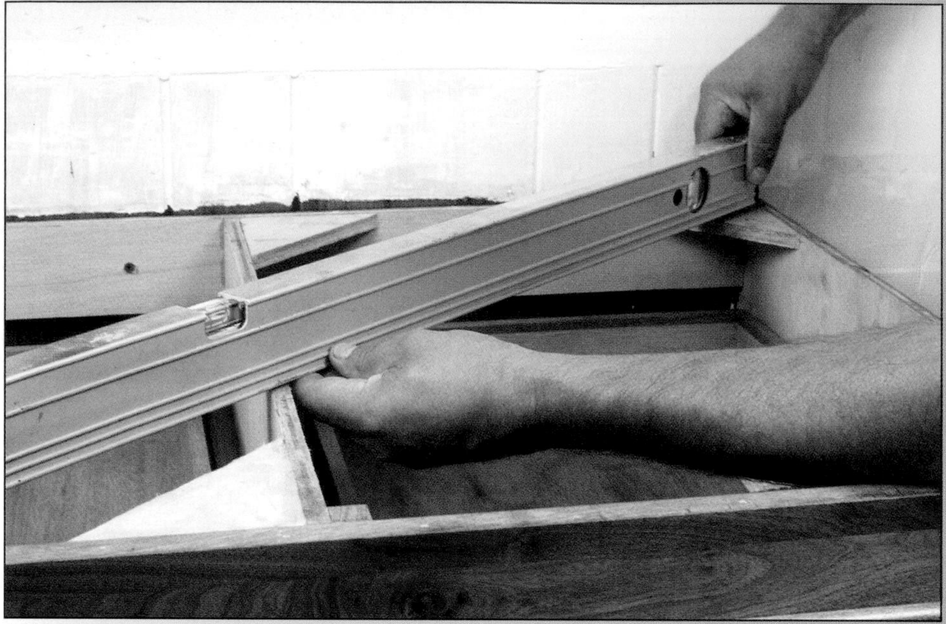

Although an out-of-level countertop will not affect the actual installation of the tile, it will create unattractive tapered edges at the backsplash. Before installing a new countertop, check the cabinet frame carefully to make sure it's level. Set a 4-foot carpenter's level along the rear cabinet edge. Raise the carpenter's level, if necessary, and mark the wall for level. Check the sides of the cabinet frame, then both sides of an L-shape counter. If you are installing new cabinets, you can level them by placing shims under the frame. If not, leave the cabinets in place and level the countertop base.

COUNTERTOP BASE
Use shims to correct an out-of-level cabinet

If the results of your checking indicate the cabinet frame is not level, you can add shims to correct the problem instead of removing the cabinets and leveling them.

Cut the countertop base to the correct dimensions and set it in place on the cabinet. Do not anchor it at this time. Place a 4-foot level against the rear of the plywood at the wall and insert shims under the countertop base at locations that will level it. Mark the wall at the locations of the shims. Repeat the process for the sides and the front of the cabinets, being careful not to dislodge shims already in place. Recheck the countertop for level before installing the new plywood base.

Install the new base as noted above, driving the screws through the plywood and the shims into the cabinet frame.

Building a new countertop base

Measure the outside of the cabinet and cut a piece of ¾-inch exterior-grade plywood wide enough to overhang the door fronts by ½ to ¾ inch. Set the plywood on the cabinet and fasten it with 2-inch coated screws.

Cutting the sink hole

1 If available, use the manufacturer's template to mark the sink cutout. Otherwise set the sink upside down on the plywood base and trace its outline. Remove the sink and draw parallel lines about 1 inch (or equal to the width of the lip of the sink) inside the outline.

2 Drill a starter hole and cut the interior line with a jigsaw. Keep the base plate of the saw flat on the plywood base and push the saw into the wood slowly. As you cut the final turn, have a helper carefully support the cutout from below to keep the saw blade from binding.

Making appliances fit

The combined thickness of new floor tile and backerboard may raise the dishwasher and other appliances too high to fit under an old countertop. Notching the countertop edge to make the appliance fit creates an unattractive gap and weakens the structure. Instead of cutting, remove the sink and take up the countertop (carefully if you will reuse it). Install shims on the cabinet edge to raise the counter height; reinstall the old countertop or build a new one.

Cutting faucet holes

Some sinks, especially decorator models, require faucets mounted in the countertop (deck-mounted faucets).

If the faucet manufacturer has provided a template for marking the faucet holes, position the template at the appropriate location to the sink hole and use a center punch (a nail or nail set will work also) to mark the points at which to drill.

If a template is not available, you can make one from stiff cardboard, punching out holes and tracing the outline of the faucet plate.

If the faucets have individual spouts, mark the countertop base for each faucet, spacing them at the appropriate location and at an equal distance from the center of the sink basin hole.

Use a holesaw with a diameter equal to the faucet mounts to drill the faucet holes.

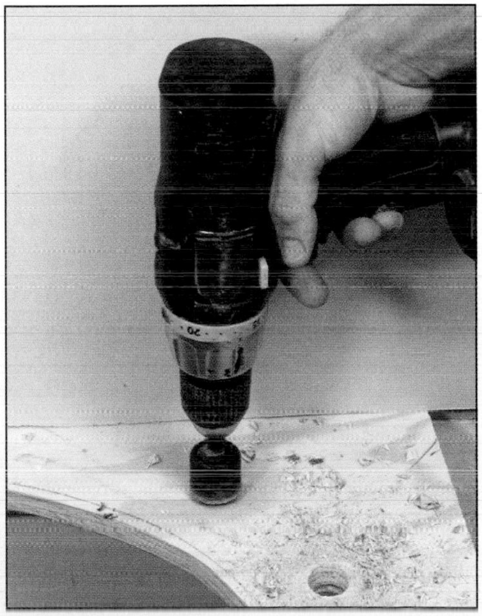

INSTALLING RADIANT HEATING

Radiant floor heating has been around since the Romans channeled hot air under their floors. Modern systems use electric mats or hot water pipes. Underfloor mats may install more quickly, but above-floor mats are more efficient because the heating element is in direct contact with the finished flooring materials.

Hydronic systems carry hot water through PEX tubing, a plastic material that stays flexible and withstands heat. Putting in PEX tubing is an easy do-it-yourself project, but hooking up the pipes and installing a boiler calls for a licensed plumber.

PRESTART CHECKLIST

☐ **TIME**
Underfloor mats: three to four hours for an 8×10-foot room
Above-floor mats: eight to twelve hours
Hydronic: six to seven hours

☐ **TOOLS**
Mats: Drill, ½- to ¾-inch bits, stapler, wire strippers and cutters, scissors, hammer, ohmmeter, drywall saw, fish tape, chisel, hot-glue gun, needle-nose pliers
Hydronic: ½-inch right-angle drill, forstner bits, hammer, tubing cutter

☐ **SKILLS**
Mats: Drilling, stapling, stripping and connecting wire, installing boxes and cable
Hydronic: Measuring, working overhead

☐ **PREP**
Underfloor: Snip protruding floor nails
Above-floor: Install or repair subfloor

☐ **MATERIALS**
Underfloor mats: Staples, splice sleeves, electrical tape, fiberglass insulation
Above-floor mats: 12/2 cable, mats, junction box, thermostat
Hydronic: PEX tubing, diffusion plates, nails, insulation

HEATING PATTERNS

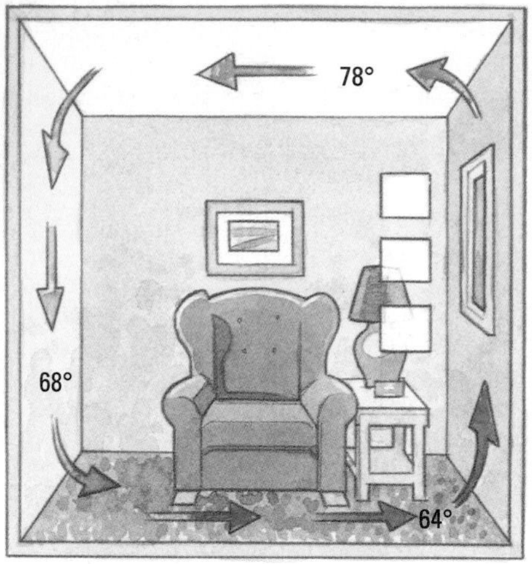

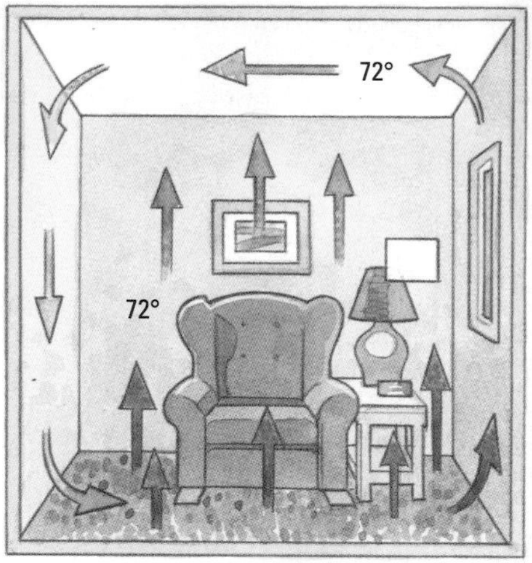

Conventional heating systems create different temperature zones in different parts of a room. These temperature zones can make different sections or levels of the room uncomfortable and prompt you to raise the heat setting to warm up the coolest spots. Radiant floor heating warms the entire area to a more consistent, comfortable temperature. It also heats without blower noise and doesn't raise dust.

FINISHED FLOORING

Radiant heat for most floors

You can install almost any finished flooring over radiant heat, but the key to the system's performance is how well the flooring material conducts heat.

Ceramic tile and stone are the best conductors and will allow the system to run more efficiently than other materials. Parquet and laminate are also good conductors. Carpet tile is thinner than broadloom carpet but still acts as insulation and won't distribute heat as well as solid materials. Vinyl tile has almost no R-value at all so it's a good choice but should not be heated above 85°F.

No matter which system you install, put separate thermostats in each room. That way you can customize the heat for maximum comfort and efficiency.

Heating bathrooms and kitchens

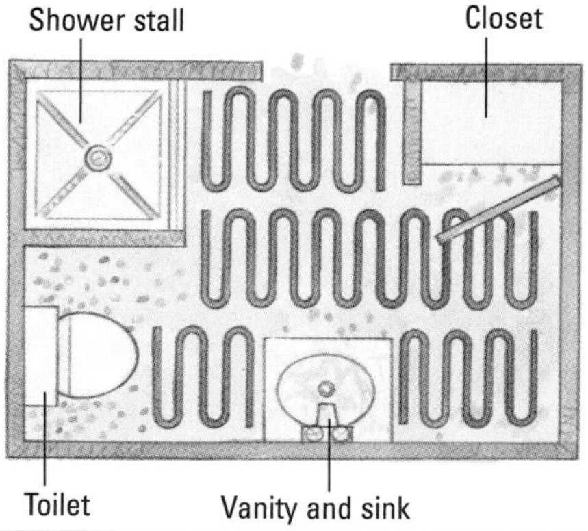

Before you purchase a radiant system, sketch the room it will be heating. Mats or piping are not required under closets, major appliances, and vanities. In bathrooms, about 50 percent of the floor area should be heated; in kitchens and living areas, about 60 percent.

Installing underfloor electric mats

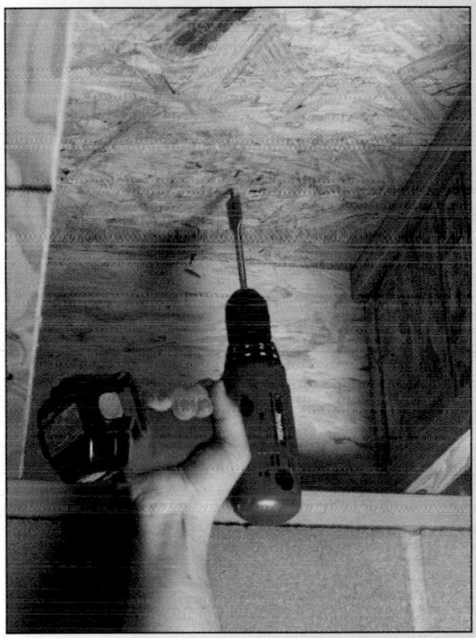

1 Make sure you can drill through the floor and the bottom plate of the wall directly below the thermostat. Drill a hole through the subfloor and wall plate for the switch/thermostat wiring. Clean out any waste in the hole with a ½-inch chisel.

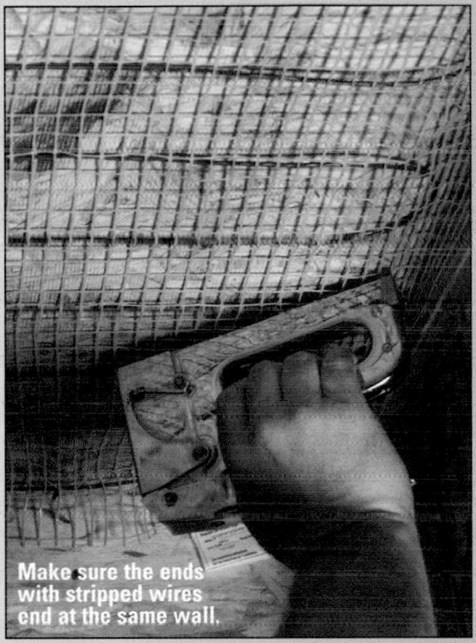

Make sure the ends with stripped wires end at the same wall.

2 Cut the mat to fit the the spaces between the joists (some mats have dotted cut lines). At one end of each mat, strip ¾ inch of insulation from the power wires. With a helper, raise the mat and staple it to the subfloor with ½-inch staples.

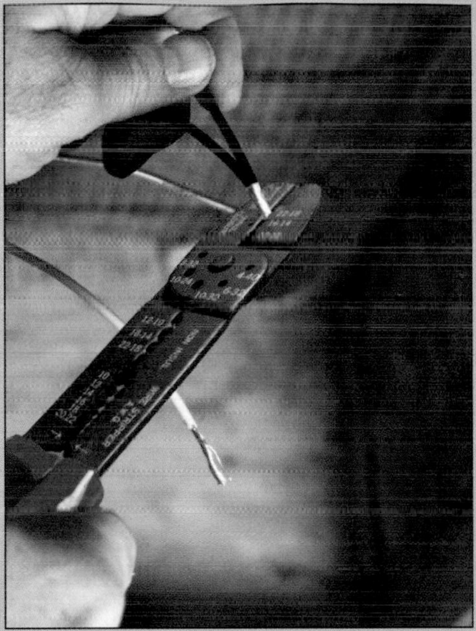

3 Connect the wires together according to the manufacturer's instructions. Splicing sleeves are a quick and easy method to make secure connections. Strip about ½ inch of insulation from the ends and slide the bare wire into a splicing sleeve. Squeeze the sleeve with wire crimpers.

THE THERMOSTAT
Plan ahead for interior walls

Carefully sketch the system wiring on a dimensional plan. Note the location of the thermostat and any other electrical switches or outlets in the room. Measure the location of the switch/thermostat from a reference point such as an adjoining wall and transfer this measurement to the subfloor in the room below.

If possible, locate the thermostat on an interior wall; this will make drilling through the floor plate easier. Place the thermostat as close to the power source as possible. Long lead wires from the power source can reduce the efficiency of the system.

WIRING THE SYSTEM

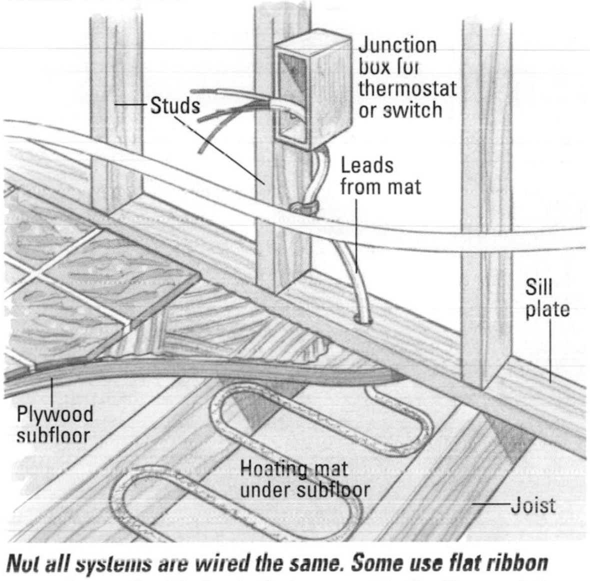

Not all systems are wired the same. Some use flat ribbon strapping and cable leads that connect to the thermostat. Others must be wired to a switch. The illustration shows a typical wiring for a thermostatically controlled system. Follow the manufacturer's instructions exactly.

SAFETY FIRST
Don't blow the fuses

Mat systems vary widely in how much power they consume (and how much heat they deliver)—from as little as 8 watts to as much as 18 watts per square foot. In an average living room, they create a sizable electric load. To avoid overloading circuits, you may need to install the new heating system on a separate circuit with its own breaker. Check the rating of the system and the load already carried by any circuit you plan to use for it.

Installing underfloor electric mats *(continued)*

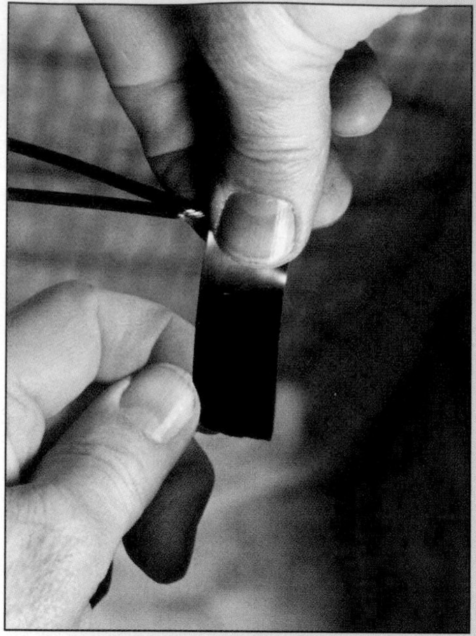

4 Cut a 3-inch piece of electrician's tape and, starting at the insulation, wrap the tape tightly around the sleeve. Make sure to cover the joint from the insulation at one end of the sleeve to the other. Fasten the bare wires at the end mat to the circuit wires and tape these joints also.

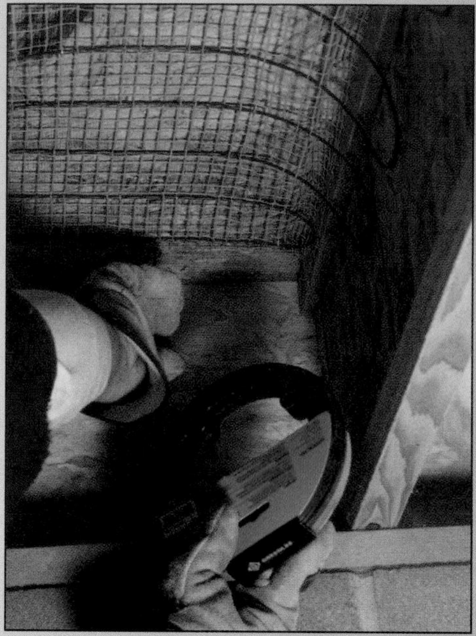

5 Before installing the junction box, push a fish tape through the hole in the floor plate. If your helper can't grab the end of the tape after a couple of attempts, try hooking the tape with a bent coat hanger. Pull the tape through the hole with the wiring. Install insulation between the joists.

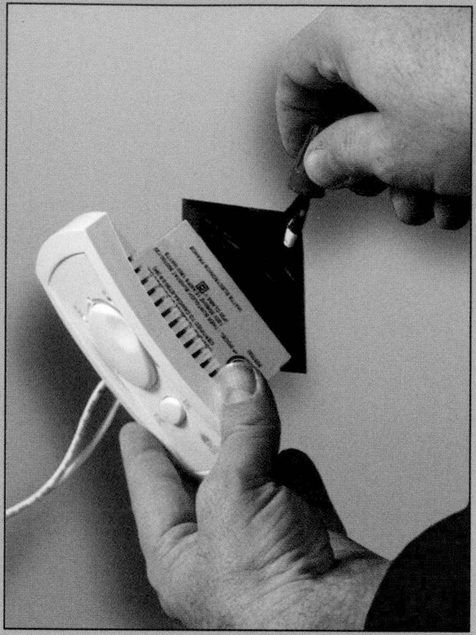

6 Remove the knockouts on the junction box and slide the box over the wires toward the wall. Fasten the box to the wall using its tabs or screws and tighten any wiring clamps inside the box. Attach the wires to the switch or thermostat with wire nuts.

Keep the heat in the room

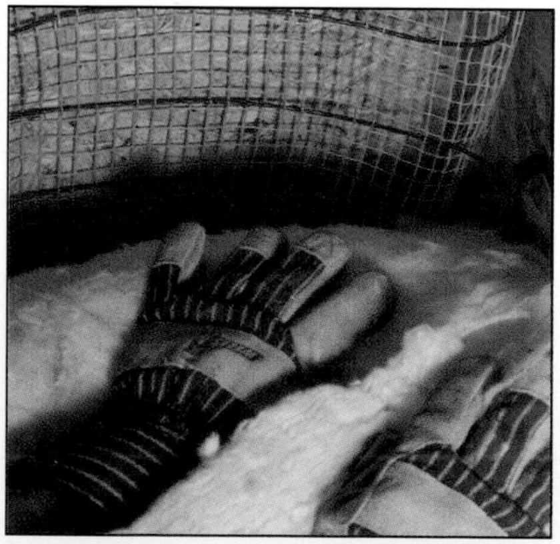

Once all the mats are in place and the system is properly wired, install fiberglass batts between the joists. Staple the batts through the paper tabs or keep them in place with metal fasteners or with 20-gauge wire inserted between staples driven into the joists.

JUNCTION BOX

Retrofit boxes are available for any installation

In new construction, installing a junction box for the thermostat is easy—just hang a box on a stud and drill a hole for the wiring through the bottom wall plate.

Installing a junction box in a finished wall is more difficult because you don't have access to the studs or other framing members.

Retrofit junction boxes are designed to solve this problem. Some mount with clips that grab the back of the drywall when screws are tightened. Others have plastic ears that swing out as the screws are tightened. Still others hold the wall between metal wings attached to the sides of the box.

Installing above-floor electric mats

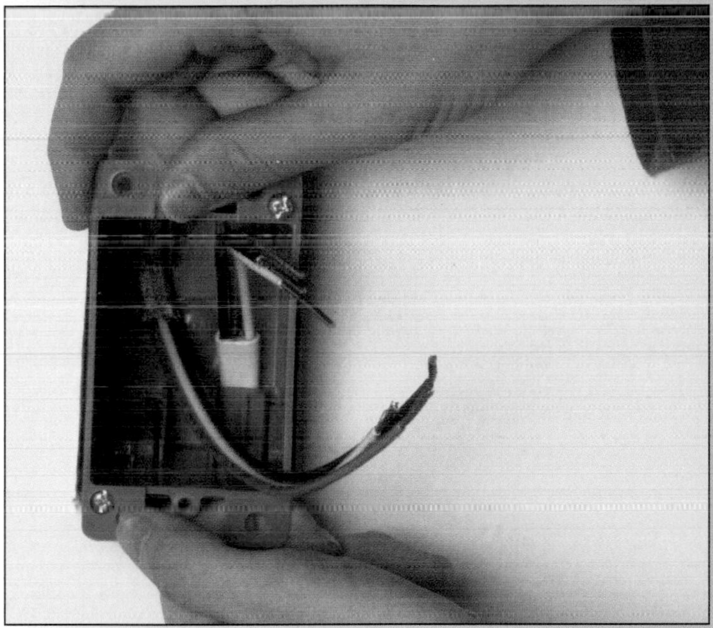

1 Using your dimensional plan, mark the location of the thermostat on the wall and install a junction box. Use a flanged box in new construction and a retrofit unit for an existing wall *(page 84)*. In both cases, install the box 60 inches above the floor. Using 12/2 cable, add a new circuit or extend an existing circuit but **do not connect the circuit to the power source.**

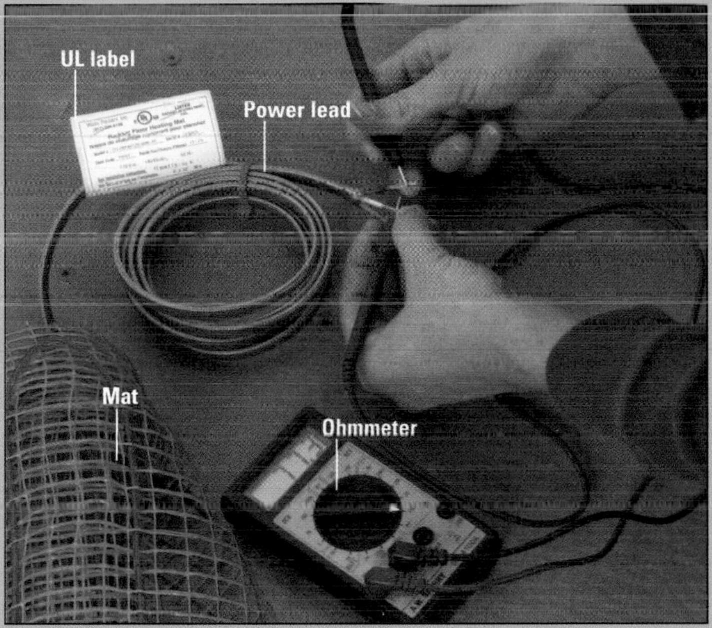

2 Unpack the mat. Check the resistance using an ohmmeter. The reading should be within 10 percent of the rating listed on the UL label. Write the reading on a piece of paper. You will need it when installing the mat to make sure that the heat cable is not nicked during installation.

Controlling the heat

Some above-floor mats are equipped with a thermostatic wire that reduces the electrical flow (and therefore the heat) as the mats warm up. When the resistance in the wire reaches the setting of the thermostat, the system shuts down. Other systems employ a sensor bulb that "tells" the thermostat when the floor requires heat.

Most sensors are designed to be "threaded" into the mat netting between the heating wires and about 6 inches into the heated area. Be sure to note the manufacturer's directions for locating the sensor. Most are about 15 feet from the thermostat. When you finish the installation, treat the sensor as you would another part of the mat, covering it with thinset as you mortar the floor.

INSTALLING ABOVE-FLOOR ELECTRIC RADIANT HEATING

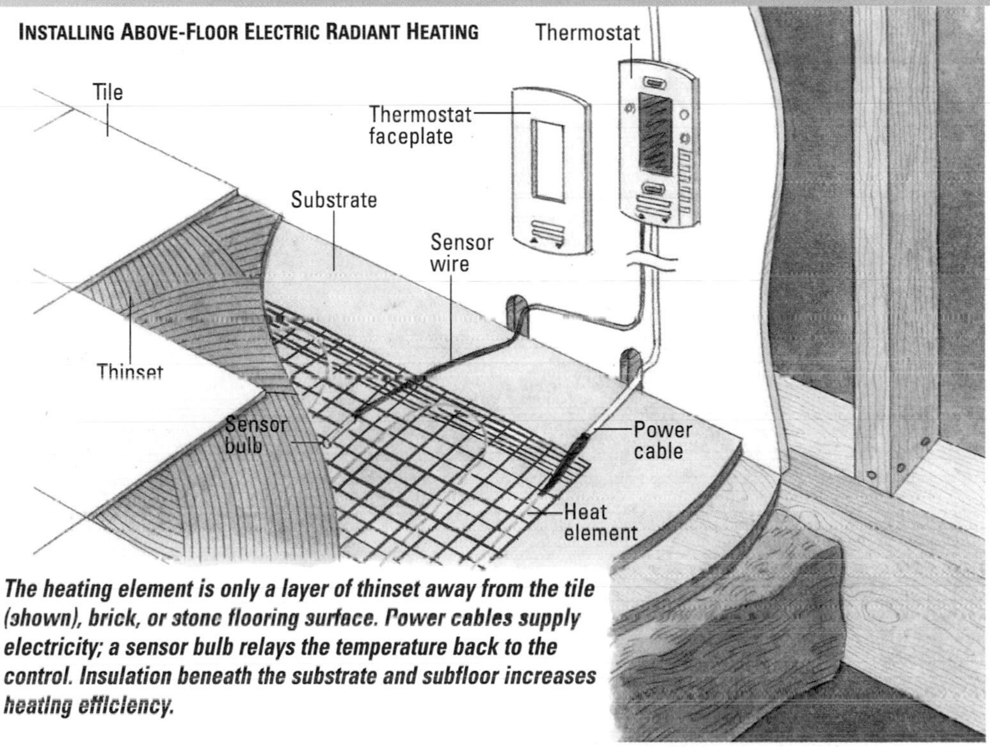

The heating element is only a layer of thinset away from the tile (shown), brick, or stone flooring surface. Power cables supply electricity; a sensor bulb relays the temperature back to the control. Insulation beneath the substrate and subfloor increases heating efficiency.

Installing above-floor electric mats *(continued)*

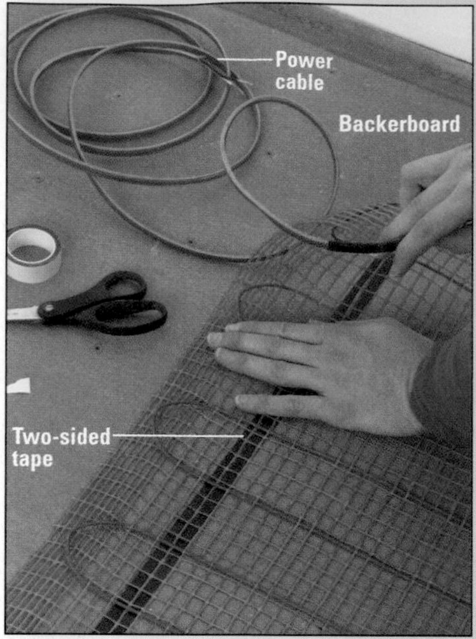

3 Roll out the mat so it's no closer than 3 inches to walls and fixtures. Staple the mat to a subfloor with ½-inch staples or fasten it with strips of double-faced tape. Press down on the tape on the backerboard, then pull off the backing and firmly press the mat onto the tape.

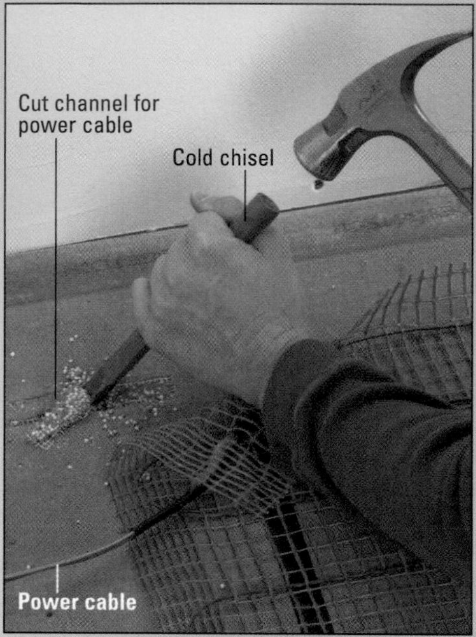

4 If the power lead is thicker than the mat (some come with flat ribbon leads) you can sink it into the substrate if you've used cement backerboard. Use a cold chisel to cut a channel for it. If you don't recess the lead, you'll have to make sure it's adequately covered with thinset.

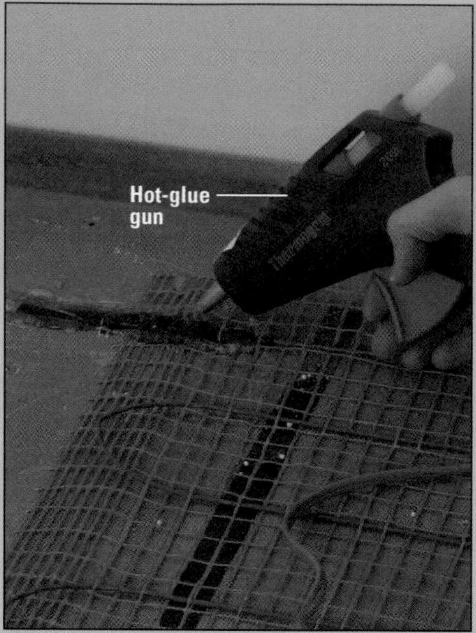

5 Hot-glue the power cable to the substrate. Mark along the power cable and slide it to one side. Working a few feet at a time, run a continuous bead of hot glue. Press the lead into the bead of hot glue. Make sure the lead wires don't cross each other or run perpendicular to a heater wire.

Strategies for running cable

Remove the baseboard in the room in which you're working *(page 52)* and drill a locator hole next to the wall. Mark the hole by pushing a wire through it to the floor below. Drill a ¾-inch hole and use a fish tape to pull the cable to where it is needed.

By cutting away drywall (save the cut piece for replacing and taping later) you can run cable horizontally. This allows you to tap into a receptacle (check that the circuit can bear the additional load) in the same room.

Placing mats in tight quarters

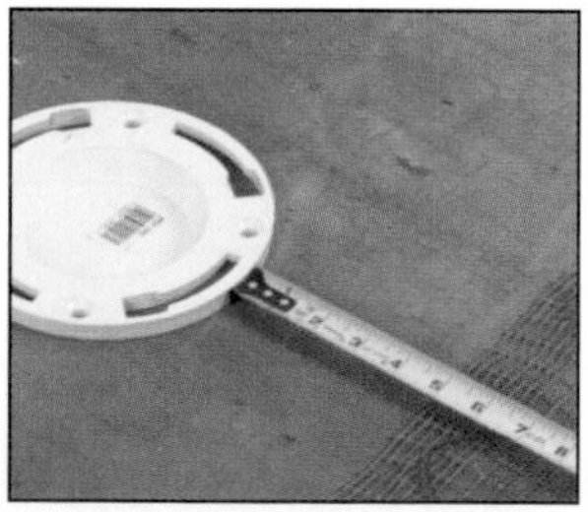

It's OK to run a mat under a toilet but it must be 3 inches from a toilet (or any) drain flange. In addition, you can run a mat beneath the kick plate of a vanity. Never overlap mats, never cut a mat to fit, and never attempt to repair a cut or nicked heating wire. If the wire is damaged, you must replace the entire mat.

SAFETY FIRST
Don't overload circuits or components

Checking the amperage demanded by a new installation will tell you if an existing circuit can carry the load or if you'll have to install a new circuit. Each square foot of electric radiant heating mat typically draws 0.1 amp. That means adding radiant heating mats to the work area of an average-size kitchen will add 5 or 6 amps to the circuit (50–60 square feet of mat). But each component included in the system also has to be up to that amperage. Check dimmers and timers to make sure they are rated to take the amperage.

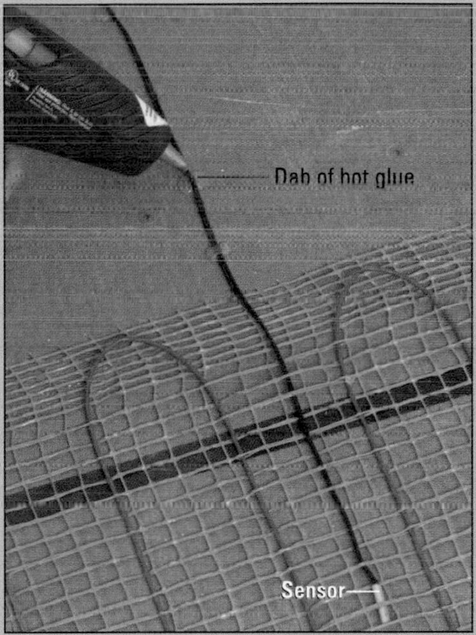

6 If your system uses a thermostatic sensor, weave the sensor bulb between two heating elements. Adhere the bulb wire with dots of hot glue. Now check the mat resistance with an ohmmeter. If the reading falls outside the manufacturer's tolerances, find the damaged mat and replace it.

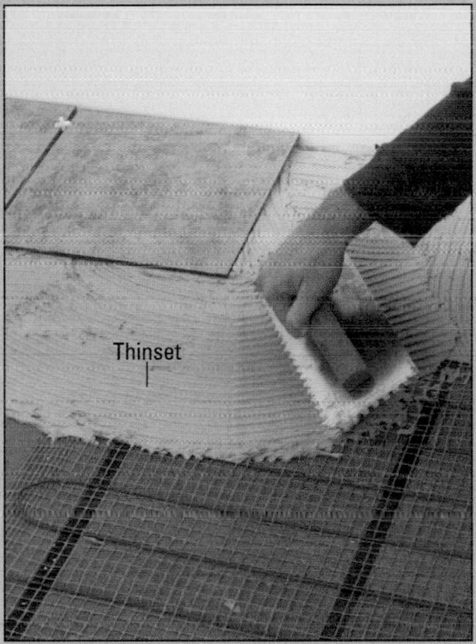

7 With the flat side of a ⅜-inch notched trowel, apply thinset over an area of the mat. Then turn the trowel over and rake the thinset to ¼-inch uniform depth. Be careful not to snag the mat. Do not clean the trowel by banging it on the mat. Tile the area of the floor covered with thinset.

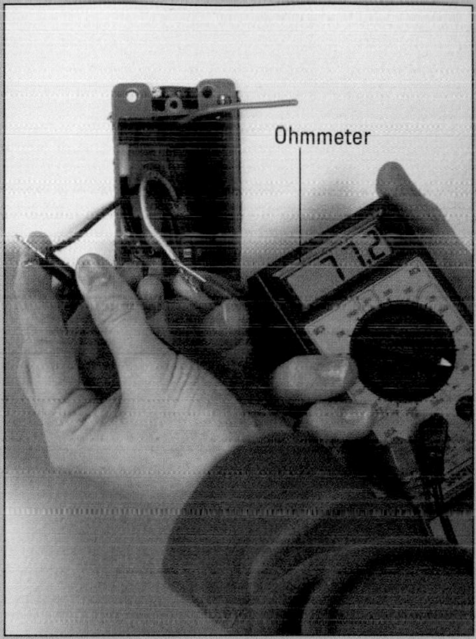

8 Check mat resistance once again, using the ohmmeter. If the ohm reading drops to 0 or infinity, the heating element has been damaged, and you must remove and replace the mat. Take extra care when grouting over a heating grid to avoid damage to the mat.

Wiring the thermostat

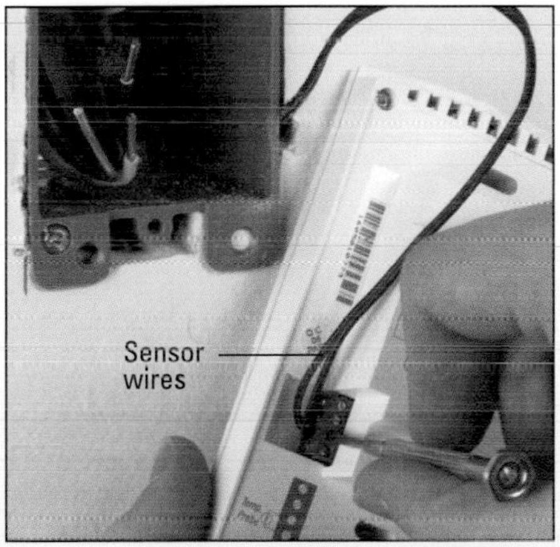

1 Using a jeweler's screwdriver, attach the two sensor wires to the screw terminals on one side of the control. Connect the ground from the mat power lead directly to the house ground. Wire the rest of the thermostat connections following the manufacturer's instructions.

2 Attach the face plate. Connect to the power source or connect the line to a new breaker. Turn on the power and follow the manufacturer's instructions for setting the temperature and timer.

WHAT IF...
You can't level the thinset?

Spreading thinset evenly on electric mats can be difficult. To apply thinset properly, you need to use a notched trowel, but the notches are prone to catch in the netting. The result is a marred, uneven surface and the possibility of a damaged mat.

Before you undertake this job, try spreading a small amount of thinset in a corner. If you can't get the hang of it, hire a pro. Or find a company that installs self-leveling gypsum. This material is force-fed through a hose and will dry to a level, thin slab of the proper thickness. Once it dries, you can install tile just as you would on a typical slab. In bathrooms, kitchens, and other wet areas, lay a moisture barrier between the gypsum and the tile.

Installing an underfloor hydronic system

1 Plan a hydronic system so you can locate the holes for the PEX tubing as close as possible to the subfloor and to the end of the joists. Using a drill and holesaw or forstner bit ¼ inch larger than the tubing (a spade bit will wear out quickly), drill all the holes in the joists before you begin threading the tubing.

2 Lay a coil of tubing on the floor at one end of the room. Walk the end of the tubing down the length of the room and thread the tubing through the first joist. Have a helper unwind the tubing from the coil and push the tubing through the holes as you walk it down the bays between the joists. Untwist the tubing from the roll so it does not kink as you thread it through the holes.

PLANNING HYDRONIC SYSTEMS
A job for the pros

Hydronic tubing is relatively easy to install. The real work lies in the planning. Plan your system room by room, using grid paper to draw the tube spacing and the location of the manifold stations (the place where each circuit begins). Have a professional design the layout based on your plans.

PEX tubing comes in different diameters. Make sure the flow of water through the pipes is sufficient for the room you're heating. For example, ½-inch tubing needs a manifold station every 300 feet; ⅝-inch tubing needs one every 450 feet.

Space the tubing lines closer together along exterior walls. This increases the output of heat in the coldest areas of the room. Provide access panels to manifold stations so you can make repairs easily.

HYDRONIC THIN-SLAB INSTALLATIONS

Concrete thin-slab

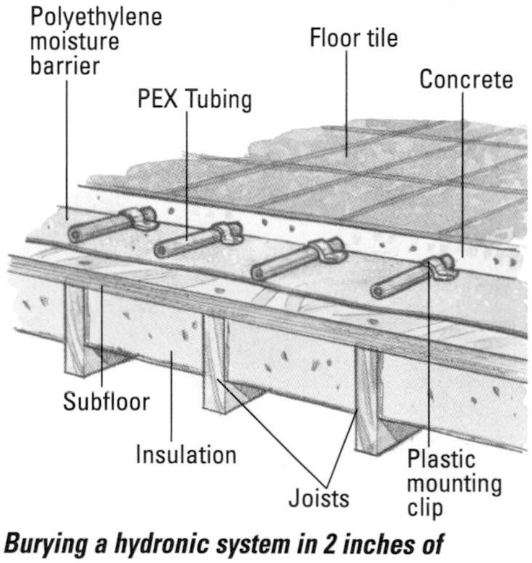

Gypsum thin-slab

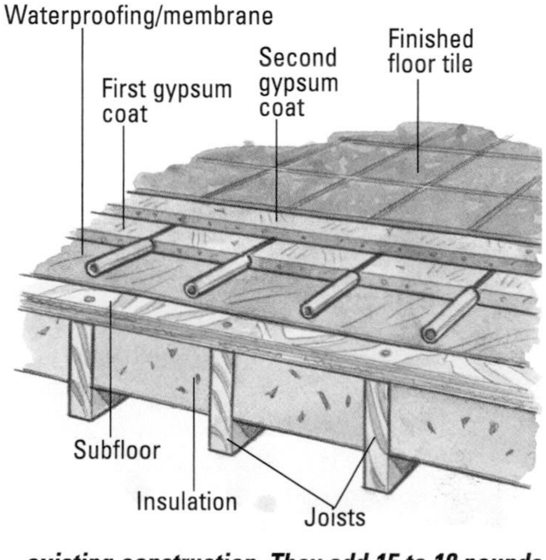

Burying a hydronic system in 2 inches of concrete results in a heavier load than most wood-frame floors can handle. Even thin slabs, which are perfect for adding radiant heat in an addition to your home, may not be suitable in existing construction. They add 15 to 18 pounds per square foot. Thin slabs also raise the floor level, which requires raising base cabinets and toilet flanges, and shortens the floor-to-sill distances of windows.

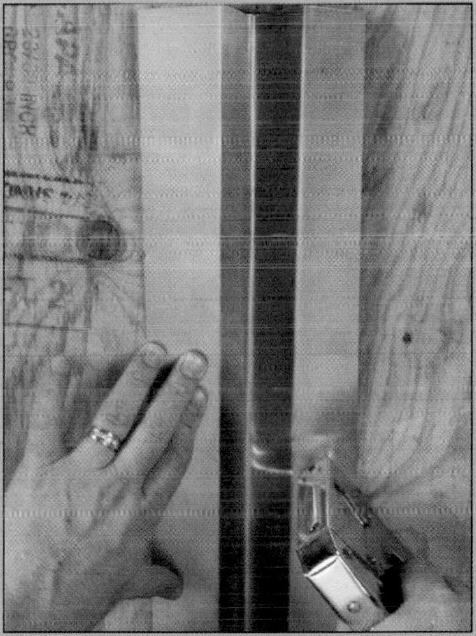

3 Staple the diffusion plates to the subfloor, spacing the plates and tubing as directed by the manufacturer. One-coil systems are generally centered between the joists. If you're working with a system that has a return line, label the inflow and outflow lines and connect the lines to a boiler.

Installing an above-floor hydronic system

Cut ¾-inch plywood or 1× sleepers to a width that will space the tubing consistent with the manufacturer's specifications. Make sure the ends of the tubing will bend without crimping. Mark the locations of the sleepers on the subfloor and fasten the first two with 1½-inch decking screws. Dry-lay a run of tubing to make sure it won't crimp, then fasten the remaining sleepers. If using a diffusion-plate system, snap and fasten the plates between the sleepers. Then press the tubing into the recesses of the plates. Cover the installation with plywood or thinset as recommended by the manufacturer.

CONNECT THE LINES TO A BOILER

Supplying hot water to hydronic systems

Although building codes in some localities may allow water heaters to be used for small hydronic systems, most systems require a hot-water boiler or geothermal heat pump. Boiler manufacturers generally make models with and without a self-contained water heater for home use. When planning a hydronic system, make sure the output of the boiler or heat pump meets the heat-load requirements of the room.

Using precut underlayment

Avoid having to cut and fasten sleepers by using plywood underlayment with channels precut in its surface. Fasten the panels to the subfloor, snap in the diffusion plates (if required), and press the tubing into the channels. Cover the installation with the proper substrate.

MASTERING BASIC INSTALLATION TECHNIQUES

Not too long ago, setting ceramic tile was beyond the skills and abilities of most homeowners. Ceramic tiles were soaked in water overnight and set in thick mortar. With the introduction of thinset adhesives and backerboard, installation of ceramic tile moved well within the reach of any do-it-yourselfer.

The same holds true for other kinds of tile. Techniques for setting parquet, resilient tile, carpet, cork, and laminates are simple and easy to learn because they're repetitive. This chapter focuses on the installation of ceramic tile. Specific instructions for resilients, parquet, laminates, cork, and carpet tile are found in their respective chapters.

Practice makes perfect

If you are starting a ceramic project for the first time, practice each step before applying it to your floor, wall, or countertop.

Create a practice station with a couple of pieces of backerboard. Mix and spread a small amount of mortar, set the tile, cut a few tiles for the edges in your mock-up, then grout and clean it. If your results don't satisfy you, pull up the installation or start a new one and try again.

A day's work

If you're tiling a floor, you'll discover that it's easier to lay the field tiles and come back the next day to lay the cut tiles on the edges. That way you won't have to walk on freshly laid tile and risk dislodging it, and you can measure the edges precisely and cut tiles to fit. You will also save money on rental tools by limiting all the cutting to one day.

If your tool box does not include tile installation tools, purchase the best you can afford. Most tools have many applications, and you'll use them for years to come. Gather all tools and materials ahead of time, think through the installation steps before you start, and take your time.

Most of the techniques presented in this chapter are shown as they are applied to a floor surface, with exceptions for other surfaces noted.

Tile installation is a series of repetitive steps—your skills will improve quickly as a project proceeds.

CHAPTER PREVIEW

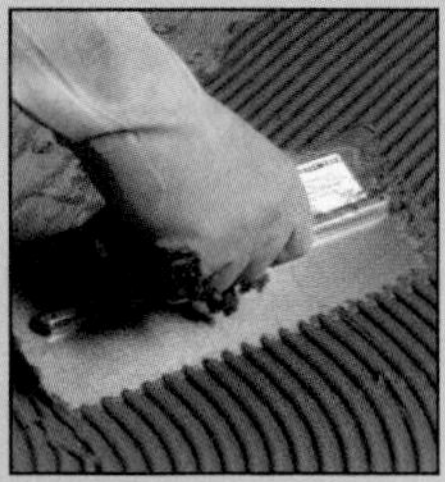

Installing new backerboard

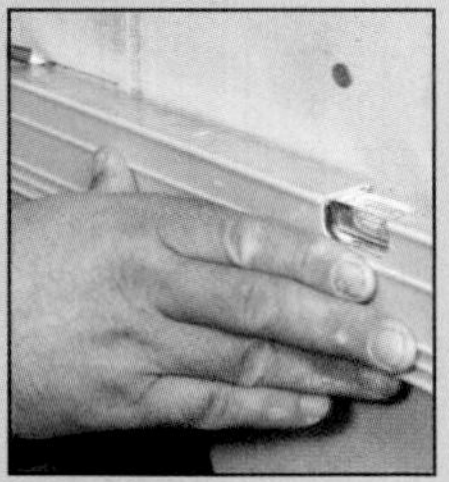

Marking layout lines

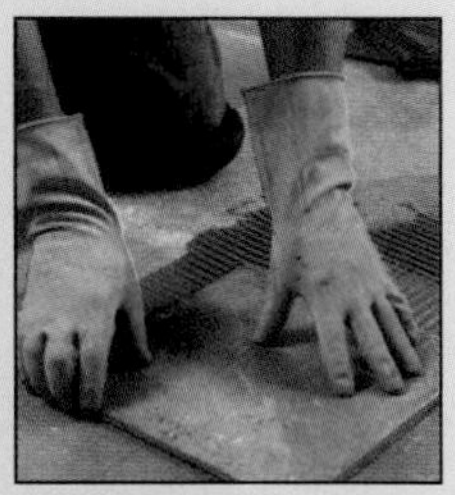

Installing ceramic tile

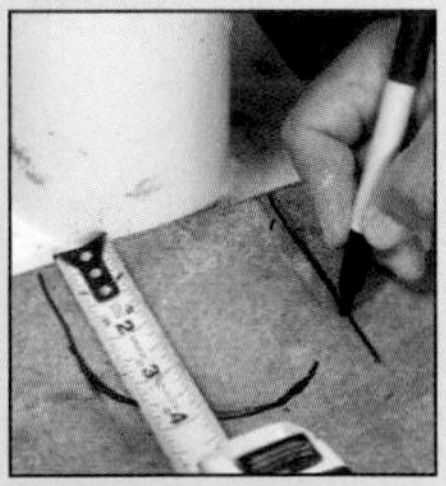

Cutting ceramic tile

Sort tile for consistency in dye lots or mix tiles from different cartons to spread colors of hand-made tile across the room.
Layout lines snapped on surface to be tiled
Cover cracks in slabs with isolation membrane.
Stack tiles close to sections in which you will lay them.

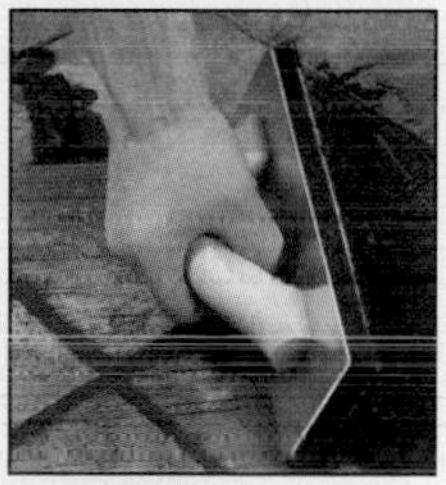

Grouting, caulking, sealing
page 104

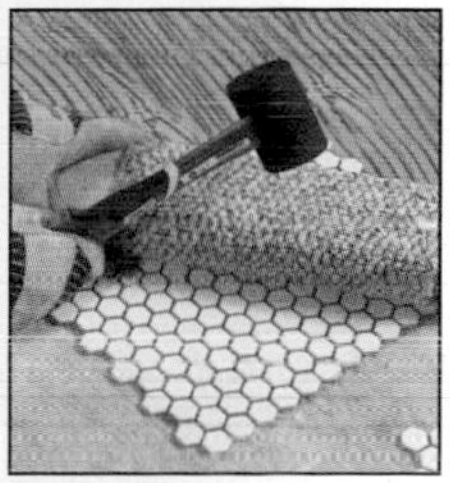

Installing mosaic tile
page 106

Installing stone tile
page 108

Installing baseboards and transitions
page 110

STANLEY PRO TIP

Snap a chalkline

To snap a chalkline accurately, the line must be held tightly on the surface. Pull the line from its housing. Place the metal tab at one end of the surface and the housing at the other. Keeping the line tight, reach out as far from the housing as you can, lift the line about 4 inches off the surface, and let it snap back.

You may be able to hook the metal tab in the perimeter recess of a slab or wood floor. If you can't, snapping the line is a two-person task: one holds the tab, the other holds the housing.

INSTALLING NEW BACKERBOARD

Because you must install backerboard with its edges centered on joists and studs, mark the joist and stud locations before you start. Because you won't be able to see marks after you have troweled on the thinset, mark joist locations on the wall and stud locations on the ceiling.

Offset by half a sheet the joints where the sheets meet, where possible. Leave at least a ⅛-inch gap between sheets (use an 8d nail) and a ¼-inch gap at the walls (about the diameter of a pencil).

Scoop thinset out of the bucket with a margin trowel, then spread it with the notched trowel recommended by the adhesive manufacturer.

PRESTART CHECKLIST

☐ **TIME**
About 30 to 45 minutes per square foot of surface

☐ **TOOLS**
Cutting backerboard: drywall square, carbide scriber, utility knife, rasp
Cutting holes: tape measure, cordless drill, carbide holesaw, compass, utility knife, and hammer for large holes
Installing backerboard: trowel, margin trowel, corner drywall knife, cordless drill, utility knife

☐ **SKILLS**
Precise measuring and cutting, driving fasteners with cordless drill, troweling

☐ **PREP**
Prepare, vacuum, and damp-clean surfaces; install waterproofing membrane in wet locations; cut and install new countertop base

☐ **MATERIALS**
Installing backerboard: thinset, backerboard, 1¼- and 2-inch backerboard screws, 2-inch gummed fiber mesh tape, 2×4 lumber for blocking (walls only), 8d nails

Cutting backerboard

1 If you are not finishing the floor, protect it with a tarp. Backerboard particles will easily scratch a floor. Mark the line to be cut and position a drywall square or metal T-square on the line. Using a carbide backerboard scriber and firm pressure, scribe the cut line. Make several passes.

2 Stand the sheet on edge or turn the sheet over; working from the side opposite the scored line, snap the board.

Cutting small holes

1 Set the board against the pipe or other obstruction. Mark the diameter of the hole to be cut. Use a tape measure to locate the center of the hole. For faucets, measure the location of each faucet hole from the wall and from the tub or floor.

2 Use a cordless drill and carbide-tipped holesaw or coring saw to cut small holes in backerboard. Place the drill point of the saw on the mark you made, and use light pressure and high speed to cut through the backerboard.

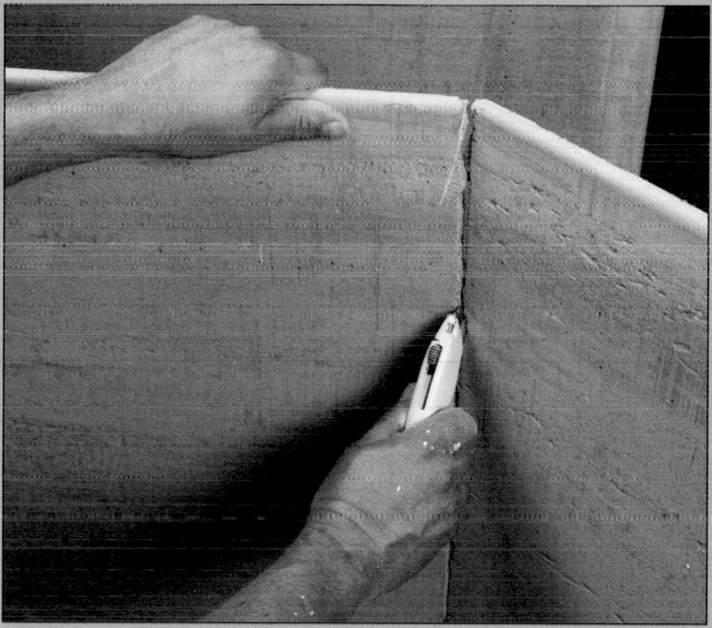

3 Using a utility knife and keeping the pieces at an angle, cut through the board to separate the two pieces. Depending on how deeply you made your first cut, you may have to make several passes with the knife to separate the pieces.

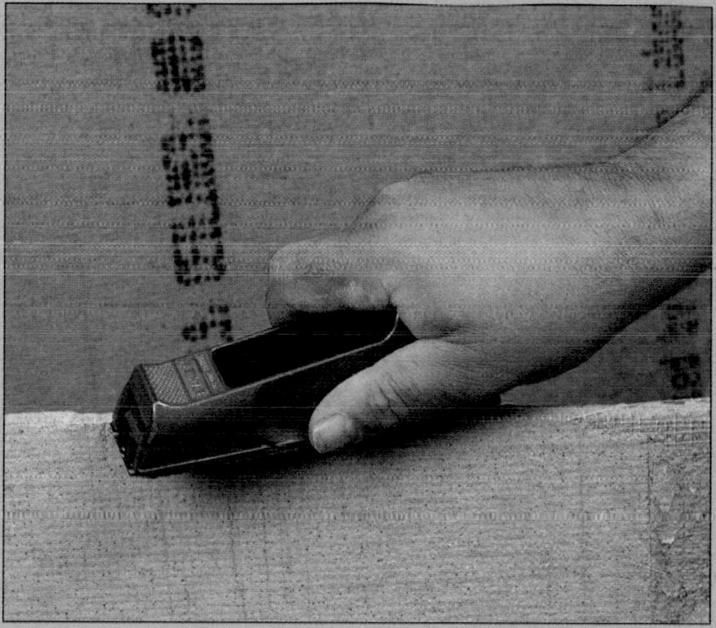

4 Backerboard cuts are rough, whether made with a carbide scriber or a utility knife. Pieces being joined should have as smooth an edge as possible. Use a contour plane with a serrated blade, a rasp, or a masonry stone to smooth out the edge. Keep the tool perpendicular to the edge of the board and pass over the board several times until its surface is flat.

Cutting large holes

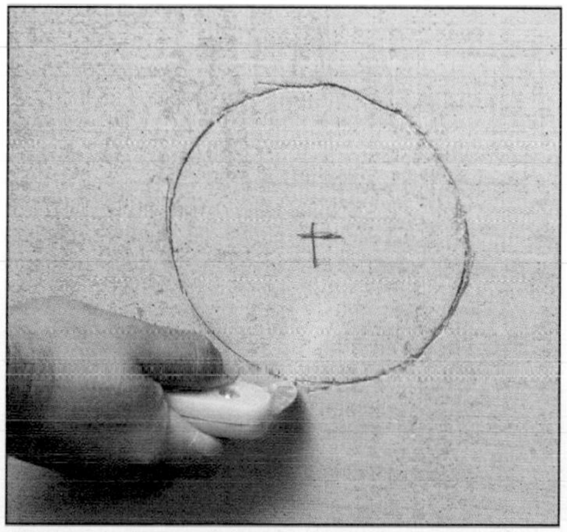

1 When the diameter of a hole to be cut exceeds the size of available holesaws, measure the obstruction and use a compass to mark its location on the backerboard. Then score completely through the backerboard mesh with a utility knife or carbide scriber.

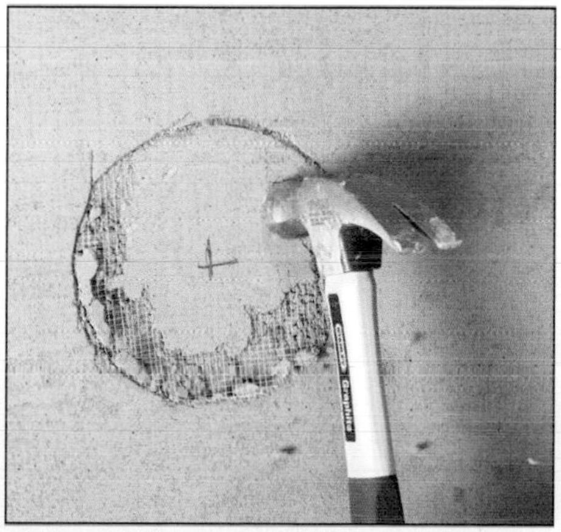

2 Support the cutout with the palm of one hand, if necessary, and tap the scored edge with a hammer. Continue tapping until the surface around the circumference crumbles. Alternatively, drill a series of small holes around the circumference.

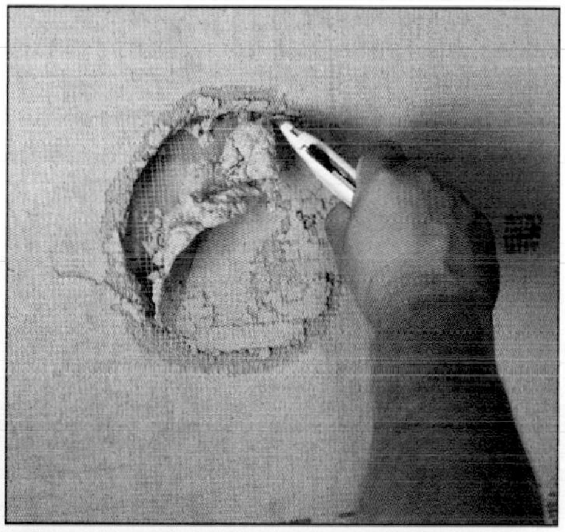

3 Using a utility knife, cut through the mesh on the opposite side of the board. Push the cutout through and smooth the edges with a rasp, serrated contour plane, or masonry stone.

Installing backerboard on floors

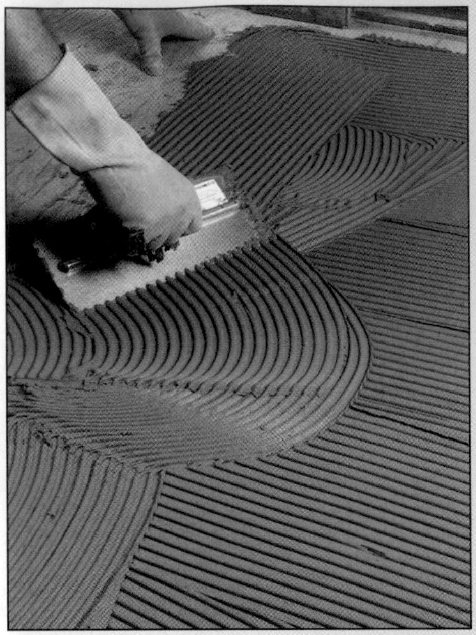

1 Mix and pour thinset *(page 98)*. Hold the smooth side of a notched trowel at a 30-degree angle and spread the mortar in a thick, even coat, forcing it into the subfloor. Then, keeping the notched side of the trowel in contact with the floor and at a 45- to 75-degree angle, work the mortar into ridges.

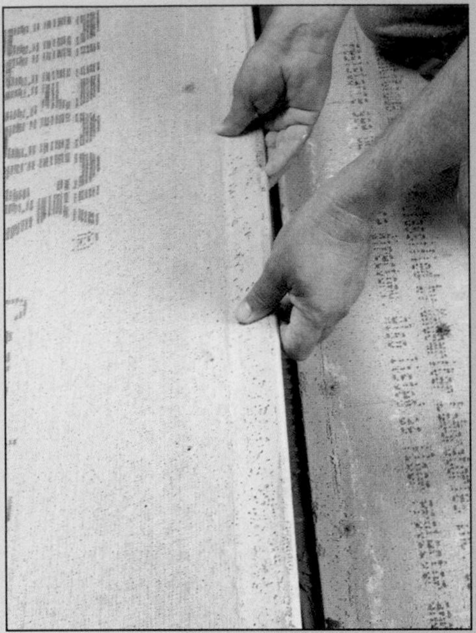

2 While the mortar is still wet, tip the board on a long edge and hinge it toward the floor. Line the first board on a joist and keep a gap of ⅛ inch between boards, ¼ inch at walls. Manufacturers' directions may vary, but typically you should stagger the joints. Walk on the board to set it in the mortar.

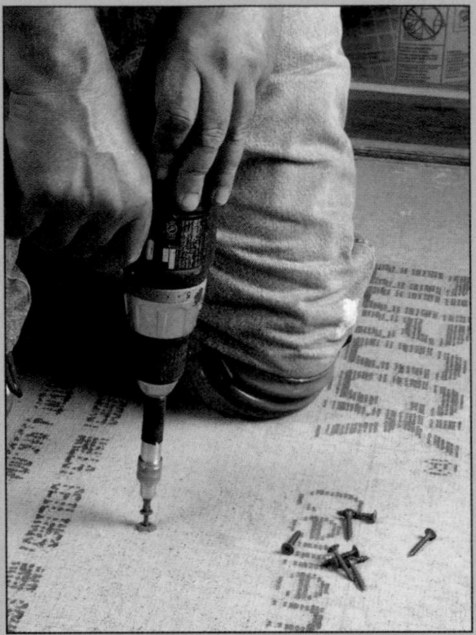

3 Using a cordless drill and phillips bit, drive backerboard screws through the board and into the subfloor at about 8-inch intervals. Use 2-inch backerboard screws at the joists and 1¼-inch screws in the field. Set the screws so they are flush with the surface of the board.

Installing backerboard on walls

1 Nail blocking between studs to support joints, if necessary. Apply construction adhesive to the studs. Screw the board to the studs and blocking. Rest the next pieces on ⅛-inch spacers (8d nails) before fastening.

2 Use 2- or 4-inch gummed tape over each backerboard joint. Press the tape into the joint and unroll it as you go. Use a utility knife to cut the tape at the end of the joint.

3 Apply a thin coat of thinset mortar to the taped joint with a margin trowel. Trowel on enough mortar to fill the joint and level it with the backerboard. Feather the edges smooth.

4 Apply 2-inch pregummed fiberglass mesh tape over each joint, pressing the tape firmly on the backerboard. The tape cuts easily with a utility knife. Use 4-inch tape (if available) for increased strength. Alternatively, you can embed ungummed tape in a thin coat of mortar applied to the joints. Use this method where stronger joints are required—in stone tile installations, for example.

5 Whether you have used ungummed or pregummed tape, finish the joint by applying a thin coat of thinset mortar over the tape. Use a margin trowel to scoop mortar from the bucket. Apply the mortar so it levels the recess in the joint from side to side. Feather the edges to avoid creating high spots under the tiled surface.

Taping corners

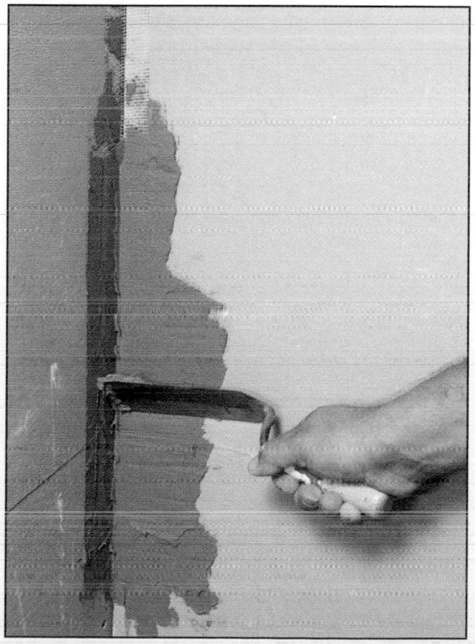

Tape corners with either 2-inch or 4-inch gummed fiberglass mesh tape. In either case, do not precut the tape to length. Unroll it as you press it into the joint and cut it when you reach the end. Precut lengths of gummed tape may roll up and stick to themselves before you get them on the board.

If using 2-inch tape, place one length along one edge and another length along the other edge. Bridge the central edges of the corner with a third length of tape. Four-inch tape hastens the job. Fold the tape in half as you press it into the corner.

If using ungummed tape, first spread a thin coat of mortar into the corner joint and smooth it with a drywall corner knife. Then embed the tape in the mortar. With any kind of tape, finish the joint with a thin coat of mortar, feathering the edges smoothly.

STANLEY PRO TIP

Fix backerboard screw snaps

Backerboard fasteners, unlike drywall screws, are made to withstand the rigors of tile installations. Occasionally, however, one will snap off. Check the torque setting of your cordless drill to make sure the clutch slips when the screw just dimples the board. If a backerboard screw snaps, remove the loose piece and drive another about 1 inch away from the first one.

MARKING LAYOUT LINES

Perhaps no other task requires more precision than marking reference and layout lines. These lines keep your tile square to the room and evenly spaced.

Mark reference lines perpendicular to each other. Save time setting tiles by locating these lines where a grout joint will fall when you install the tile. You can use your layout sketch to find this point, but it's better to dry-lay and space at least one row of the actual tiles in both directions. Mark the edge of the tile, then snap the lines.

Next mark layout lines to establish grids for laying tiles in sections. How many you use depends on how complicated your layout is, how quickly the adhesive sets up (its working time), your skill level (if you're less skilled, use more lines), and the size of the tile (larger tile will generally mean fewer lines). Establish a grid with which you feel comfortable (about 2-foot squares are a good size to start). Measure from the reference lines in both directions by an amount that equals several tiles (plus grout joints) and snap lines at these points.

PRESTART CHECKLIST

☐ **TIME**
About five minutes to measure and snap each line, more if dry-laying tile to establish lines

☐ **TOOLS**
Laying out floors: tape measure, chalkline
Laying out walls: tape measure, 4-foot level, chalkline

☐ **SKILLS**
Reading a spirit level, measuring accurately

☐ **PREP**
Surface preparation, installation of backerboard

☐ **MATERIALS**
Layout sketch, loose tile, spacers

Marking layout lines on floors

1 Using your layout sketch *(page 42–43),* mark the floor several feet from one wall where a grout joint will fall. To double-check your layout, dry-lay and space the tiles along each axis. Mark the ends of this line at both walls.

2 Snap a chalkline at the points you have marked. Repeat the process between the other walls. Use the 3-4-5 triangle method *(page 44)* to square the lines. Measure from each of these reference lines distances equal to an even number of tiles and joints, and snap layout lines at these points.

LAYOUT IS COMPLICATED
Snap additional layout lines

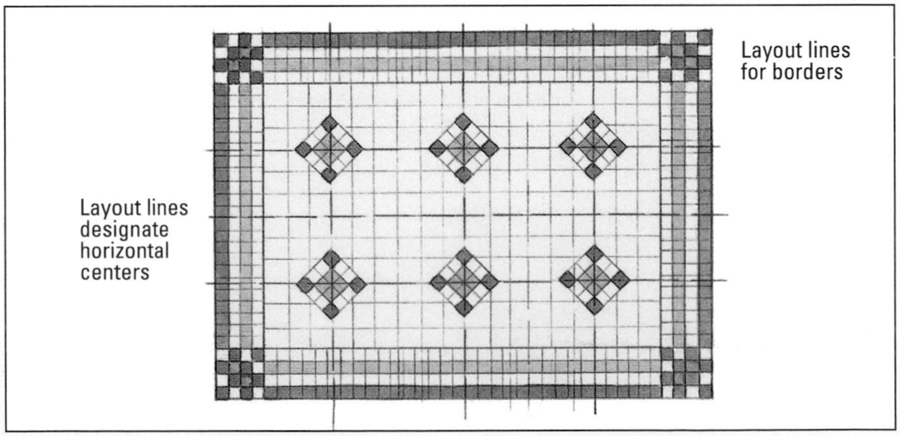

Layout becomes more complicated with decorative tiles and borders. Although you can lay such decorative items by eye, the job will go more quickly and the result will be much more attractive if you snap additional layout lines.

Once you have snapped the major layout grids on the floor or wall, measure and mark the position of decorative tiles or borders. Snap a line on both axes at each point the pattern or the tile size changes.

Marking layout lines on walls

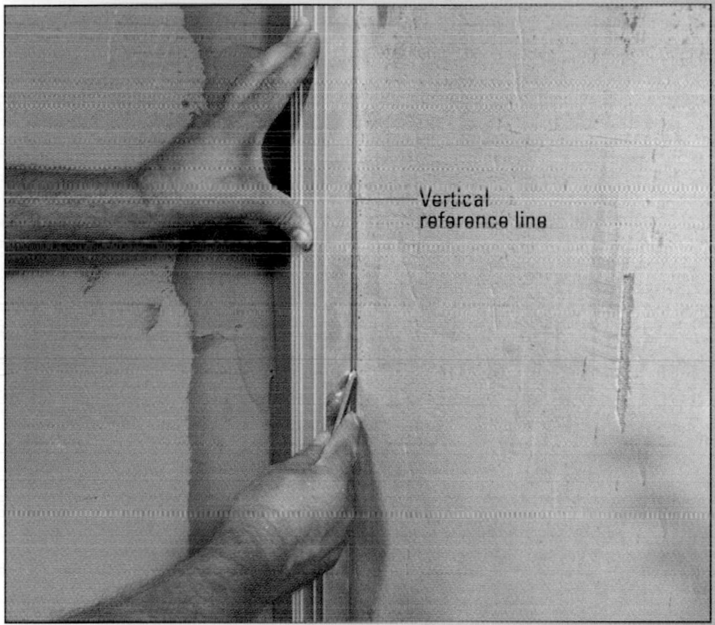

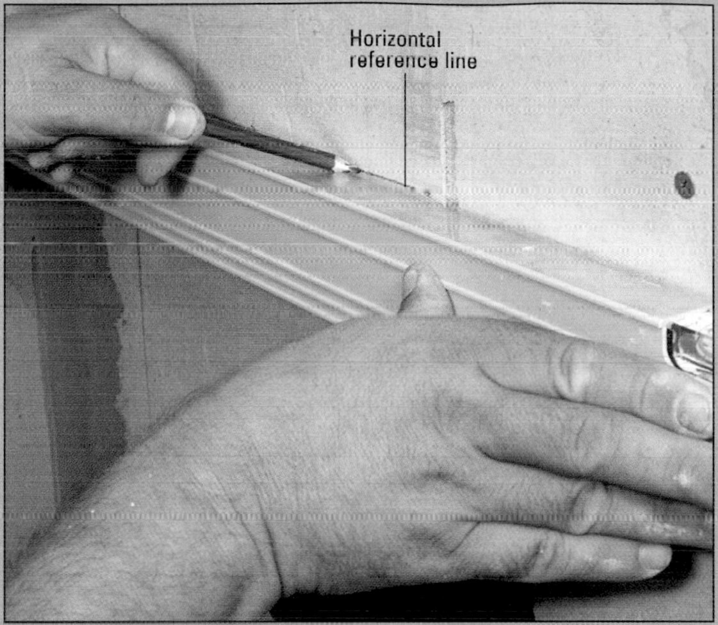

1 Hold a 4-foot carpenter's level vertically on the wall and at least 2 feet from a corner, preferably on a plane where a grout line will fall. Adjust the level until the spirit bubble indicates it is straight up and down. Taking care not to disturb the level, trace a penciled line down its edge. Extend the line to the floor and ceiling by snapping a chalkline over the one you have marked.

2 Position the level horizontally on the chalkline, about midway up the wall, and preferably on a plane where a grout joint will fall. Adjust the level until the bubble is centered in the glass and scribe a line along the level. Extend this line with a chalkline. You don't have to check the intersection for square with the 3-4-5 triangle method.

From each line, mark the wall at intervals that correspond to an equal number of tiles (include the grout joints) and snap layout lines.

STANLEY PRO TIP

Protect layout lines on the floor

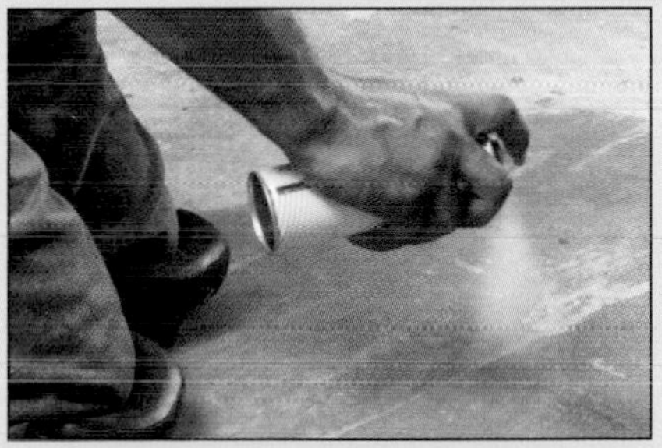

Chalk layout lines on the floor easily become erased or blurred as you walk and work in the room. To protect them, spray each of the lines with an inexpensive hair spray. Purchase a spray with a heavy hold. Apply a fairly thick coat, but not enough to obscure the lines. The spray dries almost immediately, will not wear off, and won't interfere with the adhesive bond.

Where to start?

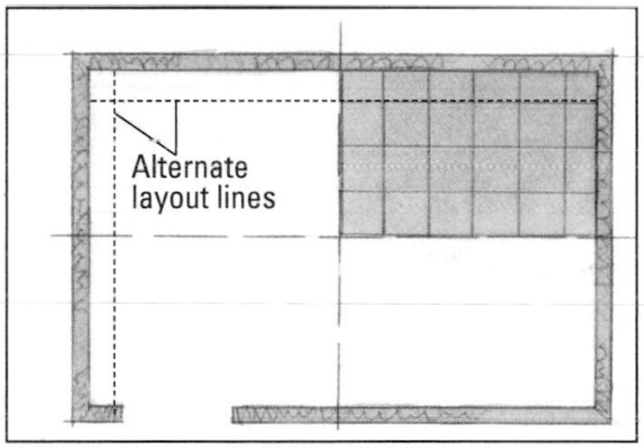

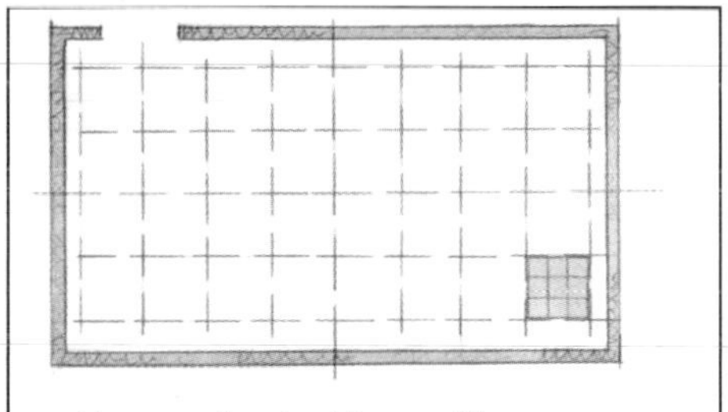

Lines mark out grids equal to width of multiple tiles

Snapping layout lines in grids will help you lay the room in manageable sections and keep each section straight. Although there is no rule that governs how many grids to snap, one rule will keep you from tiling yourself into a corner: Always start your project at a location away from a doorway.

You may be able to get by in a small room with only one pair of lines, although grids are recommended. Lay the field tiles in the corner first, then proceed toward the doorway. Let the mortar dry for a day, then come back and lay the cut tile on the edges.

Large rooms require more grids than small rooms. They also tend to lend themselves to quadrant installations. Set out the tile and lay it in the quadrant most removed from the doorway. Then go back and set the adjacent quadrant, the corner quadrant, and finally the section that exits to the door.

INSTALLING CERAMIC TILE

Prepare the surface using the methods described on *pages 48–71.* Slab floors and drywall or plaster in nonwet areas may not require the installation of backerboard. Install backerboard on wood surfaces and walls in areas that will get wet, such as bathrooms or entryways.

Before you trowel on the mortar, sweep the floor clean. Figure out how many tiles you need in each layout grid and stack them around the room close to each section. That way you won't have to go back and forth to supply yourself with fresh tiles when you start laying each grid.

Sort through all the tile boxes to make sure the dye lots match and separate out any chipped tiles. Use these for cut pieces.

If you are installing saltillo or handmade tile, its color may be consistent within each carton but may vary from box to box. Sort through the tiles; at each layout grid, mix some from each box. Doing so spreads the colors evenly in the room and keeps them from occurring in patches.

PRESTART CHECKLIST

☐ **TIME**
About an hour to trowel and set 4 to 6 square feet (varies with tile size)

☐ **TOOLS**
Mortar mixing paddle, ½-inch electric drill, notched trowel, 4-foot level, utility knife, grout float, sponge, beater block, hammer or rubber mallet

☐ **SKILLS**
Mixing with power drill, troweling

☐ **PREP**
Install backerboard, clean surface, snap layout lines

☐ **MATERIALS**
Five-gallon bucket, thinset, spacers, ¾-inch plywood squares

Setting the tile

1 Pour the water in a bucket, then add about half the thinset. Mix the thinset with a ½-inch drill and a paddle designed for mortar. Keep the speed below 300 rpm and the paddle in the mix to avoid adding air. Add thinset a little at a time. Let the mix set for 10 minutes before applying.

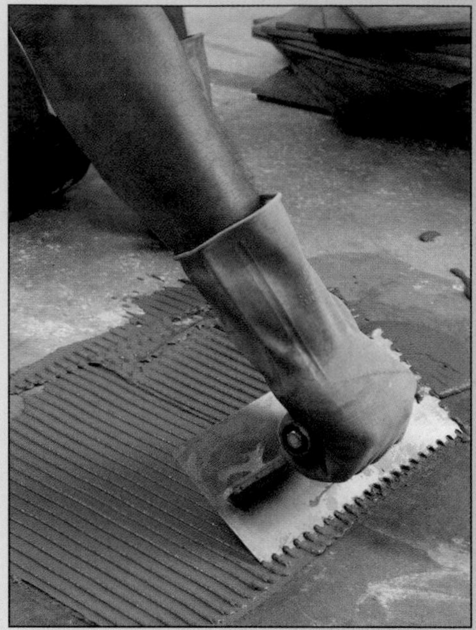

2 Pour enough mortar to cover a layout grid. Holding the straight edge of the trowel at about a 30-degree angle, spread the mortar evenly, about as thick as the depth of a trowel notch. Spread the mortar to the layout line; comb it with the notched edge at about a 45- to 75-degree angle.

Mix the thinset

Whether you have chosen thinset or organic mastic, bring it into the room to acclimate it to normal room temperatures—ideally between 65° and 75° F. Mix thinset with water that is clean enough to drink and clean out the bucket after each mix; mortar and adhesive residue can cause a new batch to cure prematurely.

Adding the powder to the water a little at a time reduces airborne mortar dust and makes mixing easier. Let the mixture set for 10 minutes so the water will penetrate any remaining lumps. Then mix again to remove lumps. To test the consistency, load a trowel with mortar and hold it upside down. If the mortar falls off the trowel easily, add more dry powder and remix. The ideal consistency is about as thick as peanut butter. Clean the bed before troweling.

STANLEY PRO TIP

Choose the right trowel

The size of the notches in the trowel you use will depend on the thickness of the tile. The depth of the notch, and therefore the ridge it forms in the adhesive, should be about two-thirds the tile thickness.

Use 1⁄16- to ⅛-inch V-notched trowels for thin tiles, such as glazed wall tiles. For 6- to 8-inch floor tiles, use a ¼- to ⅜-inch square-notched trowel; for large tiles (more than 12 inches), use a deep (½-inch) square-notched trowel.

Combing adhesive so it forms the right-size ridges requires that you hold the trowel at about a 30-degree angle and keep the edges of the trowel in constant contact with the substrate. If you have trouble making ¼-inch ridges with a ¼-inch trowel, switch to a ⅜-inch notch and hold the trowel at a slightly lower angle.

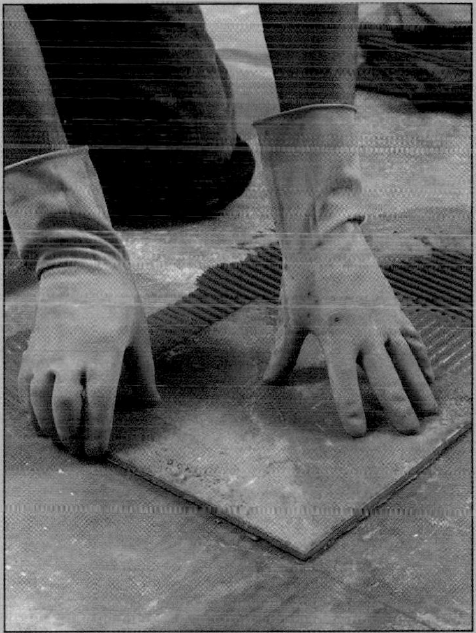

3 Set the first full tile at the intersection of your layout lines, positioning it with a slight twist as you embed it in the mortar. Do not slide the tile in place—sliding can reduce the thickness of the thinset and build up mortar between the joints. Keep the edges of the tile on the layout lines.

4 Using the layout order you have chosen *(page 123),* lay the next tile in place with the same twisting motion, keeping the tile aligned on your layout line. Insert spacers between the tiles and adjust the tiles to fit.

5 Continue laying tiles along both legs of the layout lines (for a jack-on-jack design, as shown above, see *page 123)* or in the order of your design, spacing the tiles as you go.

Testing the mixture

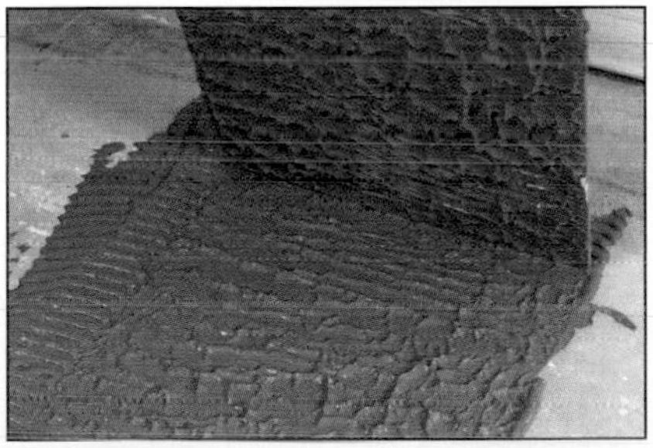

Properly applied thinset forms ridges that compress to cover the entire back of the tile when it is embedded. If thinset is applied too wet, it will not hold these ridges. A dry thinset application will not compress and will result in the tile adhering to the top of the ridges only.

Test a thinset mixture occasionally by pulling up a tile and examining the back. If the thinset completely covers the surface, the mixture is correct, as shown above.

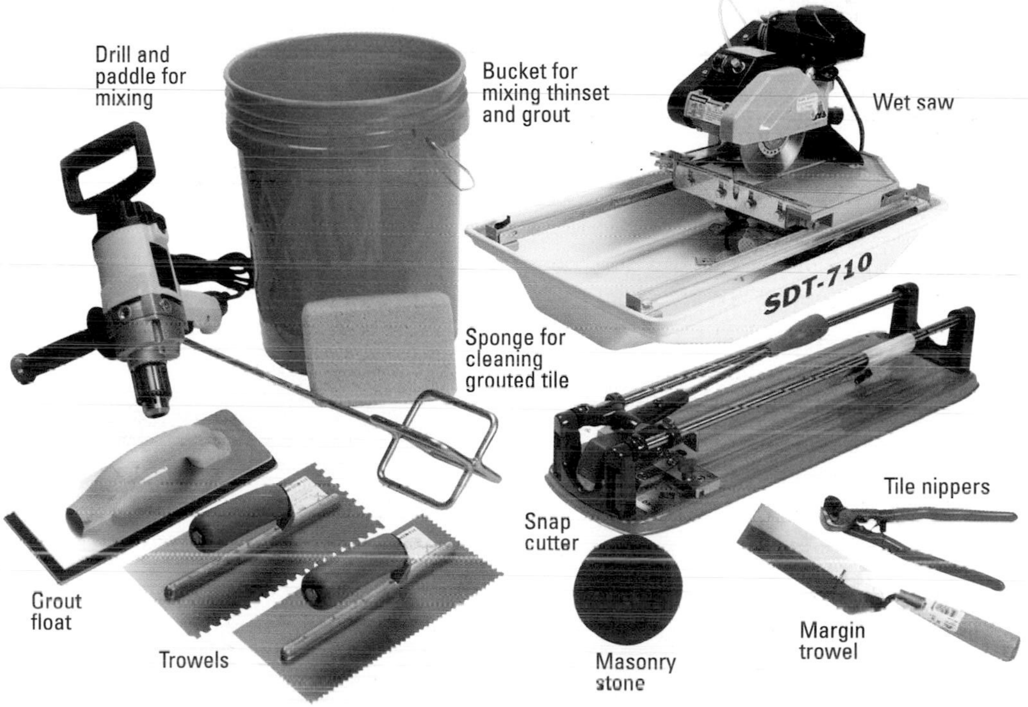

Setting the tile *(continued)*

6 Periodically check to make sure the tile conforms to the layout lines in both directions. Lay a long metal straightedge or 4-foot level on the edge of the tile. This edge should align itself with the layout lines. Each joint within the pattern should also be straight. Scrape off any excess thinset that may have spread over a layout line. Adjust the tiles to straighten the joints, if necessary.

7 Continue laying the tiles according to your chosen pattern, spacing and checking them as you go. Don't kneel or walk on set tiles. If you need to straighten a tile that is out of reach, lay down a 2-foot square of ¾-inch plywood to distribute your weight evenly and to avoid disturbing the tile. Cut at least two pieces of plywood to use, so you can position one while kneeling on the other.

Setting spacers

When laying loose tiles (not sheet-mounted), use plastic spacers to keep the tiles the proper width apart.

Insert spacers vertically in the joint after you set each successive tile. That way the tile will move into the correct placement after it is embedded in the mortar. Once you reach a point where tiles form corners, flip the spacer down into the corner. Pull the spacers before grouting, even if the manufacturer's instructions indicate that you can leave them in place. Spacers may show through the grout.

Working with mosaic tile

Mosaic sheets require special care when you are setting them. Their numerous edges can tip within the sheet or rise higher than the adjoining sheet. To keep them flat, use a grout float to gently tap them level both within the field of the sheet and at the edges. Use this same technique when aligning them to the contour of a drain recess on a shower floor.

Leveling the tile

1 When you have finished laying one section or grid of tile, place a long metal straightedge or a 4-foot carpenter's level on the surface and check for any tiles that are higher or lower than the overall surface. Make a beater block out of a 12- to 15-inch 2×4 covered with scrap carpet. Tap high tiles in place using the beater block and hammer.

2 If you discover tiles that are lower than the rest, pry them up with the point of a utility knife and spread additional adhesive on the back of the tile. Set the tile back in place and level it with the beater block. Clean excess mortar from the joints while the mortar is still wet. Run the blade of a utility knife in the joint, flicking out the excess as it accumulates on the blade. Pick up loose bits of mortar with a damp sponge. Let the thinset cure at least overnight.

WHAT IF...
The tiles have uneven edges?

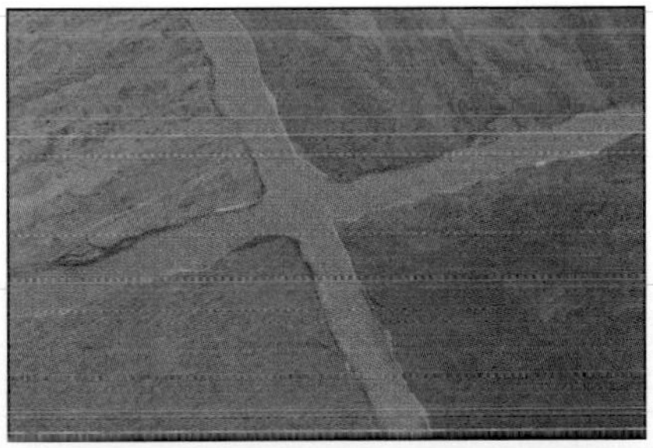

Tiles with irregular edges, such as saltillo and handmade pavers, may be difficult to keep straight, and spacers will not align the uneven edges. To keep such tiles aligned, make your layout grids small—a nine-tile (three-by-three) layout works well.

Trowel adhesive one grid at a time and set the tiles in place. Adjust the tiles until the appearance of the joints is consistent, and expect to make a few compromises.

Setting stone tiles

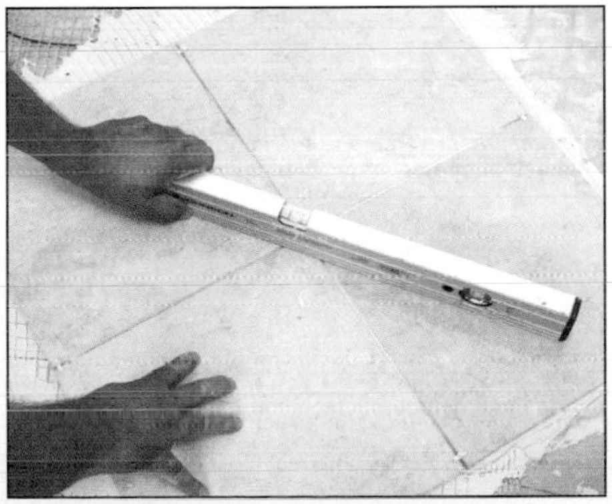

When setting marble or translucent stone, use white thinset; colored mortar may show through. Marble, granite, and travertine tiles look best with thin 1⁄16-inch grout joints.

Stone tiles are more brittle than ceramic tile and therefore more prone to cracking. Make sure the setting bed is stable and flat. Dampsponge any dust off the back of the tiles, if necessary. Apply the mortar recommended by the distributor or manufacturer of the stone.

Check each tile for level with a straightedge (above, left), pulling up and back-buttering tiles that are low (above, right). Make sure the edges of one tile are not higher than another.

CUTTING CERAMIC TILE

Cutting tile requires a little skill and patience—save yourself installation time by practicing a few cuts first.

If the cut tiles in your project will be the same width, cut all of them at once, trowel on the adhesive, and lay the tiles. If the tiles will not be uniform, cut each one separately. Do not let adhesive set longer than its working time while you're making the cuts.

Tile cutting is accomplished with a variety of tools. For only one or two cuts, you need only a tile nipper or a rod saw with a carbide blade. A snap cutter makes quick work of cutting thin tile, such as most wall tiles.

Rent a wet saw to cut thicker tiles. If you have several tiles to cut, the wet saw will prove well worth its cost. Water is used to cool wet-saw blades. It comes from an outlet or from water in a trough below it. Do not use the wet saw without water.

Cut tile edges are rough. Either hide them under toe-kicks or smooth them with a masonry stone.

Sizing the cut

Straight cut: Place the tile to be cut flush to the wall or obstruction, lined up on top of an installed tile. Place another tile over the tile to be cut, with its edge against the wall. Trace the edge with a marker. Draw the cutting line parallel to the mark but shorter by the width of two grout lines.

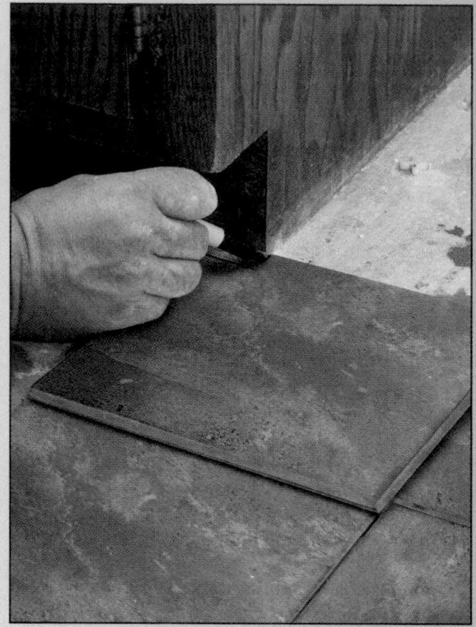

L-shape cut: Place the tile to be trimmed first on one corner, then the other, marking the cut lines with a full tile as you would for a single straight cut. Cut each side shorter than the mark by the width of two grout lines.

PRESTART CHECKLIST

☐ **TIME**
Less than five minutes to mark and cut each tile

☐ **TOOLS**
Felt-tip or china marker, tape measure, snap cutter, wet saw, masonry stone, tile nippers

☐ **SKILLS**
Measuring and marking tile precisely; cutting tile with nippers, snap cutter or power saw

☐ **PREP**
Install backerboard and field tile

☐ **MATERIALS**
Tile

STANLEY PRO TIP

Don't wash away the line

The blade of a wet saw is cooled with water, which will wash away a cut line made with a felt-tip marker. When marking tiles that will be cut with a wet saw, use a china marker so the line won't wash away.

SAFETY FIRST
Protect your eyes when cutting

Cutting tile with a snap cutter is not especially dangerous, but you should wear eye protection to guard against any fine chips, especially from glazed tile.

A wet saw can discharge chips and larger pieces of tile at high speed, so eye protection is a must. Wear ear protection to guard against damage from the noise of the saw.

Wear safety glasses when cutting tile with nippers too.

Save on rental costs
Cut all your edge tiles in one day. That way you pay only one day's rental for a wet saw.

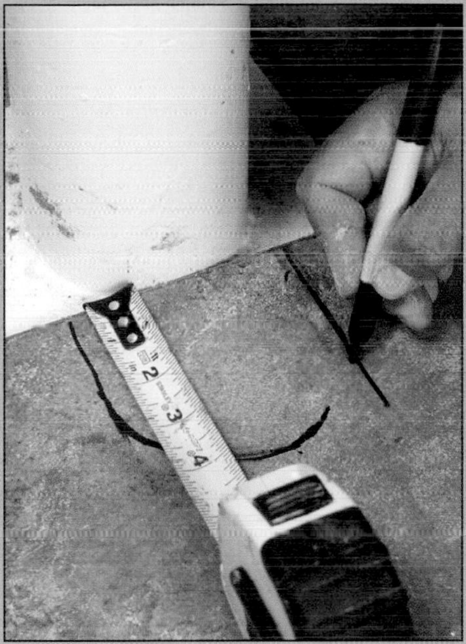

Curved cuts: Set the tile to be cut against the obstruction, lining up its edges with tile already laid. Mark the width of the cut by setting a tape measure on each edge of the obstruction. Move the tile to one side of the obstruction and use the tape to mark the depth of the cut.

Making straight cuts

Snap cutter: Insert the tile in the cutter, aligning the scoring wheel on the cut line. Pull or push the scoring wheel across the cut line, using firm pressure throughout the stroke. Score the tile in one pass. Hold the tile firmly in place and strike the handle with the heel of your hand.

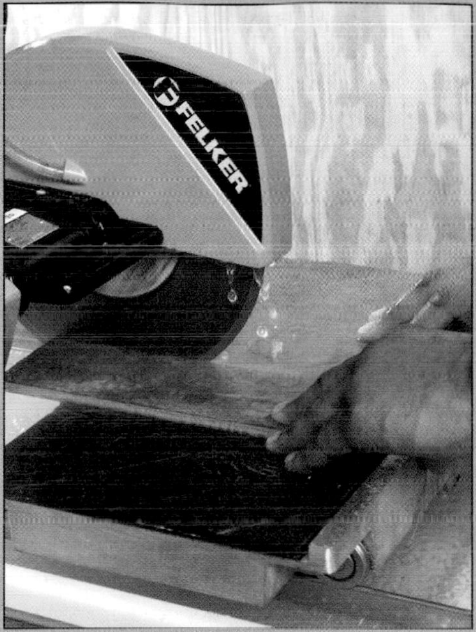

Wet saw: Set the tile securely against the fence with the cut line at the blade. Turn on the saw and feed the tile into the blade with light pressure. Increase the pressure as the saw cuts the tile and ease off as the blade approaches the rear of the cut. Keep the tile on the table at all times.

Making curved cuts

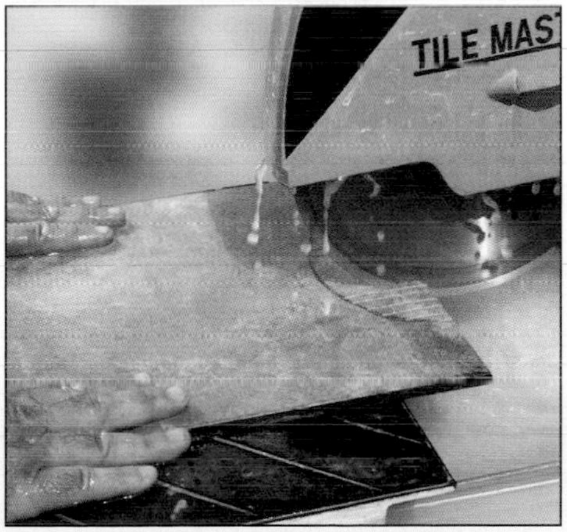

1 Using a wet saw, make several relief cuts from the edge of the tile to the curved cut line. Relief cuts do not have to be exactly parallel to each other, but make sure they stop just short of the curved line.

2 Place the jaws of tile nippers about an inch away from the curved line and carefully snap out the waste at the relief cuts.

3 Working the nippers on the cut line, snap away the remaining excess. Don't try to "bite" through the tile with the nippers. Instead, grasp the tile tightly with the tool and use a prying motion.

GROUTING, CAULKING, AND SEALING

Grouting, caulking, and sealing are not difficult tasks, but they do take time. Don't rush these activities—they affect both the final appearance of your tiling project and its longevity.

Bring all materials into the room to acclimate them to its temperature, preferably between 65° and 75°F. Prepare the surface by removing spacers and cleaning excess mortar from the joints and surface. Lightly mist the edges of nonvitreous tile with water so they won't take too much moisture from the grout. Vitreous tiles do not require misting.

Use a margin trowel to mix grout in clean containers, following the manufacturer's instructions, adding powder to liquid a little at a time. Let it set for 10 minutes and restir it to loosen its texture. Grout should be wet enough to spread, but not runny.

PRESTART CHECKLIST

☐ **TIME**
From 15 to 30 minutes to mix, float, and clean a 4-foot-square section (varies with tile size). About five minutes to caulk a 10-foot joint, 45 minutes to seal a 15×20-foot floor, longer if applying sealer to joints only.

☐ **TOOLS**
Utility knife or grout knife, grout float, nylon scrubber, margin trowel, grout bag (optional), applicator or mop for sealer, caulk gun

☐ **SKILLS**
Spreading grout with float; using caulk gun

☐ **PREP**
Install all tile and let mortar cure

☐ **MATERIALS**
Grout, bucket and water, rags, sponge, sealer, caulk

Grouting tile

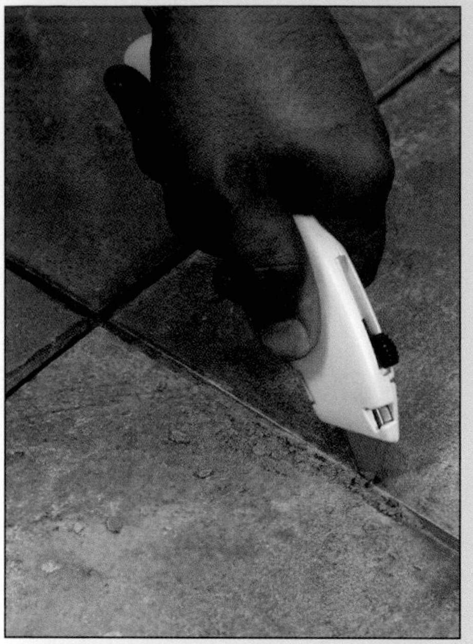

1 Remove spacers if you have not done so already. Inspect the joints for any remaining adhesive and scrape it out with a utility knife or grout knife. Remove any remaining hardened mortar from the tile surface with a nylon (not metal) scrubber.

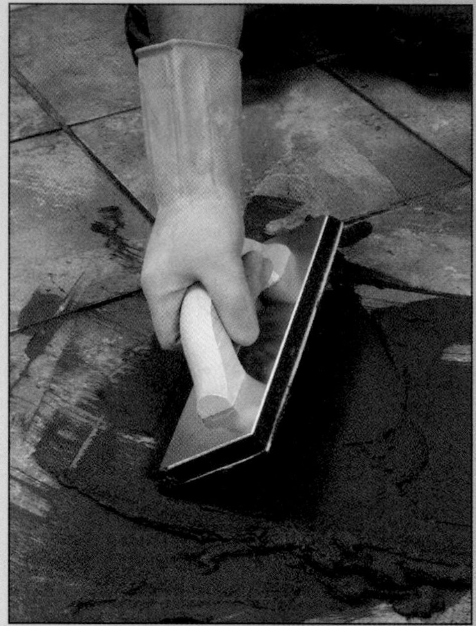

2 Mix the grout to the consistency recommended by the manufacturer; dump or scoop out a small pile with a margin trowel. Working in 10-square-foot sections, pack the grout into the joints with a grout float. Hold the float at about a 30- to 45-degree angle; work it in both directions.

WHAT IF... The grout joints are wide?

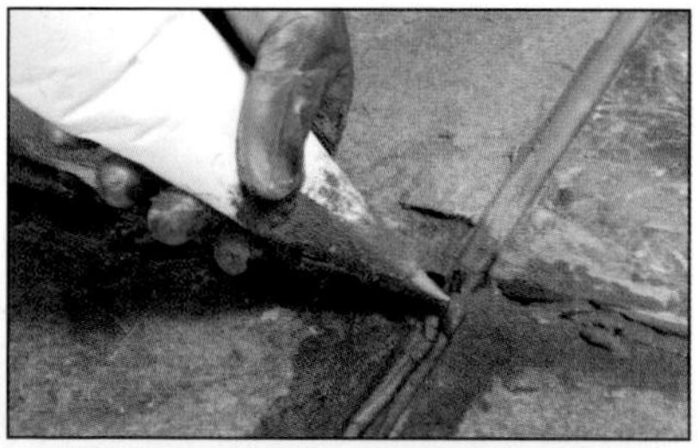

Irregular tiles look best with wide grout joints, but wide joints may be hard to fill with a grout float. Use a grout bag for these tiles and for rough tiles whose surfaces will be difficult to clean.

Fit a metal spout on the bag equal to the width of the joint. Fill the bag with grout. Working down the length of a joint, squeeze the bag, overfilling the joint slightly. Compact the excess and sweep loose grout with a stiff broom when dry.

STANLEY PRO TIP

Avoid voids when power mixing grout

Power mixing can introduce air bubbles in grout and leave voids in it. Mix grout by hand with a margin trowel, adding the powder to the water. Let the mix set for 10 minutes, then remix before applying.

Tips for grouting stone

Use the grout recommended by the manufacturer. Nonsanded grout tends to recede when curing, so you may need to apply it twice if the joints in your stone installation are set at 1⁄16 inch. Seal stone before grouting to ease cleaning and again after grouting.

3 Once you have grouted a section, hold the float almost perpendicular to the tile and scrape the excess off the tile surface. Work the float diagonally to the joints to avoid lifting the grout. If you remove grout, replace it in the joint and reclean the surface. Let the grout set.

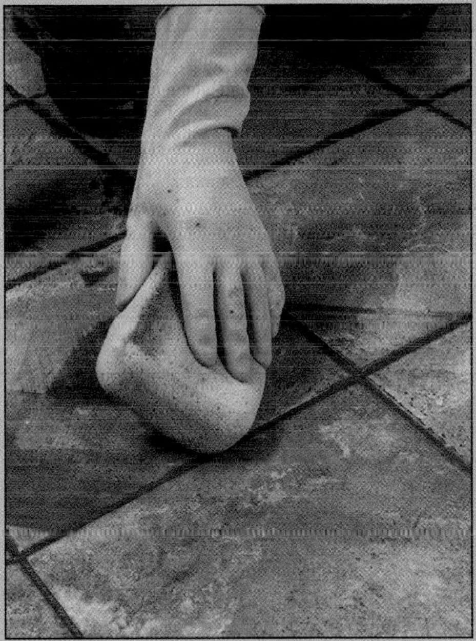

4 When a just-damp sponge won't lift grout from the joint, you can start cleaning. Wring out all excess water from a damp sponge and rub the surface in a circular motion. Rinse and wring out the sponge often. Repeat parallel to the joints to make them neat, and once more to finish cleaning.

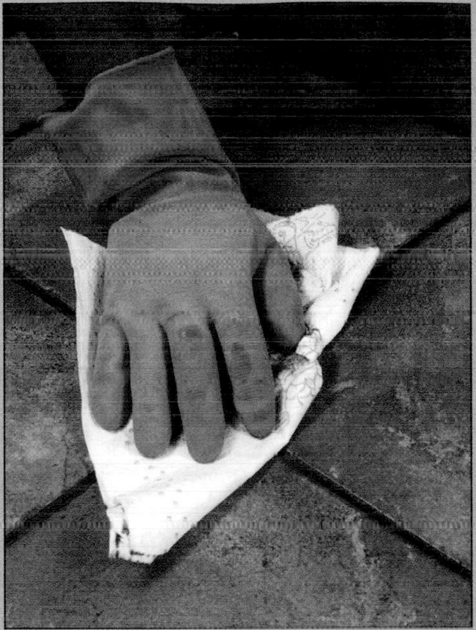

5 Let the surface dry about 15 minutes, then remove the grout haze from the surface with a dry, clean rag. Avoid terry cloth material, it can lift out uncured grout. Tile with a matte finish may require another cleaning with fresh water and a clean sponge.

Sealing grout and tiles

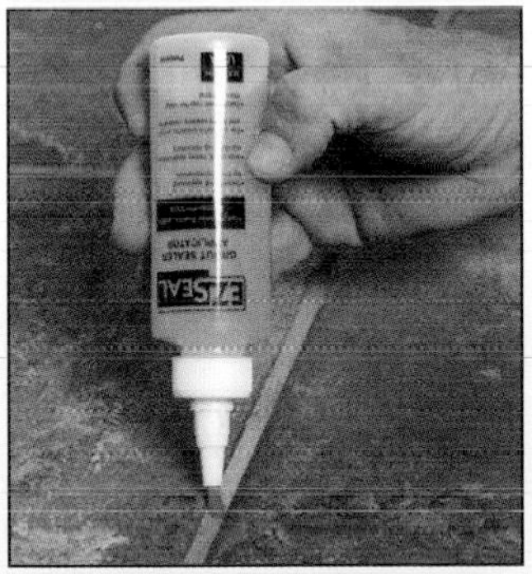

Although latex or polymer-modified grouts resist staining, you'll get the best protection from stains by sealing the grout.

On glazed and other impervious tiles, apply the sealer only to the joint using an applicator designed for this purpose.

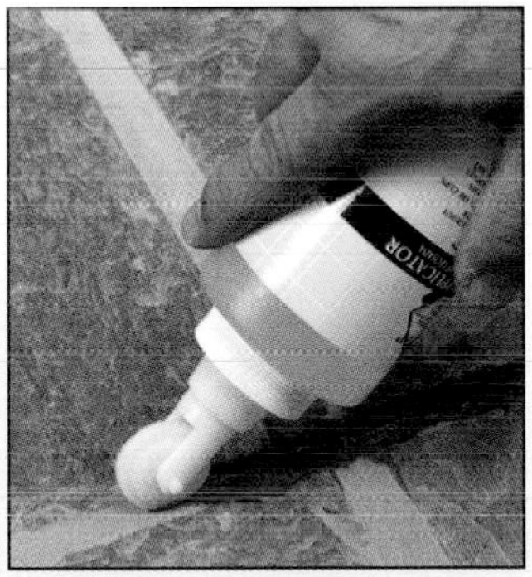

To protect saltillo and other soft-bodied tiles, seal the entire surface with a mop or applicator as recommended by the manufacturer.

Different sealers can leave stone in its natural color or enhance its richness.

Caulking the joints

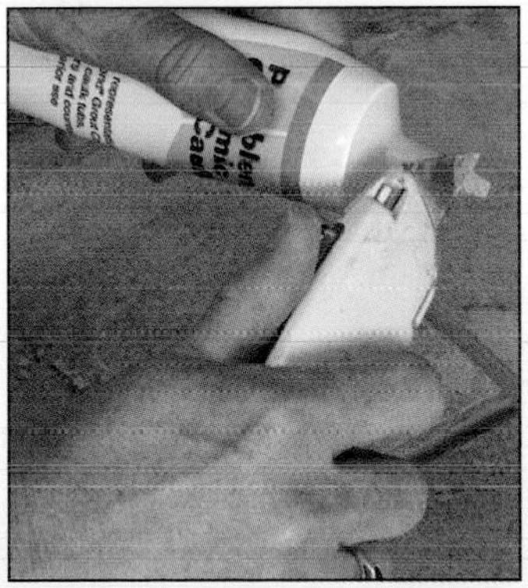

Use a utility knife to cut the nozzle to the width of the joint and at a 45-degree angle. Cut through the nozzle in one pass. Before you apply the caulk, you may want to practice the techniques on scrap.

Starting in one corner, squeeze

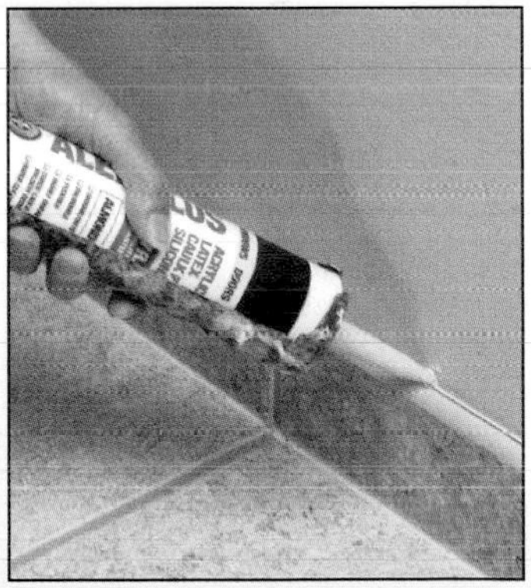

the handle of the caulk gun gently and apply the caulk to the joint. Keep the caulk gun moving as you squeeze so the caulk won't overrun the joint. Finish the surface of the caulk with a wet finger or sponge. Light pressure will avoid gouging.

INSTALLING MOSAIC TILE

Not long ago, setting mosaic tile meant embedding each small piece in a mortar bed. Later developments, notably sheets of mosaic held together by paper adhered to their face, helped reduce installation time. These early face-mounted sheets, however, were difficult to line up.

Modern mosaics have taken improvements a step further. Each small mosaic tile is bonded to the sheet with plastic dots or on a plastic mesh, paper, or threaded backing.

You'll find mosaics in many colors and in squares, rectangles, random designs, and all forms of geometric figures. Most mosaic tiles are glass or high-fired porcelain, so they're impervious to moisture. Porcelains come with glazed surfaces for walls and with nonslip surfaces for floors.

If the style you've chosen is available only in dot-mounted sheets, make sure the dots are free of any residual manufacturing oil. This oil interferes with adhesive bonding. Check two or three sheets in each carton, wiping them with a paper towel.
If replacing a carton is not an alternative, either change your design or wash the back of each sheet with a mild detergent.

PRESTART CHECKLIST

☐ **TIME**
About 5 to 6 hours (not including grouting) for an 8×10-foot room

☐ **TOOLS**
Chalkline, tape measure, carpenter's pencil, power drill, mixing paddle, notched trowel, beater block, rubber mallet, 4-foot metal straightedge

☐ **SKILLS**
Measuring, setting tile

☐ **PREP**
Remove existing flooring, repair or replace underlayment

☐ **MATERIALS**
Epoxy mortar, mosaic tile sheets

1 Lay out perpendicular lines in the center of the room *(pages 96–97)*, and snap grid lines at intervals of the same dimensions as the mosaic sheet. Mix the epoxy adhesive, and using a ¼-inch notched trowel, spread and comb it on a small area, just inside the layout lines.

2 Set the corner of the first sheet just inside the corner of the layout lines. Square the sheet to the lines and embed the tiles firmly into the mortar with a beater block and rubber mallet. Make sure the entire surface of the sheet is level in the mortar—mosaics show depressions dramatically.

Arranging random patterns

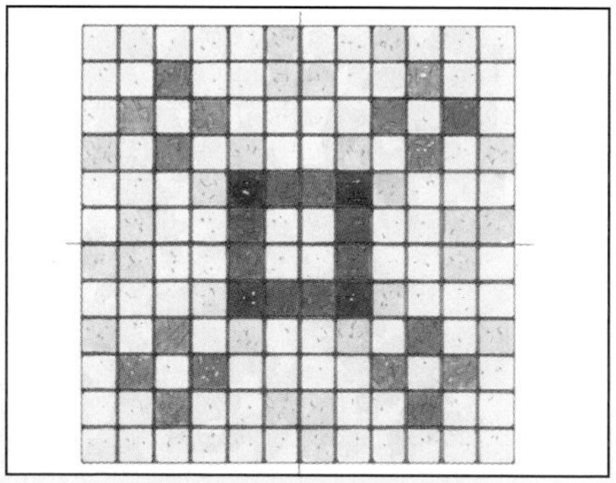

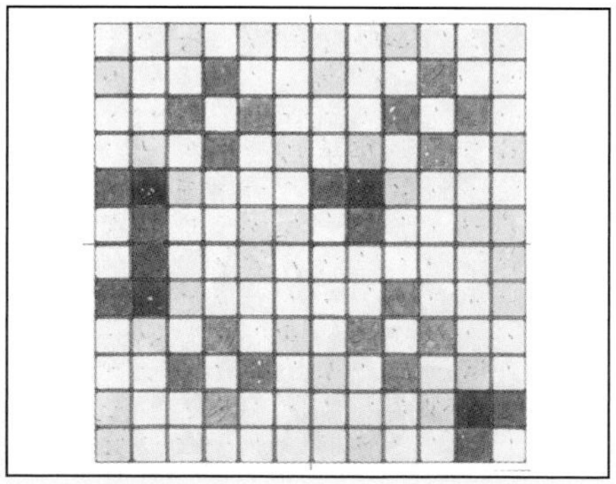

A mosaic pattern that features randomly placed colored tiles is more difficult to set than one that has regular geometric patterns—you have to make sure the color schemes throughout the design balance each other.

Lay the sheets on the surface in a dry run, changing their positions until you get the arrangement right. Then take up the sheets and number them so you can mortar them in the same order.

Such experimentation produced the balanced pattern, left, but this pattern with its centered square is not the only balanced design possible with these tiles. Avoid patterns like the one shown, right. Although it is composed of the same tiles, it appears unbalanced and chaotic.

3 Pull the sheet up and check it for full coverage. If some of the tiles show bare spots, apply more mortar. Lay the sheet face down on a clean surface and skim more mortar on the back. Recomb the mortar bed with a larger notched trowel and reset the sheet with the beater block.

4 Set the next sheet using the same techniques. After four or five sheets, you should have a feel for the proper amount of mortar. As you embed the tiles with the beater block, make sure the edges of each sheet are level with its neighbors; then line up all the joints.

5 Continue setting the tiles, using a metal straightedge to keep the joints straight. Wipe excess mortar from the surface of the tile with a damp (not wet) sponge. Make sure you remove all of the excess—dried mortar is very difficult to remove. Let the mortar set, then grout and clean the tiles.

STANLEY PRO TIP

Keep colors consistent

It's impossible to set mosaics without some of the mortar creeping up into the grout joints. To keep your work from looking blotchy when you apply the grout, use the same product for both the mortar bed and the grout—100 percent solid epoxy of the same color. Alternatively, you might be able to color the mortar to match the grout, but such attempts often result in noticeably different shades.

Embedding the mosaic sheets into the mortar will inevitably force some mortar onto the surface of the tiles. Before you set the next section, use a synthetic scrubbing pad to clean the tile, then wipe it with a dampened sponge. Don't use too much water—it will wash out the epoxy from the joint and weaken it.

WHAT IF...

Mosaic tiles need to be cut?

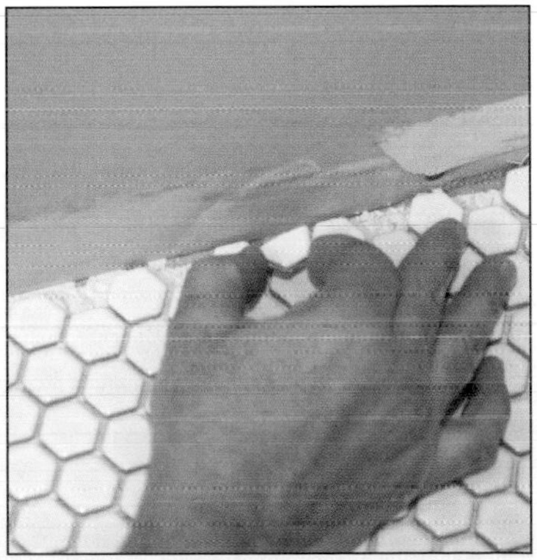

One advantage of mosaics is that the small size of the individual tiles can often fit around obstacles without cutting them. Use a utility knife to cut the backing in the contour of the obstacle and strip away the tiles. If you need to cut an individual tile, remove it from the backing and cut it with a snap cutter. Then back-butter the cut piece and set it in the mortar.

INSTALLING STONE TILE

Stone tile requires the same firm and level setting bed as ceramic tile—only more so. Because stone is brittle and the minerals that make up its pattern are not perfectly "cemented" to each other, it is subject to fracture along the grain lines.

Stone also suffers from the normal physical inconsistencies found in any natural material. Some pieces might not be exactly as wide or thick as the others. Adjust length and width by cutting the tile with a wet saw and accommodate differences in thickness by adjusting the amount of mortar you spread.

When set, the top edges of all tiles should be flush. Back-butter each tile before you set it in the mortar bed and test it to make sure its edges are flush with its neighbors.

Most stone tile comes from the factory with beveled edges, so cutting a tile will leave it with an unbeveled edge. Hone the edge of the cut tile with a rubbing stone or with sandpaper wrapped around a block of wood. To polish a tile to a high sheen, use progressively finer grits of carbide sandpaper (from 120 to 600).

1 Stone tile often has a dusty residue on its back, and this dust weakens the adhesive bond. Wipe your finger across the back of the tile and if it comes up dusty, clean the backs of the tiles with a sponge and water. Let the tiles dry before bedding them.

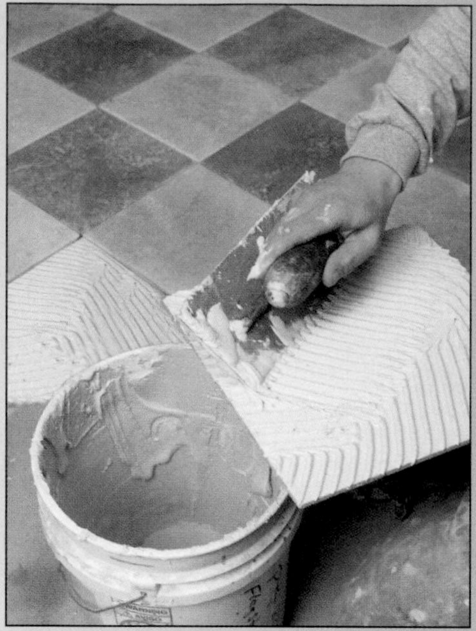

2 Lay out a dry run so the edge tiles are the same size *(page 43)*. Then snap lines as guides. Using white thinset for light-color tiles, trowel thinset on the subfloor and back-butter the tile. Set and level the tiles, adding mortar to the back as needed. Line up the tiles with a straightedge.

PRESTART CHECKLIST

☐ **TIME**
About 10 hours for an 8×10-foot room. Allow 3 to 4 hours for grouting and cleanup on the next day.

☐ **TOOLS**
Chalkline, tape measure, carpenter's pencil, power drill with mixing paddle, notched trowel, beater block, rubber mallet, grout float, 4-foot metal straightedge, wet saw, dry-cutting saw

☐ **SKILLS**
Marking, setting, and cutting tile

☐ **PREP**
Remove existing flooring, repair or replace underlayment

☐ **MATERIALS**
Thinset mortar, stone tile

WHAT IF...
You have to cut a hole in the stone?

Cutting holes for obstacles such as electrical outlets becomes a relatively easy task with a dry-cutting saw equipped with a diamond blade. The saw allows you to get almost all the way into the corners to make a clean cut.

Mark the outline with a china marker (not a felt-tip, which may bleed). While a helper steadies the tile, lower the saw into the middle of the line. Work the saw forward to one end of the line, then back to the other corner. Knock out the cut piece with tile nippers and trim the corners square. Don't worry if the cut line is slightly errant; it will be hidden under the wall plate.

3 When the mortar for the field tiles has set sufficiently (usually overnight), cut the edge tiles with a wet saw and lay them in a mortar bed, back-buttering each tile as you go. Measure for each individual edge tile—it's unlikely that the room will be square and all the tiles the same size.

4 Let the mortar for the edge tiles cure for 24 hours. Then mix a batch of unsanded grout, just enough to cover a small section. To keep the stone tiles from absorbing too much water from the grout, wet them with a spray bottle. Apply the grout with a float. Remove excess grout from the surface of the stone. When the grout has set for about 15 minutes, wipe the haze with a damp sponge. Finish grouting the entire installation, working in sections so you can clean the excess before it hardens. When the grout has completely cured, seal the tiles as necessary.

WHAT IF...
Edge tiles are not available?

Some manufacturers produce stone bullnose, but if your selection doesn't come with them, you can make your own by rounding the edges with a rubbing stone. As an alternative, start with coarse carbide sandpaper wrapped around a wood block and polish with finer grades.

STANLEY PRO TIP: Use adhesive alternatives for stone

Granite tiles make an attractive substitute for a granite slab on a countertop. If your tiles are cut to a consistent thickness, you can use silicone adhesive instead of thinset. Lay the tiles in a dry run. Then lift one at a time, apply silicone to the substrate, and press the tiles in place. Line up the tiles with a straightedge.

For some stone tiles, expensive epoxy mortar is the preferred adhesive, but you might be able to get around the cost by sealing the back of the tile with a nonporous epoxy sealer. Once the coating has cured, you can set the tiles in regular thinset mortar.

INSTALLING BASEBOARDS AND TRANSITIONS

Baseboards and transitions not only serve as accents, they also hide structural defects and rough edges.

Baseboards hide the gap between the wall and the floor. Transitions—metal, stone, wood, or laminate—bridge the gap between every possible combination of flooring materials *(page 113).* They help prevent tripping and protect the edges of tiles and other surfaces.

Baseboards come in many choices of styles and contours. Choose the wood for your baseboard according to the kind of finish you'll apply. If you plan to paint the baseboard, get paintable pine or medium density fiberboard (MDF). If you plan to apply stain and varnish, you'll need a higher quality wood. Poplar and hardwoods are good choices.

To get a seamless joint, you can cope (or back-cut) the joint. If you don't want to go to the trouble of coping the joints, install no-cope baseboards with corner pieces and butt joints.

PRESTART CHECKLIST

☐ **TIME**
About 45 minutes for an 8-foot section

☐ **TOOLS**
Hammer, nail set, stud finder, cordless drill, tape measure, pencil, combination square, miter saw, circular saw, wood file, caulking gun, coping saw

☐ **SKILLS**
Basic carpentry skills: measuring, marking, cutting, drilling

☐ **PREP**
Remove old baseboard, install finished flooring

☐ **MATERIALS**
Baseboard, corner pieces, shoe molding, 8d finishing nails, sandpaper, threshold or transition, caulk

Installing a coped baseboard

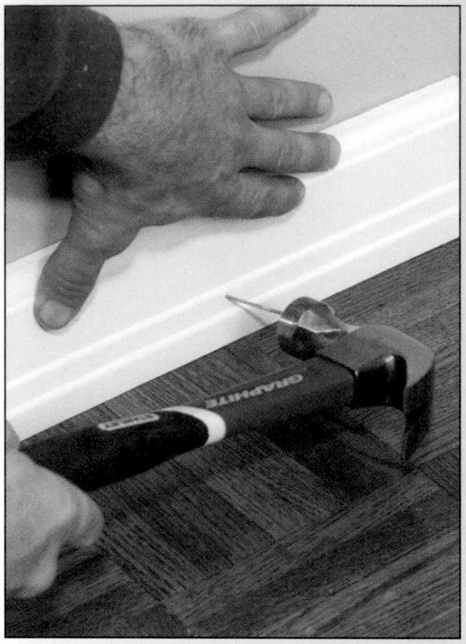

1 Measure from the edge of the door trim to the nearest corner and cut a piece of baseboard to fit. Cut butt joints on both ends of the baseboard and predrill it for 8d finishing nails. Drive the nails into the studs and bottom plate of the wall.

2 Using a power miter saw, miter the end of the adjoining corner piece as if you were cutting it for an inside corner. Then set the baseboard on a firm work surface and outline the edge of the profile with a pencil.

STANLEY PRO TIP: **Drill guide holes to avoid splitting trim**

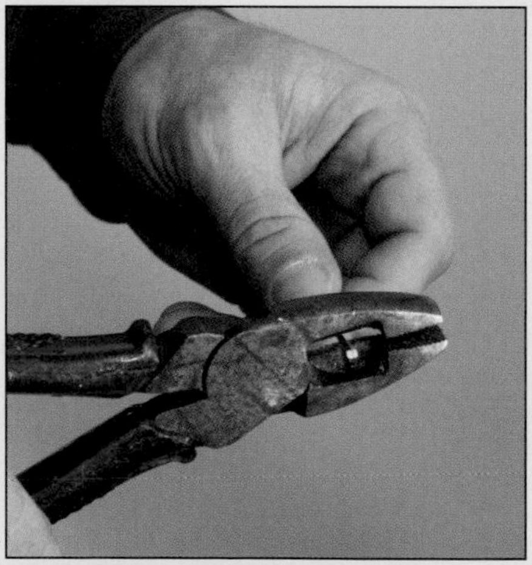

1 Using side cutters or diagonal cutters, snip the head off the 6d or 8d finishing nail. Insert the nail into the chuck of your cordless drill.

2 Using moderate pressure and high speed, drill guide holes into the baseboard. Then drive finishing nails through the holes and into the wall. Use a nailset to drive the nails below the surface.

3 Clamp or steady the baseboard on a work surface and hold a coping saw with a fine-tooth blade at right angles to the mitered end. Carefully cut the board along your penciled outline. The goal is to create a thin edge at the front of the baseboard—one that follows its contour and will fit almost seamlessly into the profile of the adjoining corner piece.

4 Test-fit the coped piece against the baseboard already in place (or a piece of scrap), sanding and filing to correct your contour until it mates with the baseboard. Use 80-grit sandpaper where it will fit the contour and a fine round wood file in tightly curved sections. Don't worry about small gaps—you can fill them with caulk later. If you've made large mistakes, miter the board again and start over.

Installing baseboard on outside corners

1 Stick a piece of masking tape on the floor at the outside corner (to protect the floor from the marks you will make). Set a piece of scrap baseboard against one wall and pencil a line along its outer edge past the corner. Pencil another line along the adjoining wall.

2 Hold an adjustable bevel against one wall and set it against the corner of the wall. Adjust the angle until the "T" intersects the penciled corner. Tighten the bevel screw. Transfer the angle to the top of the baseboard and line up the mark with the blade of your miter saw. Clamp the board to the miter saw fence. When you cut the piece, lower the blade slowly.

STANLEY PRO TIP

Fit and splice baseboard

Baseboards often generate some stubborn challenges. Here are a few tips to make their installation easier.

- To get a tightly fitting coped joint, cut baseboard sections about $\frac{1}{16}$ inch longer than the measured length of the space on the wall. The piece may bow slightly when you first fit it, but the coped edges will snug into the recess of the neighboring piece as you nail it.
- Locating a stud for nailing is sometimes tricky, especially in older homes where door trim often extends beyond the studs. Wherever you know you'll have trouble anchoring the baseboard, lay a bead of construction adhesive on the back of it.
- On long walls, join sections of baseboard or shoe molding with angled (scarf) joints.

Installing a coped baseboard *(continued)*

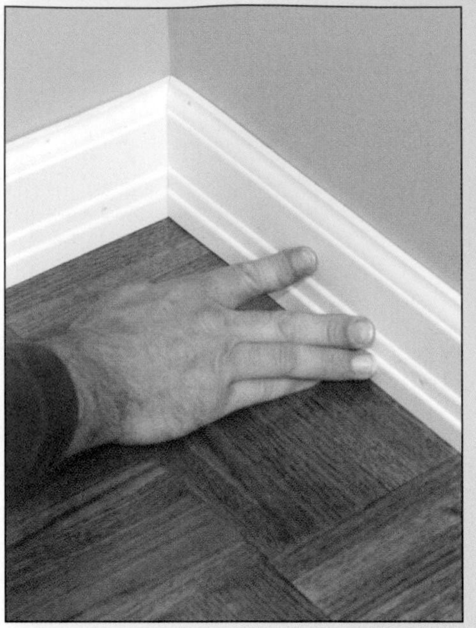

5 Cut the other end of the coped piece, if necessary, to fit its section of wall. Cut the end square if the board goes all the way to the corner. Miter it to create a scarf joint if you need another board to complete this section. Fasten this piece to the wall with finishing nails.

6 Cut a piece of baseboard to fit the next wall. Then cut, miter, and cope the left corner, employing the same techniques you used for the first piece. Fit the final piece of baseboard against the door trim with a butt joint.

7 Cut shoe molding to length for each section of wall, duplicating coped and butt joints where they fall on the baseboard. Predrill the shoe molding and nail it at an angle into the baseboard. Make sure its bottom edge is flush with the surface of the finished floor.

WHAT IF... You're installing capped baseboards?

Install the baseboard *(pages 110–112)*. Then, using the pattern of your choice, measure, cut, and fasten the first piece of cap molding to the baseboard. Cope the remaining pieces. Predrill the stock. Use the heaviest finishing nail that does the job without splitting the cap pieces.

Installing no-cope baseboards

1 Cut and install inside and outside corner pieces longer than the width of the baseboard (to the height of your choice). Hold a combination square against a corner piece and scribe a line on the baseboard. This line will conform to any out-of-plumb conditions in the walls. Scribe both ends of each baseboard section and cut the first piece.

2 Drive 8d finishing nails into the predrilled baseboard and use the same techniques to install the remaining pieces between the corners. Drive the nails below the surface with a nail set. Fill and sand them smooth, and stain, paint, or varnish.

Installing thresholds and transitions

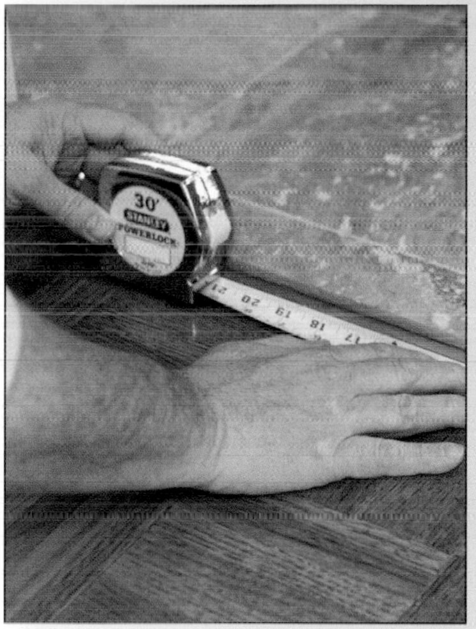

1 Measure the width of the doorway or opening carefully and subtract 1⁄16 inch from your measurement to allow the transition to fit snugly. Using this measurement, cut a piece of thin scrap to the same length and test-fit it in the opening.

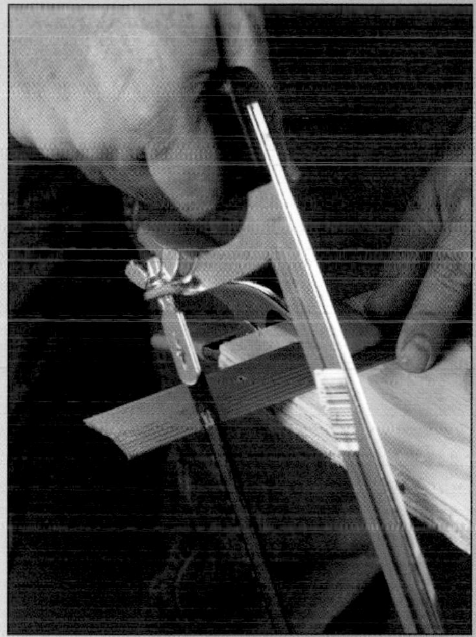

2 Adjust the measurement, if necessary, and mark your transition stock to the test dimension. Clamp the transition securely to a work surface and cut it. Use a hacksaw with a fine-tooth blade to cut metal stock and apply moderate clamping pressure to avoid bonding it.

3 Slide the transition in place in the opening and fasten it with ringshank nails, brass wood screws, or the fasteners recommended by the manufacturer. Predrlll the transition and the subfloor at the same time. Drive in the screws to secure the transition to the floor.

STANLEY PRO TIP

Cut stock thresholds to fit

Parquet tile, like hardwood floors, must have room to expand under thresholds. Ready-made units come with a recess precut for this purpose. If you're cutting stock for a threshold, use a table saw to cut a dado in the edge facing the parquet.

Easing the transitions

A reducer strip eases the transition from a thicker to thinner floor, from wood to vinyl, for example.

A universal threshold is used when wood flooring butts up against a carpeted floor.

T molding is used as a transition between floors of the same height.

Carpet edging is an inexpensive transition between carpet and an existing floor.

TILING FLOORS, WALLS & COUNTERTOPS

You'll find that setting the tile is less tedious and more rewarding than preparing a surface for tiling. This is when you begin to see the results of your planning. If you have several projects planned, start with the least complicated. That way you can build your skills and gain experience. The information in this chapter pertains to ceramic tile; you'll find complete instructions for installing other kinds of tile in later chapters.

Mixing mortar and thinset

Before you begin to mix adhesives, read the manufacturer's directions carefully. Always mix mortar and grout in a clean container. Any residue in the bucket may cause the material to cure prematurely. Clean buckets and utensils after each mixing to save time and avoid problems.

Carefully heed the "working" time—how long it takes the material to set up. Once the setting up has started, tile will not adhere. Grout that has exceeded its working time will not work properly into the joints and will pop out when dry. If either material has begun to set up before you are finished working with it, scrape it off the surface, remix, and reapply.

It takes some practice to discover how much material will cover an area before it sets up. Installation of large tiles will go more quickly than small tiles. Start with a small batch and work up to larger areas.

Heat and humidity affects mortar and grout. You may need to mix a wetter consistency in hot or dry conditions. However, do not add water to mortar that has begun to set up in the heat; doing so weakens its strength. Discard the mixture and start over.

Working with mastics

Mastic ingredients may settle in the can, leaving an oily-looking liquid on top. Stir it until the consistency is smooth.

If you open a can of mastic and it has begun to harden, throw it out and purchase fresh stock.

Application techniques remain essentially the same no matter what surface you're tiling.

CHAPTER PREVIEW

Tiling floors
page 116

Tiling walls
page 122

Tiling a kitchen countertop and backsplash
page 126

Hold the grout float at a 45-degree angle when forcing grout into joints.
Use a dampened sponge to smooth grout and clean excess off tiles.

You can plan to tile a countertop and backsplash together as a single project or as separate projects. Because backsplashes are hard to reach, the work goes slowly; work in small sections to avoid the grout setting up before you're finished.

TILING FLOORS

Ceramic tile is the most stable finished floor covering, but it's best to acclimate it to the room before setting it. Bring tile and other materials into the room at least a day in advance.

Sort tiles for consistent coloring and according to design or texture patterns. Stack tiles around the room near the sections in which you'll lay them, counting out enough to fill each section. Organizing your materials reduces trips to another room to get more tiles.

If you haven't done so already, verify the accuracy of your dimensional layout plan by setting a row of tiles in each direction in a dry run on the floor.

Leave outswinging doors in place. Remove inswinging doors as needed.

PRESTART CHECKLIST

☐ **TIME**
About 30 to 45 minutes per square yard to prepare and set tile

☐ **TOOLS**
Four-foot level, small sledge and cold chisel, right-angle grinder (slab) or belt sander (wood floor), chalkline, margin trowel, notched trowel, straightedge, utility knife, carbide scriber, snap cutter or wet saw, nippers, masonry stone, grout knife, caulk gun, grout float, hammer, cordless drill, putty knife, tape measure, china marker or felt-tip pen

☐ **SKILLS**
Power sanding, snapping chalklines, driving fasteners, troweling, laying tile, grouting

☐ **PREP**
Repair structural defects

☐ **MATERIALS**
Bucket, thinset, isolation membrane, roller, tile, spacers, caulk, grout, rags, sponge, water, backerboard, screws, tape, foam backer rod, tile base or bullnose tile, nylon wedges, threshold and fasteners

DIMENSIONAL KITCHEN DRAWING

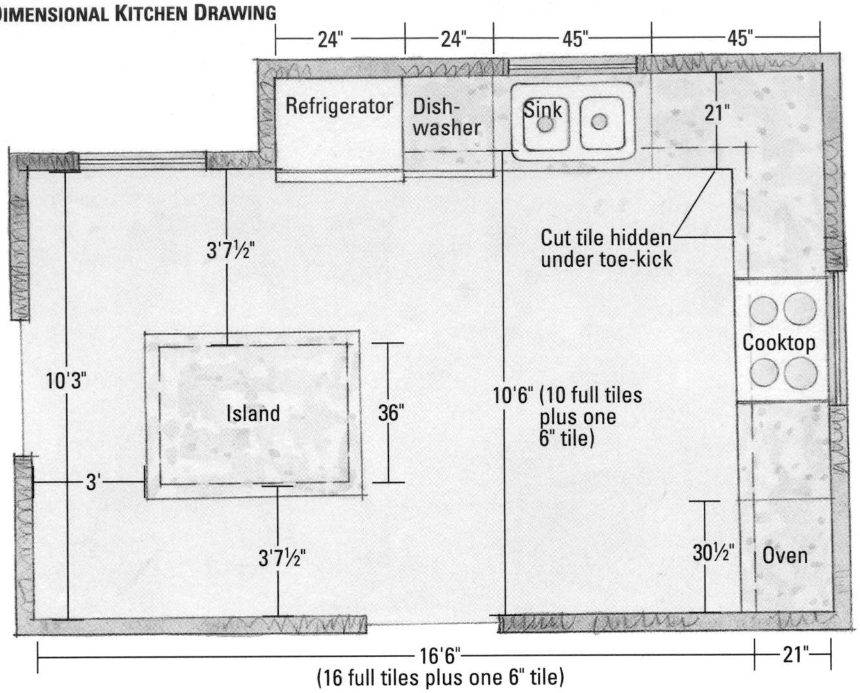

A dimensional drawing for a kitchen floor includes spaces that currently house appliances. When you note dimensions on the plan, add the thickness of any baseboard that you will remove. Measure up to the edge of toe-kicks under the cabinets.

DIMENSIONAL BATHROOM DRAWING

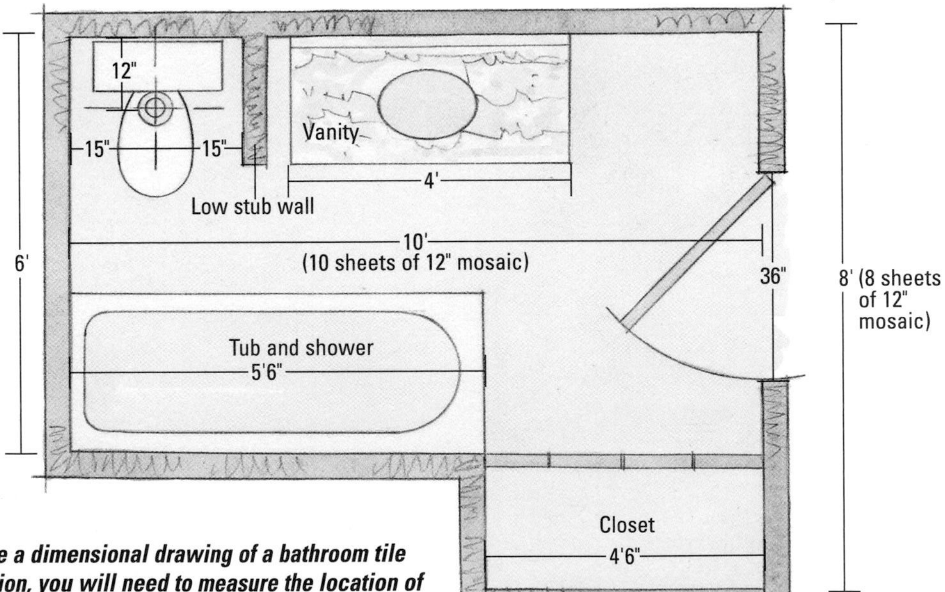

To create a dimensional drawing of a bathroom tile installation, you will need to measure the location of the toilet flange as accurately as possible. Because the toilet will likely be in place when you draw the plan, you will not be able to see the flange. Estimate its location: measure from the side wall to half the width of the toilet base and from the back wall to about one-fourth of its length.

Installing thresholds and transitions

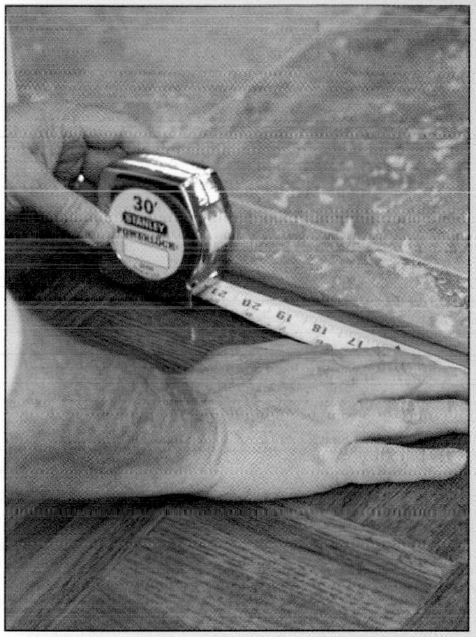

1 Measure the width of the doorway or opening carefully and subtract 1⁄16 inch from your measurement to allow the transition to fit snugly. Using this measurement, cut a piece of thin scrap to the same length and test-fit it in the opening.
.

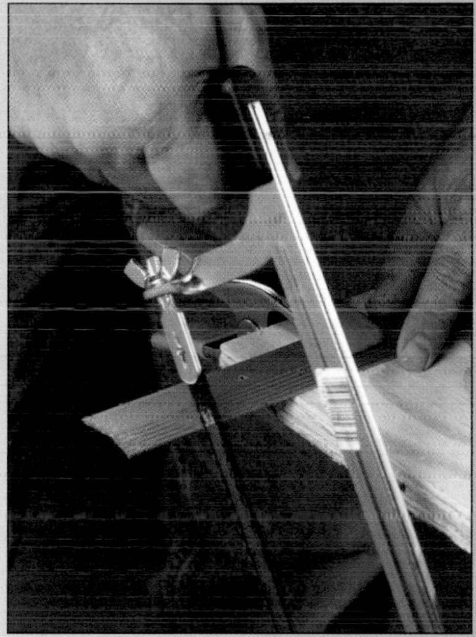

2 Adjust the measurement, if necessary, and mark your transition stock to the test dimension. Clamp the transition securely to a work surface and cut it. Use a hacksaw with a fine-tooth blade to cut metal stock and apply moderate clamping pressure to avoid bending it.

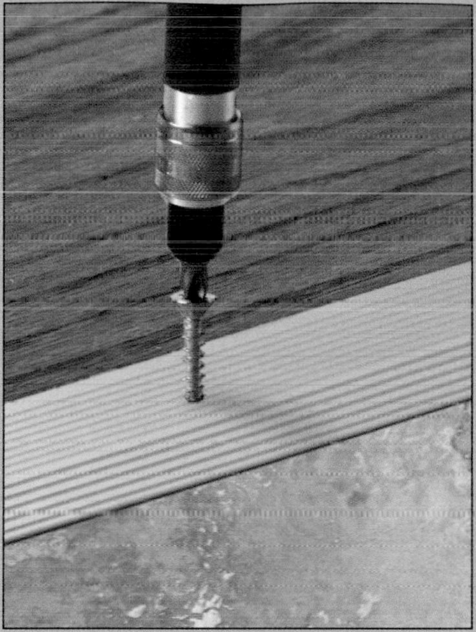

3 Slide the transition in place in the opening and fasten it with ringshank nails, brass wood screws, or the fasteners recommended by the manufacturer. Predrill the transition and the subfloor at the same time. Drive in the screws to secure the transition to the floor.

STANLEY PRO TIP

Cut stock thresholds to fit

Parquet tile, like hardwood floors, must have room to expand under thresholds. Ready-made units come with a recess precut for this purpose. If you're cutting stock for a threshold, use a table saw to cut a dado in the edge facing the parquet.

Easing the transitions

A reducer strip eases the transition from a thicker to thinner floor, from wood to vinyl, for example.

A universal threshold is used when wood flooring butts up against a carpeted floor.

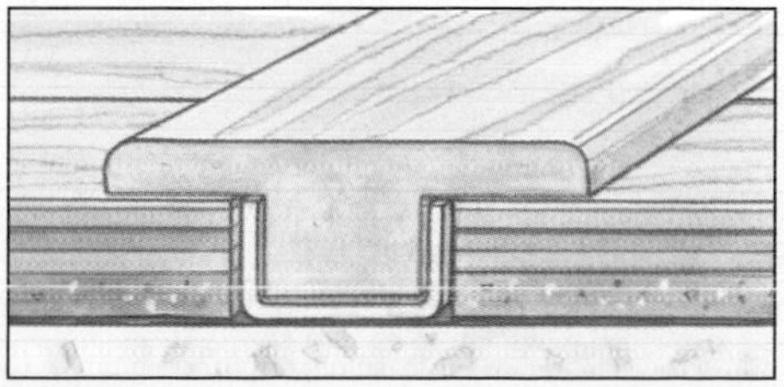

T molding is used as a transition between floors of the same height.

Carpet edging is an inexpensive transition between carpet and an existing floor.

Tiling Floors, Walls & Countertops

You'll find that setting the tile is less tedious and more rewarding than preparing a surface for tiling. This is when you begin to see the results of your planning. If you have several projects planned, start with the least complicated. That way you can build your skills and gain experience. The information in this chapter pertains to ceramic tile; you'll find complete instructions for installing other kinds of tile in later chapters.

Mixing mortar and thinset

Before you begin to mix adhesives, read the manufacturer's directions carefully. Always mix mortar and grout in a clean container. Any residue in the bucket may cause the material to cure prematurely. Clean buckets and utensils after each mixing to save time and avoid problems.

Carefully heed the "working" time—how long it takes the material to set up. Once the setting up has started, tile will not adhere. Grout that has exceeded its working time will not work properly into the joints and will pop out when dry. If either material has begun to set up before you are finished working with it, scrape it off the surface, remix, and reapply.

It takes some practice to discover how much material will cover an area before it sets up. Installation of large tiles will go more quickly than small tiles. Start with a small batch and work up to larger areas.

Heat and humidity affects mortar and grout. You may need to mix a wetter consistency in hot or dry conditions. However, do not add water to mortar that has begun to set up in the heat; doing so weakens its strength. Discard the mixture and start over.

Working with mastics

Mastic ingredients may settle in the can, leaving an oily-looking liquid on top. Stir it until the consistency is smooth.

If you open a can of mastic and it has begun to harden, throw it out and purchase fresh stock.

Application techniques remain essentially the same no matter what surface you're tiling.

Chapter Preview

Tiling floors
page 116

Tiling walls
page 122

Tiling a kitchen countertop and backsplash
page 126

A. Installing backerboard

1 Examine the floor carefully and mark defects—high spots, indentations and depressions, popped nails, and cracks. Fix all defects that could interfere with the adhesive, backerboard, or tile installation. Install a waterproofing membrane over the floor if necessary.

2 Mark floor joist locations on the walls. Cut the pieces of backerboard so the edges will be centered on the joists. Starting on a wall away from the door, trowel a section of thinset, lay the board, and fasten with screws. Continue the process, working toward the doorway.

3 Starting again at a wall away from the door, tape each backerboard joint with 2-inch pregummed mesh tape. Use 4-inch tape at the corners if the backerboard goes up the wall. Trowel a thin coat of thinset over the tape.

FIX ALL DEFECTS

Level high and low spots

Work in sections and use a 4-foot level. Place the level on the floor and rotate it within a section, noting and marking defects with a carpenter's pencil.

Although the floor shown here is a wood floor *(page 68)*, the techniques for fixing defects on a slab are essentially the same *(page 70)*. First chip out and fill major cracks. Then pour self-leveling compound or trowel thinset into depressions and feather the edges level with the floor. Use a belt sander to remove high spots on a wood floor; use a right-angle grinder with a carbide abrasive wheel on a slab. Dewax surfaces and clean.

WHAT IF...

You're tiling a kitchen or bathroom?

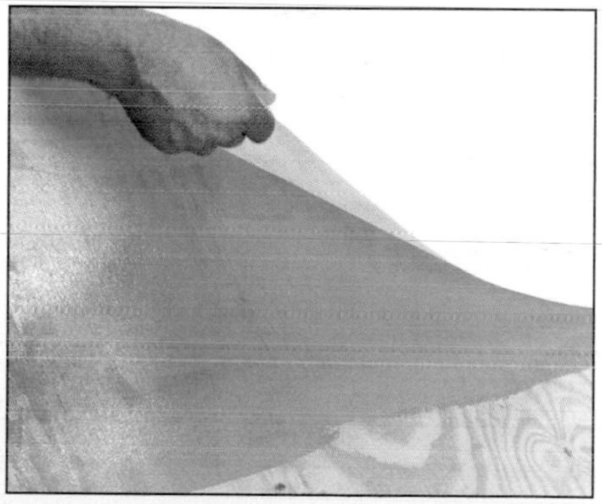

In wet areas such as bathroom floors, apply adhesive with a roller, then the membrane, then trowel on more adhesive *(page 69)*. Working in sections, start on a wall away from a door and cover the entire floor. Make sure the adhesive is spread all the way to the edge of the floor.

B. Marking layout lines

1 Use the dimensional drawing to guide the placement of layout lines. From the midpoint of the walls or at a distance equal to several tiles and grout joints, mark the location of the lines where a grout joint will fall. Dry-lay tiles and spacers in both directions to locate the line precisely. Anchor one end of the chalkline or have a helper hold it and snap the lines. Adjust the first pair so they are perpendicular and snap lines in layout grids of a manageable size.

2 If you have designed a border or accent pattern on your dimensional drawing, snap layout lines where the field tile ends and the border begins. Mark lines within the pattern where the tile changes shape or size. If the design is especially complicated, dry-lay the tiles on a piece of heavy cardboard, trace and cut out the pattern, and use the cardboard as a stencil to lightly spray-paint the pattern on the floor. Tape the stencil down.

LAYOUT LINES

How to lay out different room configurations

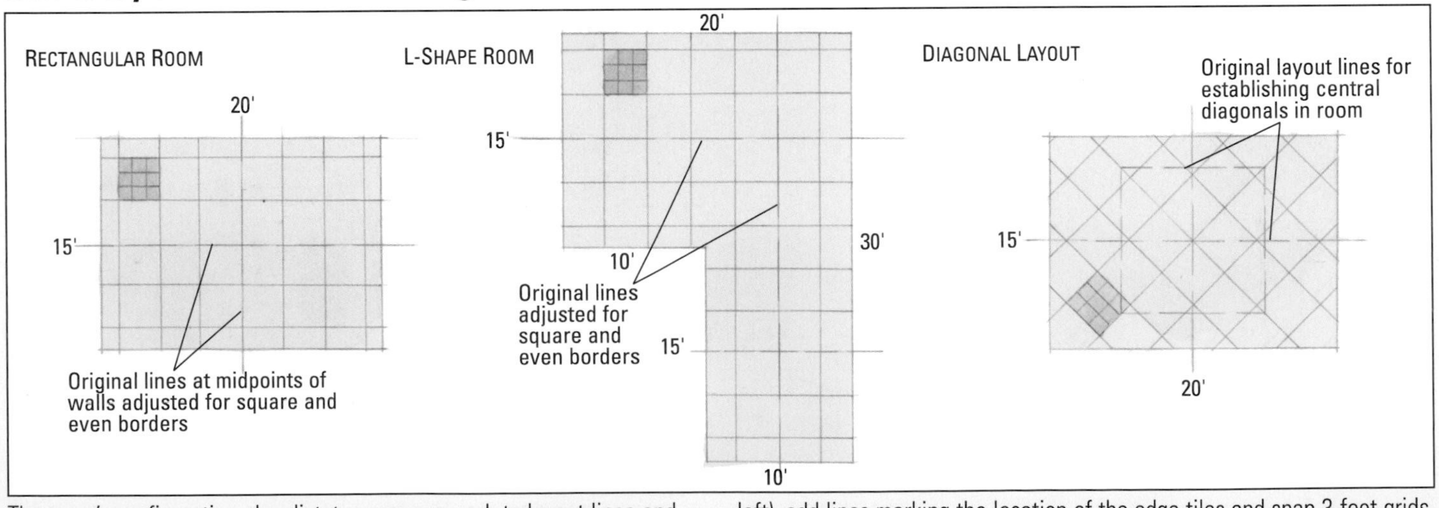

The room's configuration also dictates your approach to layout lines and grids. For small square or rectangular rooms, the number of lines will be minimal and you probably won't need a line at the edges to mark the location of cut tiles. In a large room with large handmade pavers (above left), add lines marking the location of the edge tiles and snap 3-foot grids to help keep it straight. In an L-shape room, position the lines along the longest walls so they fall in both sections. In all cases, snap the first pair of reference lines where a grout line will fall.

C. Laying the tiles

1 Mix enough thinset for the number of layout grids you will set at one time. Dump mortar in the first grid, spread it to the lines, and comb it. Lay the first tile in a corner of the grid, twisting it slightly as you embed it. Continue laying tile, inserting spacers as you go. Check each grid with a straightedge to make sure the joints are properly aligned. Clean excess thinset from the joints and surface. Cut tile for the edges and around obstructions and set it.

2 When the mortar has cured (usually overnight), mix enough grout to cover a section and apply it with a grout float *(pages 104–105)*. Let the grout set up until a damp sponge won't pull it from the joint, then scrape the excess off the tile surface with the float. Damp-sponge the residue from the surface, smoothing out the joints. Damp-sponge again. Let the surface dry. Scrub the haze from the surface with a rag. Grout the next section. Caulk the perimeter joint.

STANLEY PRO TIP

Hide the edges

A tile's cut edges look noticeably different from the molded factory edge. You can smooth the edges of cut tile with a masonry stone to make them less conspicuous, but smoothing takes time. Where possible, hide the cut edges of the tile under the cabinet toe-kicks by setting the tile with its factory edge toward the field tile.

CUT TILE

Working around pipes and flanges

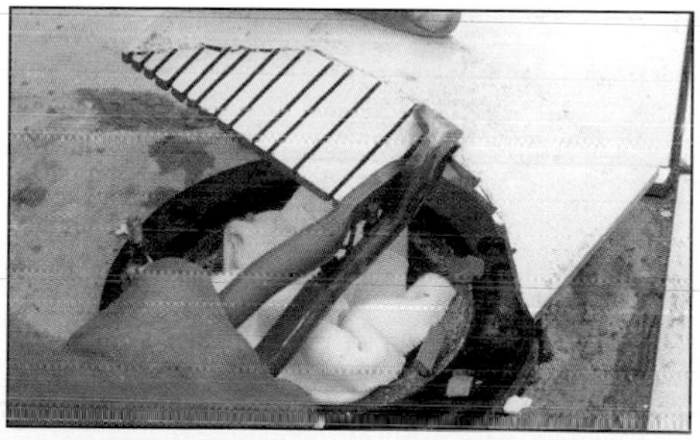

Cutting tile to accommodate pipes and flanges is easier after the field tile has been laid *(page 103)*, and you can make more precise cuts.

Set the tile to be cut on the field tile, with the cut edge against the pipe or flange. Make an allowance for the size of the grout joint. You can mark the width of the cut by eye or hold a small square against the pipe. Mark the dimensions of the cut with a felt-tip pen or china marker. Then mark the tile slightly wider than these lines, so the cut will allow for any expansion of the pipe.

If the arc of the cut is shallow, you can nibble it out with tile nippers. If not, use a wet saw to cut relief cuts from the edge to the arc. Remove the relief cuts with tile nippers and snap out the remaining material to the arc. Remove just a little material at a time. Trying to nip out too much may crack the tile.

D. Adding a tile base

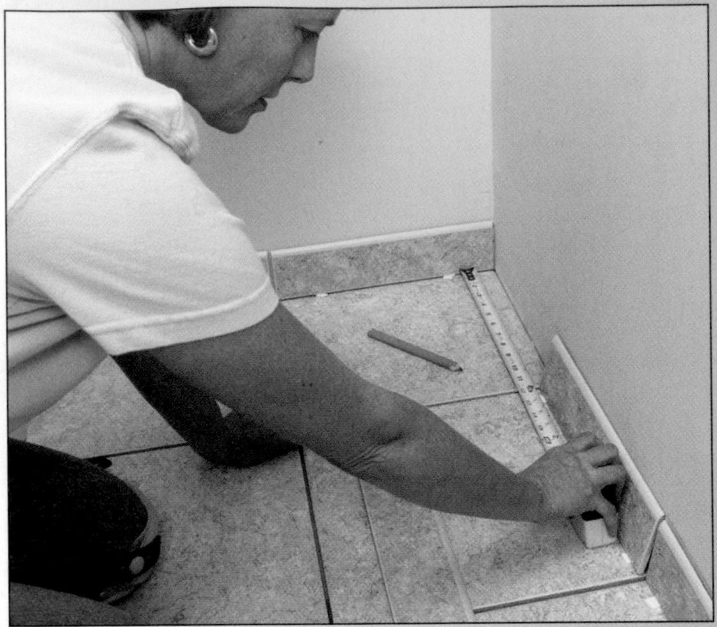

1 Out-of-level floors force you to adjust the base tiles to make their top edges level. You'll make up the difference in the joint at the floor. Lay the bullnose tile against the wall with spacers. Adjust the tile heights with plastic wedges until the top edges of all tiles are level. Make sure the joint at the floor is as even as possible from one end to the other. Continue the layout on adjacent walls. Mark the wall at the top edge of the final layout.

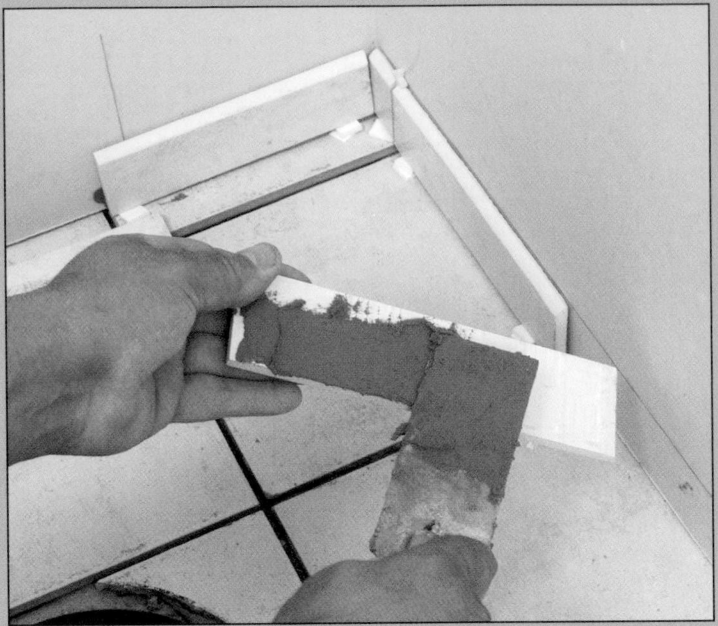

2 Remove the tiles and snap a level chalkline at the mark you made. Mark all the walls with chalklines in a similar fashion. Mix up enough thinset to cover the area in which you'll be working. Back-butter each tile and set it in place.

STANLEY PRO TIP

Wrap the corners

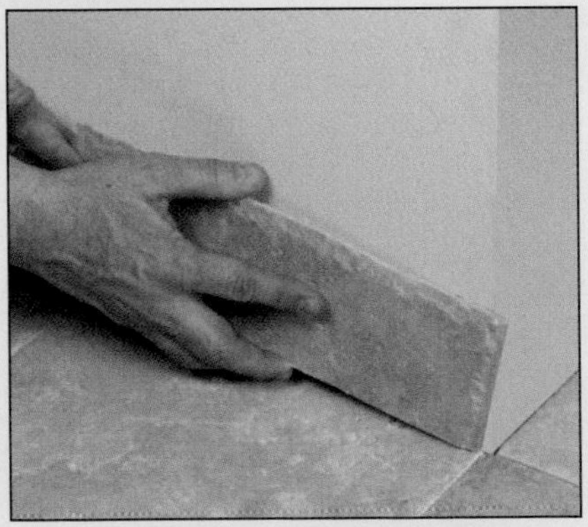

Double-bullnose tile has two rounded edges—one on top and another on the side. It is made especially to provide a smooth way to finish outside corners. The vertical rounded edge covers the square edge of the adjoining tile.

WHAT IF...

Bullnose is not available for your tile?

If bullnose trim is not available in the style you need, cut trim tile from the same stock you laid on the floor. Determine the height of the edging you want and cut enough tiles to run the entire length of the wall. Cut each piece of tile only once. Even if you can get more than one piece from a large floor tile, you'll want a factory edge on top. Install the cut tile and, if the factory edge is not finished to your liking, grout the top edge.

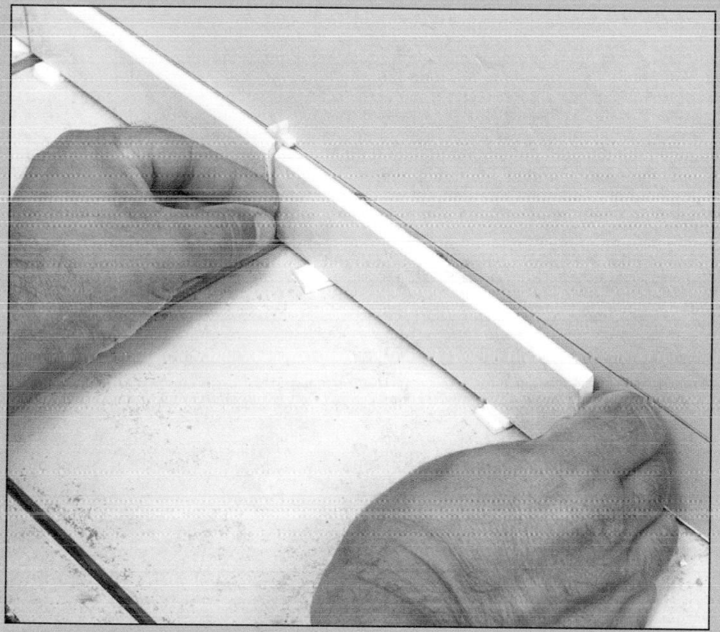

3 Press tile in place, inserting spacers. Use the plastic wedges to keep the top edge in line. About every 3 feet, use a 4-foot level to make sure the top edge is level. Adjust the tile if necessary by gently pushing or pulling on the wedges. Gently remove excess mortar from the joints with a utility knife and clean the surface. Set and clean corner tiles and let the mortar cure overnight before grouting.

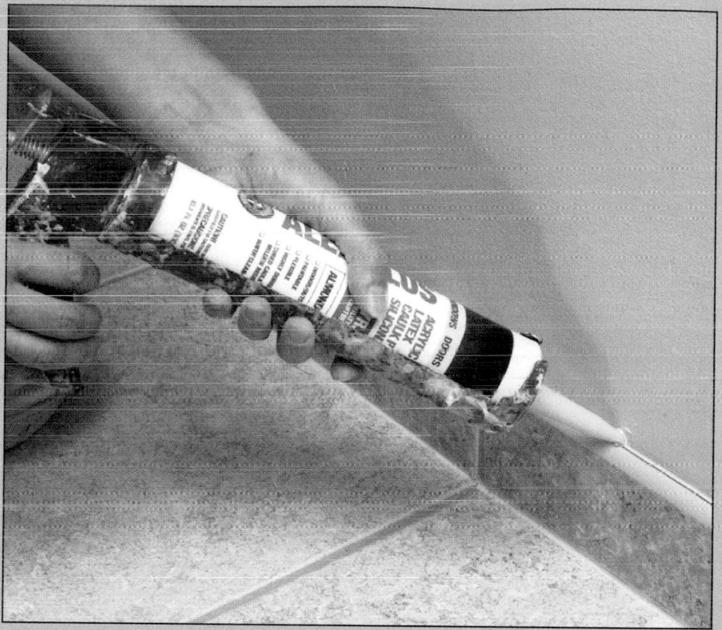

4 As a final step, grout the trim tiles and caulk the joints at the floor and top edge. Force grout into the vertical joints with a grout float. When the grout has partially cured, remove the excess from the joint at the floor with a utility knife and from the surface with a damp sponge. Sponge-clean the surface at least twice and wipe off the haze with a clean rag. Caulk the joint at the floor and along the top edge of the trim. Smooth the caulk with a wet finger or sponge.

Trimming doors

1 Remove the door if necessary. Tap the hinge pin with an 8d nail and pull the pin out with pliers. You may have to tap out a stubborn pin with a hammer and straight screwdriver inserted under the head of the pin.

Measure the distance from the tiled floor to the bottom of the lowest hinge knuckle on the door jamb.

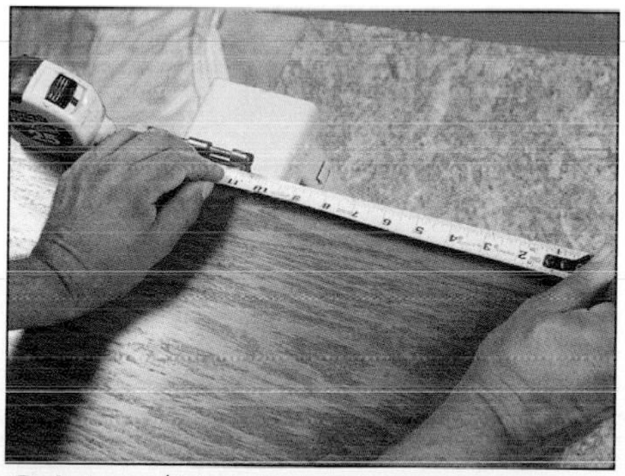

2 Subtract ¼ inch from your measurement and, using this length, measure from the top of the lower pin knuckle on the door to the bottom of the door. Use a carpenter's square and straightedge to extend the line across the bottom of the door. Transfer the line to the other side of the door.

3 Score the lines on both sides of the door with a utility knife. Use a straightedge to keep the knife on line and score deeply with several passes.

Clamp the door securely to a solid worktable and clamp a guide that will keep the saw blade on the cut line. Trim the excess off the door, sand the edges smooth, and rehang the door.

TILING WALLS

Establishing layout lines on walls is much easier than on a floor. Hold the level on the wall in both a vertical and horizontal plane, and when the bubble centers in the glass, trace intersecting lines.

Wall tiles are affected by gravity and tend to slide down the wall during installation. Organic mastic is one solution—tile sticks to it almost immediately. Mastic is not as strong as thinset mortar, however, and not as water-resistant. You can keep tile that's embedded in thinset in place with spacers, nails, or tape.

If you are tiling a wall and a floor, tile the floor first so you can continue the grout joints up the wall in the same pattern as the floor. Install a cove base, then start wall tile at the cove base. If you are tiling adjacent walls, set the back wall first. Tapered edges on a side wall are less visible.

PRESTART CHECKLIST

☐ **TIME**
About 30 to 45 minutes per square yard to prepare and set tile

☐ **TOOLS**
Wide putty knife, 4-foot level, sanding block, small sledge and cold chisel, stud finder, tape measure, chalkline, utility knife, carbide scriber, margin trowel, notched trowel, straightedge, cordless drill, grout knife, snap cutter or wet saw, tile nippers, masonry stone, caulk gun, hammer, grout float

☐ **SKILLS**
Reading spirit level, troweling, laying tile, grouting

☐ **PREP**
Repair structural defects

☐ **MATERIALS**
Deglossing agent, release agent, bucket, thinset, dimensional lumber for battens, backerboard, screws, tape, tile, spacers, caulk, grout, rags, sponge, water, tile base or bullnose, nylon wedges, nails

A. Preparing the wall

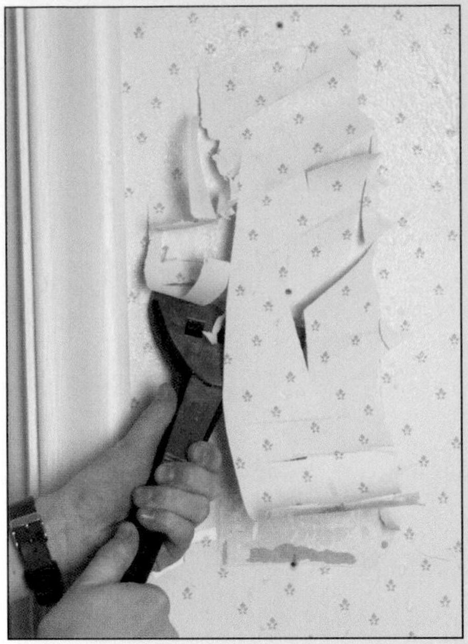

1 Remove any wallcovering and degloss paint. If removing wallpaper, sand or use a wet sponge to clean off the residue of glue and paper. Make sure the surface dries completely before setting tile on it.

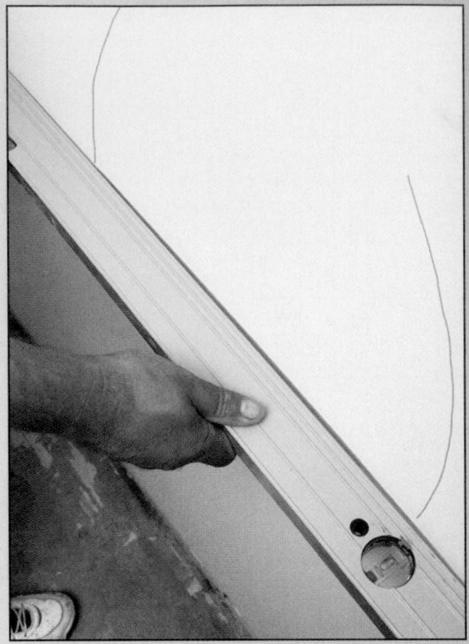

2 Using a 4-foot level, examine the wall in sections, marking high spots, depressions, and other defects that would interfere with the tile. Pay close attention to corners to check for plumb *(page 75)*. Using care in your survey of the wall at this stage will save time later.

WHAT IF...
There's a window on the wall?

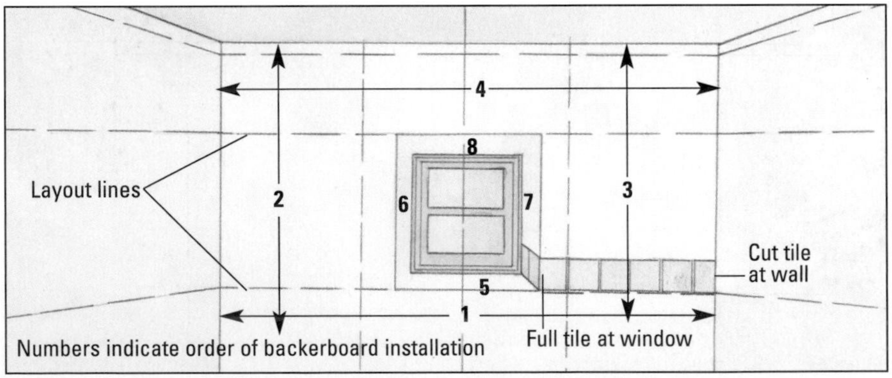

Windows complicate wall layouts. If possible, arrange the pattern with a full tile around the perimeter of the window and cut tiles at the edges of the wall. You can achieve this balance fairly easily if the window is centered and if tile covers the surface evenly or leaves at least a half tile at the corners.

If a perfectly balanced layout won't work, try adjusting the grout lines or inserting decorative tile. Trim tiles at the window's edge might even out the layout. Install the window tiles first to establish the grout lines for wall field tile, then tile the remainder of the back wall, working upwards.

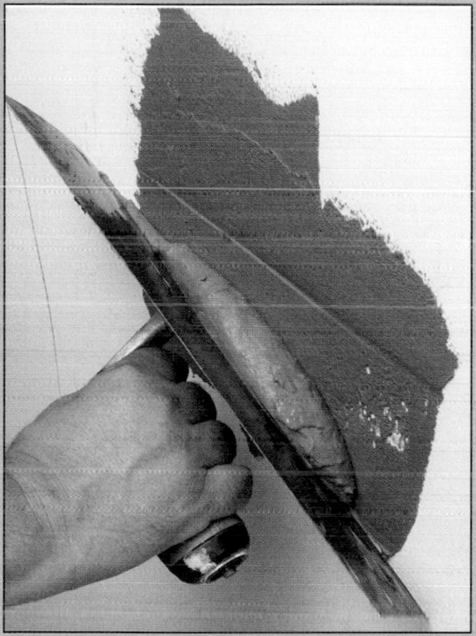

3 Skim-coat a layer of thinset on any walls that are out of plumb and fill depressions. If installing backerboard on studs, mark stud centers on the ceiling. Cut and fasten backerboard, centering its edges on the studs. Position the backerboard pieces to minimize cutting and waste.

B. Marking layout lines

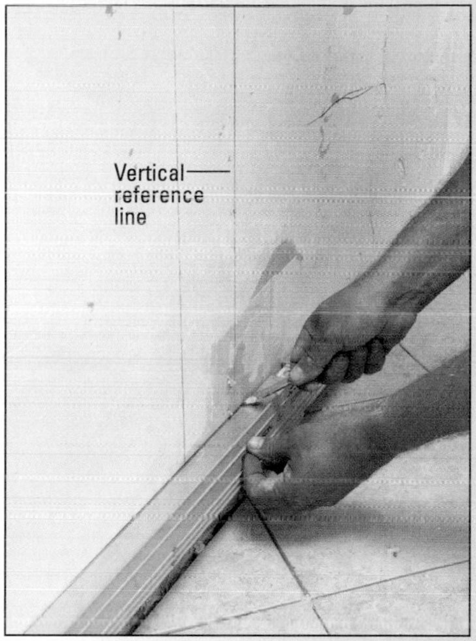

1 Set a 4-foot level vertically on the wall about 2 feet from a corner, over a grout joint. If the wall meets at an outside corner, set the level where the inside edge of a bullnose will fall. Pencil a line down the level, extend it to the floor and ceiling. Repeat the process on the horizontal plane.

2 Measure up from the horizontal line a distance equal to the size of your tile and mark the wall at this point. Continue marking the wall in the same increments. Using a 4-foot level, mark the wall across from these points and snap layout grids so you can keep each horizontal course straight.

LAYOUT GRIDS
Patterns determine the order of setting tile

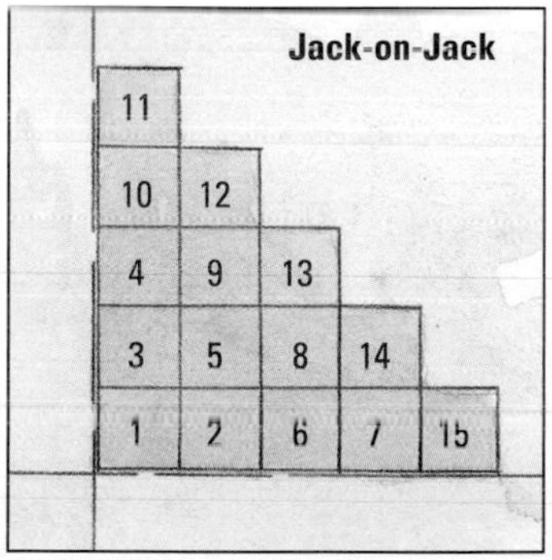

A jack-on-jack pattern is one of the easiest patterns to use. Set the first tile at the intersection of the layout grid or quadrant and lay the remaining tiles in the order shown above. As an alternative, you can set the legs of the quadrant and fill in the interior.

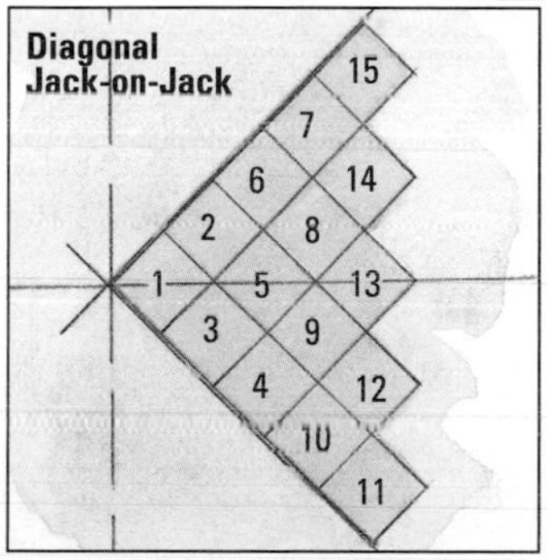

Diagonal patterns always result in cut tiles on the edges. Before choosing a diagonal pattern, work with your dimensional layout drawing to make sure these edge tiles will be as close to a full diagonal as possible. A border will frame a diagonal pattern nicely.

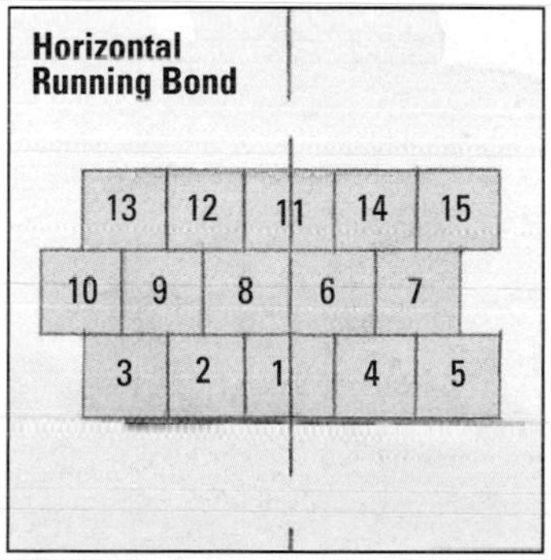

To make horizontal running bond work, find the exact center of the first tile and lay it on one axis of the layout lines. Work from that tile to the left, then to the right. Then center the next row on the same axis. Check the alternating grout lines with a straightedge.

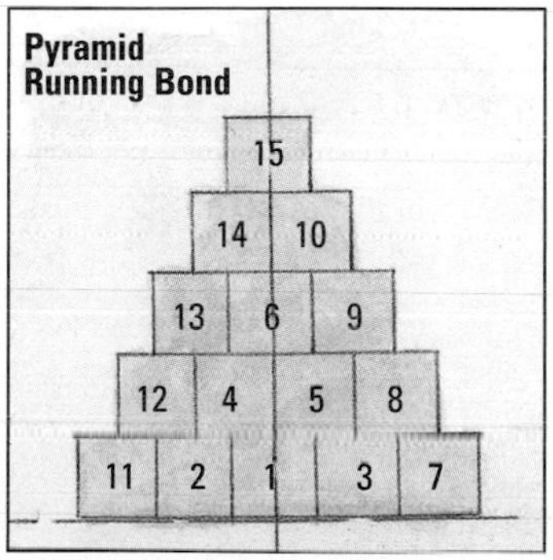

A pyramid running bond is perhaps the most difficult to keep straight because it stacks the centers of tiles not only on alternate rows but also on both sides of the vertical axis. Before laying this pattern, mark all the tiles that will be centered on this axis.

C. Laying the tile

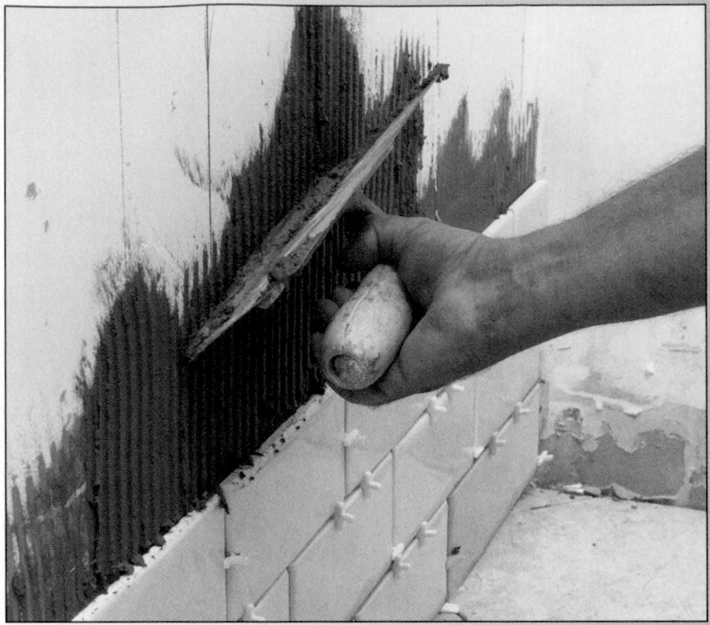

1 Mix enough adhesive to cover the size of a section you can lay within its working time (the amount of time it takes for the mortar to set up and become unworkable). Work from the bottom up, spreading the adhesive evenly and combing it with the notched edge of the trowel. Start at the bottom, and using a batten, press the tile into the mortar with a slight twist.

2 Continue laying the pattern of your choice, using spacers if your tile is not lugged. Note the placement and position of the spacers. Setting the spacers flush with the surface of the tile will make them difficult to remove. Inserting them in the manner shown above makes removal an easy task. When the field tile is set, cut and install the edge tiles.

Keeping the tiles on the wall

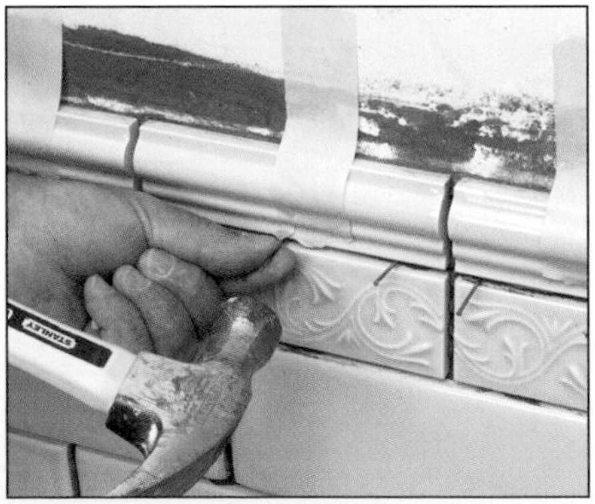

If you're not using a coved base and your layout results in cut tiles at the floor, tack a level 1× or 2× batten along the plane on which your first full tiles will be laid. The batten will keep the rows in place and prevent the tiles from sliding down the wall. Even with a coved base or a batten and spacers, you may have to take extra precautions to keep the tile on the wall while the adhesive cures. Drive nails partway into the wall at least every third of each tile's length and tape the tiles with masking tape. If your layout calls for a coved tile base, install it first, leveling it with nylon wedges. Then tile up the wall.

WHAT IF...
Tiles are lugged (prespaced)?

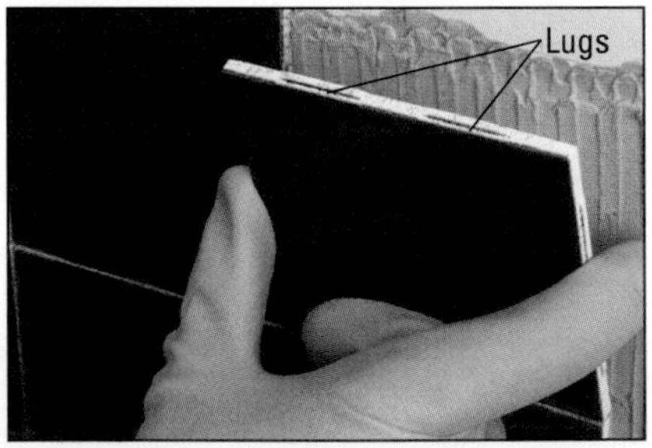

Lugged tiles make it easy to space wall installations. They come with small bisque lugs raised on the edges and don't require additional spacers to keep them aligned.

Because the lugs are fired into the tile at the time of manufacture, they don't allow you to make the grout joints narrower. Determine the actual dimensions of the tile when you purchase it so you know how much space each tile actually covers.

D. Grouting the tile

1 When the adhesive has cured to the manufacturer's specifications, inspect the joints for excess adhesive. Use a utility knife or grout knife to remove any adhesive left in the joints and clean any excess off the tile surface. Mix enough grout to cover a section and force it into the joints with a grout float, keeping the float at a 45-degree angle. Work the float in both directions to fill the joints; work diagonally to remove excess grout.

2 When the grout has cured enough that a damp sponge won't pull it out of the joints, scrape off the excess with the float held almost perpendicular to the surface. Clean the surface and smooth the joints with a damp sponge, then repeat the cleaning with clean water and a clean sponge. When a haze forms, wipe it with a clean rag. You may have to wipe with some pressure to remove the haze.

WHAT IF...
The wall has electrical outlets on it?

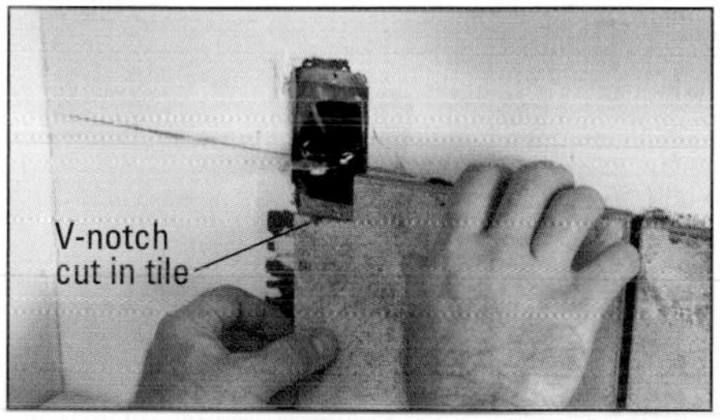

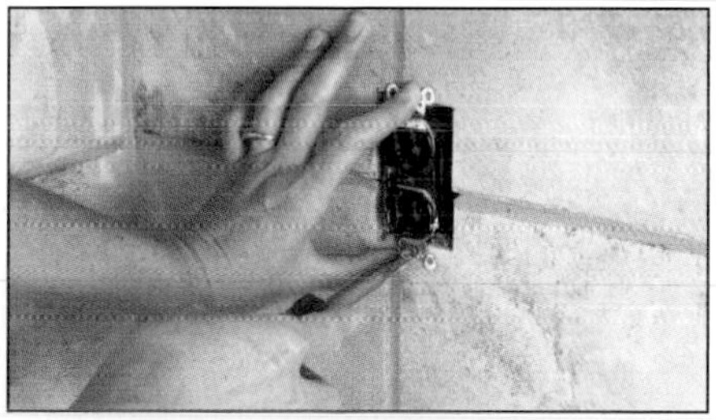

Unless you have removed the wall surface, the thickness of the finished surface will extend beyond the edges of electrical outlet boxes. As a result the receptacle screws may be too short to anchor the receptacle. A box extension will remedy the problem, but if local codes don't require an extension you can fix the problem by using longer screws.

First **turn off the power to the circuit** and remove the cover plate and receptacle screws. Remove one receptacle screw completely so you can take it to the store to buy a screw ½ inch longer. Push the receptacle into the box and out of your way.

Cut the tiles to fit around the box. Then cut V-shape notches (use tile nippers) that line up with the tabs and screw holes on the top and bottom of the box. Spread adhesive to within ¼ inch of the box and embed the tile. When the mortar cures, pull out the receptacle from the box and fasten it with the longer screws inserted through the notches.

Turning an outside corner

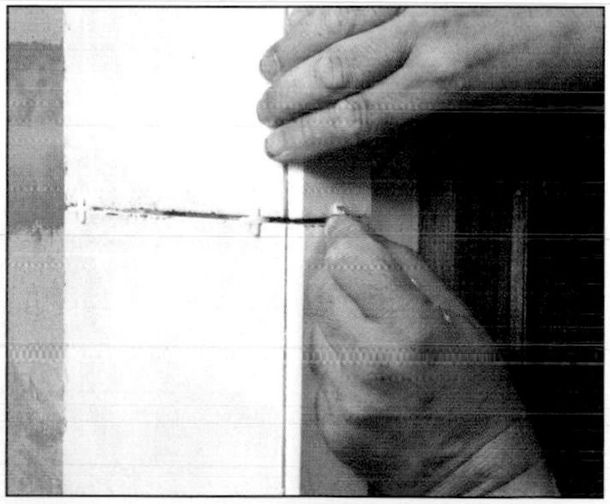

Outside corners can present problems, especially if they are not plumb. You can hide slightly out-of-plumb situations by skim-coating the wall with thinset. Then overlap bullnose tiles or edge tiles on the full tiles on the other wall. As long as the tiles meet crisply, the out-of-plumb wall should not be as noticeable.

TILING A KITCHEN COUNTERTOP AND BACKSPLASH

A countertop and backsplash can be planned as a single project or as separate projects.

If you are setting a countertop and backsplash, lay the backsplash tiles before the countertop front edge to avoid disturbing the edge tiles when you lean over the counter. If possible, hide cut tiles at the top of a backsplash, under wall cabinets. Design the layout so decorative molding avoids electrical outlets.

The installation shown here includes a waterproofing membrane, necessary if the surface will be subject to spills or frequent cleaning. Use latex- or acrylic-modified adhesives and grout. Seal the grout joints to protect them from staining.

PRESTART CHECKLIST

☐ **TIME**
About 20 minutes per lineal foot of countertop to prepare and set tile

☐ **TOOLS**
Utility knife, stapler, hair dryer, 4-foot level, tape measure, chalkline, carbide scriber, margin trowel, notched trowel, straightedge, cordless drill, snap cutter or wet saw, nippers, grout knife, masonry stone, caulk gun, grout float

☐ **SKILLS**
Reading a level, troweling, laying tile, grouting tile

☐ **PREP**
Repair structural defects, remove old countertop and build new countertop base

☐ **MATERIALS**
Asphalt mastic and 15-pound felt paper, staples, bucket, thinset, backerboard, screws, tape, tile, spacers, caulk, grout, rags, sponge, water, bullnose or V-cap edge tile, nylon wedges, sink

A. Preparing the surface

1 Measure and cut polyethylene sheets or 15-pound felt paper to the size of the countertop, including the backsplash, if desired. Allow enough for the overhang. Staple the sheets to the plywood base.

2 Cut backerboard to fit both sides of the sink. If the sink has reinforcing bars, cut grooves in the pieces to match. Set the sections at both sides of the sink cutout, but do not fasten them. Measure the remaining spaces at the rear and front of the sink, and cut and groove backerboard to fit.

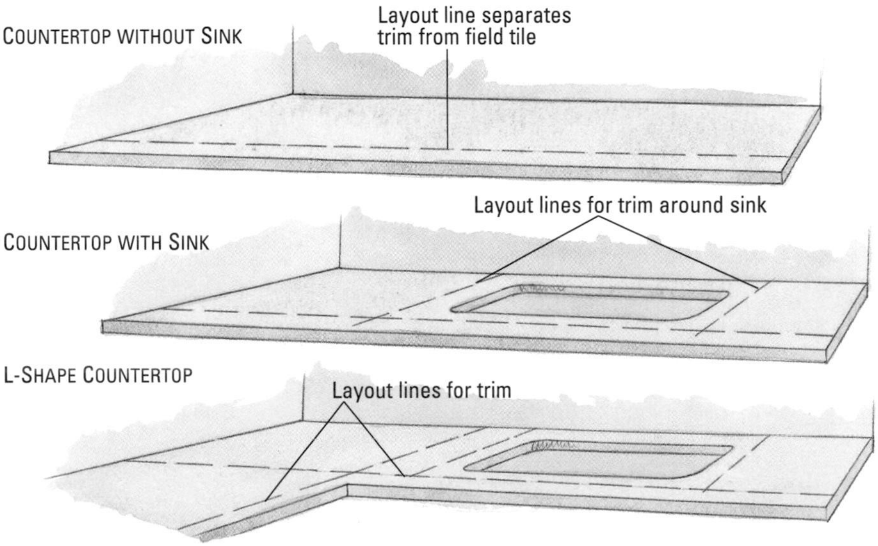

The number of layout lines required for a countertop installation varies with the job's complexity. At a minimum, a counter with no sink needs a line that locates the front edge tile. Counters with a sink require lines for the front edge and the perimeter of the sink. For a tiled backsplash, carry the lines up the wall.

3 Drop in the sink to make sure its reinforcing bars fit, then fasten the board to the plywood base with backerboard screws. If using backerboard on the backsplash, back-butter it to make the job easier. Tape all joints and edges and apply a thin coat of thinset over the tape.

B. Laying the field tile

Snap reference and layout grids on the countertop and backsplash as necessary to help you keep the layout straight. Be sure to snap a line where you will lay the edge tiles, both on the front of the countertop and around the perimeter of the sink. Dry-lay as many tiles as necessary to make sure the lines are located correctly. Pull up a section of the dry-laid tiles and apply thinset to the section. Install all of the field tiles first. Clean the grout lines with a utility knife and remove excess mortar from the tile surface. Let the adhesive cure overnight.

STANLEY PRO TIP

Carry grout joints up the wall

If you are tiling a backsplash with the same tile as the countertop, establish layout lines on the counter at a point on which a grout line will fall. Then carry the lines up the backsplash area so the backsplash joint will match the joints on the countertop.

If the backsplash tiles are different from countertop tiles, you must lay out the backsplash separately.

WHAT IF...

The countertop is L-shape?

L-shape countertops require a slightly different approach than rectangular counters.

Snap a layout line on the front of both legs to locate the position of the edge tiles. Make sure that this line extends the full length of each leg. Then snap the remaining lines for the rear edge tile and tile around the sink. Dry-lay the tiles to keep the location accurate.

Begin the installation of the tile at the intersection of the two legs, working first on the leg without the sink. Then set the field tiles on the second leg, then the backsplash tiles. Clean the joints and the tile surface. Set the V-cap or bullnose edge tiles last to avoid the risk of disturbing them when you lean over the countertop.

Layout lines
You don't have as much working room on a countertop, so make your layout lines precise.

C. Setting the trim tile and grouting

1 Measure and cut the trim tile to be set around the sink. If using bullnose tile, cut corners on a wet saw. Dry-fit the corners to make sure the grout line will be the same width as the others. Spread thinset on the backerboard and back-butter tiles so they adhere properly. Let the adhesive cure until it just begins to set up. Carefully remove any excess from the joints and perimeter with a utility knife.

2 If using bullnose tile on the top edges instead of V-cap edging, you can keep the tile in line with a thin batten on the edge of the plywood base. Trowel on thinset and lay the bullnose tile in place on the top of the plywood base. Let the mortar cure, then remove the batten. Back-butter the front edge tiles with thinset. If necessary, tape the tiles in place until the mortar cures.

STANLEY PRO TIP

Level stone countertops

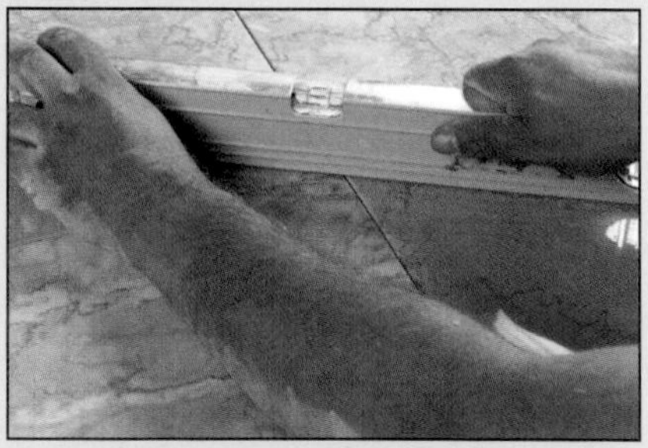

Stone countertops must be level to avoid cracking. Check each section as you lay it. For a high-sheen finish that matches the surface of the tile, you'll want to polish it.

Polishing stone edges and surfaces is a tricky business, and the tools are expensive to buy for just a one-time use. Ask your supplier for the name of a professional who can do the job for you.

KEEP THE TILE IN LINE

Working with bullnose or sheet-mounted tiles

Keeping both field and edge tiles lined up properly on a countertop can be difficult if you do not have the room to maneuver a long straightedge.

To help keep bullnose edges in line, cut a strip of wood to the thickness of the front edge tile. Tack this batten to the front of the plywood base flush with the top. Install the bullnose so its front edge is flush with the front of the batten.

Sheet-mounted tiles often shift as the mesh backing softens in the thinset. To prod them back in line, use the smooth edge of a trowel as a short straightedge.

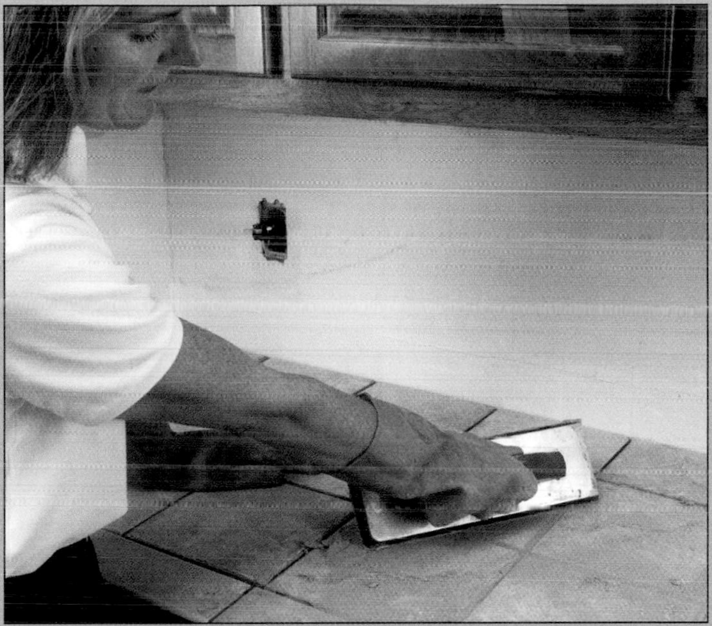

3 When the mortar is dry, clean any residue if necessary. Mix the grout thoroughly to remove any trace of lumps. Spread it into the joints with a grout float held at about a 45-degree angle. Make sure all the joints are completely filled.

4 Clean sections as soon as the grout sets up slightly. To avoid scratches remove the grout from the surface before it hardens. Remove excess grout with the float. Use a wrung-out wet sponge to smooth the joints and remove the excess from the surface. Repeat the cleaning at least once more and wipe off the haze with a rag.

WHAT IF...
You are using V-cap or wood edge?

If you are trimming the countertop with V-cap, first trowel thinset on the countertop edge. Then back-butter the inside bottom edge and embed the cap in the mortar. V-cap firings often vary a little from field tile sizes. If so, center the cap between the grout joints. The slight difference in grout joint sizes will not be apparent.

If your V-cap extends below the edge of the plywood base, use a piece of scrap or your finger behind the open gap at the bottom edge to keep the grout in place.

To install a wood edge, measure pieces and miter-cut the corners if desired. After the tile is set, fasten the edging to the countertop base with nails or screws. Use 6d finish nails and countersink them with a nail set. Fill the holes with colored filler that matches the wood stain. If using screws, glue wood plugs to hide the tops of counterbored screws.

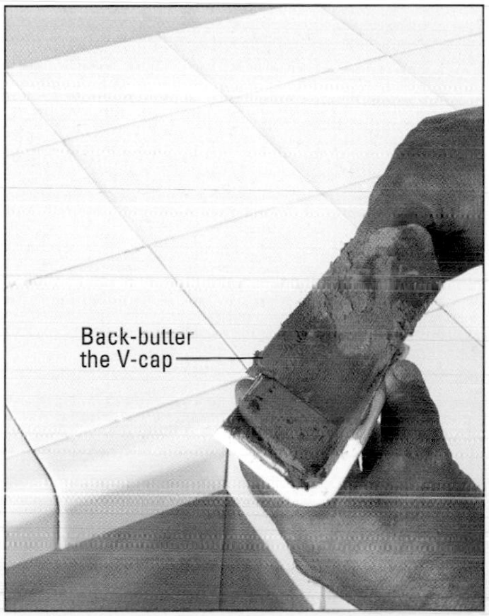

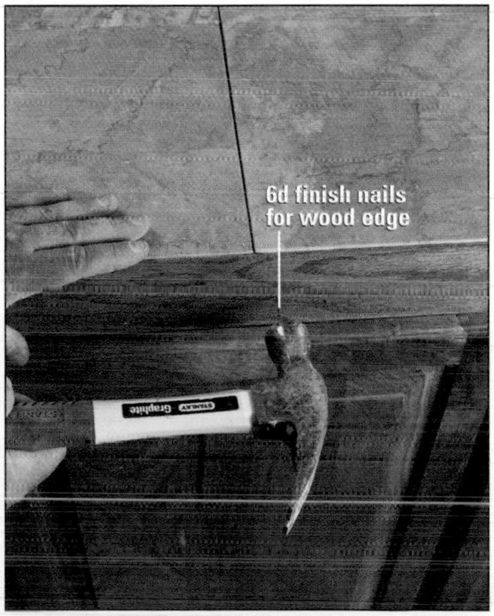

D. Tiling a backsplash

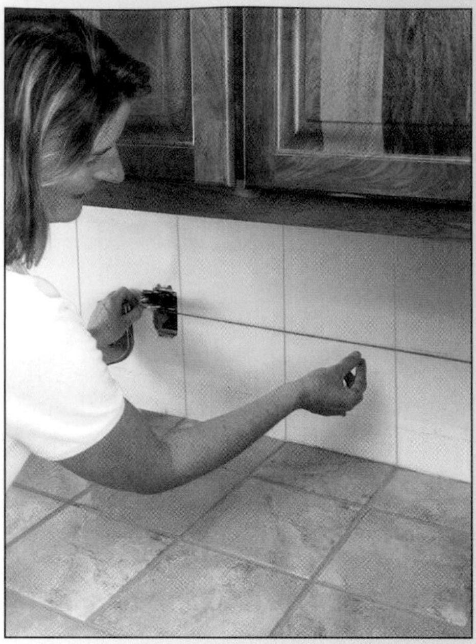

1 Snap layout lines on the backsplash area to correspond to the grout lines for the tile size used. Set up the first row of tiles in a dry run, using nylon wedges to keep their top edges level. Mark the top edge on the wall and snap a level chalkline at this point, extending it beyond the end if possible.

2 Remove the dry-laid tiles and apply thinset. If the backsplash continues up to the cabinets, work in small sections. Some areas may be hard to reach and will require more time for placing the tile. Working in small sections will avoid the risk of the adhesive setting up too soon.

3 Set the bottom row of tiles using the wedges to bring it level with the line you have marked on the wall. Set the remaining tiles, cleaning the grout lines with a utility knife as you go. Use spacers if appropriate to your tile and check the lines with a straightedge. Let the mortar cure.

Installing a vanity countertop

The techniques for tiling a backsplash and countertop are not limited to the kitchen. You'll find a complete step-by-step discussion about tiling a bathroom vanity on *pages 170–171*.

WHAT IF...

Backsplash tiles are different from the countertop?

Backsplash tiles do not have to be the same as those on the countertop. You can achieve interesting decorative effects by using accent tiles or wall tiles of different dimensions.

Plan the layout carefully on paper and by laying out the tiles without mortar so that you achieve a pleasing effect with the offset grout joints.

Once you have established the layout with dry-set tiles, mark their position on the walls and snap layout lines that conform to their dimensions.

Install the tiles with the same techniques as you would other backsplash tile.

4 Remove the wedges from beneath the bottom row of tiles. Apply grout to the joints with a grout float. Do not grout the joint below the bottom row. Work the float in both directions to fill the joints. Completing an upward stroke is difficult under a cabinet; instead pull the float down.

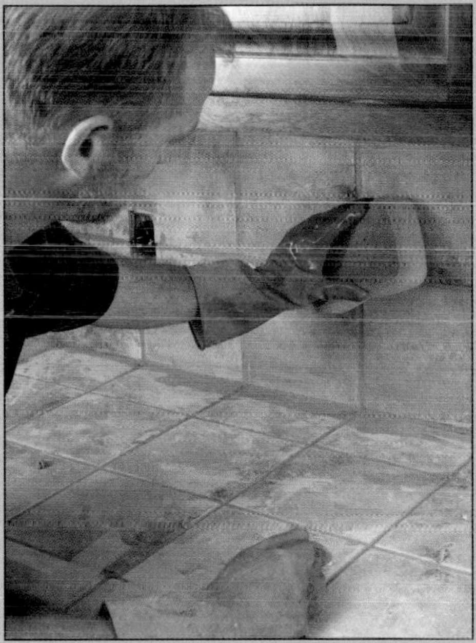

5 Let the grout set until it doesn't pull out of the joint when you run a damp sponge lightly across it. Then scrape the excess grout off the tile surface. Wring out a sponge completely and smooth the joints, removing the excess from the surface. Repeat the cleaning at least one more time.

6 Using a sealant or caulk that matches the color and consistency of the grout, caulk the joint at the base of the backsplash. Apply the caulk at a consistent rate into the joint. Smooth the caulk with a wet finger.

Laying a diagonal backsplash

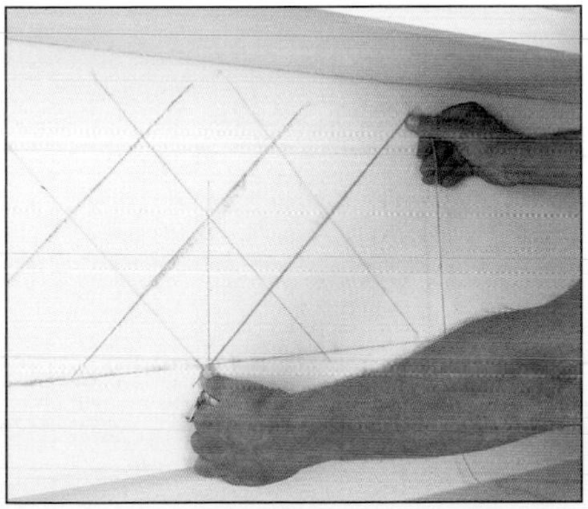

1 At the horizontal and vertical midpoints, snap perpendicular chalklines. From their intersection, measure out an equal distance on each line. At these points, draw lines perpendicular to the original lines, extending them until they intersect. Draw diagonal lines connecting the intersection points.

2 Using the diagonal lines as quadrants, trowel on thinset in one quadrant. Set tile within that quadrant and clean it. Then set and clean the remaining quadrants in any order. Remove any excess mortar from the joints. Let the mortar cure, then cut and install the edge tile.

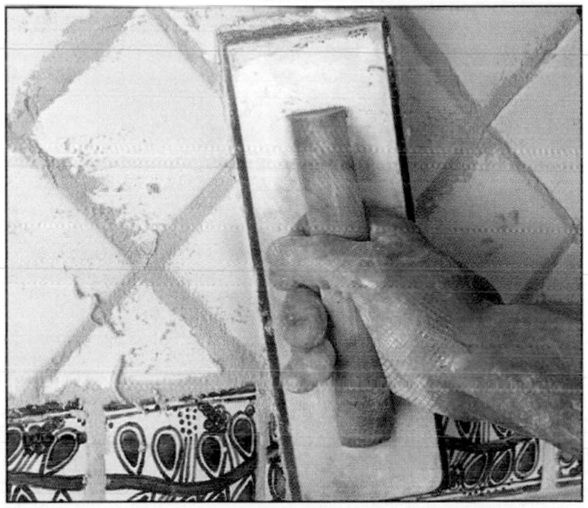

3 Force grout into the joints with the grout float, working at right angles to the joints. Let the grout set up slightly and remove the excess grout from the tile with the float. Clean the surface at least twice with a damp sponge and clean water. Scour the haze from the surface with a clean rag.

TILING SPECIAL SPACES

Although most tiling projects fall into one of three categories—floors, walls, and countertops—some installations require special treatment. These projects employ the same basic setting techniques as others, but with a few slight yet significant differences.

Tiling a small entryway, for example, calls for the same methods as tiling any floor. Their narrow configurations, however, make them more susceptible to design and installation errors. An entryway also opens up into several rooms, so the tile pattern must be designed with an eye toward its most viewed perspective.

Tiling a window recess calls for the same methods as tiling walls. This project, however, is complicated by design and layout choices created by the wide variety of window styles, from a double-hung window in a turn-of-the-century home to a casement window in a 1960s ranch-style residence.

Tiling hot spots

Tiling a fireplace and the surfaces around a wood-burning stove are essentially the same as setting tile on a floor and wall, but these installations require the use of special materials. Heat-resistant mortar is needed. Chances are, you'll drop a piece of firewood or a fireplace tool in the lifetime of a fireplace or stove, so you should use hearth tiles that can stand up to rough usage.

The tiling projects in this chapter may be small in scope but they still benefit from careful planning. Start with a sketch rather than a formal plan—a rough outline of the tile pattern places less restrictions on your creativity. The early stages of any project are the time for experimentation. Your initial design may go through several versions. Several factors may cause you to alter your plans: your budget and time, the size of the tile, and your skills and abilities. Work with all of the elements until they come together in a plan that's just right for you.

The following chapters, "Tiling Bathroom Fixtures" and "Tiling Outdoor Projects," present more specialized tile applications.

The basics of setting tile remain constant, but each special installation requires a unique strategy.

CHAPTER PREVIEW

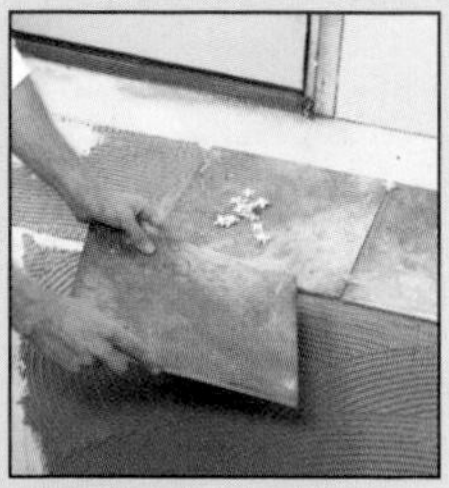

Check local building codes for requirements on the use of fire-resistant materials. Combustible materials, such as a wood mantlepiece, may need to be a specific distance from the firebox.

Draw a design to scale using actual dimensions of the fireplace and tile. Layout the pattern on the floor to check its fit.

Tiling a fireplace requires the use heat-resistant epoxy when tiling over wood or heat-resistant cement-based mortars on masonry surfaces.

TILING A SMALL ENTRYWAY

A small entryway is a good beginning tile project, requiring a straightforward application of basic skills. An entryway opens to many rooms; lay it out so it looks best from its most viewed perspective.

PRESTART CHECKLIST

☐ **TIME**
About 30 to 45 minutes per square yard to prepare floor and set tile

☐ **TOOLS**
Four-foot level, small sledge and cold chisel, right-angled grinder or belt sander (for wood floor), tape measure, chalkline, margin trowel, roller, notched trowel, straightedge, carbide scriber, utility knife, snap cutter or wet saw, nippers, masonry stone, grout knife, caulk gun, grout float, hammer, cordless drill, putty knife

☐ **SKILLS**
Troweling, snapping with chalkline, setting tile, grouting with float

☐ **PREP**
Repair structural defects

☐ **MATERIALS**
Bucket, thinset, isolation membrane, tile, spacers, caulk, grout, rags, sponge, water, threshold and fasteners, backerboard and tape (for wood floor), foam backer rod

Tiling an entry slab

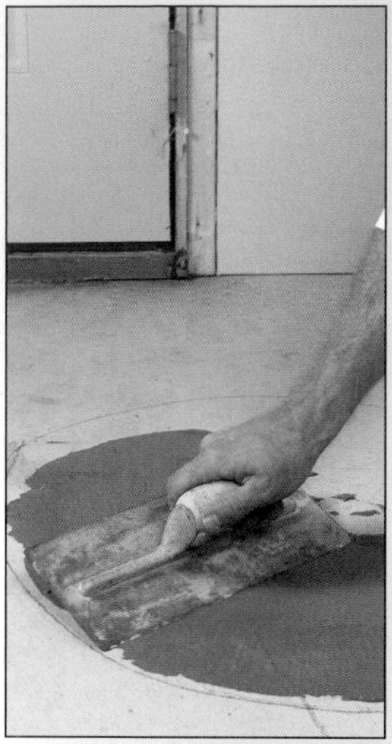

1 Examine the entryway slab for high spots, depressions, cracks, and other defects. Work in sections with a 4-foot level and mark the defects. Fill depressions, level high spots, and roughen slick surfaces.

2 "Bandage" each crack in the slab with an isolation membrane. Apply the adhesive with a roller, let it cure (follow the manufacturer's directions), and cover the adhesive with the membrane *(page 71)*.

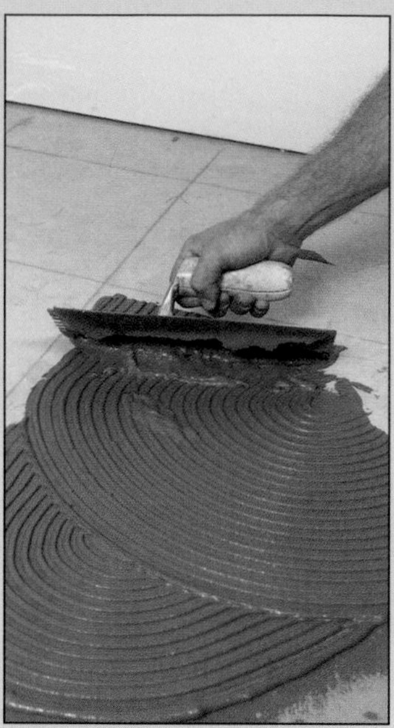

3 Dry-lay tiles to test your layout, keeping small cut tiles to a minimum. Then snap a reference and as many layout lines as the pattern needs *(pages 96–97)*. Start at the door and trowel on thinset *(page 98)*.

LAYOUT LINES
Measure and make square

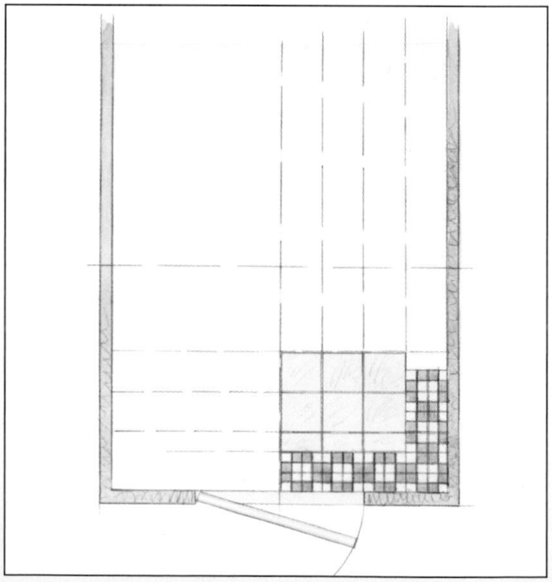

Snap perpendicular reference lines either at the midpoint of the walls or at least 2 feet from them. Snap the line at a point over which a grout joint will fall in the installation. Use the 3-4-5 triangle method to adjust the lines, if necessary, to form a right angle at the intersection *(page 44)*.

Measure from the reference lines (not from the wall) to locate the start of any border tiles. If you measure from the wall, you may be thrown off by discrepancies in the surface and transmit them to the layout.

Establish layout grids by measuring in each direction a distance equal to the width of several tiles and grout joints. Snap layout grids at these points. Double-check the marks before you snap the lines so the grids will be the same size and square.

4 Set field tile first on the layout lines. Insert spacers as you go and check the sections with a straightedge to make certain they're straight. Clean excess mortar from the joints with a utility knife.

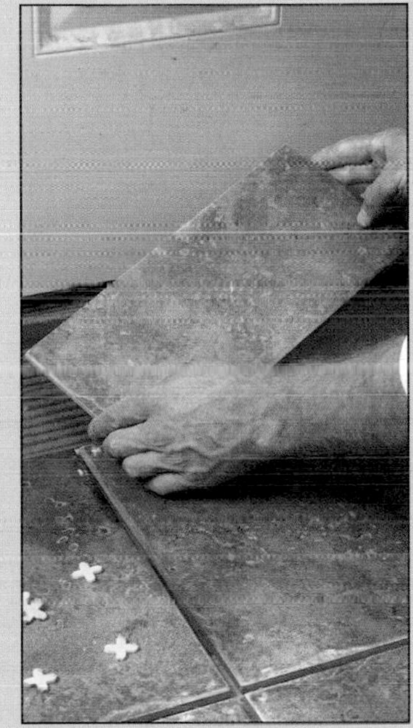

5 When the mortar under the field tiles is dry, cut and set the edge tile *(page 102)*. Round the cut edges with a masonry stone to give them a finished appearance. Clean the joints and caulk the joint at the wall.

6 Let the edge tiles cure before you grout. Force grout into the joint with a grout float, let it set slightly, then scrape the excess off the surface. Clean the grout from the surface and wipe off the haze with rags.

7 If the threshold didn't require installation before the tile, install it now. Cut the threshold to fit the doorway, if necessary, and install it with fasteners recommended by the manufacturer.

Tiling an entry on a wood subfloor

Shore up the joists and the subfloor, if necessary *(page 68)*, and prepare the surface with the same methods used for a slab. Mix enough thinset to allow you to use it within its working time (the time it takes to "skin" over) and trowel it on the floor, smoothing first with the straight edge of a trowel and combing it with the notched edge.

Screw down cement backerboard with the edges centered on the joists, offsetting subsequent joints and spacing the edges ⅛ inch apart. Drive screws into the backerboard on the edges and within the field.

Tape the backerboard joints with 2-inch pregummed tape and spread a thin coat of thinset over the tape.

Don't forget the expansion joint

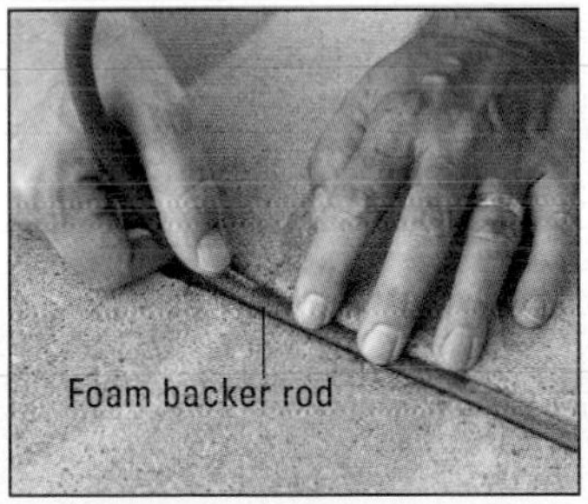

Tile floors expand and contract with changes in temperature. Expansion joints cushion the expansion of tile against the wall and keep the tile from cracking.

An expansion joint is a gap filled with a compressible material and topped off with caulk. Foam backer rod is available in a variety of thicknesses. Purchase backer rod that fits snugly *(page 39)*.

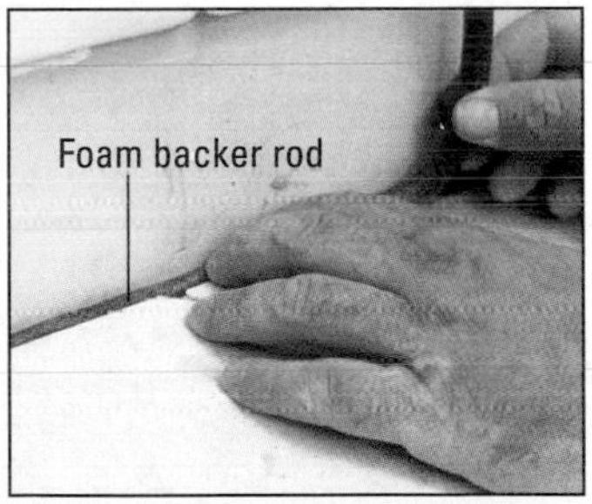

On a slab, insert foam backer rod into any control joints in the field of the slab and also along the perimeter at the wall. Push the backer rod into place with a wide putty knife.

On a tiled wood floor, insert the backer rod into the ¼-inch gap between the cement backerboard and the wall. Finish the joint with caulk colored to match the grout.

TILING A WINDOW RECESS

Tiling a window recess adds a whole new feeling to the design scheme of a room. With the right color, texture, and shape, window tiles provide the effects of a makeover without the costly expense of redecorating. And a tiled window adds a practical dimension as well: Tiles won't rot or stain, and they won't get scratched by cats seeking a sunny refuge.

Choose the color first, then the texture (most often they go hand in hand). A neutral color will cause the window to recede or blend in with the wall. Terra-cotta tiles are a good choice. If you want to call attention to the architecture of the window, use decorative tiles but design judiciously. Too many bright colors and designs can overwhelm a room and defeat the purpose.

If the window is situated on a wall that you're going to tile, the color choice is already made. Use bullnose tiles to round off the edges of the window frame and tile the wall first. That way you can make sure the grout lines of the recess are on the same plane as the wall.

PRESTART CHECKLIST

- ☐ **TIME**
  About four to five hours for a standard 36×40-inch double-hung window
- ☐ **TOOLS**
  Pry bar, hammer, handsaw, margin trowel, notched trowel, grout float, wide putty knife, caulking gun, bucket, sponge
- ☐ **SKILLS**
  Prying, troweling, sanding, setting tile, grouting
- ☐ **PREP**
  Repair structural defects
- ☐ **MATERIALS**
  Joint tape, joint compound, mortar, tile, caulk, sandpaper, spacers, grout, rags, water, nails, fiberglass insulation

1 Remove the window casing with a pry bar and hammer, inserting a piece of scrap wood under the pry bar to keep from damaging the surfaces. Remove the stop molding if the tile will extend all the way to the sash. Remove the sill, cutting it with a handsaw if necessary.

2 Stuff insulation into the gap between the jamb and the wall but don't hinder the movement of the sash weights in an old double-hung unit. If you're tiling the wall, apply fiberglass drywall tape and compound. Feather the compound level with the wall. Let it dry and sand smooth.

WHAT IF... You're painting the wall?

If you plan to paint the wall around the window, fasten metal corner bead to the jamb and trowel on two coats of joint compound. Feather the compound level with the wall. Let each coat dry and sand it smooth.

Create a tiled molding

You can achieve an eye-catching effect with a tiled molding. Pry off the trim and build a molding from milled stock. Make the internal width of the molding ¼-inch larger than the tile. Set the tile in thinset (applied with a margin trowel) or silicone adhesive.

3 Spread and comb thinset on the sill plate and set these tiles before the sides. Then mortar the jambs and set the side tiles, holding them in place with 8d nails *(page 124)*. Pounding nails into hardwood causes tiles to shift, so insert finishing nails in a drill and spin them in. Grout tiles with a float.

4 To create a straight grout line at the edge, install wall tiles flush with the jamb. Then set the ceiling tile in mortar and support it with three boards (battens). To avoid pushing the end tiles too deeply into the mortar, don't force the supports. Let the mortar dry.

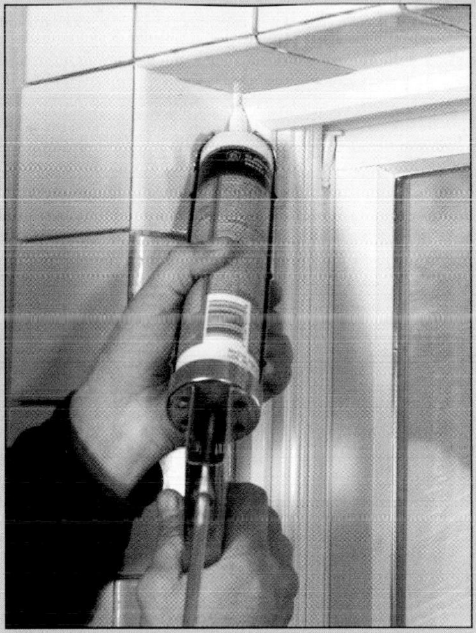

5 Caulk the joint between the tiles and the window to prevent water damage. Choose a caulk that's the same color as the grout and smooth it with a caulking tool or a wet finger.

Edging options

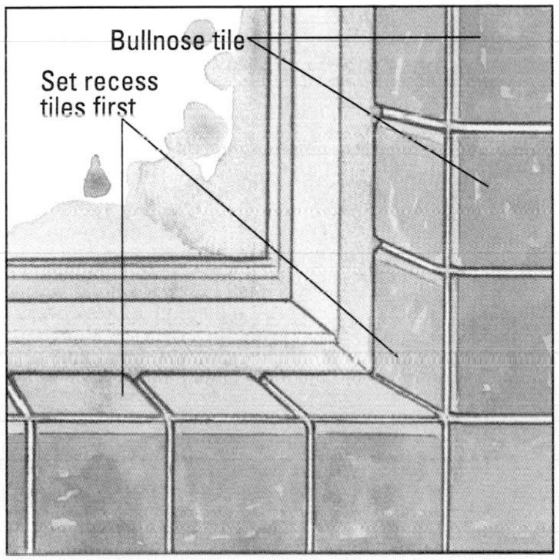

To finish the edge of a tiled window, you have several options other than the one shown at the top of the page. Instead of setting bullnose inside the recess, set it on the wall surface. Set the recess tiles first, then the bullnose.

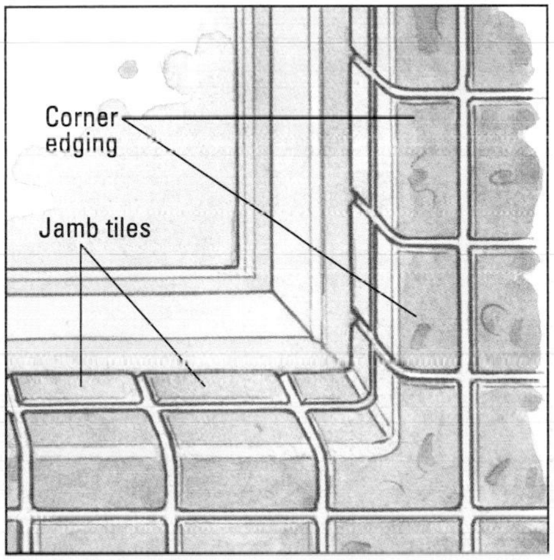

Use corner edging tiles, similar to countertop V-caps (but without the raised lip that forms the front edge of the counter). Mark the wall where the edges of the corners will fall. Set the wall, then the corners, then the jamb tile.

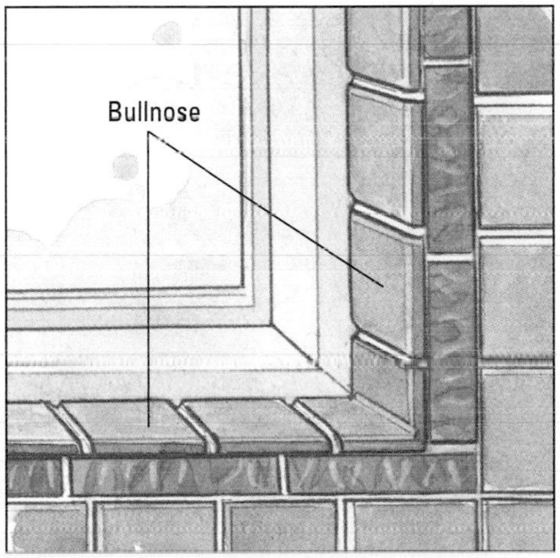

Apply a decorative border strip around the recess with bullnose or rounded field tiles on the jambs. Use bullnose if the border tile does not have a finished edge. Set the wall tiles and border first, then set the jamb tiles.

TILING A FIREPLACE

For a modest cost, tile will alter the look of a fireplace and dramatically improve the overall character of a room.

The major difference in tiling a fireplace compared to other surfaces is the type of mortar required. Use heat-resistant epoxy (up to 400°F) when tiling over wood; use heat-resistant cement-based mortars on masonry surfaces.

If a brick surround and hearth are stable and in good repair, you can tile over them. Clean them thoroughly, removing any soot, which interferes with adhesive, and flatten any high spots with a rubbing stone. Spread a thin coat of heat-resistant mortar over the brick surface, leveling the mortar with a 2×4 set against ½-inch screed boards tacked into the mortar joints on either side of the opening. Let the skim coat dry and use it as a base for the tiles.

If the surface is in poor repair or you don't want to apply a skim coat, cover it with backerboard. Backerboard must be used when applying tile to a metal surround because most metal surrounds are not strong enough to support the weight of tile.

PRESTART CHECKLIST

☐ **TIME**
Surround: four to six hours (not counting prep time); hearth: about three hours

☐ **TOOLS**
Cordless drill, mixing paddle, trowel, tape measure, straightedge, utility knife, snap cutter or wet saw, notched and margin trowels, grout float

☐ **SKILLS**
Installing backerboard, troweling, cutting and setting tile, grouting

☐ **PREP**
Clean the fireplace face; level the surface

☐ **MATERIALS**
Bucket, mortar, tile, spacers, fiberglass tape, grout, rags, sponge, water, backerboard, nails or screws, sealer

Tiling a fireplace surround

1 Measure the dimensions of the surfaces and cut backerboard to fit. Install the backerboard with thinset mortar and self-tapping masonry screws.Tape and finish any joints in the backerboard using fiberglass tape and joint compound *(pages 94–95)*

2 Using your dimensional drawing as a guide, lay out the tile pattern on the floor. Be sure to put spacers between the tiles so the pattern will fit the installation.

DIMENSIONAL DRAWING
Guiding your layout

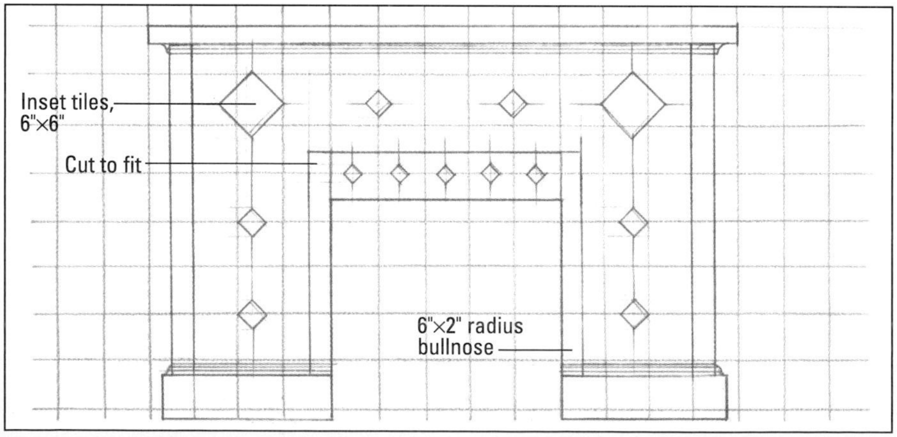

Measure the dimensions of the surface to be tiled and transfer them to graph paper with a ¼-inch rule. Experiment with several designs until you come up with the one you want to pursue. Draw the design to scale using the actual dimensions of the tile, including grout joints. If you find that the dimensions result in unattractive narrow pieces along any of the edges, you may want to use a wider grout joint or larger tile.

3 Place any insets on the field tile and mark their outlines with a china marker. Cut the field tiles and test-fit them in the design. You may have to trim the field tiles to make the design fit and still leave enough room for grout joints. Number the tiles to indicate their location before you pick them up.

4 Set the edges of the opening with trim tiles or bullnose tiles. Keep them straight with a batten. If bullnose is not available for the tile you've chosen, set field tiles and, when the mortar has cured, round the edges with a rubbing stone.

5 Spread and comb mortar for the field tiles. Line up the bottom edges with a metal straightedge and support the tiles with 8d finishing nails driven into the backerboard. Repeat the process for the rest of the rows, setting the insets as you go. Finish setting the tiles and grout them.

WHAT IF...

You're adding tile inside the opening?

If you want to tile the inside edge of the opening, use bullnose tiles and support them with a 2×4 batten until the mortar has cured. Push the "legs" of the batten just hard enough to keep it in place without compressing the tiles into the mortar.

STANLEY PRO TIP

Finish the edges

Instead of tiling up to the edges of the fireplace opening, you can leave the firebox exposed. However, this also leaves the edges of the last row of tiles exposed, a problem that radius bullnose solves quickly.

If a matching bullnose isn't available, grout the inside edge of the tiles and bevel the grout with a margin trowel. Or cut a template in the shape of a curve or other design and pull it through the grout to form a beaded edging.

Tiling a fireplace hearth

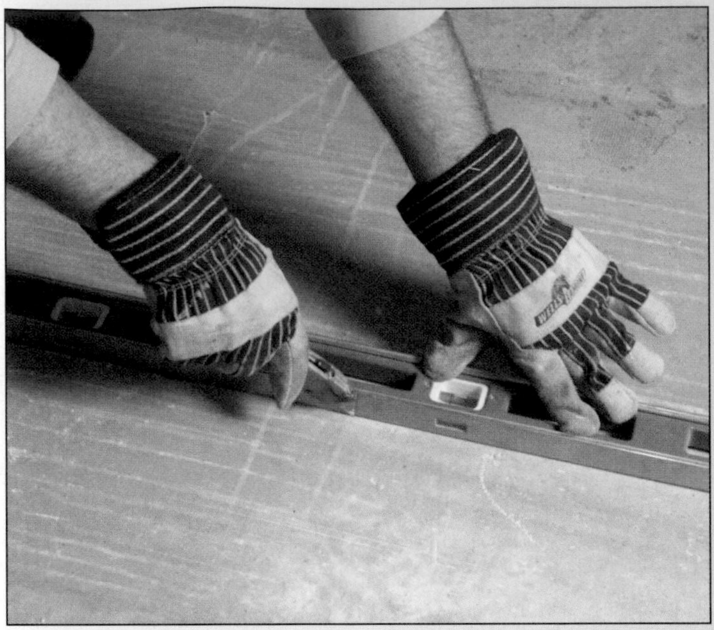

1 Hearths take a beating: A tiled hearth needs a sturdy 1¼-inch setting bed to withstand the shock of dropped logs. Make the bed from backerboard. Cut two strips of backerboard to the finished dimensions of the hearth. Use a carbide knife and a straightedge to cut the board to length *(pages 93–94)* and a circular saw with a masonry blade to notch any corners that have to fit around trim or the outside corners of the fireplace.

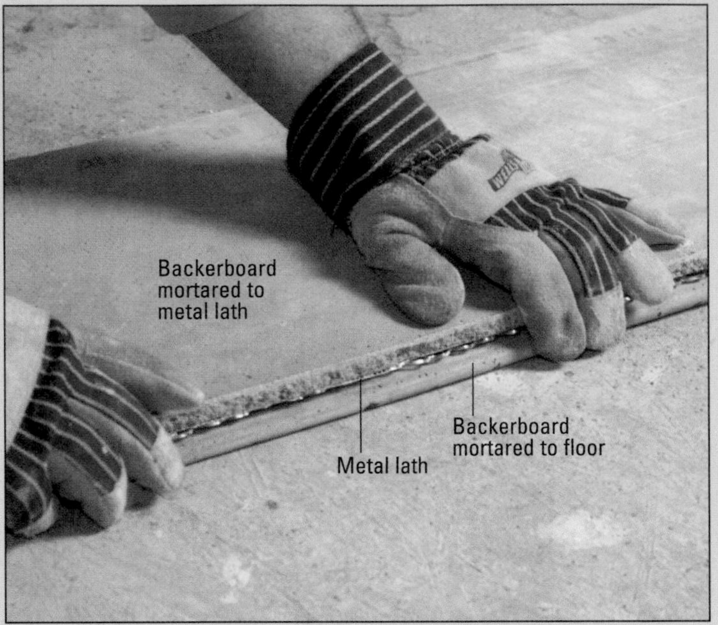

2 Spread heat-resistant mortar on the existing hearth or subfloor and set one piece of backerboard in it. Embed the board in the mortar. Spread mortar on the top of the backerboard and lay metal lath in it. Then apply mortar to the second piece of backerboard and lay it mortared side down on the metal lath. Embed and realign this piece so the corners of both boards are flush with each other. Clean the excess and let the mortar set for 48 hours.

Handle antique tiles carefully

If your hearth has antique tiles, you may want to think twice about replacing them with modern counterparts. Certain antique tiles add value to your home, especially those made around 1900 or earlier and those with high artistic character. You can reset the loose tiles and regrout even those that are cracked. Consider engaging the services of a restoration specialist. Skilled artisans can camouflage the cracks with the right application of tints and paints.

Tile over a hearth
If your hearth is structurally stable, you can tile right over it. Chip out any loose tile and level the surface with mortar.

Abide by codes

Tiling an existing fireplace may not seem to be new construction in your home, but many local building codes will classify this renovation as new construction. You may even have to take out a permit before you do the work.

Building codes are understandably fussy when it comes to anything that concerns fire, so before you choose tile and purchase materials, check with your building code officials. For example, you may have to keep combustible materials, such as the mantel shelf, a specified distance from the firebox. Local codes may also require an inspection of your fireplace to make sure the damper and chimney are in good working condition. If they're not, the addition of a new metal insert may satisfy building code requirements.

STANLEY PRO TIP

Ease the edges

Adding tile to an existing hearth will invariably raise its level above the existing floor. You can install square trim as shown above or apply a more eased edging with coped trim. Curved molding allows for a less abrupt transition between the floor and hearth and is easier to keep clean.

3 Cut and miter wood trim to frame the hearth using the same species as the surrounding floor, if possible. If not, stain and finish the trim to match the floor finish as closely as you can. Fasten the trim to the floor with 8d finishing nails. Countersink the nails and fill the holes with tinted wood filler.

4 Spread and comb heat-resistant mortar on the backerboard bed and, starting along an edge with full tiles, set the tiles in place. Be sure to leave a ¼-inch gap along the wood trim. If your hearth design includes insets, set them as you go—don't wait until you've set all the field tiles.

5 After the mortar has cured (at least overnight), grout the joints with unsanded grout, cleaning the tiles thoroughly to remove the excess grout and haze. Caulk the joint along the trimmed edge and seal the tiles with a penetrating sealer. Apply the sealer liberally. It will help keep the hearth clean.

Maintaining a hearth

Even with the proper bedding, tile is not indestructible. The best maintenance for a hearth is preventive maintenance. Prevent cracked tile by using the hearth carefully. Some tiles stand up to the task of chopping firewood. Others don't. Ceramic and porcelain floor tiles are tough and should be able to take a beating. Saltillo and marble will crack. Marble also stains easily, so keep it well sealed to minimize black marks from sooty wood or thrown embers. Hang a high-quality glass or mesh screen. If a tile does crack, chisel it out and replace it *(pages 224–225)*.

WHAT IF...

You need to expand the hearth?

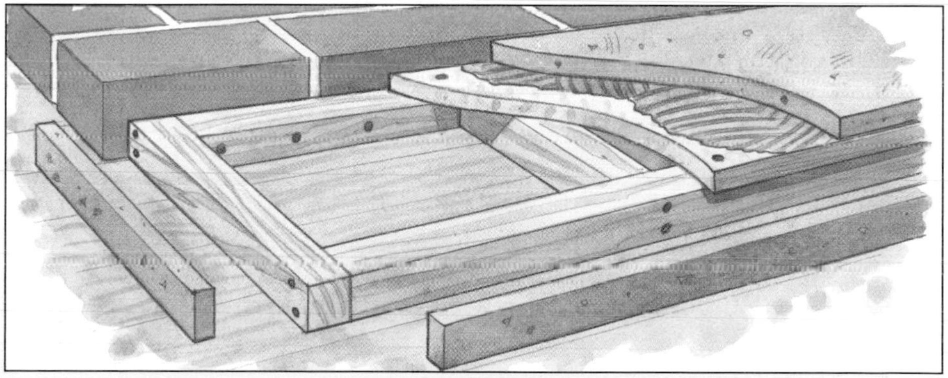

An extension to a hearth must be the same height as the original hearth or the new tile could crack. Measure the height of the existing surface and rip 2× lumber 1¼ inches thinner than that measurement. Adding two sheets of ½ inch cement backerboard and metal lath mortared together will bring the extension level with the original. Locate the floor joists and mark their positions on the floor. Fasten the 2× frame to the floor with screws that penetrate into the joists. Then fasten the first piece of backerboard to the frame, mortar it, embed the metal lath, and fasten the second piece of backerboard.

TILING A STOVE ENCLOSURE

A wood or gas stove brings warmth and a touch of the old-fashioned into a family room or den. If you're considering a stove, decide whether you will treat it as an addition to your design or as a reason to completely redecorate the space.

Your first concern is how and where to vent the unit, followed by aesthetic considerations. Do you want the stove to be housed in a three-sided enclosure or simply set against a wall with a tiled base and rear heat shield? A corner stove installation can fit right into the current design scheme of the room without requiring major alterations.

Using the manufacturer's specifications and any requirements set by local codes, draw a dimensional plan of the stove location. Don't scrimp on the size of the space. Large areas of tile look attractive and are easy to clean—a backdrop and base of about 54 inches is a good place to start. Make sure the floor structure can hold the combined weight of the stove and tiled base.

PRESTART CHECKLIST

☐ **TIME**
Stove base: four to six hours
Heat shield: three to four hours

☐ **TOOLS**
Hammer, tape measure, 4-foot level, stud finder, cordless drill, notched and margin trowels, float, carbide scoring tool, circular saw, snap cutter or wet saw, chalkline

☐ **SKILLS**
Measuring; cutting, setting, grouting tile;

☐ **PREP**
Remove carpet and padding, remove/repair wood flooring

☐ **MATERIALS**
Mortar, backerboard, joint tape, tile, grout, hat channel, strapping, screws, shim, tile spacers, plywood, lumber

Tiling a stove base

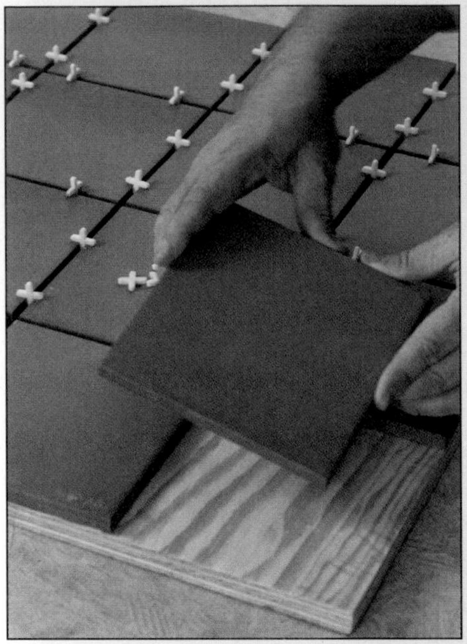

1 Remove carpet *(page 65).* Cut baseboard to leave an opening for the tiled base. If tiling a wood floor, install backerboard and tile *(pages 92–95).* For a raised base, dry-lay tile and spacers on ¾-inch plywood. Cut the plywood to dimensions of a layout that utilizes full-width tiles.

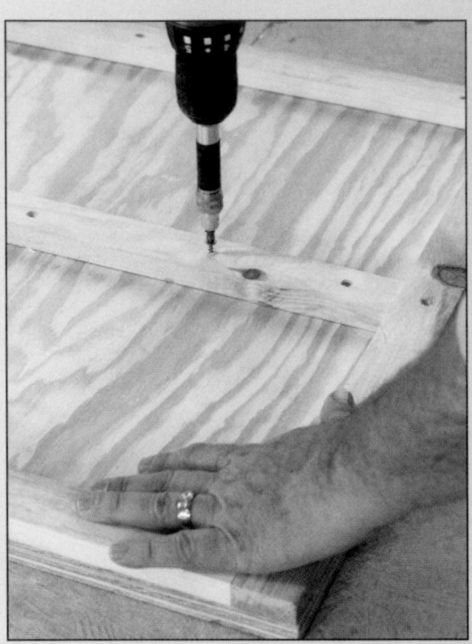

2 Build up the base with 1× or 2× sleepers (depending on the height the platform will be), tacking the sleepers to the plywood every 16 inches on center. Cut backerboard to the exact dimensions of the plywood.

TYPICAL STOVE CLEARANCES

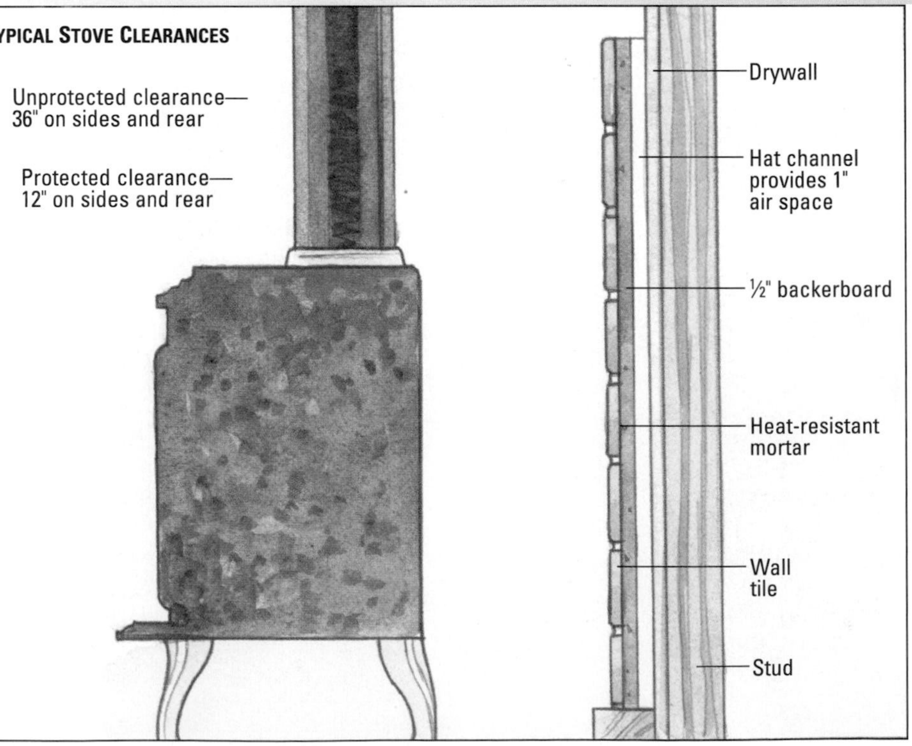

3 Turn the base over and secure the plywood to the sleepers with screws. Then spread and comb heat-resistant mortar on the plywood. Use a ¼×¼-inch notched trowel, taking care to make the mortar bed even and level.

Snap chalk
lines to keep
tiles straight

4 Set the backerboard on the mortared plywood and fasten it with backerboard screws at no more than 8-inch intervals. Tape any joints in the backerboard, fill with compound, and sand. If the layout requires edge tiles, snap chalklines on the backerboard as guides for the tile layout.

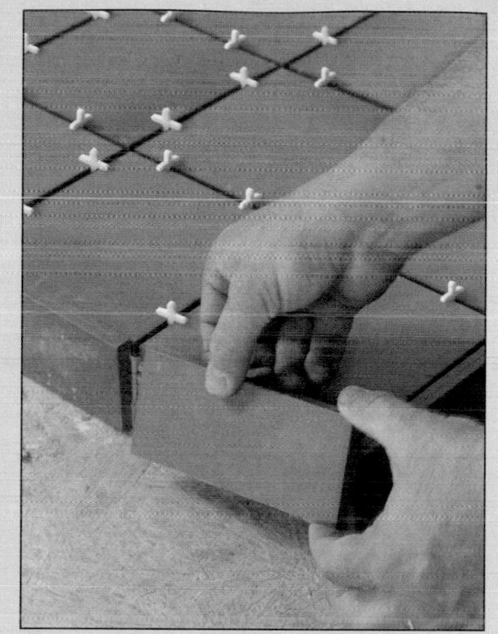

5 Spread and comb mortar on the backerboard to the layout lines. Set the tiles flush with the edges. Begin setting whole tiles in a corner and work outward. If the layout has edge tiles, set field tiles, then edges. Back-butter bullnose or trim tiles for the sides of the platform. Grout the joints.

Moving the base

Even if you assemble your stove base in the same room in which you'll install the stove, you'll need to set the base in its final location once you've finished tiling it. And that means moving it.

A tiled stove base is extremely heavy and moving it will prove next to impossible unless you can get your fingers under it.

To give yourself some clearance and to make moving it easier, slide a stiff putty knife under each end of one side of the platform before setting the tile. That way you can use the putty knives to lift the finished unit enough to give yourself a handhold. Be careful to avoid straining your back: Bend at the knees and enlist the aid of a helper, if possible.

STANLEY PRO TIP

Set the tiles flush

Any tile that's set crookedly on a small surface like a stove base will be obvious. Keep the platform's edge tiles flush by tacking wood strips to the sides of the platform before you spread the mortar and set the tile.

Rip ¼-inch-thick strips from a 2×4. Then use brads to tack the strips to the sides of the platform. The strips needn't be perfectly level, but you will need to extend them above the backerboard by about ½ inch. Remove the strips after the mortar has cured.

Tiling a heat shield

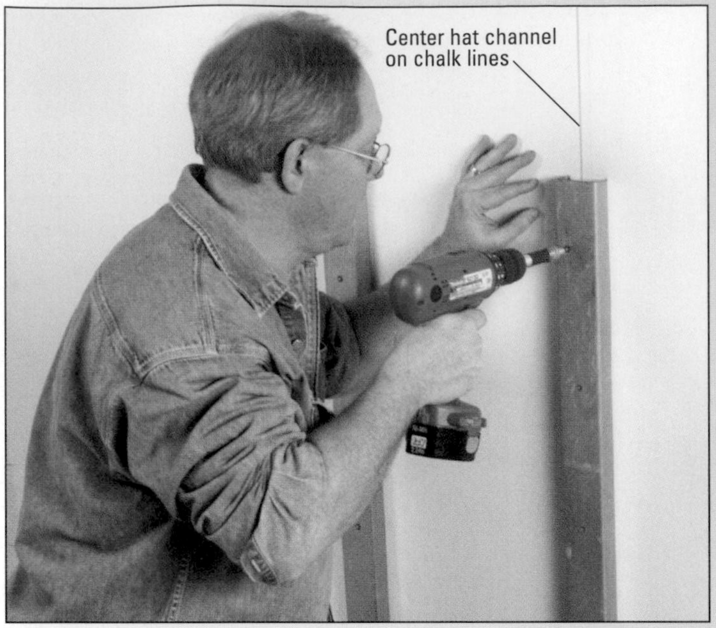
Center hat channel
on chalk lines

1 Building codes require an air space between the tile and a combustible wall surface. Hat channel, light-gauge sheet-metal track, is the ideal material for this purpose (don't use 2×4s). Using a stud finder, locate the centers of the studs and mark them on the wall. Holding a 4-foot level vertically on the mark, extend this center line down the wall. Cut the hat channel to the height of the heat shield and fasten it to the wall with 2½-inch screws.

Mark locations
for fasteners

2 Cut two sheets of backerboard to the dimensions of your heat shield. If you're using a raised tile panel for the stove base, set the backerboard on a shim that's the same thickness as the base. Position the backerboard and mark the hat channel centers on the surface. This will allow you to keep your screws in line toward the bottom of the channel.

SAFETY FIRST
Maintaining a stove

Modern wood-burning stoves are a marvel of efficiency. They burn logs completely and send only a little heat up the chimney. Most models are sold with the appropriate chimney, but if you're installing a secondhand stove, be sure to vent it up a masonry chimney or a class-A metal flue. Clean the flue regularly to remove the creosote that accumulates as a byproduct of burning wood. Creosote can ignite in the chimney and burn through the roof.

No matter how well you maintain it, a wood stove increases the possibility of fire damage in your home and may necessitate a change in your insurance policy and rates. Check with your agent before installing a stove.

Zero-tolerance stoves

Some stove manufacturers offer zero-clearance models, which take up less useable floor space because they require little or no clearance between the firebox and a wall or other combustible material. Although these models reduce the amount of space required and eliminate the dead air space, you still should mount them on a hearth or platform to minimize damage to the floor caused by dropped firewood and sparks.

Get creative
Be creative with a stove base design. Lay out a fan shape, a large circle, or even a tile mural.

WHAT IF...
You want to tile a ceiling?

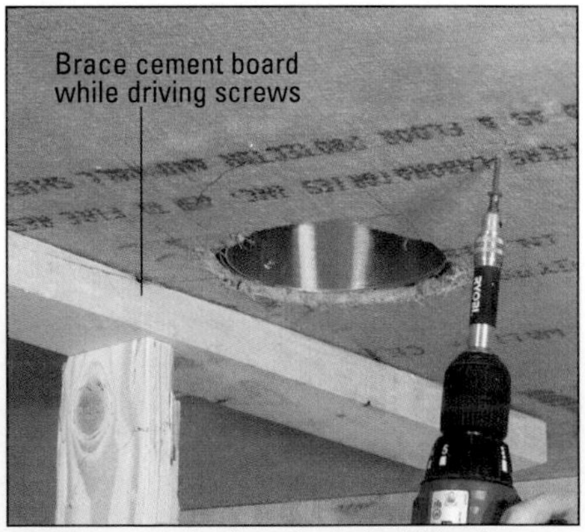
Brace cement board
while driving screws

1 Measure the length and width of the ceiling area, and if the adjoining walls are covered, subtract ¼ inch from this measurement. Cut cement backerboard to fit and with the aid of a helper or brace, fasten the backerboard to the ceiling with backerboard screws.

3 Assemble the two sheets of backerboard with a thin coat of thinset between them. Set the assembly against the hat channel with the edges flush and the marked sheet facing you. Line up the backerboard on the hat channel and fasten it every 4 inches with 1½-inch self-tapping sheet metal screws. Drive the heads flush with the backerboard surface. Tape and finish any joints. Leave the shim in place if you need a guide to keep the first row of tiles straight.

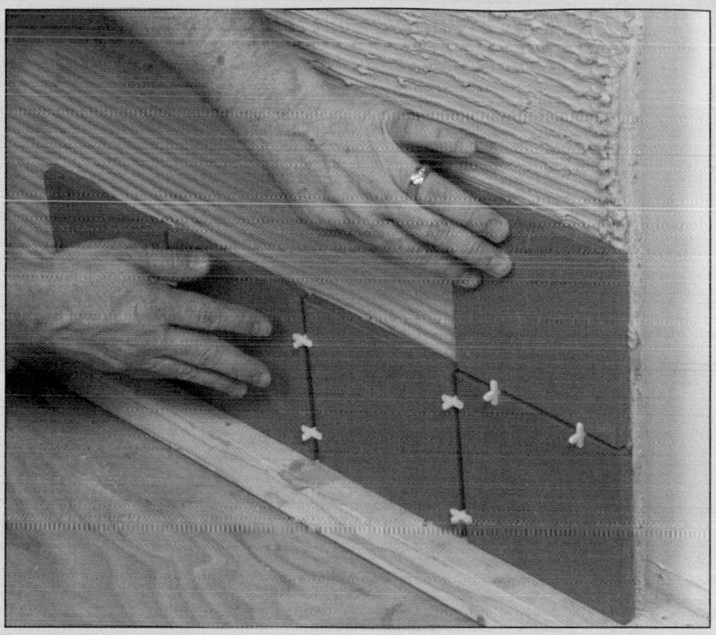

4 If you're installing a stove base, set it in place before you set the wall tile. Spread a coat of heat-resistant epoxy mortar on the backerboard. Set the bottom row of tiles—field tiles first, then the edge tiles, if any—inserting spacers as you go. Hold a piece of 1× lumber against the sides of the heat shield to keep the edge tiles flush. Let the mortar cure for 24 hours, grout the tiles, and remove the bottom shim.

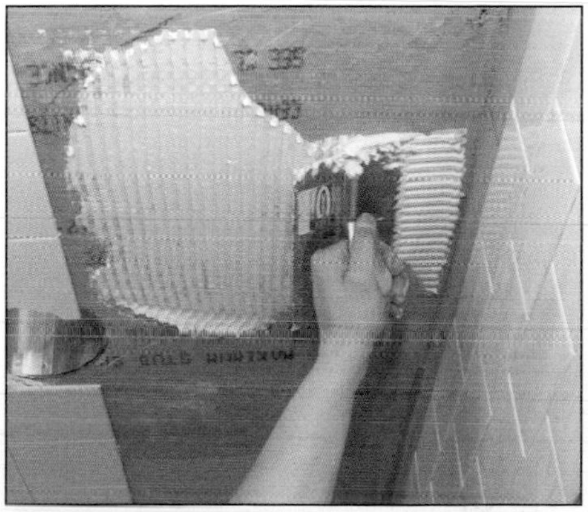

2 Comb thinset mortar on a section of ceiling. Spread thinset only over an area you can tile before the mortar begins to set. For heavy tiles, use a "doadman," a piece of ⅜-inch plywood supported with 2×4s, to keep the tiles in place until the mortar dries.

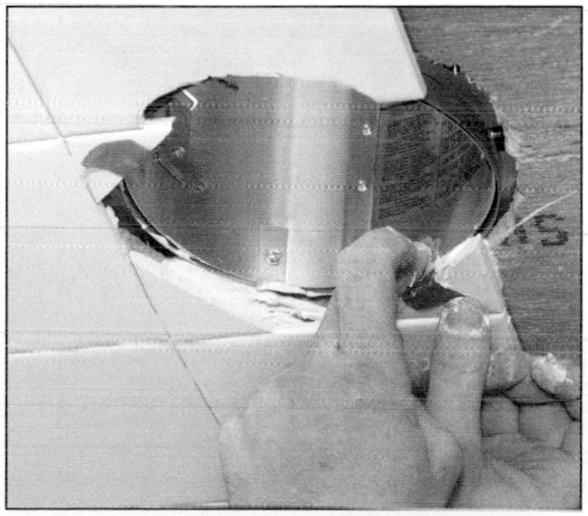

3 Back-butter each tile and set it in the mortar with a slight twist. Working overhead and laying ceiling tile is more difficult and more time-consuming than setting floor or wall tile. Take breaks if necessary to minimize mistakes.

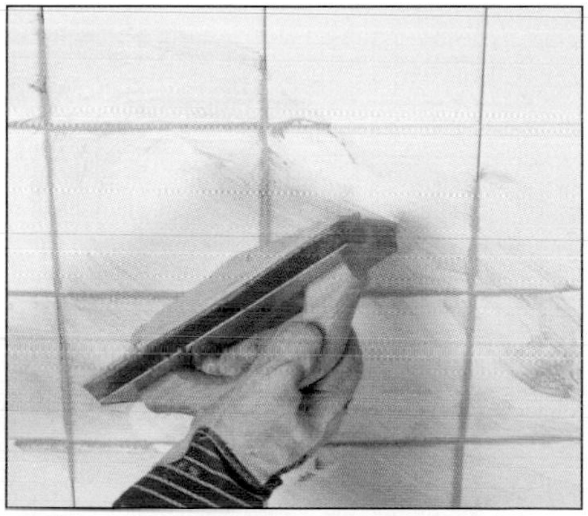

4 After the mortar has cured, grout the tiles with a grout float, applying grout only to an area you can finish and clean before the grout begins to set. Clean off excess grout and remove the haze.

TILING DECORATIVE ACCENTS

If you're at all uncertain about how skillful you are at installing tile, any one of the projects in this chapter can help you get started and develop confidence. While you're busy honing your skills, you'll be creating an object that's both useful and decorative.

These projects range from a few easy tasks, such as tiling a small tabletop or house numbers, to more complex endeavors, such as adding a border to a tiled floor. You can finish many of them in a little over an hour, none will take you more than a weekend, and everything in these pages is very affordable. Even a border need not be expensive if you purchase mesh-backed borders and less expensive field tiles. Let the border carry the design.

If you're looking for a project for the whole family or one that will give you a chance to express your creativity, browse through these pages. There's a good chance you'll find something here.

But don't limit yourself to the projects you see on these pages. The same techniques used to tile a birdbath with homemade mosaics work well with other items: flowerpots, window boxes, outdoor furniture, and mirror frames, to name just a few.

Start small

Like any new activity, learning to install tile seems formidable at first, so start with an easy project and progress to something more complicated.

An old adage about spreading mortar may well have been around since the Egyptians decorated the rooms of the pyramids: "It's all in the wrist." What this age-old saying implies is that successful tiling involves developing a feel for the material and working in a rhythm that is both pleasant and productive. The best way to develop that feel is with practice.

Make yourself some practice pads (2×2-foot pieces of hardboard or similar inexpensive material), purchase some cheap tiles (get "seconds" or anything that's on sale) and mix up a small batch of thinset mortar.

Spread the mortar on the board with the straight edge of the trowel, holding it at the proper angle. Scrape off the mortar and try it again, until you can apply it in a relatively level coat of the appropriate thickness. Then practice combing out the mortar until you get just the right ridges. When you have that step mastered, practice setting the tiles in the mortar with a slight twist. Then check your work by taking up the tiles to make sure their backs are completely covered with mortar. When you feel ready to move on, practice grouting the tiles. In time you'll be ready to tackle all of the projects in this chapter, or for that matter, a floor, wall, or countertop.

You can create accents with tile in less than an hour. Most take less than a weekend.

CHAPTER PREVIEW

Tiling a tabletop
page148

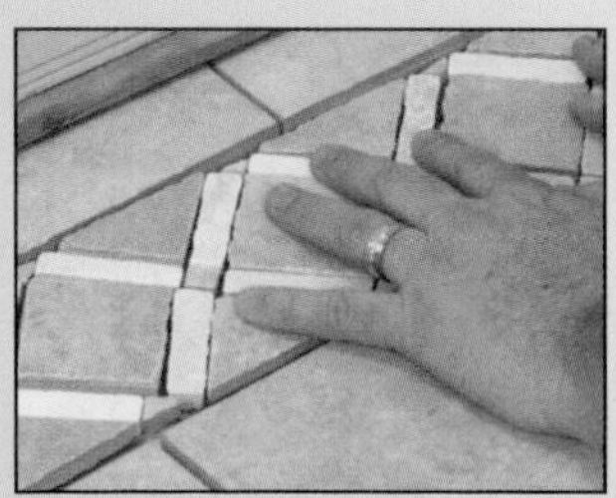

Installing a border and mural panel
page 150

Tiling a birdbath
page 152

Make your own mosaic pieces by breaking and timming tiles of the colors you want.
Use latex-modified thinset and grout for this underwater application.

Transform a plain concrete birdbath into an eye-catching yard ornament with ceramic tile. The same techniques used to make and set mosaic pieces can be used to create other decorative tile projects.

Tiling a precast bench
page 154

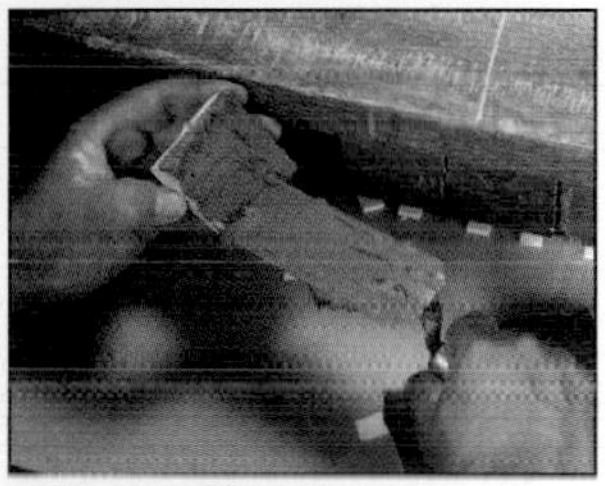

Tiling rails, risers, and rosettes
page 156

TILING A TABLETOP

Before you tackle a full-scale floor, wall, or countertop, you may want to take on a project that gives you a chance to practice each step. Tiling the top of a small table provides this ready-made opportunity.

Here's a surface on which you can carry out tile installation techniques on a small scale: prepping the surface, dry-laying tile, snapping layout and reference lines, applying mortar, and setting and grouting the tile. If the dimensions of the table won't accommodate a setting of full tiles, you can practice cutting edge tiles too.

Tile can add new life to an old table. If the top is a little warped, you can set small tile, which doesn't crack as easily as large tile. If the table is severely warped, sand it with a belt sander first. The tabletop installation shown here uses thinset for the adhesive, but if the table is primarily decorative and won't receive heavy use, use organic mastic as the adhesive.

PRESTART CHECKLIST

- ☐ **TIME**
  About one hour to tile a small table, slightly more if edge tiles are cut; 15 to 20 minutes for tiled house numbers
- ☐ **TOOLS**
  Tabletop tiles: chalkline, framing square, utility knife, margin and notched trowels, grout float, masonry stone
  House numbers: margin trowel, square
- ☐ **SKILLS**
  Snapping precise layout lines, troweling mortar, laying tiles
- ☐ **PREP**
  Clean surfaces
- ☐ **MATERIALS**
  Tile, thinset or mastic, grout, rags, spacers, duct tape

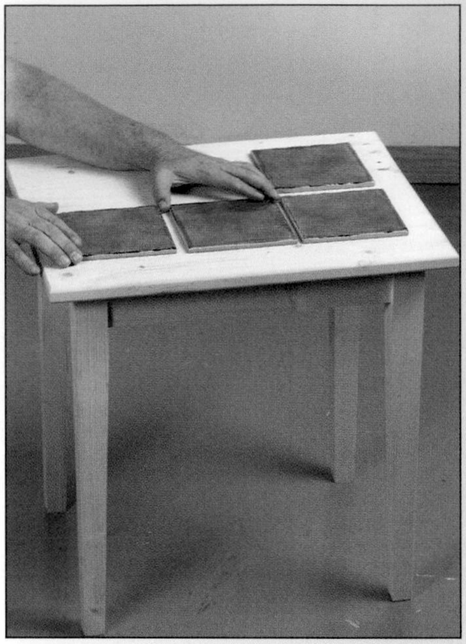

1 Lay one course of tiles without thinset on the table across its width and another course across its length. Adjust the courses to leave at least a half tile at the edges, if possible. Mark the ends of the table at the edges of each row.

2 Remove the dry-laid tile; snap reference lines at the marks on the table. Test the intersection of the lines with the 3-4-5 triangle method *(page 44)* or a framing square. Adjust the lines if necessary to make them perpendicular to each other. Snap additional layout grids if necessary.

REFRESHER COURSE
Mix and spread the thinset

Pour the water into a bucket, then add about half the thinset. Mix the thinset with a ½-inch drill and a paddle designed for mortar. Keep the speed below 300 rpm and the paddle in the mix to avoid adding air. Add thinset a little at a time. Adding the powder to the water a little at a time reduces airborne mortar dust and makes mixing easier. Then mix again to remove lumps. The ideal thinset is about as thick as peanut butter. Let the mix set for 10 minutes before applying. Clean the bed before troweling.

Pour enough mortar to cover a layout grid. Holding the straight edge of the trowel at about a 30-degree angle, spread the mortar evenly, about as thick as the depth of a trowel notch. Spread the mortar to the layout line; comb it with the notched edge at about a 45- to 75-degree angle.

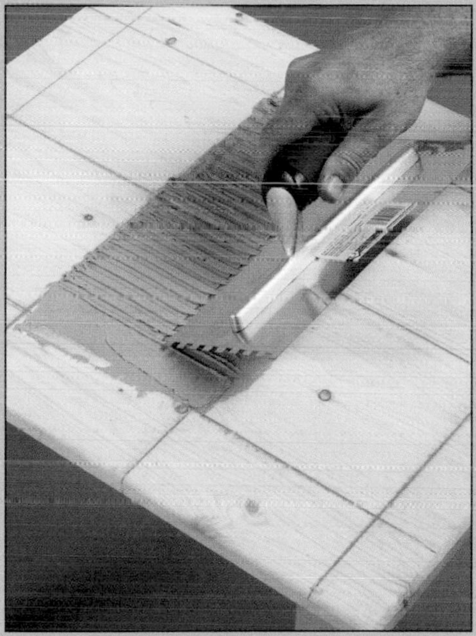

3 Mix enough thinset to cover the table (or a section of it) and pour the mortar on the table. Spread it to an even thickness with the straight edge of a trowel, keeping it along the layout lines. Then use the notched edge to comb the mortar to create ridges.

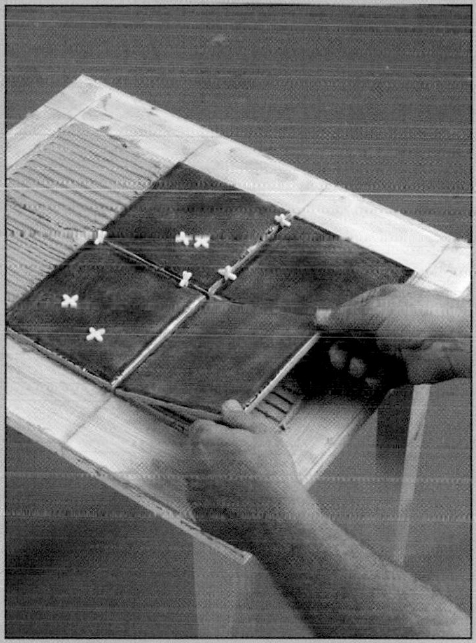

4 Starting at the intersection of a layout grid, lay the field tiles in the pattern of your choice, keeping them on the layout lines and spacing them as you go. Remove excess mortar from joints and let the mortar set up. Measure and cut any edge tiles, rounding the cut edge with a masonry stone.

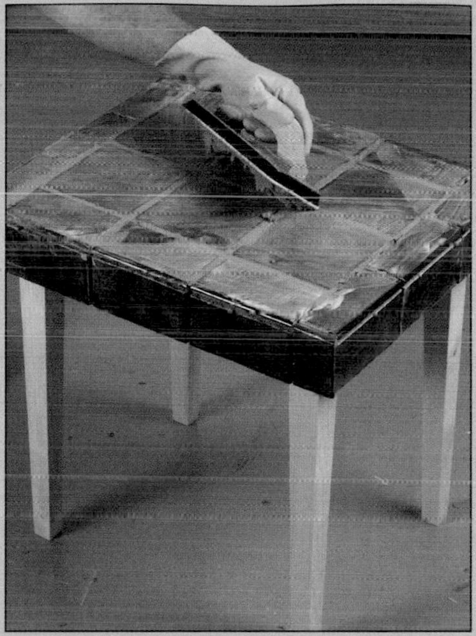

5 When the mortar is dry, set the edge tiles with the factory edge to the outside of the table. Let the mortar cure and force grout into the joints with a grout float. Let the grout set up and scrape the excess off with the float. Clean the tiles at least twice and remove the haze with a soft rag.

Applying tiled house numbers

1 Lay the numbers on a flat surface, spacing them to allow for any joints. Measure the dimensions of the layout. Using a level, mark the outline on the outside house wall.

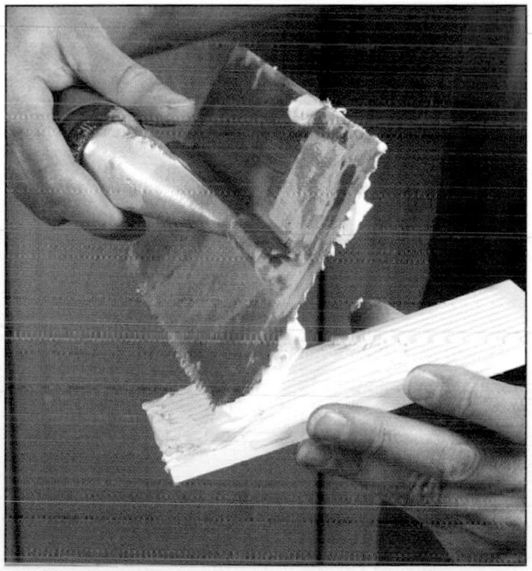

2 On siding, use organic mastic to anchor the tiles. Use thinset on masonry surfaces. In both cases, back-butter the tiles and press them firmly on the surface.

3 As soon as you have applied each tile, tape it in place with duct tape. Let the adhesive cure for at least 12 hours, then remove the tape.

INSTALLING A BORDER AND MURAL PANEL

Borders and murals solve design problems that might otherwise plague a tile installation.

A border emphasizes a floor design, setting off the field tiles from the rest of the floor. Installing a rectangular border around a layout of diagonal field tiles minimizes the effect of cut diagonals on a floor that's severely out of square. For a modest price, you can create a stunning floor design with mesh-backed border sheets and affordable field tile.

A tiled mural panel is common in kitchens, but it can brighten any room. Use an outdoor scene to complement a solid office wall. Cooking scenes or floral designs go well behind a countertop range or behind the food prep area on kitchen backsplash.

Layout is crucial to both borders and murals. Draw a dimensional plan. When planning a border, be sure to allow for the likelihood that the room is not square.

PRESTART CHECKLIST

- ☐ **TIME**
  About eight to ten hours for a border on an 8×10 floor, four to six hours for a mural
- ☐ **TOOLS**
  Tape measure, carbide scorer, chalkline, cordless drill, framing square, china marker, wet saw, beater block, rubber mallet, notched trowel, grout float
- ☐ **SKILLS**
  Measuring, attention to detail, setting tile, grouting
- ☐ **PREP**
  Repair and clean surface to be tiled
- ☐ **MATERIALS**
  Backerboard, tile, mesh-backed border tile, mortar, grout, backerboard screws, joint tape

Installing a border

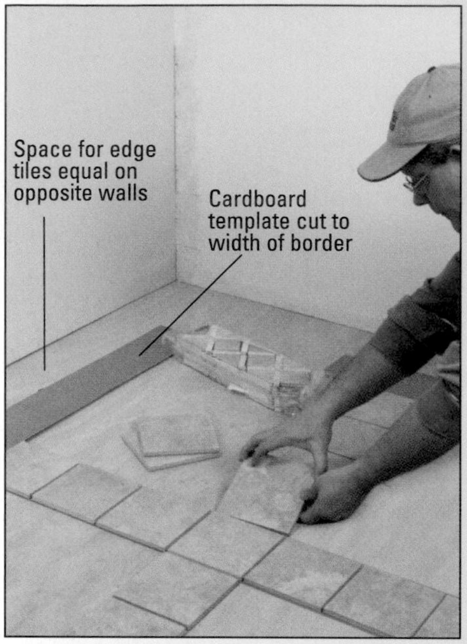

1 Snap chalklines at the midpoints of opposite walls and square them *(pages 96–97)*. Dry-lay tiles on each axis. Insert a cardboard template as a place holder for the border. Adjust the lines until you have space for a half-tile or more along the edges.

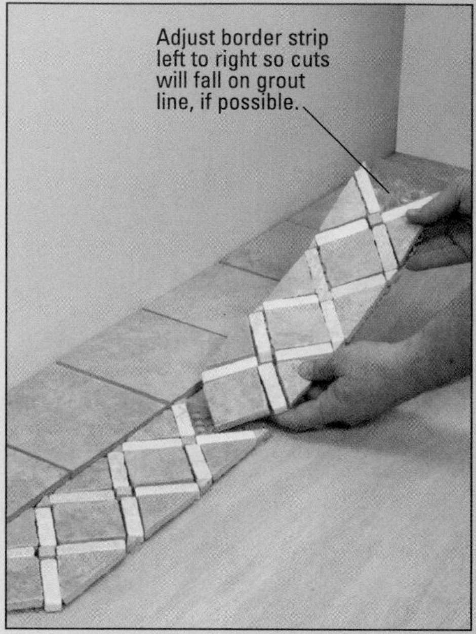

2 Leave the dry-laid tiles in place, and if using mesh-backed border sheets, dry-lay the border. Adjust the border so any cuts you have to make will fall on a grout line, if possible. If using individual border tiles, measure the pattern and determine cut lines using the measurement.

Installing a mural

1 If the mural will be set on a wall in a wet area such as a kitchen or bath, cut backerboard to fit and fasten it to the wall with backerboard screws.

2 If using a wood frame, set the bottom piece along your layout line. If using a listello *(page 29)* or no border, tack a batten along your level line.

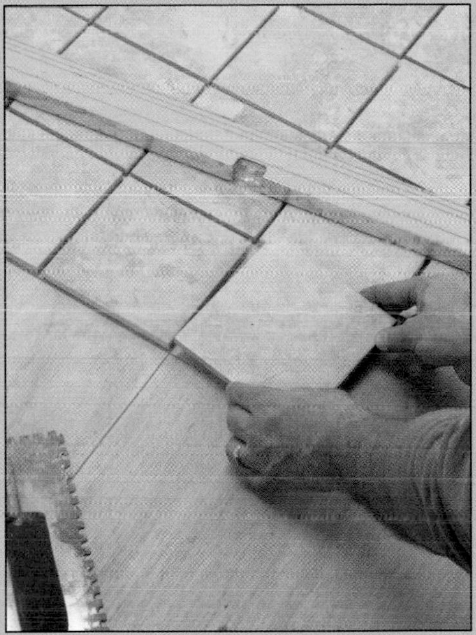

3 Using the quadrant method *(pages 194–197)*, set the tile in two adjacent quadrants, lining up the tiles in each section with a metal straightedge. This will complete the field tiles along one wall. You can lay the field tiles in the remaining quadrants or set the border on each wall separately.

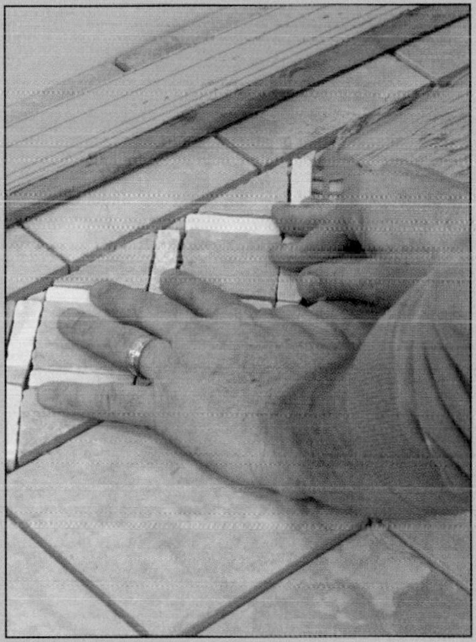

4 Spread mortar for the border and lay it, taking care to space all the pieces evenly, both along the edges and within the field of the border. Embed the tiles with a beater block as you would any mosaic tile *(pages 106–107)*. If you haven't done so already, measure, cut, and set the edge tiles.

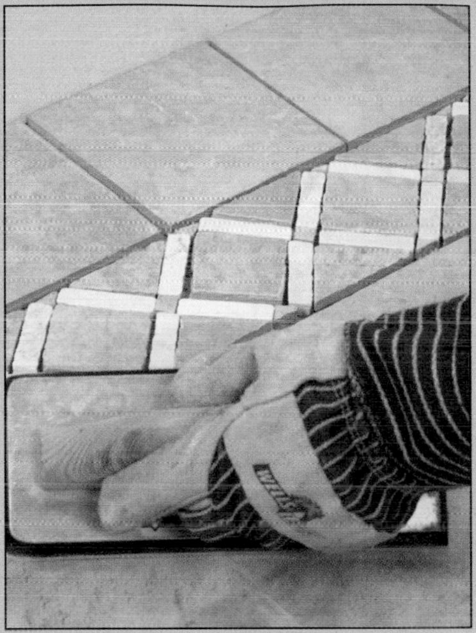

5 Let the mortar cure. Mix just enough grout that you can use before it sets up. Using a grout float, force the grout between the tiles, removing any excess from the surface of the tile as you go. When the grout has set, clean the tile with a dampened sponge and wipe off the remaining haze.

3 Spread and comb thinset mortar on the backerboard, then set the bottom tiles of the mural in the mortar, using a slight twisting motion. Keep the joints tight and adjust the tiles to keep the pattern lined up. It's more important that the pattern is cohesive than that the tiles are set right on the lines.

4 Set the remaining wall tiles, stand back a few feet and make sure the pieces of the pattern are lined up with each other and that the mural is centered in the frame, if you have installed one. Make adjustments as necessary. Grout the tile when the mortar cures and seal the grout if the mural is in a wet area.

TILING A BIRDBATH

A precast concrete birdbath is inexpensive and functional but not very attractive. A handmade mosaic design will transform it into an eye-catching ornament for your backyard.

Birdbaths come in different sizes—the larger the unit, the easier it will be to work with. Get the largest one you can afford.

The decorative tile in the bottom center of the bowl is an optional feature. Shop around at tile outlets or home centers to find one you like.

The mosaics are actually broken pieces of plain glazed wall tile. Choose colors that complement the center tile. Calculate the area of the bowl by multiplying the radius squared times 3.14 and buy twice as much tile. You need this much because breaking the tiles into mosaic results in about 50 percent waste and the area of the bowl is actually larger than the circle it represents.

Purchase 1-inch bead tile for the row around the rim. Lay a string on the rim and measure it to compute the number of bead tiles you'll need.

PRESTART CHECKLIST

☐ **TIME**
About three hours for a 24-inch birdbath

☐ **TOOLS**
Tape measure, rubber mallet, tile nippers, putty knife, notched plastic spreader, rubber spatula, burlap bag or heavy towel, plastic scrub pad

☐ **SKILLS**
Measuring, calculating, mixing mortar, setting tile, grouting

☐ **PREP**
Spray-wash surface of the bowl to remove dust

☐ **MATERIALS**
Decorative tile, 1-inch bead tile, assorted glazed wall tile, latex-modified thinset mortar, latex-modified grout, sealer

1 Set the rim tile first by back-buttering the pieces and pushing them in place. To get the tiles flush with the rim, place a piece of scrap wood on the top edge of the rim and push the tiles up to it. Back-butter the decorative art tile and center it in the bottom of the bowl.

2 Cut the width of a plastic spreader to conform roughly to the contour of the bowl. Then use a hacksaw to cut a few teeth in the edge of the spreader. Comb out latex-modified thinset across the entire surface of the bowl.

How much tile do you need?

The amount of glazed tile you need to purchase is determined by the size and depth of the birdbath bowl. Compute the area of the bowl using the formula for the area of a circle. The area of the bowl will be more than its circle, but you can adjust for that difference (and for waste) by purchasing twice that figure.

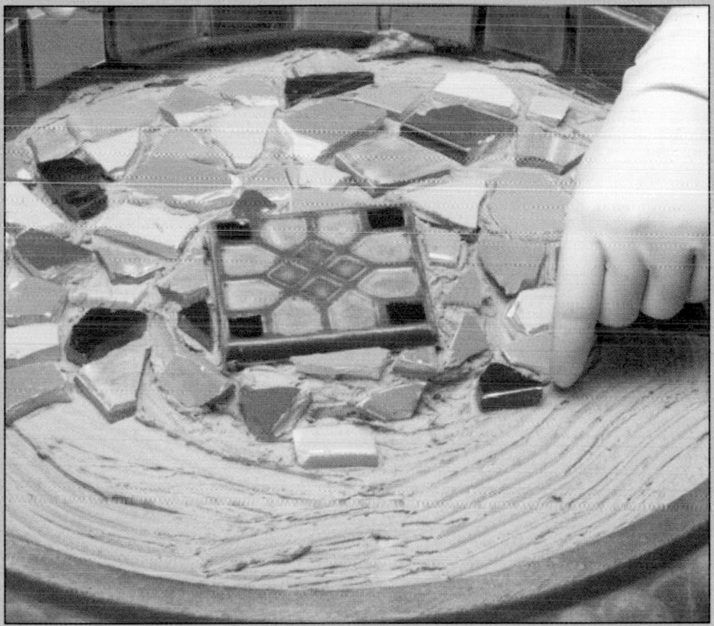

3 If you haven't done so already, tumble your handmade mosaics in a paper bag so different-color pieces mix. Set the mosaics in the mortar, pushing them in place with a margin trowel or putty knife. Make sure the surfaces of the pieces conform to the shape of the bowl and that the edges tilt only slightly, if at all. Try to space the pieces as consistently as possible so the grouting will look regular. Let the mortar dry.

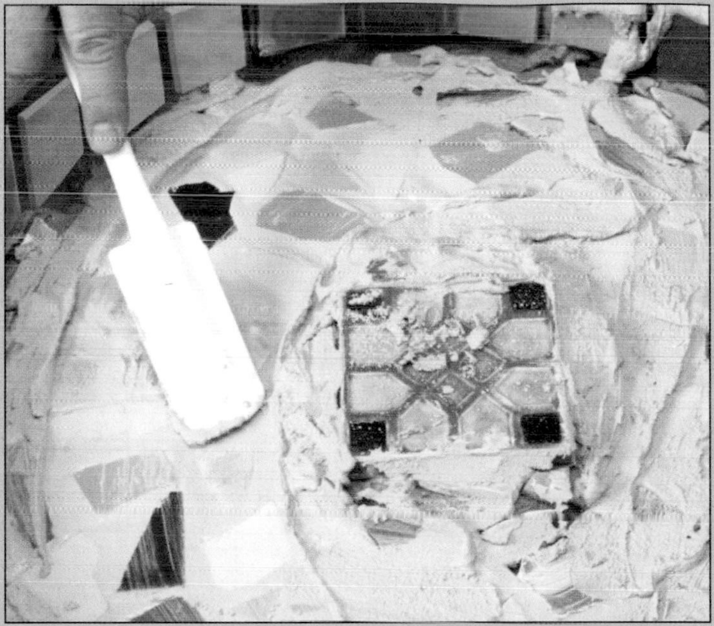

4 Mix up a batch of latex-modified grout and spread it on the mosaics with a rubber kitchen spatula. Force the grout into the joints and remove as much excess as possible from the surface using the spatula. Let the grout set from 5 to 15 minutes, then remove the excess with a slightly dampened sponge. Let the grout set for another 5 to 10 minutes, then sponge it again. When the grout hardens, remove excess with a plastic scrubber.

HANDMADE MOSAICS
Make your own mosaic pieces

1 Place several tiles in a burlap bag or in the folds of a large heavy towel and set the bag on a solid work surface. Pounding the mosaic can leave dents in the surface you work on, so don't use your dining room table. Pound the tile with a rubber or wooden mallet until the pieces are about 1 to 1½ inches at their widest dimension.

2 Pour out the pieces and break another tile in the same fashion. Trim the fragments, if necessary, with tile nippers. When all the tile is broken and trimmed, place the pieces in a paper sack and gently mix them up so that no one color predominates.

TILING A PRECAST BENCH

Garden benches come in many sizes and styles, most of them quite plain. But with just a little investment of time and cash, you can turn an unadorned bench into an attractive backyard accent.

Choose a bench whose style matches other features of your landscape. Most large home centers offer a wide selection with various embossed patterns. Perhaps the simplest of models—those with flat, plain legs—offer the greatest creative potential. Tile the legs in addition to the seat and back of the bench for a contemporary addition to your landscape.

The treatment of the edges affects the amount of time you need to devote to this project. If you select a field tile for which bullnose (for the edges) and down-angle trim tile (for the corners) is available, the job will go more quickly. If you have to set field tile on the edges, you will need to round them with a masonry stone. Squared-off edges invite chipping. If possible, purchase tile that fits the bench seat without cutting.

PRESTART CHECKLIST

☐ **TIME**
Two to four hours, depending on whether you have to round the edges or not

☐ **TOOLS**
Tape measure, rubber mallet, beater block, snap cutter or wet saw, notched spreader, grout float, chalkline, pencil

☐ **SKILLS**
Measuring, mixing mortar and grout, setting tile

☐ **PREP**
Spray-wash the surface to remove dust

☐ **MATERIALS**
Field tile, bullnose tile, down-angle trim tiles, latex-modified thinset mortar, grout, scrub pad, sponge, rags

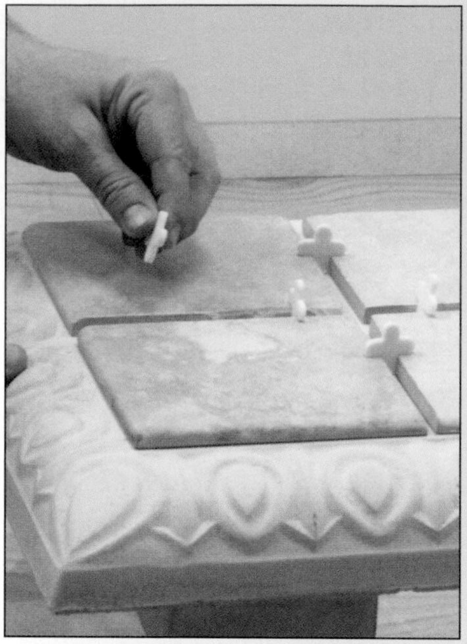

1 Lay out the tile in a dry run, using spacers and covering the entire surface. Center the middle row (if you'll have an odd number of rows) or the middle grout joint (for an even number of rows) on the bench and cut edge tiles if necessary. Place the cut edge facing inward.

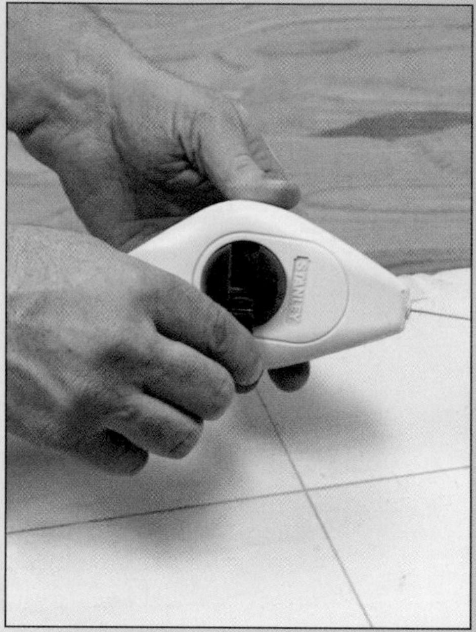

2 Make a mark at the edges of the tiles at each row and at each column of tiles. Remove the tiles and snap chalklines between the points you have marked. Use these lines as a layout grid to guide you when setting the tile.

Precast benches provide comfortable places to sit in your backyard or along a path, while adding a touch of color and texture to the landscape.

3 Comb mortar onto the top with a plastic trowel, but don't hide the layout lines. Set the tiles with a downward twist and embed them with a beater block. Keep the tiles evenly spaced and aligned with spacers or a metal straightedge.

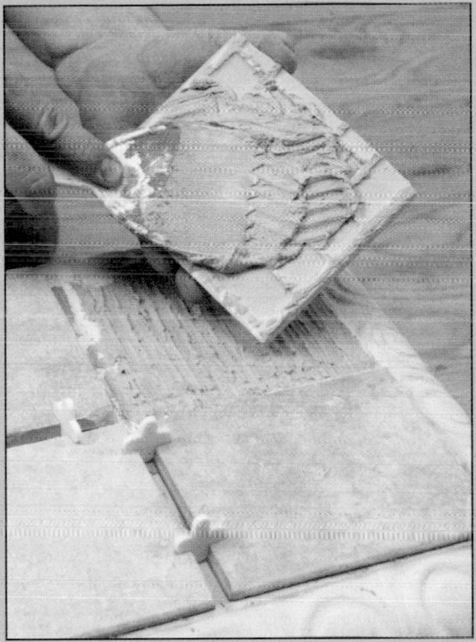

4 Lift every third or fourth tile to make sure their backs are fully covered with mortar. Back-butter the tiles when necessary and reset them. Keep each row level with the rest. Clean out excess mortar from the joints with a matchstick and scrape the excess from the edges.

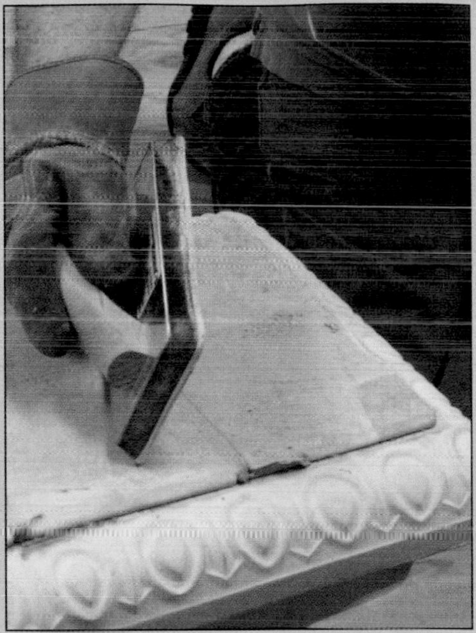

5 After the mortar has cured (overnight), grout the tiles with a latex-modified grout (sanded or unsanded). When the grout is just hard enough that you can dent it with a thumbnail, wipe it with a dampened sponge and remove the haze. Remove stubborn spots with a plastic scrubber.

REFRESHER COURSE

Checking the thinset

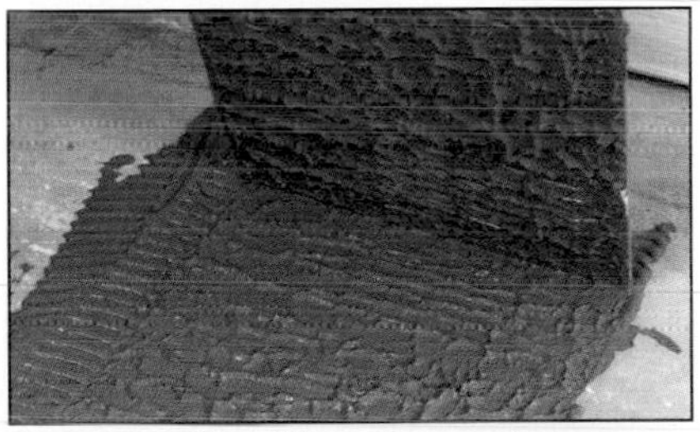

Properly applied thinset forms ridges that compress to cover the entire back of the tile when it is embedded. If thinset is applied too wet, it will not hold these ridges. If it is too dry, it will not compress and will result in the tile adhering to the top of the ridges only.

Test the thinset mixture by pulling up a tile and examining the back. If the thinset completely covers the surface, as shown above, the mixture is correct.

STANLEY PRO TIP

Make a plastic trowel

Make your own custom trowel from a plastic spreader, cutting the notches with a hacksaw and breaking them out with needle-nose pliers.

WHAT IF...

You need to round the edges?

Round the edges after you grout the tiles. Use a masonry stone (available from your tile retailer): Apply the stone to the edge with steady pressure. Use a long stroke and a rolling action to round the edges of the tile in sections.

TILING RAILS, RISERS, AND ROSETTES

Tiling a chair rail, stair risers, or the corners of a window frame are simple, inexpensive projects you can start and finish in a single afternoon.

Because the tile for each of these projects functions as a decorative accent, choose tiles that enhance the overall color scheme of the room. Ask a tile dealer for suggestions if you are having trouble making up your mind.

Each of these projects requires a small amount of preparation. When installing a chair rail on a painted wall, you must roughen the paint a little to give it "tooth" to which the mortar will adhere. The same goes for installing stair risers—sand any finish lightly before spreading the mortar.

If you're installing a chair rail over wallpaper, make sure the paper is bonded tightly. Properly applied latex papers are usually strong enough to hold the weight of tile. Old wheat-pasted papers are not.

PRESTART CHECKLIST

☐ **TIME**
About an hour for every 10 feet of chair rail, two risers, or pair of rosettes

☐ **TOOLS**
Tape measure, 4-foot level, pencil, wet saw, trowel, margin trowel, tablesaw, backsaw, hammer, cordless drill

☐ **SKILLS**
Measuring, leveling, setting tile, basic carpentry

☐ **PREP**
Roughen wall and riser surface

☐ **MATERIALS**
Eighty-grit sandpaper, listello tile, latex-modified thinset, masking tape, lauan plywood, cove molding, brads, drywall screws, tiles, silicon adhesive

Installing a chair rail

1 Mark the wall 36 inches above the floor. Using a 4-foot level, extend this mark in a horizontal line from one end of the wall to the other. This is your layout line. If the wall is painted, use 80-grit sandpaper to roughen the surface of the paint below the line.

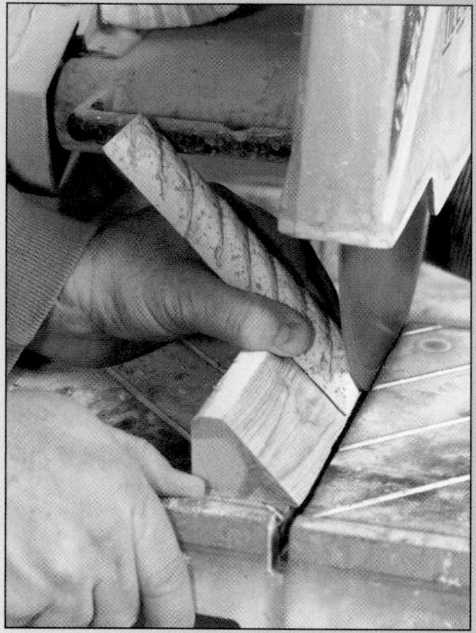

2 Using a scrap piece of 2×4, make a 45-degree cutting jig with a tablesaw. Clamp the jig on the bed of a wet saw and miter two pieces of your tile at 45 degrees. These are the corner pieces and must be at least 6 inches long.

Installing door or window rosettes

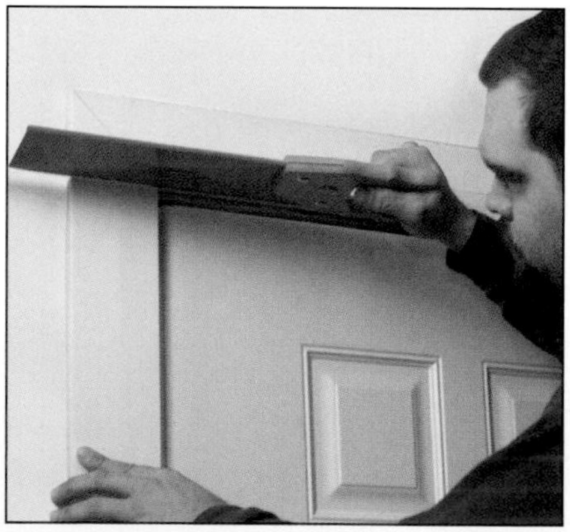

1 Using a combination square, mark the corner of the door or window casing to be cut. Make sure the lines are clear and exactly parallel to the edges of the casing. Cut the corners out with a backsaw. If the cut loosens the remaining top casing, drive 6d finishing nails into the framing.

2 Cut lauan plywood to fit the square corners you have removed. Using the cove molding in the pattern of your choice, construct a four-sided frame for the tile by fastening the the plywood to the molding with brads.

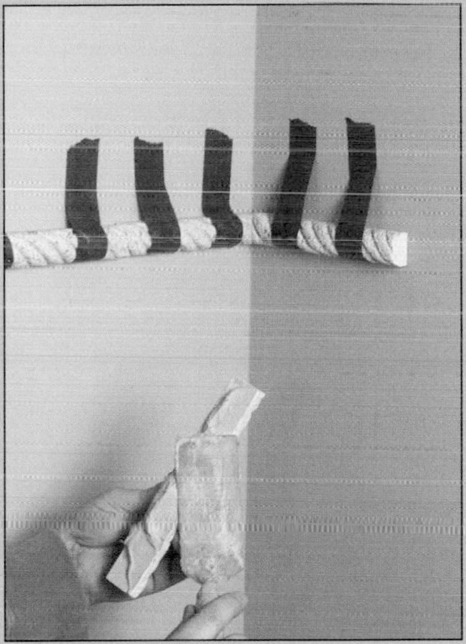

3 Back-butter each section of tile with latex thinset mortar, covering the entire back of the tile. Don't make the coat so thick that it creates excess mortar. Push the tile on the wall exactly on the layout line. Clean off excess mortar immediately. Support the tile with masking tape.

Tiling stairway risers

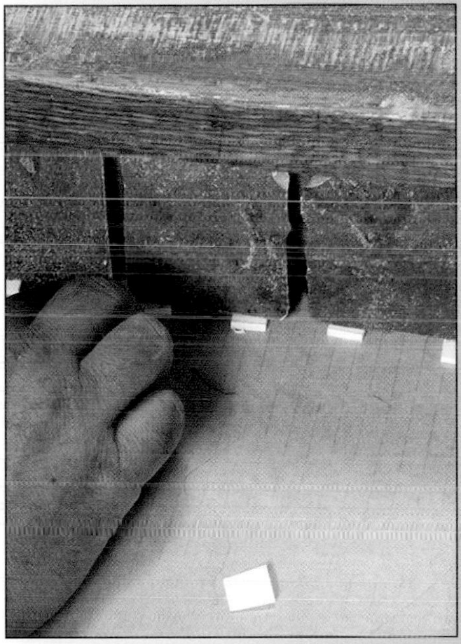

1 It is not necessary to avoid cut tiles on stair risers, but the installation will be easier if you purchase tiles that will cover the riser evenly. Set out the tiles to mark any that must be cut.

2 Back-butter each tile with thinset, about two-thirds the thickness of the tile. Press the tile against the riser. Tape the tiles to hold them till the mortar cures. Grout if using thinset and if appropriate to the tile.

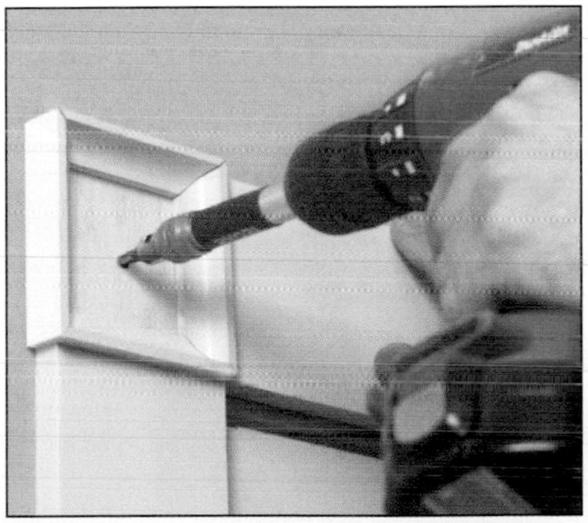

3 Predrill the plywood backing before you attach the tile frames to the recesses. Then drive three or four 1⅝-inch drywall screws through the plywood and drywall, and into the framing behind it.

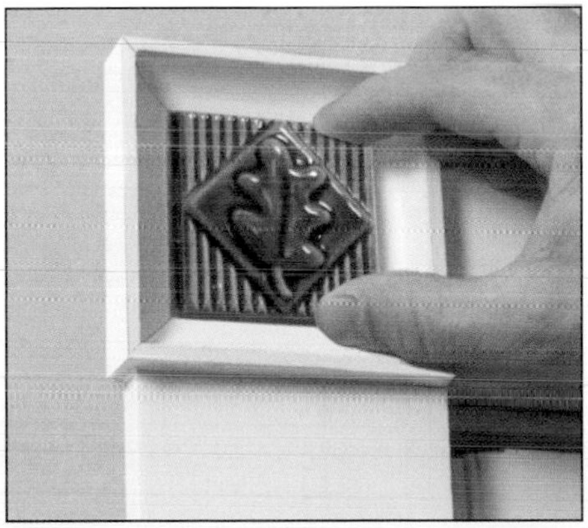

4 Apply a ¼-inch bead of silicone adhesive to the back of the frame (the front surface of the plywood) and press the tile into the recess. Make sure the tile is centered and square with the frame.

STANLEY PRO TIP

Use cut tiles on stair risers

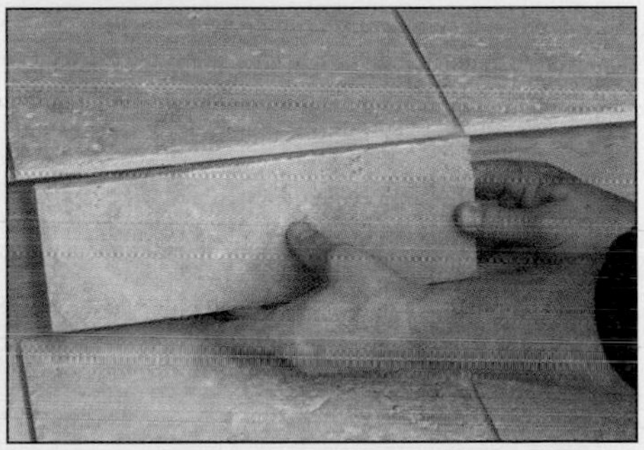

The rise of most indoor stair treads from the top of one tread to the top of the next is about 7 inches, resulting in an actual riser height of between 6 and 6½ inches. If you have to use cut tile to fill the space, install the cut tile at the top of the riser. This way it won't be as visible, and the cut edge will be hidden from view.

TILING BATHROOM FEATURES

All materials used to cover bathroom surfaces have to meet three standards: They must be durable, resistant to water and humidity, and easy to clean. No material does a better job of meeting those criteria than ceramic tile. Tile offers another advantage: Carefully chosen, it will unify the design of the entire room.

Designing your bath

Many homeowners first consider tile as a replacement surface for their bathroom floor or a tub or shower enclosure. But if you're planning to put tile in your bathroom, don't stop there. Think of the tub enclosure or floor as part of an ensemble—the tub, vanity, sink, walls, floor, and fixtures—and experiment with designs for the entire room. Take tile samples home so you can judge their appearance and don't focus too much on single-color themes. A little variety can improve your design. Use accents sparingly—they'll overwhelm a small space.

As you shop for ceramic tile for your bath, think small, at least at first. Tiles four inches or less fit more easily around sinks, tubs, and toilets, and require less cutting. Choose impervious tile, either glazed or unglazed. Glazed tiles on the walls are much easier to clean than those with a matte finish.

Be wary of glazed tiles on floors—they're slippery. Use tiles with a matte finish and seal them with enough sealer that water beads on the surface. Mosaic tiles are great for the floors. Their abundance of grouted joints makes the floor virtually slip-free.

Tiling a bathroom floor

In this chapter, you'll find techniques for tiling almost any bathroom surface except floors. Tiling a bathroom floor relies on the same methods as tiling any other floor. Remove the fixtures *(pages 56–61)* for a better finish that requires less tile cutting. Tiling over existing tile is OK if the surface is sound, but doing so will raise the floor level and may require an extension flange for the toilet *(page 57)*. Dry-lay tiles to test your design before installing them.

Nothing beats ceramic tile for standing up to the rigors of a bathroom installation.

CHAPTER PREVIEW

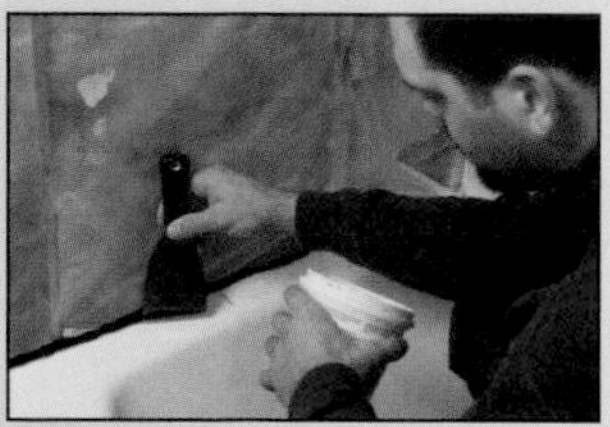

Tiling a shower enclosure or tub surround
page 160

Installing a mortared shower pan
page 164

Tiling a vanity
page 170

A tiled vanity countertop and backsplash, with a new self-rimming sink and faucet are a fairly simple upgrade for any bathroom. You may need to reinforce the base cabinet to handle the additional weight of the substrate and tile.

STANLEY PRO TIP: **Plan for safety bars**

Make tub and shower safety bars an integral part of your plans—not an afterthought. Fasten them securely to the framing.

Wherever possible, mount the flange of a safety bar on a stud, but if the flange will fall between two studs, install 2×6 blocking. Make sure the bars will be centered 33 to 36 inches above the floor.

TILING A SHOWER ENCLOSURE OR TUB SURROUND

Because a shower enclosure is a wet installation, you must waterproof the walls and the framing. Use felt paper with cement backerboard but not with greenboard or waterproofed gypsum board *(page 34).*

A bathtub introduces additional challenges. If the tub is level, set a full tile at its top edge. To help hide the awkward appearance of an out-of-level tub, make the bottom row of tiles at least three-fourths of a tile high.

For a shower enclosure, extend the tile and the backerboard at least 6 inches above the showerhead. For a tub surround only, install the backerboard and tile 12 inches above the tub.

PRESTART CHECKLIST

☐ **TIME**
About 20 minutes per square yard to prepare and set tile

☐ **TOOLS**
Utility knife, stapler, hair dryer, 4-foot level, tape measure, chalkline, carbide scriber, margin trowel, notched trowel, straightedge, drill, snap cutter or wet saw, nippers, grout knife, putty knife, masonry stone, caulk gun, grout float

☐ **SKILLS**
Ability to use hand tools, cordless drill, and trowels

☐ **PREP**
Repair structural defects, remove finished wall material to studs

☐ **MATERIALS**
Asphalt roofing cement, 15-pound felt paper, staples, bucket, thinset, dimensional lumber for battens, backerboard, screws, tape, tile, spacers, caulk, grout, rags, sponge, water, tile base or bullnose, nylon wedges, accessories

A. Preparing the substrate

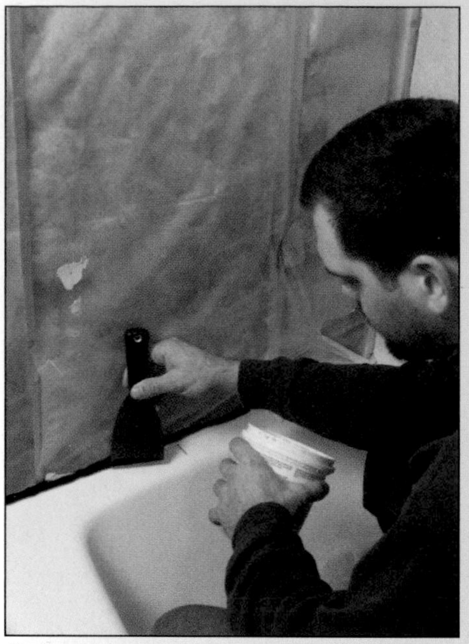

1 Apply asphalt roofing cement to the flange of the tub. This is the place where most tub and shower surrounds fail, and water that gets into this joint will migrate upwards and down into the floor. The asphalt cement seals the tub to the waterproofing felt or 4-mil poly sheet.

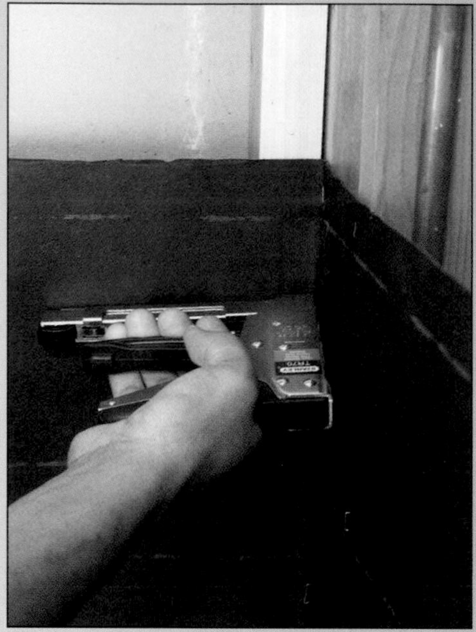

2 Cut a piece of felt paper long enough to turn all corners and cover the surface in a single run. Apply asphalt mastic to the studs, then staple the paper, warming it with a hair dryer before pressing it into the corners. Overlap top pieces on lower ones and seal overlaps with asphalt mastic.

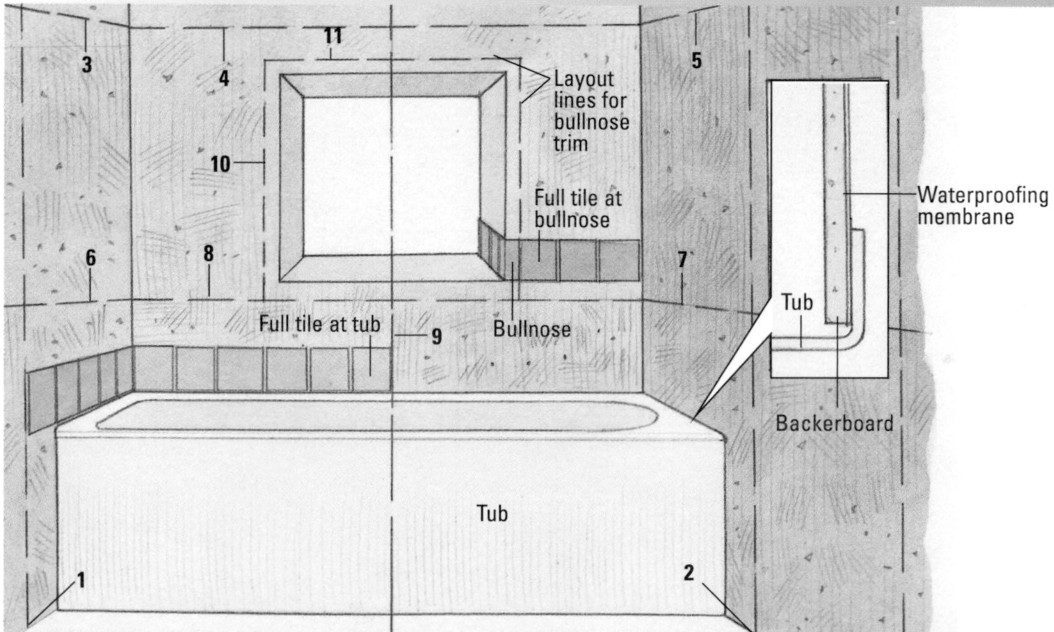

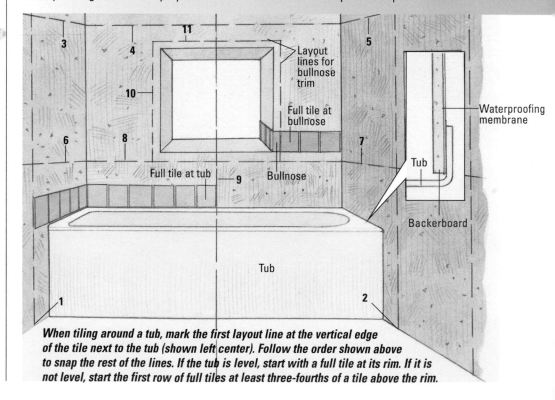

When tiling around a tub, mark the first layout line at the vertical edge of the tile next to the tub (shown left center). Follow the order shown above to snap the rest of the lines. If the tub is level, start with a full tile at its rim. If it is not level, start the first row of full tiles at least three-fourths of a tile above the rim.

3 Cut backerboard so its edges will be centered on the studs and fasten it to the studs with backerboard screws. When fitting backerboard above a tub, leave a ¼-inch gap between the bottom edge of the board and the tub rim.

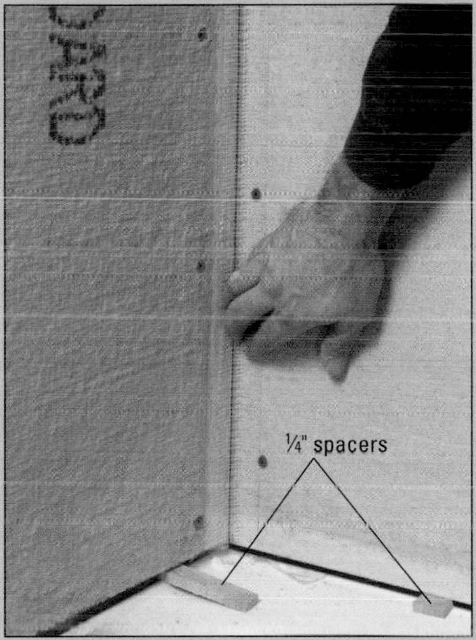

4 Reinforce the corners of the backerboard with fiberglass mesh tape. Skim-coat the tape with thinset, let it dry, and sand smooth. Repeat the process, feathering the edge of the thinset. The spacers create a ¼-inch gap for the bead of caulk.

5 Caulk the gap at the bottom of the backerboard with clear or white silicone caulk. The caulk seals the joint between the tub and backerboard and allows for some expansion and contraction of the different materials.

Installing a prefab shower pan

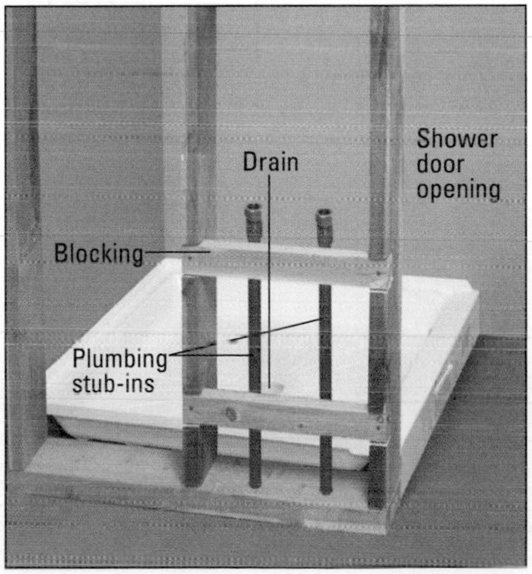

1 Using a dimensional plan for the shower stall, build the 2×4 frame, making sure it's plumb and square to the surrounding walls. Use blocking to support the plumbing stub-ins.

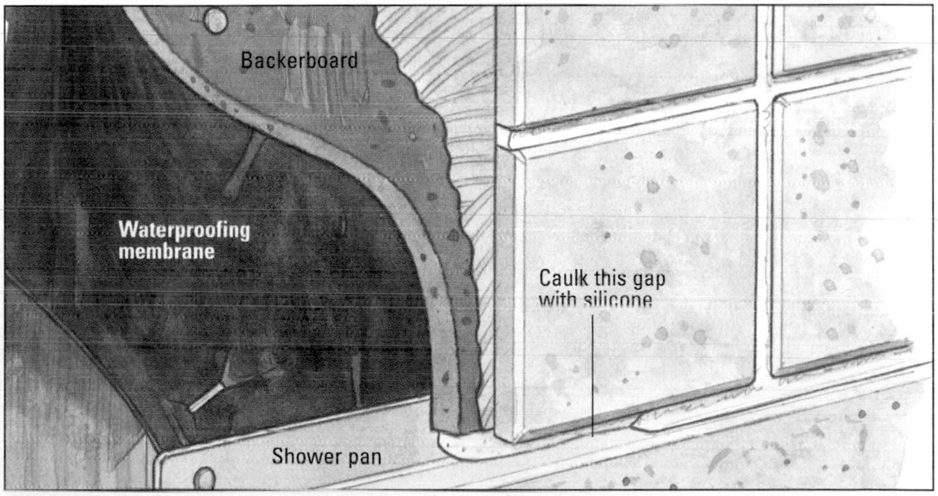

2 Set the pan in place and check it for level in both directions. Attach the drain to the pan and to the drain line and test it for leaks by pouring buckets of water down the drain. Most pans have a flange that fits tightly against the wall. Install the backerboard ¼-inch above the flange and caulk the joint with silicone caulk.

B. Installing the tile

1 Using a dimensional layout drawing, locate the point on which a horizontal and vertical grout line will fall. Hold a 4-foot level on both planes and mark reference lines. Then snap layout grids whose dimensions equal the width of the tiles and grout joints.

2 Tack a batten on the bottom of the wall, if necessary *(page 124)* and prepare enough adhesive to cover the number of layout grids you can lay before the adhesive begins to set up. Set field tiles on the back wall first. Don't set tiles around fixtures yet.

3 When the back wall is done, set the side walls. Start from the front, leaving cut tiles for the back edge at the corner of the adjoining wall. Tape the tiles if necessary to hold them in place *(page 124)*. Remove excess adhesive from the joints; let it cure.

STANLEY PRO TIP

Cut the corners

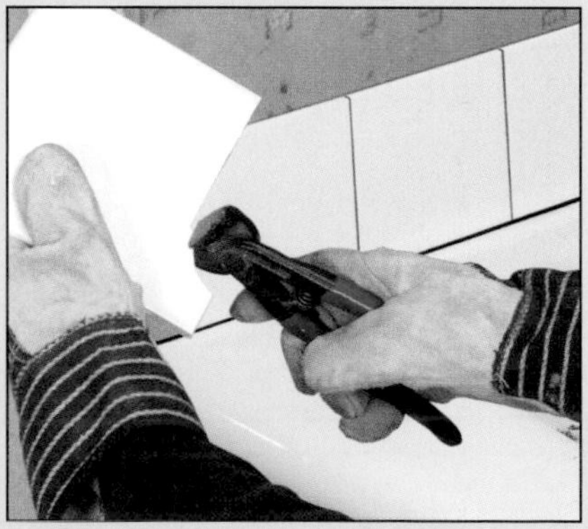

Cut the tile at the corner of the tub carefully. This cut can be somewhat tricky, so it's best to lay out the curve on a cardboard template and transfer the line to the tile. Make relief cuts and bite out the curve with nippers.

TACK A BATTEN

Keeping the tiles level

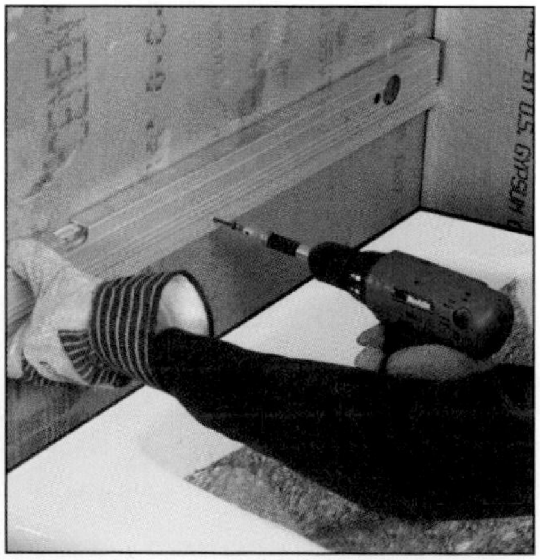

To keep the first row (and all that follow) level, tack a 1× batten to the backerboard one full tile width above the tub. Cover the tub with heavy paper to protect it from damage it might incur as you tile the wall.

REFRESHER COURSE

Measure the thread length

If you are tiling over existing wall tile or installing new tile with backerboard, the combined thickness of the new materials may exceed the length of the threads on the faucet valves. The threads of the valves need to extend beyond the new wall.

Before you install any tile, measure the depth of the threads. If they are less than the thickness of the new materials, you'll have to install new faucets—a job best left to a plumber.

4 When the adhesive has dried overnight, cut and set the edge tiles and remove excess adhesive from the joints. Then mark, cut, and install the tile around the showerhead and faucets. Leave at least ¼ inch around the fixtures and fill that recess with silicone caulk. Let the adhesive cure.

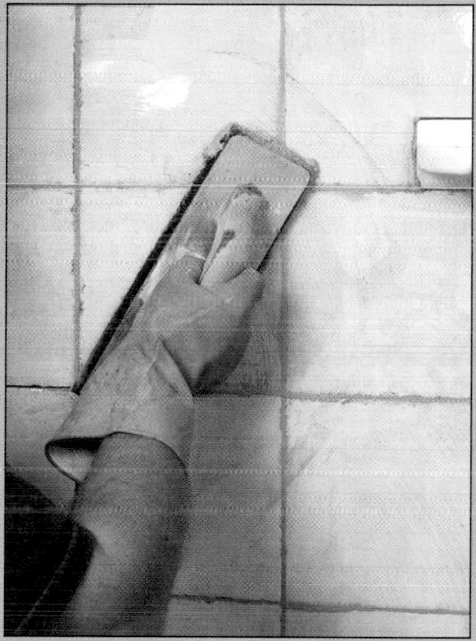

5 When the adhesive is dry, clean the surface and joints of any remaining excess. Mix grout and apply it with a grout float, forcing it into the joints in both planes. Let the grout cure until a damp sponge won't lift the grout out of the joints.

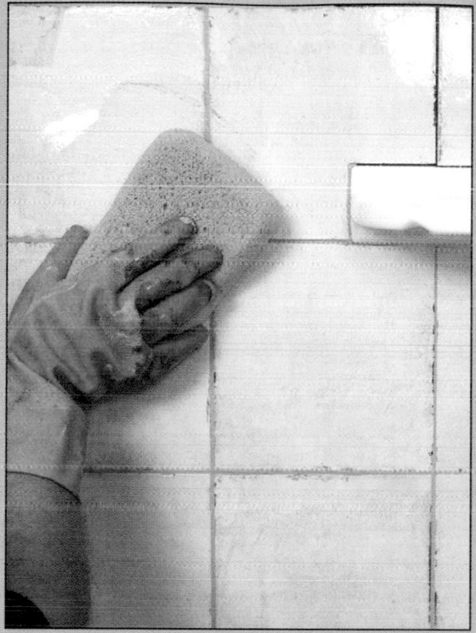

6 To scrape excess grout off the surface, hold the float almost perpendicular to the tile and work diagonally to avoid pulling the grout from the joints. Dampen a sponge, wring it out thoroughly, and clean the surface twice, smoothing the joints. Scrub off the haze with a clean rag.

Framing a shower bench

1 Make sure your plan for a bench includes exact dimensions. Measure each framing member before cutting and fastening it. Mistakes in shower stalls are certain to leak. Frame the rear wall of the bench first, then each front wall.

2 Cover all the framing with a waterproof membrane and backerboard. Caulk all seams with silicone. Tile the seat surfaces first, followed by the wall tile. Use bullnose for the edges or round the field tile with a masonry stone.

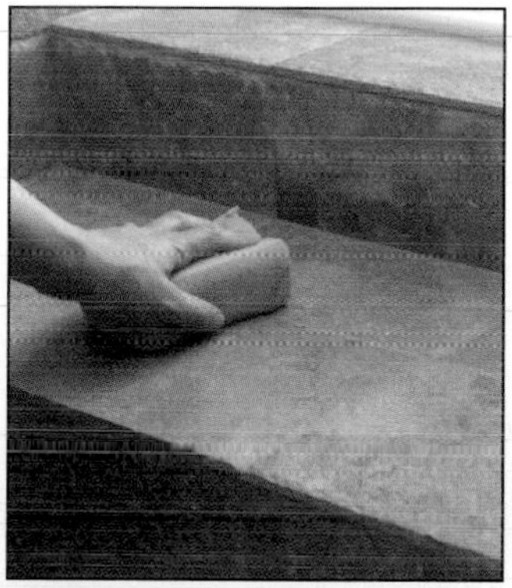

3 When the mortar has cured, grout the joints and clean the tile. When the grout has cured, seal the grout lines.

Installing surface-mounted fixtures

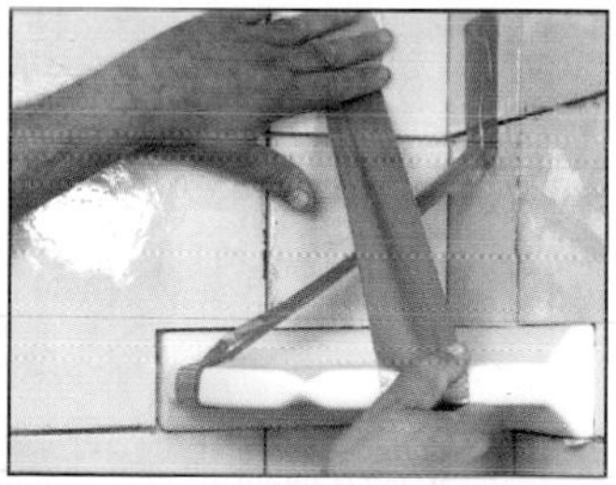

When you set the wall surface, leave a space for surface-mounted accessories, such as soap dishes, cutting the tile around it if necessary. Use a margin trowel to apply mortar to both the recess and the back of the accessory and press the unit into place. Keep it centered with wedges. Tape it in place until the mortar dries, then caulk the joint.

INSTALLING A MORTARED SHOWER PAN

A mortared shower pan allows you to custom-fit a shower enclosure. The key to a successful installation lies in the use of a chlorinated polyethylene (CPE) or PVC membrane, tough but flexible plastics that form the pan of the enclosure and make the floor waterproof. Over the membrane, a mortar bed floor supports the tile. Smaller tiles work best to conform to the slope.

This thick-bed installation relies on a troweled mortar mix, which when properly mixed is like a sandy clay. Floating a thick bed takes two steps: floating the sloped sub-base for the membrane and floating a reinforced top floor that follows the slope of the sub-base. Because of its considerable weight, you should install it only on a slab or properly supported wood subfloor.

PRESTART CHECKLIST

☐ **TIME**
Two to three days to frame the enclosure, float the floor, and tile and grout the interior

☐ **TOOLS**
Carpenter's hammer, framing square, tape measure, 4-foot level, carbide scorer, utility knife, wrench, scissors, tinsnips, stapler, ½-inch drill, mixing paddle, notched trowel, grout float, jigsaw, marker, circular saw

☐ **SKILLS**
Basic framing skills, mixing and floating mortar, setting tile, grouting

☐ **PREP**
Strengthen and repair subfloor

☐ **MATERIALS**
Dimensional lumber, ¾-inch exterior plywood, backerboard, backerboard screws, dry mortar mix, metal lath, felt, staples, 4-mil polyethylene, thinset, CPE or PVC membrane and solvent, nails, masking tape, shower drain, tile, grout

A. Framing the stall

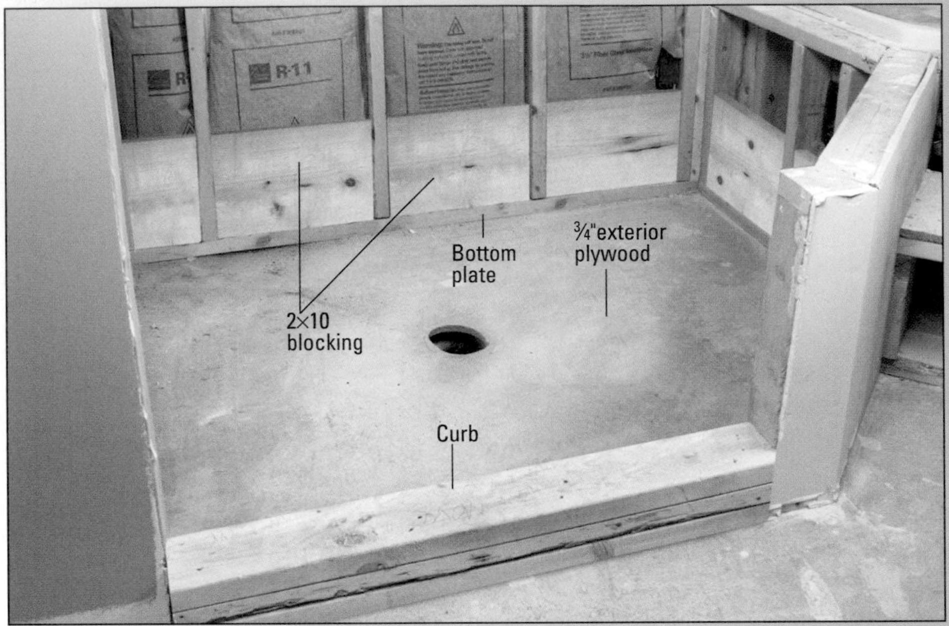

Replace an unsound subfloor with ¾-inch exterior plywood. Cut pressure-treated bottom plates and pre-assemble the walls, centering the studs every 16 inches. Erect and brace the walls. Fasten the bottom plates to the floor with 3-inch decking screws and tie the top corners together. Toenail 2×10 blocking between the studs to support the sides of the membrane. Build the curb from three pressure-treated 2×4s. Tack ¾-inch guides around the perimeter (not necessary for stalls larger than 4 feet on both sides). Cut a hole in the center of the floor and fit the lower drain plate.

FIT THE LOWER DRAIN PLATE
Seal the drain to prevent leaks

1 Cut a hole in the floor with a hole saw or jigsaw (drilling a starter hole first). Coat the bottom of the lower drain with beads of silicone—one outside and one inside the bolt circle.

2 Coat the interior of the drain with PVC primer and cement and twist the drain onto the waste line. Let the cement dry and insert the drain bolts into the lower drain plate, leaving about ¾-inch exposed.

B. Building the sloped sub-base

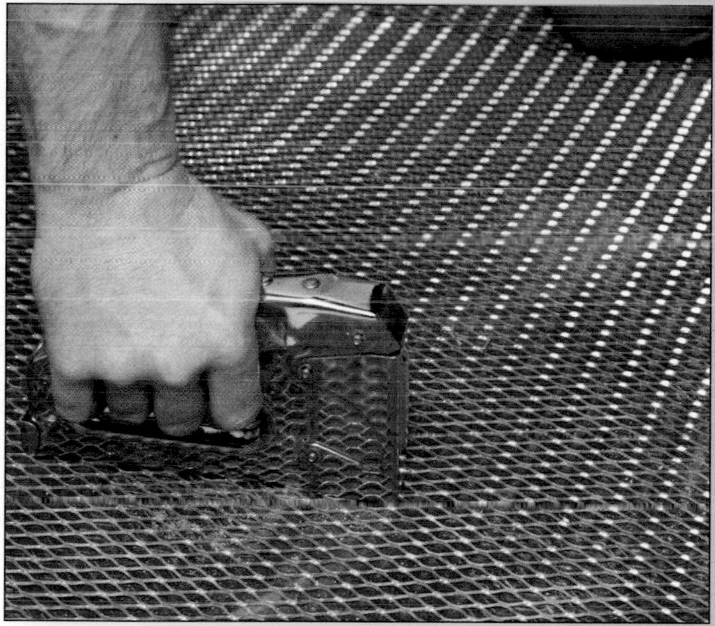

1 Cut a piece of 15-pound felt to fit the floor area between the bottom plates or the ¾-inch float guides and staple the felt to the floor. Cut a section of metal lath to the same dimensions. The metal gives the floor a "tooth" for the mortar. Set the metal lath in place and snip out a circle about an inch wider than the circumference of the drain. Staple the entire sheet of metal lath securely to the floor, flattening any bumps which could weaken the sub-base.

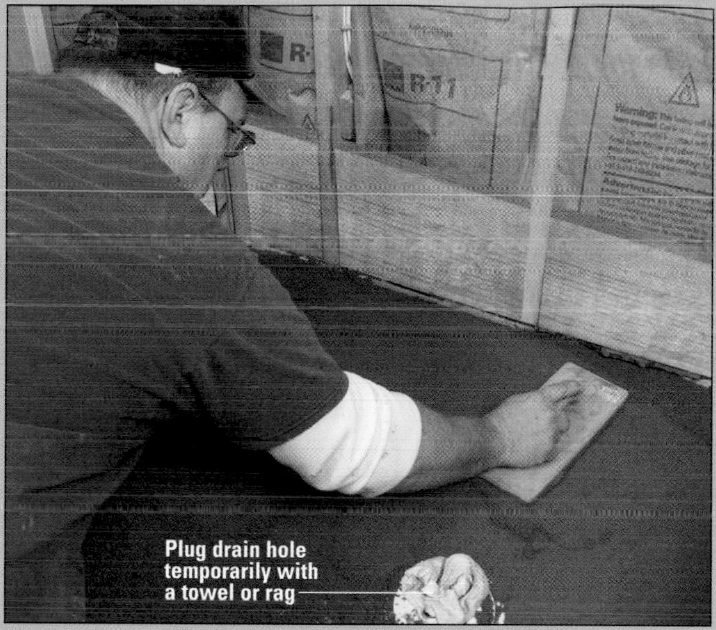
Plug drain hole temporarily with a towel or rag

2 Using bagged sand mix from your home center (or 4 parts sand, 1 part portland cement), mix up a batch of dry deck mud with latex additive (not water). Mix the mortar in a wheelbarrow (not a bucket). Dump the mortar onto the floor, spreading it with a wood float and sloping it from the top of the guides (or the bottom wall plate on larger stalls) to the top of the drain flange. Compact the mortar into an even surface and let it dry overnight.

WHAT IF...
You want to install a mortared shower bench?

1 Spread mortar on the shower pan and set concrete block in the mortar. Plumb and level the block. Mortar the side pieces in place and repeat the process for the next course(s) of block. Then spread a level coat of thinset on the surfaces to be tiled.

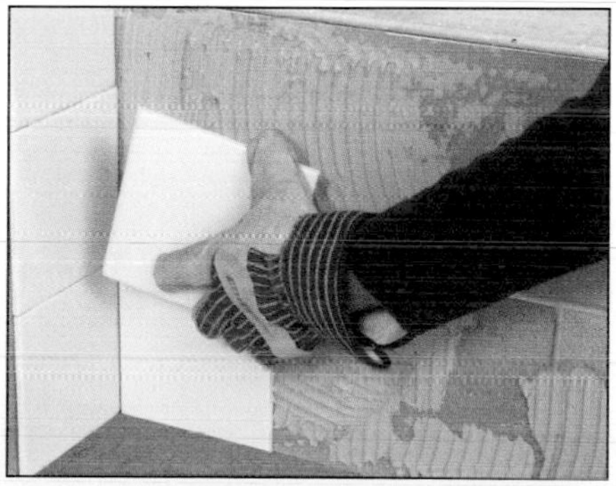

2 Tile the bench as you would a wall, lining up the courses on the front of the bench with the courses on the walls. Finish tiling the shower and grout the entire installation. Seal the grout with the product recommended by the manufacturer.

DRY DECK MUD
The squeeze test

The mortar for a shower enclosure should be just wet enough to clump together. You'll know it's right when you squeeze it and it just holds its shape.

C. Installing the membrane and upper drain plate

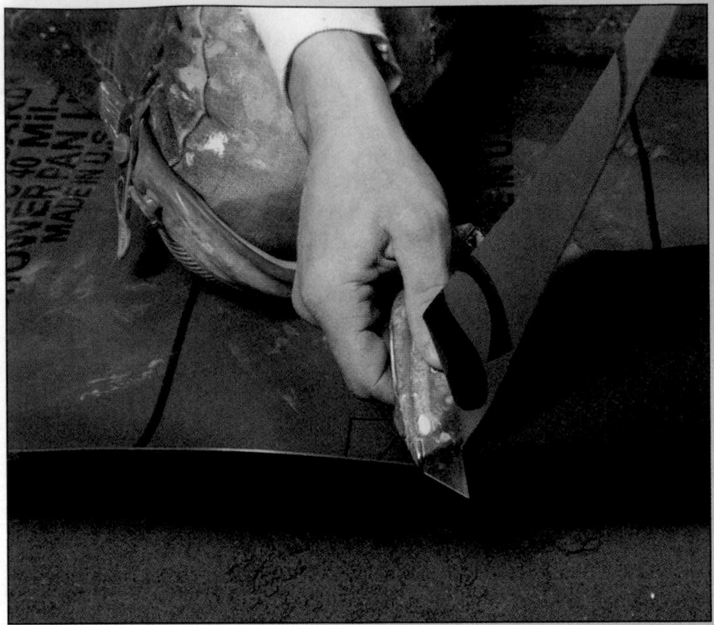

1 Roll out the membrane on the surrounding floor. Mark the cut lines 9 inches larger than the shower floor on the sides and back, and 16 inches larger in the front (to cover all faces of the curb). If the stall is larger than the membrane, solvent-weld additional sections. Reinforce the drain area by solvent-welding a 10-inch circle of membrane in the center, folding the edges, and rolling or folding the membrane so it fits easily in the enclosure.

2 Set the membrane on the floor of the enclosure and unroll it from front to back, pulling it forward until it covers the front of the curb. Working from the drain outward, smooth out the air bubbles. Then staple the top 1 inch of the sheet to the blocking. Weld the corners and cut the sheet at the bottom of the jambs. Fold the sheet over the curb and tack it only on the front. Solvent-weld a dam corner (available from the manufacturer) over the jamb cuts.

STANLEY PRO TIP

Keep the membrane flat

Shower pan membranes must lie flat on the sub-base and against the sides. Wrinkles create air pockets that weaken the bed. It can be difficult to keep the membrane flat on the sloped sub-base, especially in large enclosures. To keep the membrane flat as you smooth out the air bubbles, trowel on a thin coat of asphalt mastic or laminating adhesive on the sub-base and blocking. Make sure the adhesive you use is compatible with the membrane material.

WHAT IF...

You need to add another section of membrane?

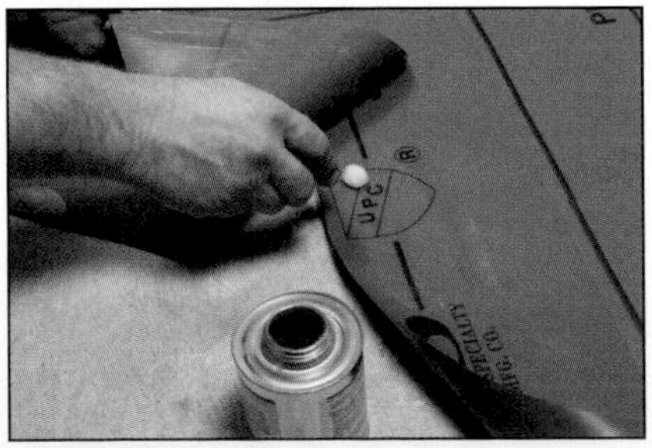

If the shower enclosure is larger than the CPE or PVC sheet, you will need to seam an additional section. Coat both sides of the seam with the primer or sealer appropriate to the material, covering about 4 inches from the edges. Let the primer dry. Overlap the edges and roll them tightly. After 5 minutes, try to separate the seam. If it comes apart, repeat the process.

WELD THE CORNERS

Make the membrane watertight

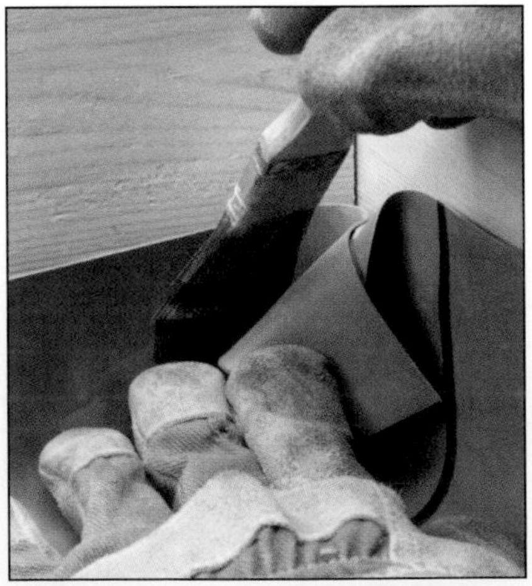

After stapling the membrane along its length, you will have excess material at the corners. Fold the corners into triangles and solvent-weld the folds in place.

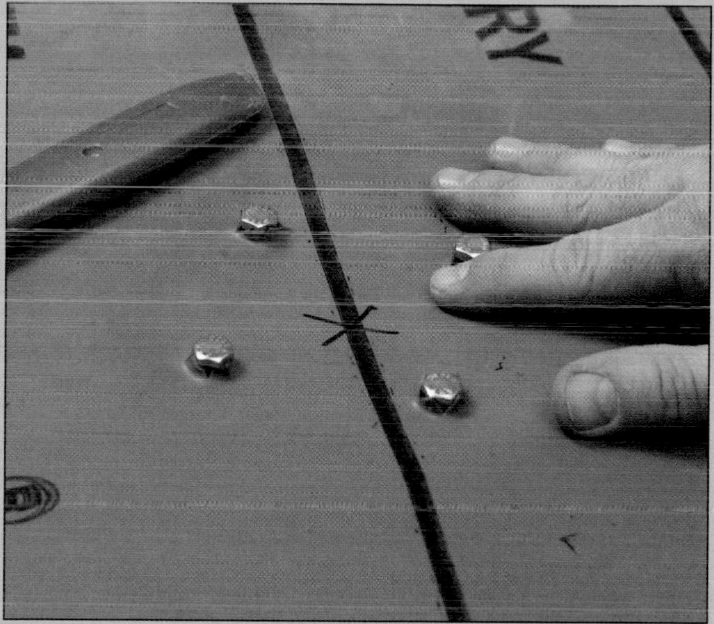

3 To cut the membrane so the bolts will be exposed, feel around each raised bolt head and press the membrane down until the profile of the bolt shows clearly. Then with a sharp utility knife, cut a ⅜-inch "X" in the membrane over the bolts—just enough to allow you to push the membrane over the bolt head. Then unscrew the bolts so you can fasten the upper drain plate.

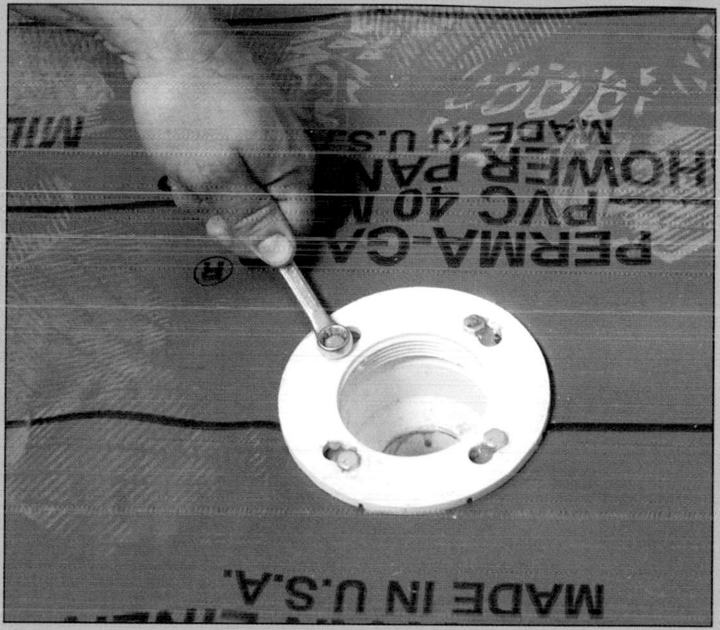

4 Position the upper drain plate so the holes are directly above the X-cuts in the membrane. Don't seal the underside of this plate with silicone—it will clog the weep holes. Reinsert the bolts in the holes, turn the plate to lock it, if necessary, and tighten the bolts evenly with a wrench. Using a long sharp knife, carefully cut away the membrane in the drain hole. (Don't use a utility knife. Its blade is not long enough to make a clean cut.) Then check for leaks.

Check for leaks

To check for leaks in the membrane, plug the drain hole with an expandable stopper, which you can purchase at a hardware store.

Fill the pan with water to about an inch from the top of the membrane. Let the water come to rest, mark its level on the side of the pan, and let the water sit for 24 hours. Then check the level. If it's still at the mark, the pan is watertight. If the water is below the mark, the membrane has a leak somewhere.

Check the surrounding floor for water, which would have come from a leak in the side. If there's no evidence of water, pull the plug, expand its diameter a little, and repeat the test.

If the water has drained out completely, it's probably leaking at the drain flange, which is either too loose or too tight (and may have cut the membrane). Tighten the bolts if they feel too loose. If the flange has cut the membrane, remove the drain plate, let the membrane dry completely, and solvent weld a patch at least 2 inches larger than the puncture.

Installing the strainer

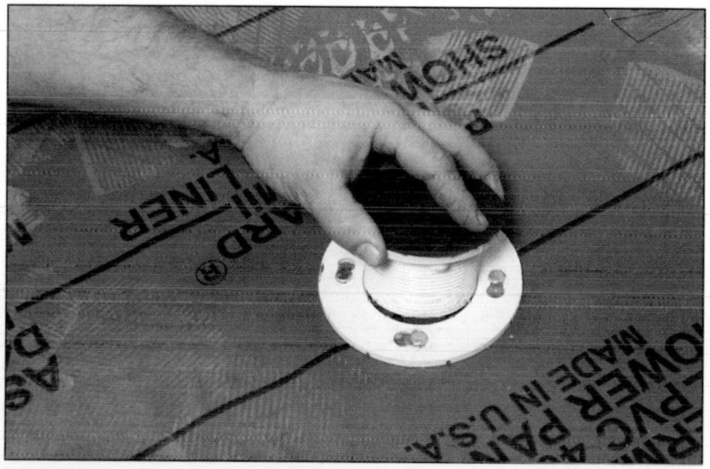

Wrap the threads of the strainer with four or five turns of plumber's tape and screw the strainer into the flange. To protect the strainer and drain from stray mortar and thinset, apply two layers of crisscrossed masking tape. Overlap the tape and cut it flush around the edge of the strainer.

D. Installing the mortared floor

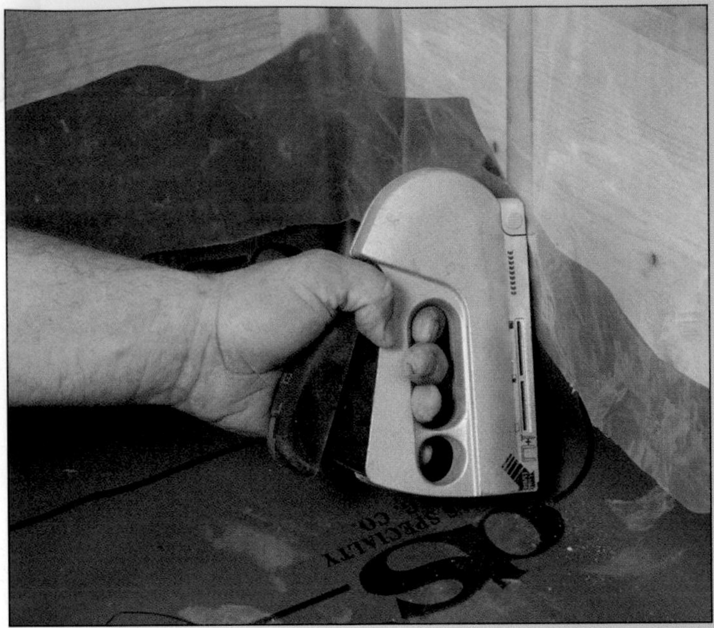

1 If any of the walls are outside walls, insulate them with fiberglass batts. Then cut sheets of 4-mil polyethylene waterproofing membrane long enough to hang from the top of the walls down to 3 or 4 inches below the top edge of the pan membrane. Use only four or five staples on each stud to attach the poly, the minimum necessary to keep it in place. Make sure you don't put staples through the pan membrane lower than 1 inch from the top.

2 Clean off any grit with a damp cloth. As added protection you can cover the liner with a drop cloth to prevent a backerboard corner from puncturing it. Cut backerboard to fit the walls and set it on ½-inch shims. Fasten the backerboard to the studs with backerboard screws *(page 94);* keep the screws within the top 1 inch of the pan membrane. Remove the shims and caulk the space at the bottom with silicone. Tape and mud the seams with modified thinset.

Sloping the floor

1 Using a torpedo level or 2-foot level (the longest size that will fit the enclosure), transfer the plane of the bottom of the strainer to the walls and the curb. Mark the plane on the backerboard with a felt-tip pen.

2 The floor of the pan must slope ¼ inch for every linear foot. Compute the amount of slope based on the dimensions of the enclosure and mark this point on the backerboard.

3 Mark the slope on the walls. Protect the weep holes from clogging and mix up another batch of dry mortar. Spread the mortar about halfway to your marks, keeping the slope at about one-third of a bubble on a level. Lay metal lath over the first course, then pack and level a top layer, starting at the wall, even with the marks. Work in sections, sloping the floor toward the drain. Bend lath to fit the curb and pack it also, slanting the top inward.

E. Laying the floor tile

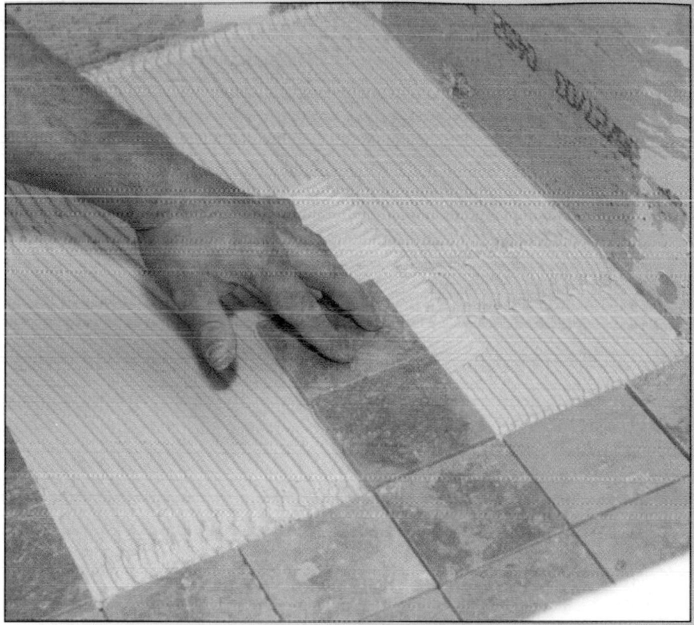

When the floor has dried, scape off any remaining imperfections with a steel trowel, then spread and comb latex-modified thinset. Press the tiles firmly into the mortar to make sure they conform to the slope of the floor. Line up all the edges with a 2-foot straightedge and let the mortar cure overnight. Grout the tiles with latex-modified grout, cleaning off the excess and wiping the grout haze.

Protect the weep holes

Weep holes allow moisture trapped in the mortar bed to escape down the drain. If the moisture can't go down, it will go up—into your grout, causing mold and mildew. To keep the weep holes from clogging with mortar, put a few spacers or pieces of gravel around them.

STANLEY PRO TIP

Prebend the lath

Metal lath is sharp, especially its cut edges, and can easily put holes in the membrane that covers the curb. To avoid puncturing the membrane when fitting the lath, prebend the lath over the 2×4s before installing the membrane. Make the bends slightly oversize so you can put the lath section down over the curb without tearing the membrane.

WHAT IF...

You puncture the membrane?

If you do happen to puncture the liner, it doesn't mean you have to take the whole thing up and start over. Clean the punctured area thoroughly and cut a patch at least 2 inches wider than the puncture. Apply the appropriate solvent to both the membrane and the patch. Roll the patch flat and let the repair dry.

Don't forget the tile
Don't mortar right to the top of the drain. Leave room for the tile so it comes out level with the top of the drain.

TILING A VANITY

A tiled vanity gives your bathroom a designer look without completely redesigning the whole room. If you plan to tile a bathroom wall, tiling the vanity will make the vanity and sink an integral part of the space.

Even if your existing base cabinet is in good condition, you'll have to build up the top. Commercial vanity countertops are made to handle less weight. Remove the top and add bracing, a ¾-inch plywood base, and polyethylene waterproofing membrane *(page 69)*.

Buy the tile for all the surfaces you'll be tiling—vanity tile, wall tile, and bullnose trim. That way you can be more certain of getting tiles of a consistent color throughout the entire project. Make sure the cartons have the same lot number.

Select the right tile to use on your vanity. Use glazed tile ⅜ to ½ inch thick. Purchase a sink whose texture matches the glaze—vitreous china and enameled cast iron are good choices. Self-rimming sinks are easy to install, and the rim will cover the rough edges of the cut tile.

PRESTART CHECKLIST

☐ **TIME**
Eight to nine hours to build the substrate and lay the tiles; an hour more the next day to grout them

☐ **TOOLS**
Circular saw, cordless drill, jigsaw, level, stapler, notched trowel, beater block, straightedge, caulking gun, grout float

☐ **SKILLS**
Basic carpentry skills, setting tile, cutting tile, grouting

☐ **PREP**
Remove existing vanity top or install a new prefab or custom unit

☐ **MATERIALS**
Drywall screws, ¾-inch exterior grade plywood, cement backerboard, backerboard screws, tile, thinset mortar, 4-mil polyethylene or 15-pound felt, grout

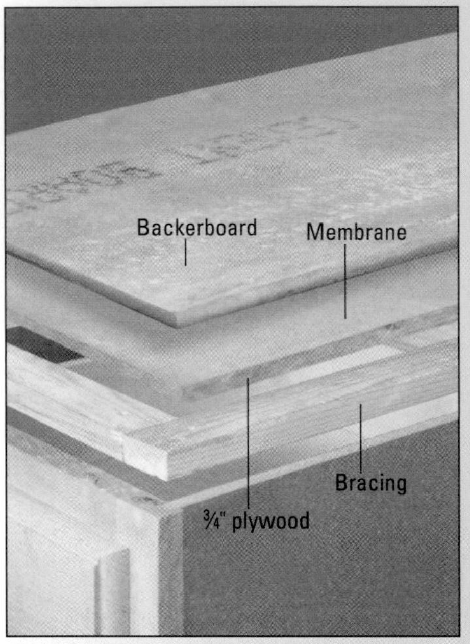

1 Build your own base or modify a commercial unit. Glue and screw bracing inside the cabinet, then install ¾-inch exterior plywood with a 1-inch overhang, according to your design. Staple waterproofing membrane to the plywood and install ½-inch backerboard *(page 126)*.

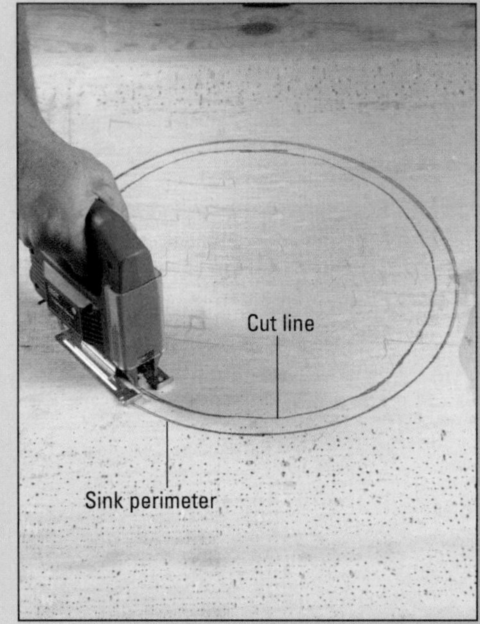

2 Mark the outline and cut line of the sink using the manufacturer's template. If a template isn't available, center the sink upside down on the surface and mark its shape. Draw a second line 1 inch inside the first line and drill a starter hole. Cut the second line with a jigsaw.

Removing a flush-mounted or recessed sink

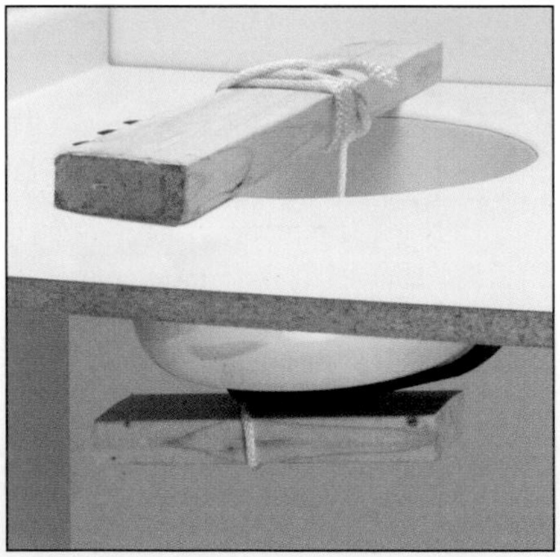

Most flush-mounted and recessed sinks are supported with clips under the cabinet. If you remove the clips without some sort of bracing, the sink will fall into the cabinet.
First unhook the plumbing, then support the sink with 2×4 braces tied with nylon rope.

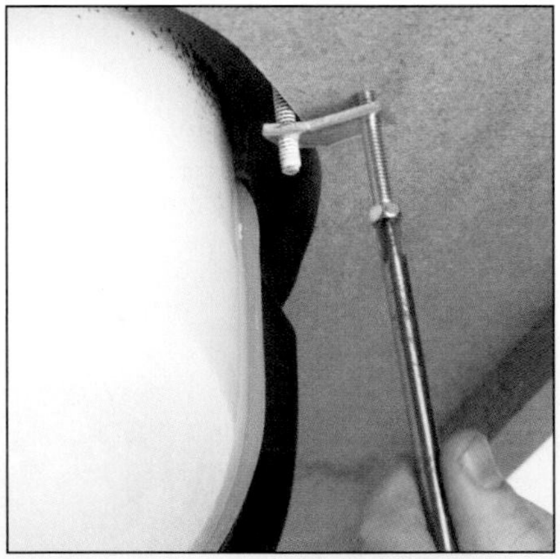

Thread one end of the rope through the drain and tie it to the bottom brace. Soak any rusted clips with penetrating oil, then remove them. Lift the sink or let it down with the braces.

3 Lay out the tiles in a dry run using spacers. Try to minimize cutting as much as possible. Mark the edges of your dry run and snap chalk lines to guide the installation. Then comb thinset onto the backerboard.

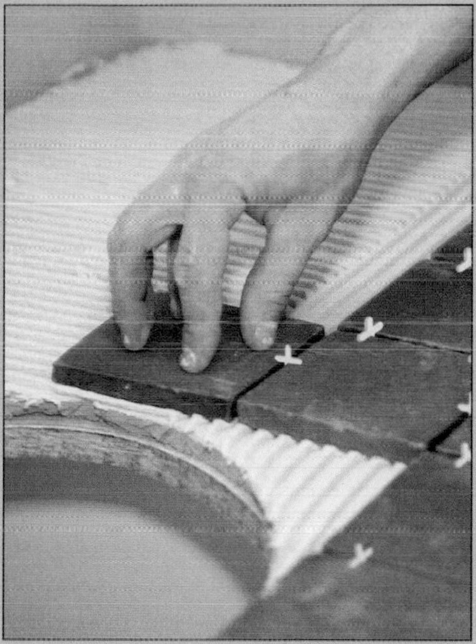

4 Set the tiles in place and level them *(page 101)*. Cut tiles don't have to fit exactly to the edge of the sink hole but must not extend beyond the edge. Keep the tiles in line using a metal straightedge. Let the mortar cure, then grout the tiles.

5 When the grout has cured, run a bead of silicone caulk around the edge of the hole and set in the sink. To avoid pinched fingers, ask a helper to support the bottom of the sink. Install and tighten any mounting clips and hook up the plumbing lines. Run another bead of caulk around the edge of the sink.

WHAT IF...
You're tiling an alcove?

If you plan to tile a sink enclosed in an alcove, design the layout carefully. First decide whether you want the grout joints on the wall to line up with those on the vanity. Draw a scaled plan to avoid ending up with small slivers of tile at the edges—you'll want the same size tile on both ends of the installation.

Tile the walls first, then the countertop, then the ledge. Finish with V-cap edging.

Other sink installations

Both flush-mounted and underhung sinks make for easier cleaning, but they require special countertop treatments.

Install a flush-mounted sink with its rim resting on plywood substrate. Install concrete backerboard around the sink and top it with tiles that partially rest on top of the sink flange.

Install and plumb an underhung sink after the substrate is installed. Then install tiles, as shown, with thin vertical pieces around the perimeter and bullnose trim overlapping them.

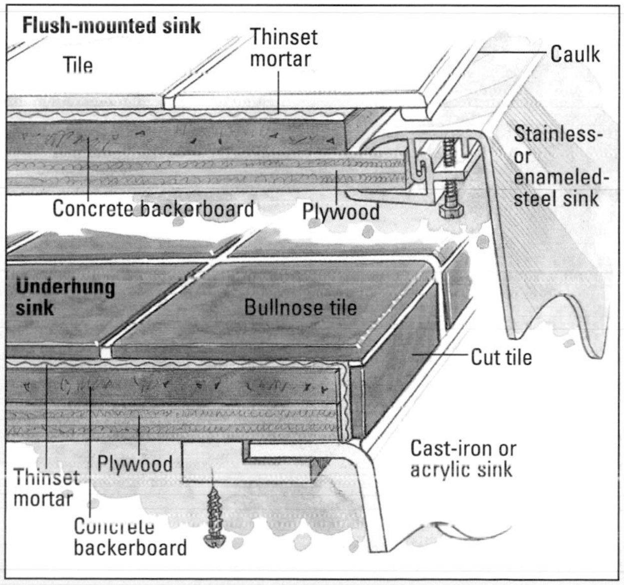

Tiling Outdoor Projects

Ceramic tile is the perfect choice for outdoor projects— patios, pool surrounds, walkways, or outdoor kitchens. Although the basic techniques for setting tile outdoors are the same as indoors, outdoor projects are studies in their own right. Your choice of tile must be tailored to your climate, for instance. And outdoor substrates are generally different from indoor substrates.

Your climate and tile

Your tile choices will be affected by the region in which you live. Saltillo and other soft-bodied tiles are fine for warm climates. Freezing climates call for hard-bodied tiles, such as porcelain, whose density repels water and won't crack when temperatures drop. No matter what tile you choose, you'll need nonslip surfaces. Ask your dealer for tiles made expressly for wet installations.

Consider the substrate

Outdoor installations require a solid foundation, and nothing short of a 3- or 4-inch concrete slab will do. Be sure to contact your local building department about the thickness of the slab, other aspects of its construction, and the need for inspections and permits.

If your project will include a roof—either now or in the future—the perimeter of the slab will need a footing (a thicker, reinforced section of concrete). It's a lot easier and cheaper to pour the footing when you pour the slab than to go back and add it later.

In most cases it's best to choose the general location of the outdoor feature first and "fine tune" its size to the dimensions of the tile.

Large-scale or smaller?

Typically the scale of an outdoors project means using 9- or 12-inch tiles, but vitreous tile now comes in much larger sizes—2-feet square and larger. Large tiles will cover more surface area faster than small ones, but they don't lend themselves to as much design "finesse." They often require more cutting, and their weight makes them harder to line up.

With its infinite variety of colors, shapes, and sizes, tile is the perfect design choice for patios, pools, or an outdoor kitchen.

Chapter Preview

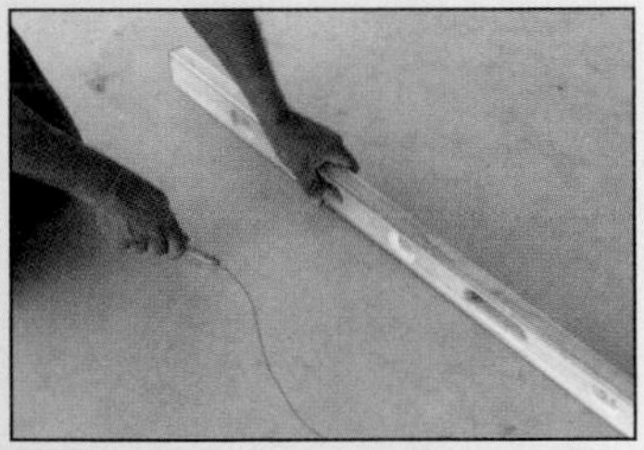

Preparing an existing slab
page 174

Installing a new concrete slab
page 176

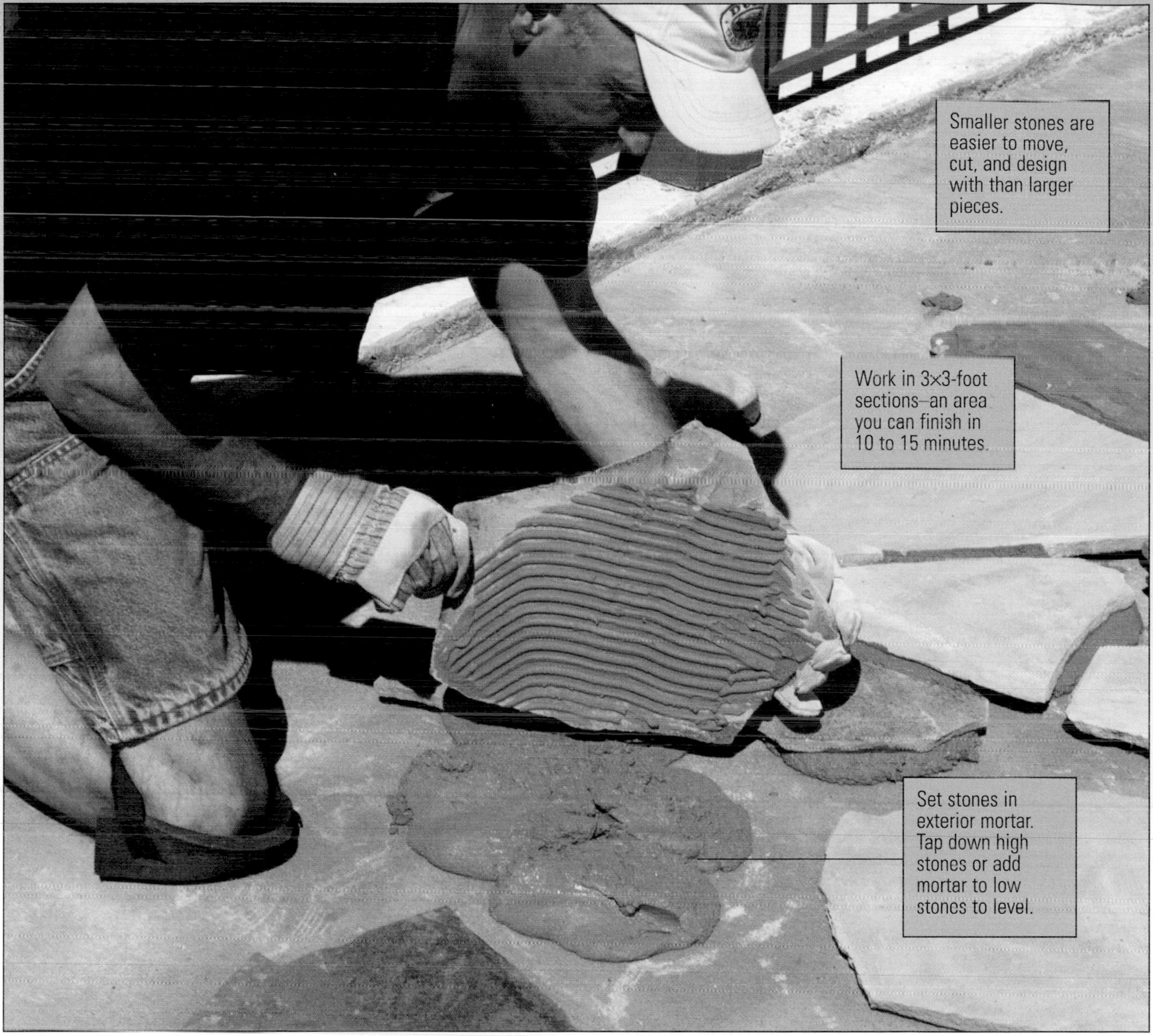
Smaller stones are easier to move, cut, and design with than larger pieces.
Work in 3×3-foot sections–an area you can finish in 10 to 15 minutes.
Set stones in exterior mortar. Tap down high stones or add mortar to low stones to level.

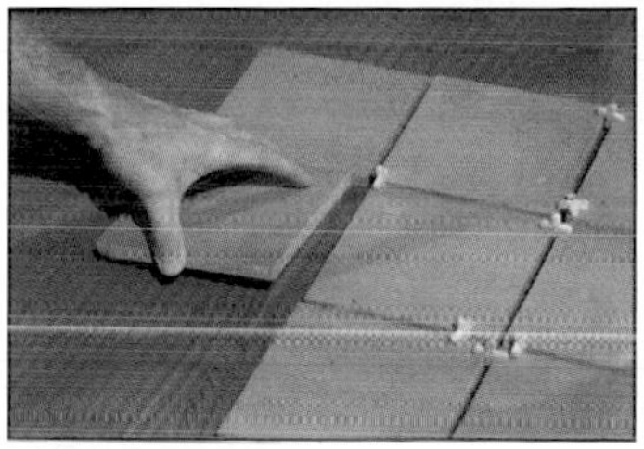

Tiling a patio
page 182

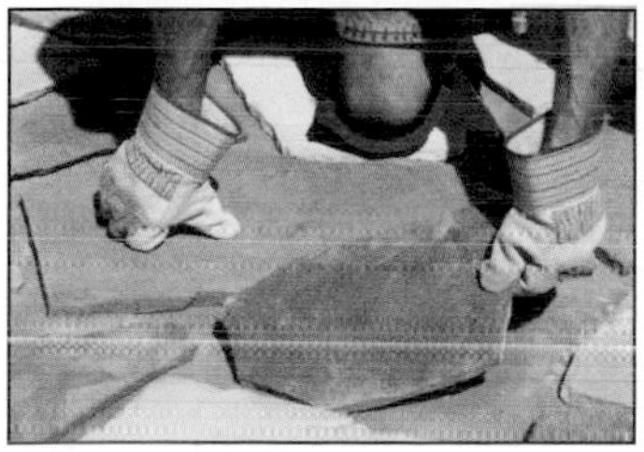

Tiling with flagstone
page 186

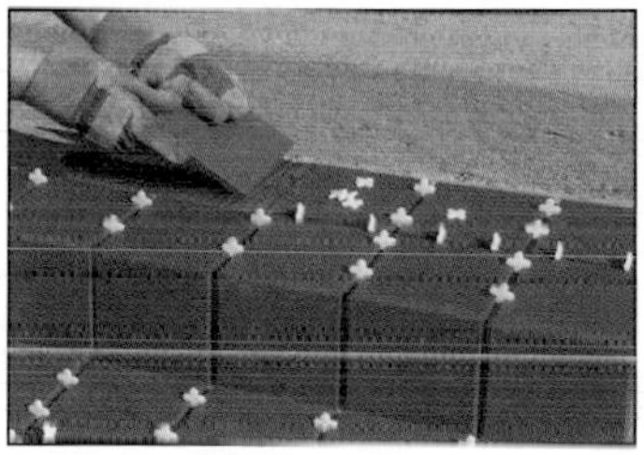

Tiling outdoor steps
page 188

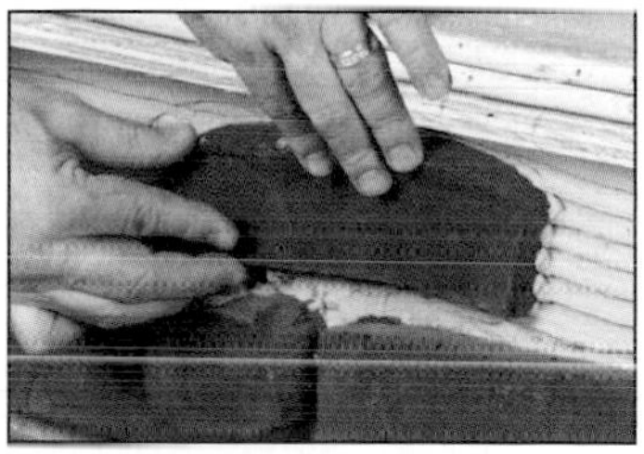

Tiling an outdoor kitchen
page 190

PREPARING AN EXISTING SLAB

Like an interior slab, an outdoor slab for a tiled patio or walkway has to be solid, smooth, and level. If you plan to tile your present slab, take an inventory of its condition before you get out the trowels and thinset. First look for large cracks and sagging sections. If they're present, the base is not adequate—you'll need to remove the slab and pour a new one.

Even if your present slab appears flawless, you need to make sure it will stay that way when it's tiled. Dig along the perimeter of the slab and look for a 4-inch gravel base and 3 to 4 inches of concrete. If an adequate subbase is present, check the surface for drainage—it must be sloped at least 1 inch for every 4 feet and should not contain high spots more than ⅛ inch in 10 feet.

If the surface is crowned in the center for drainage, that's okay, as long as the crowning is gradual. You can repair minor holes or flaking with the techniques shown here. The same goes for loose or damaged brick and tile.

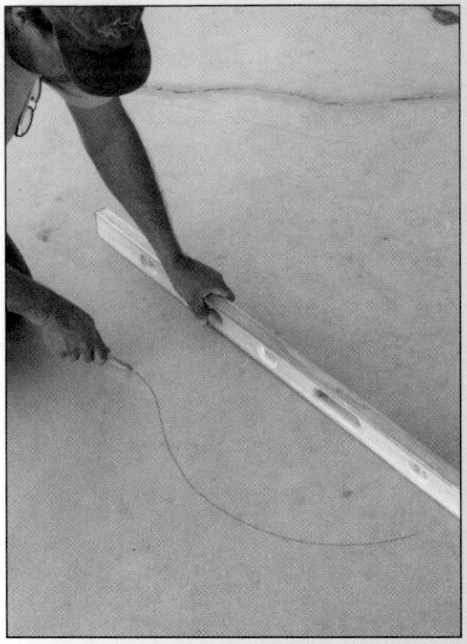

1 Working in 6-foot-square sections, check the surface with a 4-foot level. Mark any cracks, high spots, and other defects with a carpenter's pencil. Cracks may be a sign of structural problems. Some may be repairable. Others may require professional help.

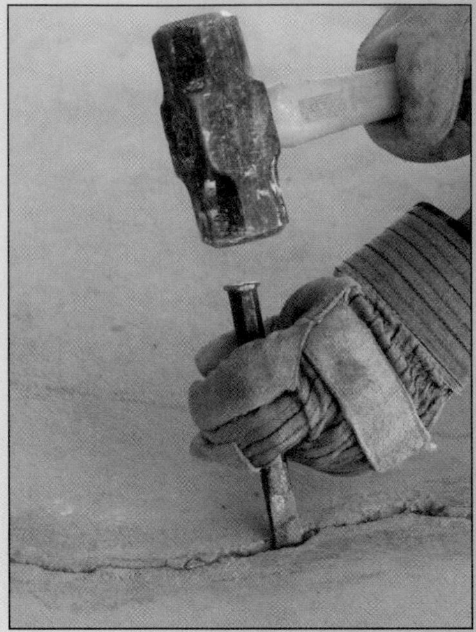

2 Use a small sledge and a cold chisel to open small cracks so you can fill them. If possible, angle the chisel into each side of the crack to create a recess wider at the bottom than the top. Doing so helps hold the patching cement more securely.

PRESTART CHECKLIST

☐ **TIME**
From 30 to 45 minutes per square yard

☐ **TOOLS**
Repair surface: level, hammer, cold chisel, trowels, grinder, vacuum, sanding block, brush
Repair structural defects: sledge, crowbar, wheelbarrow, rented concrete saw or jackhammer

☐ **SKILLS**
Leveling, troweling, grinding

☐ **MATERIALS**
Repair surface: hydraulic cement, thinset, self-leveling compound,
Repair structural defects: gravel, reinforcing wire, epoxy bonding agent, concrete mix, 2×4 screed

TYPICAL OUTDOOR SLAB CONSTRUCTION

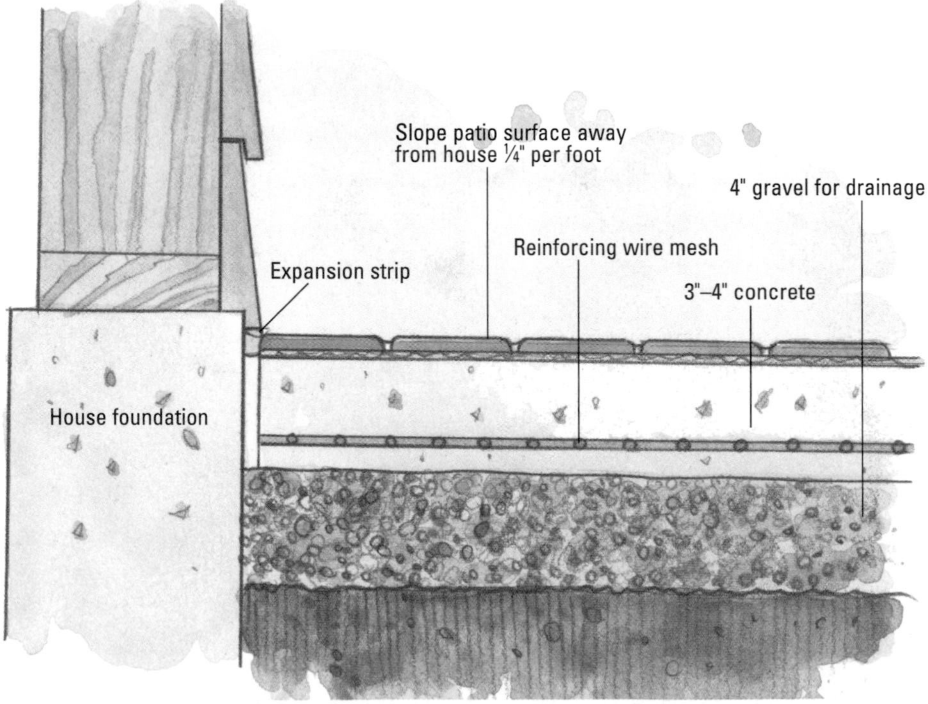

3 Wash out the crack with water and fill it with quick-setting hydraulic cement or thinset. Use a margin trowel or mason's trowel to feather out the edges until the patch is level with the surrounding surface. When the patch has cured, install an isolation membrane *(page 71)*.

4 To fill depressions in the slab, pour a small amount of self-leveling compound into the depression or trowel on a skim coat of thinset. Add thinset or compound until the surface is level. If you're using thinset, feather the edges even with the floor. Self-leveling compound will do this on its own.

5 Grind down any high spots you have marked with a grinder fitted with a masonry-grit abrasive wheel. A right-angle grinder simplifies the job. Hold a vacuum hose near the grinder to remove the dust as you work. Vacuum and damp-mop the surface thoroughly.

STANLEY PRO TIP

Repair damaged edges

If a slab has extensive edge damage, chip away any loose concrete, then clean and wet the edge. Set a 2× form against the edge extending about 1 inch above the surface. Fill the damaged area with fresh concrete, smooth it, and let it cure.

Cutting control joints

Slabs wider than 8 feet require control joints. If the existing slab has no control joints, snap chalklines at 8-foot intervals, perpendicular to the edges. Using a rented concrete saw, cut the joints (¾ inch deep). After setting the tile, fill the joint with foam backer rod *(page 135)*.

WHAT IF...

You have to remove a slab?

If your existing patio slab fails to make the grade, you'll have to get tough—concrete is stubborn. You'll need at least a 10-pound sledge—heavier is better, if you can handle it—and crowbars. If the slab is thicker than 4 inches or you have a large area to remove, rent a masonry saw or jackhammer. Save your strength for toting away the broken concrete.

Start at a corner and crack small sections. Pry out the section with a crowbar and carry it away in a wheelbarrow.

Work your way across the surface, cracking and prying. Let the crowbar do most of the work—concrete pries up more easily than it pounds down.

INSTALLING A NEW CONCRETE SLAB

The first step in installing a patio is laying out its perimeter. For very small jobs, such as a pad for a new barbecue, use an uncut sheet of plywood to mark and square the corners. Anything larger than 4×8 feet calls for batterboards.

To make batterboards, cut 2×4 "legs" 24 to 36 inches long. Point the legs with 30-degree angles so they'll penetrate the soil. Then cut 1×4s into 15- to 18-inch crosspieces and screw the crosspieces to the 2×4s. (After you've laid out the site, cut the wood into braces for the concrete forms.)

Don't pour a slab without planning for drainage. Slope the surface 1 inch every 4 feet. Let the runoff pour into a mulched flower bed or shrub border, or dig a trench, around the slab and fill it with gravel. For seriously wet sites, embed a perforated drainpipe in the trench. Crown the surface (make it a little higher in the center) so water flows away from the center and off all sides.

PRESTART CHECKLIST

☐ **TIME**
About 15 hours for a 10×10-foot patio

☐ **TOOLS**
Shovels, rototiller, plumb bob, tape measure, power tamper, 4-foot level, hammer, small sledge, trowels, screed, hand float, edger, broom, trowel, pliers, wheelbarrow, mortar box, cordless drill

☐ **SKILLS**
Measuring, cutting, assembling forms, excavating, laying tile

☐ **PREP**
Lay out site on a dimensional plan

☐ **MATERIALS**
Gravel, 1× and 2× lumber, nails, decking screws, concrete, expansion joint material, wire reinforcing mesh, dobies, tie wire, plastic tarp

A. Laying out and excavating the site

1 Set temporary stakes about a foot out from the corners of the slab and drive batterboards 3 to 4 feet beyond the stake. Tie mason's lines to nails in the crosspieces and square the site. Level the lines with a line level. Cut notches in the crosspieces so you can retie the lines.

2 At each corner, suspend a plumb bob just touching the intersection of the mason's lines. Let the plumb bob settle to the ground and mark the spot where the point of the plumb bob rests. These points represent the outside corners of the excavation. Drive a stake at each mark.

LAYING OUT A PATIO SITE

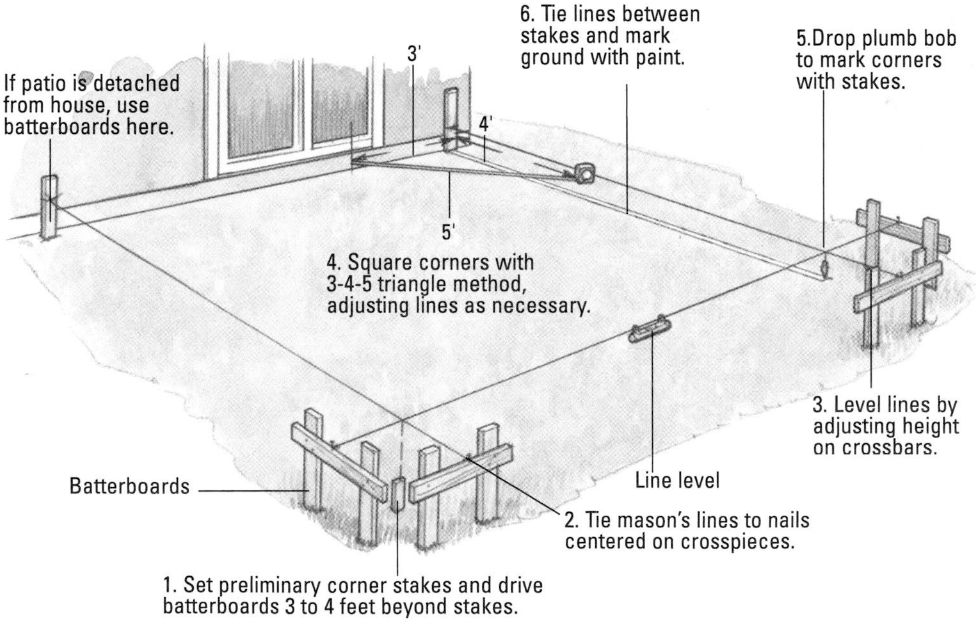

6. Tie lines between stakes and mark ground with paint.
3'
5.Drop plumb bob to mark corners with stakes.
If patio is detached from house, use batterboards here.
4'
5'
4. Square corners with 3-4-5 triangle method, adjusting lines as necessary.
3. Level lines by adjusting height on crossbars.
Line level
Batterboards
2. Tie mason's lines to nails centered on crosspieces.
1. Set preliminary corner stakes and drive batterboards 3 to 4 feet beyond stakes.

3 Tie a line between the stakes at ground level. Then using powdered chalk or spray paint, mark the ground along this line. Remove the mason's lines from the batterboards to get them out of your way, and cut the sod into 12-inch strips with a square shovel. Push the shovel handle about 2 inches under the roots to dislodge them and roll up the sod in strips. Store the sod in the shade or replant it in your landscape.

4 Excavate the site with a round-nose shovel, working from the center to the edge. Hold the shovel at a low angle to avoid digging too deeply and remove the soil in small amounts. Use a slope gauge to slope the site for drainage. Then retie the mason's lines so they intersect a foot inside the edge of the excavation. Level the lines, stake the intersections with a plumb bob, and tie a line between the stakes to represent the inside edges of your forms.

Marking the patio height

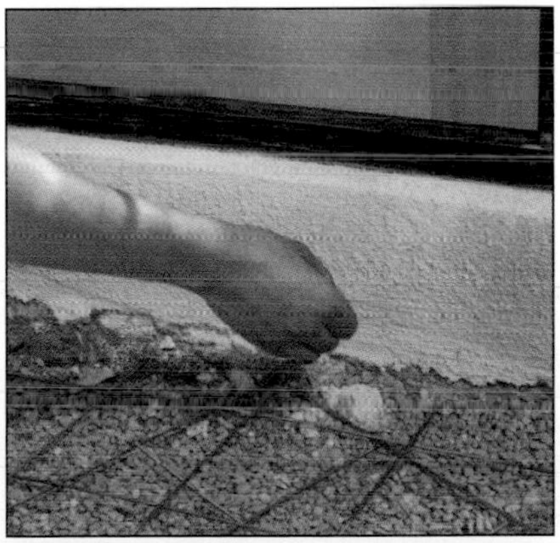

If the patio will abut the house, snap a chalkline under the door at the height of the patio surface—about 1 to 3 inches below the threshold—to keep snow and rain out of the interior. Remember to include the thickness of the tile. Use this line to set the excavation depth along the house.

STANLEY PRO TIP

Loosen the soil

You can make the job of excavating a patio a lot easier by loosening the soil with a rototiller before you dig.

Remove the sod first, then set the tiller to the depth of the substrate and tile. Take a couple of passes across the site with the tiller and remove the soil with a shovel.

USE A SLOPE GAUGE

Slope surfaces for drainage

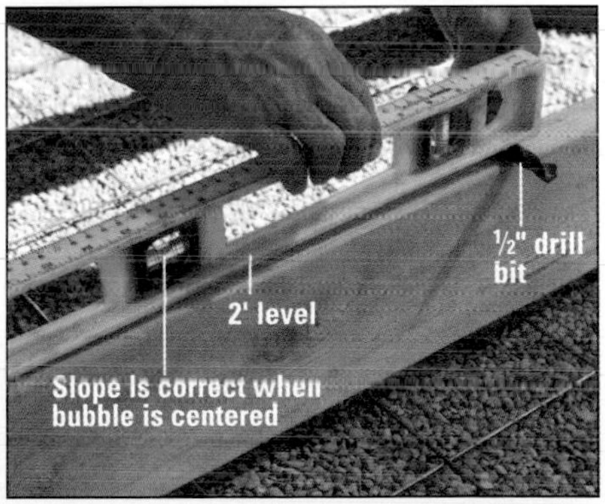

Any hard-scaped surface has to slope slightly to allow rainwater to run off. A slope of 1 inch in every 4 feet is all you need, and the handy homemade slope gauge shown above will help slope the site correctly. Set the gauge on the soil periodically as you dig and adjust the excavation to keep the bubble level.

B. Preparing the base

1 Assemble the forms using 2×4s with the inside edge directly under the mason's line. Pound stakes into the soil at the corners and every 2 to 4 feet. Attach the stakes with deck screws. Splice long sections with ½-inch plywood cleats.

2 To slope the forms, start at the house and measure the distance from the top of the form to the mason's line. Then measure at the lower edge of the form. Adjust the forms until the lower measurement is an inch less for every 4 feet of form (2 inches less over an 8-foot form, for example).

3 Spread a gravel base, then pack it with a power tamper until the surface is smooth, solid, and consistently 4 inches thick. Lay 6×6-inch 10/10 reinforcing wire mesh on 2-inch dobies, overlapping the ends of the wire by 4 inches and tying the dobies to it.

Pouring a large patio

Any patio larger than 8×8 feet can be difficult to pour and screed. Make your job easier by dividing the area into sections, installing temporary screed guides to partition the work.

WHAT IF... Codes require a footing?

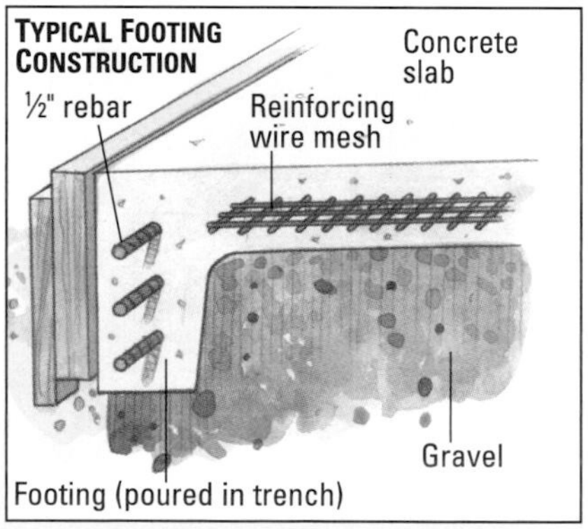

Certain patio installations (especially those including a wall) may require a footing on the perimeter of the slab. Footings are extra-thick sections of concrete reinforced with rebar. Dig the footing trench at the same time you excavate the site and pour the footing and slab at the same time.

Tying dobies to the wire

You can lay the reinforcing wire on the dobies and leave it untied, but tying it down will keep the wire at the right level. Wrap the bottom of the dobie with soft stove wire and twist it snug with pliers. Reinforcing wire can also be held up in place with wire supports, sometimes called chairs.

C. Making the pour

Put next load of concrete
where previous load ends

1 Start pouring in the corner farthest from the truck or mixing site. Fill the excavation to the top of the forms and push it into the edges of the site. Don't throw the mix. Then consolidate, or settle, it by working a shovel or 2×4 up and down in it. You may have to recenter the wire mesh with a garden rake. Add the next load of concrete as soon as you've spread the first one. Pour it where the first load ends.

2 Level the concrete with the top of the forms using a long, straight 2×4 metal stud as a screed. With one person at each end of the board, pull it along the top of the forms with a side-to-side sawing motion. If there are humps in the surface of the concrete after the first pass, screed again. Fill low spots with concrete; then screed again. Remove any temporary guides, shovel concrete into the cavity they leave behind, and screed once more.

Mixing your own concrete

If the site is 10×10 feet or smaller, it might be more cost efficient to mix your own concrete from dry ingredients. Here's a recipe.

- 1 part portland cement
- 2 parts sand
- 3 parts gravel or aggregate
- ½ part water

Combine the dry ingredients in a mortar box or wheelbarrow and stir in the water a little at a time.

The moisture in the sand and the atmospheric humidity will affect how much water you need to add to your concrete. To test the sand, squeeze a handful, then relax your hand. If the mix holds together, add just ½ part water. If it crumbles or leaves your hand wet, use less water. An ideal consistency resembles thick malted milk.

STANLEY PRO TIP

Handling a concrete pour

- A wheelbarrow makes moving concrete easier, but protect your yard from ruts with a ramp of 2×12s.
- If your concrete forms will be permanent, use redwood or cedar or pressure-treated lumber rated for ground contact. Cover the top edges with duct tape to protect them from concrete stains.
- If the forms for your patio slab will be temporary, coat the inside edges with a commercial releasing agent so you can pull the forms away after the concrete has cured.
- Don't pour new concrete against concrete that has already set up. Doing so creates a cold joint, which fractures easily.

Concrete additives

Plain, unmodified concrete works well in moderate weather, but extremely hot and cold temperatures render a mix unworkable and improperly cured. Engineers have developed additives for less-than-perfect weather.

- Air bubbles (air entrainment) in the mix help keep concrete from freezing when pouring in extreme cold.
- Accelerators help concrete set up faster in cold weather.
- Retardants slow the curing process when the weather gets too hot.
- Water reducers make the mix more workable, reducing time and labor on large jobs.

D. Finishing the surface

1 For small areas that you can reach from the edges of the slab, use a hand float or a darby that extends your reach about 2 feet. Hold the darby flat as you move it across the surface in wide arcs. Then tilt it slightly and work in straight pulls. If you have to work on the surface, spread your weight with 2×2-foot pieces of plywood. While one or more people float a section, have the finisher work right behind them.

2 Cut control joints every 8 feet by sliding the side of an edger along a guide board (1× or 2× stock that's as long as the surface you're jointing and fastened to the forms at either end). Don't try to cut a control joint without a guide; the joint will look sloppy. Tip up the leading edge of the tool slightly as you move it forward and back. Make control joints about 20 percent as deep as the thickness of the concrete (for example, ¾ inch on a 4-inch slab).

CONTROL JOINTS

Match grout lines to control joints

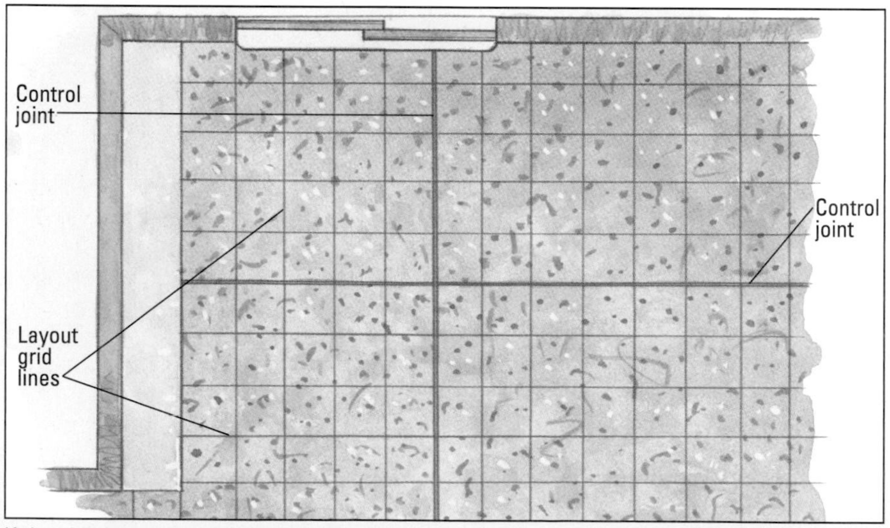

If the slab has control joints cut in its surface, make sure you start the layout lines on the control joints. That way you'll know a grout joint and not a tile falls on a control joint.

WHAT IF...

The site is too large to float with a darby?

For any site too large to float with a darby, use a bull float—a smooth board or plate attached with a swivel joint to a long handle. Push the float away from you with the leading edge slightly raised so it doesn't dig in. Pull it back in the same manner. Overlap each pass until you've gone over the entire surface.

3 Brooming creates a "tooth" in the concrete for the thinset and increases its adhesion to the surface of the slab. First trowel the concrete; then drag a dampened, stiff garage broom across it. After brooming the surface, you may need to touch up the edges and control joints.

Curing the slab

Cover the concrete with plastic to help it cure properly. Use black plastic in cool weather—it absorbs heat from the sun. Weight the edges and seams with stones or boards. If you are able to attend to your slab regularly, it is better to sprinkle it with water occasionally than to cover it. Cover the slab with old blankets or burlap and keep them wet. Don't use a curing agent—thinset will not stick to treated concrete. Snap layout lines when the slab has cured.

When to begin the final finish

Wait until the sheen of water on the surface of the concrete disappears before you attempt to broom-finish the slab. Step on the surface to make sure—your foot should leave an impression no deeper than ¼ inch. Finishing a slab while water remains on the surface can result in concrete that is dusty, or that spalls or has other problems after it cures.

Evaporation can take minutes in hot, dry weather or more than an hour when it's damp and cool. If you notice that the concrete is beginning to set up before the sheen has disappeared, sweep off the water with a push broom, soak it up with burlap, or drag the surface of the concrete with a length of hose. Whichever method you use, don't step on wet concrete.

STANLEY PRO TIP

Remove the forms

Concrete sticks to untreated wood like glue, and even with a release agent, it can be hard to remove the forms. As soon as you have floated a section, separate the concrete from the forms by slipping a mason's trowel between the two and drawing it along the form.

WHAT IF...

You're tiling a pool deck?

If you're tiling the deck around a swimming pool, engage the services of a pool contractor to tile the pool's interior and cope the edge. Tiling the deck, however, is a good do-it-yourself project. Follow the steps for tiling a patio, with only a couple of adjustments. First wait until the pool is installed and tiled before starting the slab. Then make sure the excavation is deep enough for the gravel base and slab, and it should result in the deck tile setting flush with the edge tiles. The finished deck should slope at least one inch per foot away from the pool.

Install an expansion strip around the edge of the pool and build forms, setting the perimeter forms about ¾ inch higher than the lawn or allowing for a finished cap tile to keep soil from backwashing onto the deck.

TILING A PATIO

Before you start setting the tile, test the pattern. In general you'll want full tiles in the field of the site and as few cut tiles as possible on the edges. Snap chalklines between the midpoints of each side. Starting at the center point, dry-lay tiles and spacers on both axes, extending the tiles to the edge of the slab.

If one side ends with a full tile and the opposite side has only a partial tile, move the center point so both sides will have tiles of the same size. Adjust the tiles on both axes. When the layout fits the slab, snap parallel reference lines every 2 feet or at intervals equal to the dimensions of the tile. These lines will help keep the tile straight when you lay it.

Ideally you should apply mortar in temperatures between 60 and 70 degrees F. Don't work in direct sunlight—the mortar will set up too quickly. Start with enough mortar to lay just a few tiles. As you work, you'll develop a rhythm. Work in sections you can complete in 10 minutes. When you press the tiles in place, mortar will squeeze up between them. If the mortar comes up more than half the thickness of the tile, you're using too much.

PRESTART CHECKLIST

☐ **TIME**
About 18 to 24 hours for a 10×10-foot area

☐ **TOOLS**
Five-gallon bucket, ½-inch drill, mixing paddle, chalkline, snap cutter or wet saw, square-notched trowel, beater block, rubber mallet, straightedge, grout float, caulk gun, wide putty knife, nippers, grout bag, sponge

☐ **SKILLS**
Mixing mortar; setting, cutting, and grouting tile

☐ **PREP**
Repair existing slab or install a new one

☐ **MATERIALS**
Latex-modified thinset, grout, tile, foam backer rod, caulk, spacers, sealers

A. Setting the tile

1 Start at the center of the slab and spread a thin coat of mortar with the flat side of the trowel. Lay the mortar up to but not covering the layout lines. Rake the mortar with the notched side of the trowel held at a 45-degree angle. Set each tile in place with a slight twist and tap it with a rubber mallet and beater block. Place the covered side of the beater block on the tile and tap it a couple of times to seat the tile in the mortar, leveling it with the rest of the tiles.

REFRESHER COURSE
Cutting tiles

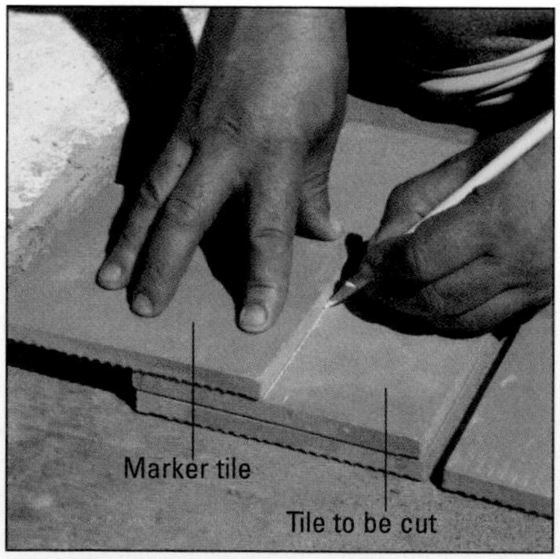

Place the tile you want to cut on top of the last set tile. Set another tile against the wall on the first tile and mark the cut line with a china marker.

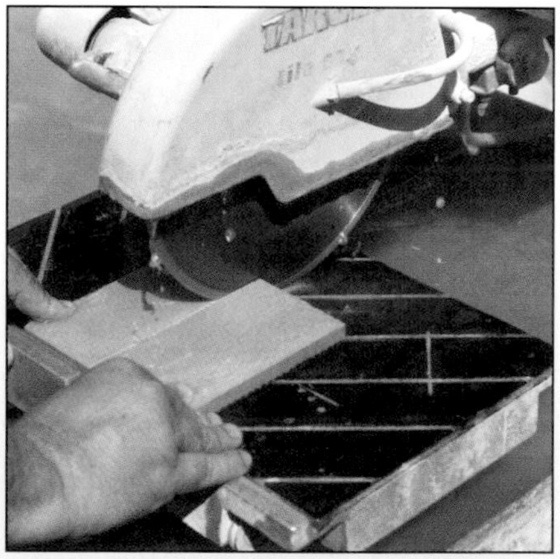

A wet saw makes quick work of cutting a large number of tiles. Even for a small patio, renting one is worth the cost. Set the tile against the fence so the cut line is in line with the blade.

2 Use spacers to keep the tiles properly spaced. Set the spacers on end so you can remove them easily. As you work, remove the spacers from tiles that have had a few minutes to set up. It's much easier to remove the spacers before the mortar has hardened completely.

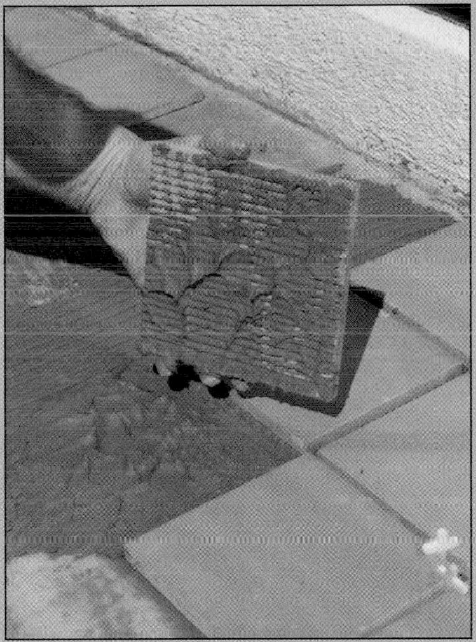

3 Every now and then, pick up a tile to make sure the mortar adheres evenly. Apply more or less as necessary. Check each section with a straightedge. If a tile is too low, pull it up, apply more mortar, and reset it. If a tile is too high, scrape off excess mortar and reset it.

4 Continue spreading mortar in both directions away from the intersection of the layout lines. Leave yourself room to work. Use a spacer to remove excess mortar before it hardens. Finish cleaning the joints with a pointed trowel. Let the mortar cure and caulk the joints where necessary.

STANLEY PRO TIP

Have cut tiles on hand

As you get close to an edge, have a supply of cut tiles ready so you can set them in place without searching for them or having to cut new ones.

SAFETY FIRST
Save your knees

Don't subject your knees to possible injury or the discomfort that can come from working on a hard concrete slab. Wear knee pads—they're less expensive than surgery.

Caulk the joints

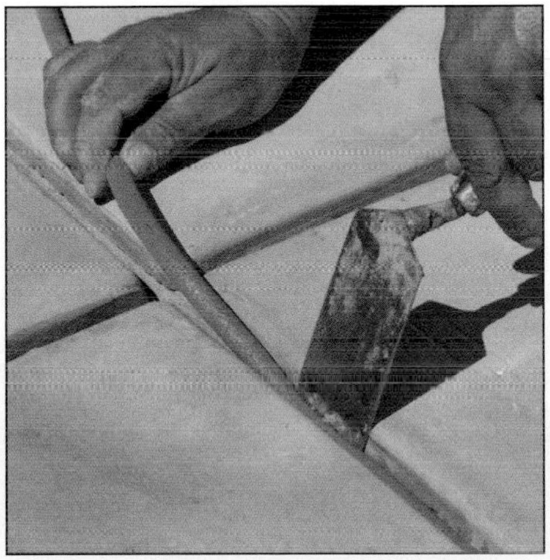

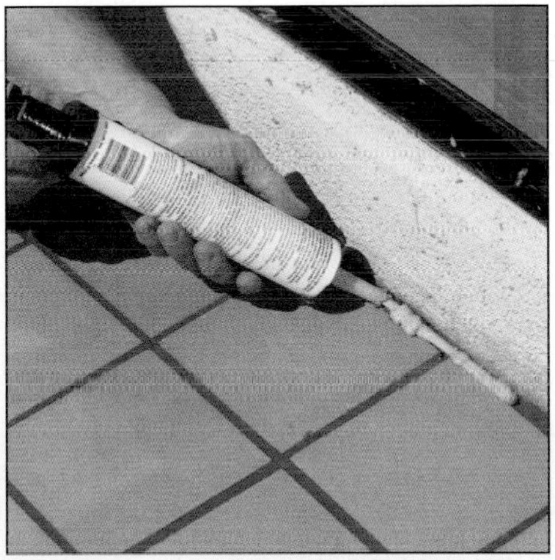

After the mortar has set, use a wide putty knife or margin trowel to stuff the control joints with foam backer rod, leaving a recess of roughly two-thirds the thickness of the tile. Apply a high-quality silicone outdoor caulk, in the same color as the grout you will use. Seal the joints where the patio meets the foundation of the house, making sure you apply enough to fill the gap all the way to the top of the expansion joint material. Smooth the caulk with a wet finger.

B. Grouting the tile

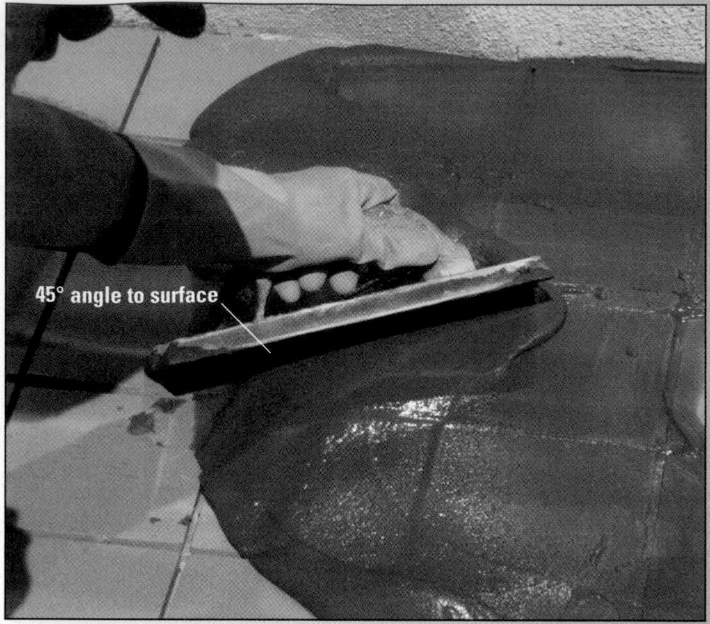

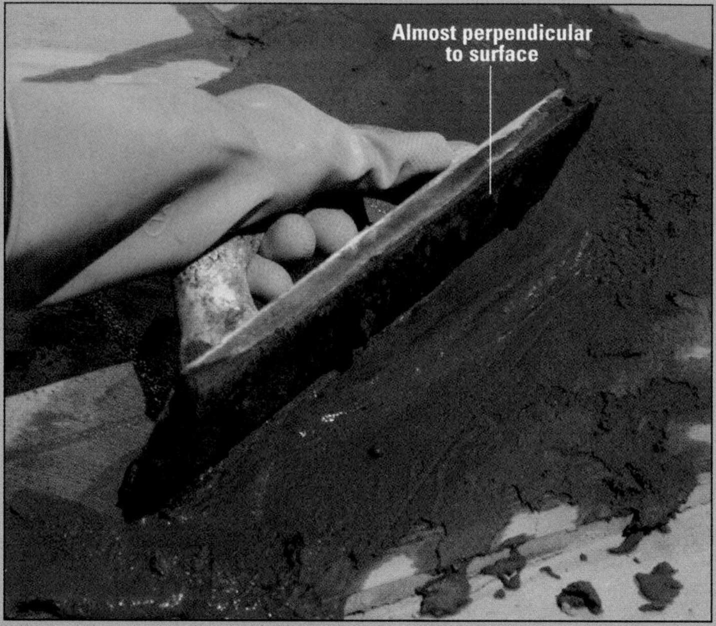

1 Mix only enough grout to cover a small section. Scoop grout from the mixing container and set it on the tiles. Angle the grout float at 45 degrees as you spread grout across the tiles, forcing it into the joints with the trailing edge. Move the float at angles to the tile pattern so the grout will fill the joints. Spread grout in alternating directions to force out any air trapped in the joints. Grout the tile in sections and clean each section before grouting the next one.

2 When all the joints in the section are full, clean off the grout float in a bucket of warm, clean water and use it to scrape excess grout from the tile. Hold the float almost perpendicular to the surface to remove the excess. Keep the float from pressing into the joints. Otherwise it will remove grout and undo all your hard work.

Mix the grout

Using a ½-inch drill and a mixing paddle, mix the grout slowly in a 5-gallon bucket. Follow the manufacturer's directions for mixing the grout and keep it in a container you can seal. For exterior applications, use grout that contains latex, which is easy to clean and needs little time to cure. If the grout you want to use doesn't come with a latex additive, ask your supplier if you can add it. If not, change brands.

Use the right drill

If you have a ⅜-inch drill handy, you may be tempted to use it to power-mix your mortar or grout—but don't. Mortar and grout are stout mixes; and the motor in a drill of this size is too small to push the paddle through it. You'll end up with an improper mix and a burned-out drill. If you can't rent or borrow a ½-inch model, buy one. You'll find plenty of other uses for it.

Estimating grout

The amount of grout you'll need depends on its chemical composition, the size of the tile, and the width of the grout joints. Grout packaging is often printed with a chart that will help you estimate how much you'll need.

Study the chart before you make your purchase—it's better to have a little left over than to have to run to your tile supplier in the middle of a grout job. The table below will give you a rough idea of how much area a pound of grout covers.

Tile size (in inches)	Joint width	Coverage per pound
2×2×¼	1/16	24 square feet
4¼×4¼×5/16	1/16	16 square feet
4¼×4¼×5/16	⅛	8 square feet
6×6×¼	1/16	28 square feet
6×6×¼	⅛	14 square feet
12×12×⅜	1/16	37 square feet

3 Scraping the excess won't remove all of it. You'll have to take up the residue with a damp sponge. Test the grout to make sure it's set up, then wipe the surface with a damp (not wet) sponge. The more often you change the water, the less haze you'll have to remove in the next step.

4 Use a clean soft cloth (old T-shirts work well) to wipe the haze off the tiles. In many cases the haze will be a somewhat stubborn adversary. Don't be afraid to scrub hard. You won't damage the tiles or the grout.

5 If the grout calls for damp curing, mist it lightly for a few minutes three times a day for three days. If the patio sits in direct sunlight, cover the tile with a sheet of plastic. After the grout has cured, seal the tile if recommended by the manufacturer.

Test the grout

To make sure the grout has set up sufficiently to clean it (so it won't pull back out of the joints), press it with your fingernail or the tip of a pointed trowel. If one or the other doesn't leave a dent, the grout is ready.

WHAT IF...
Your design calls for wide joints?

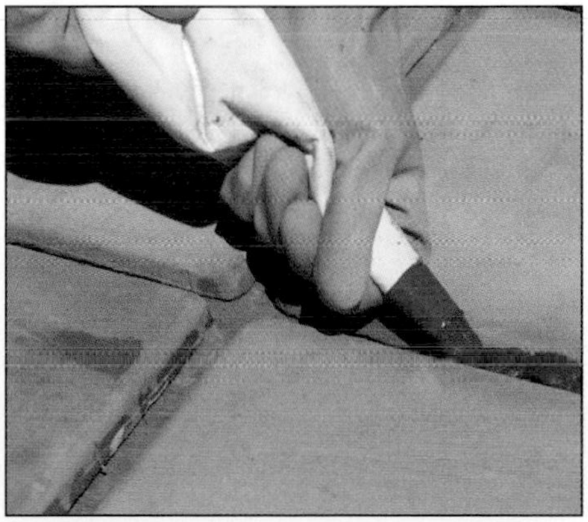

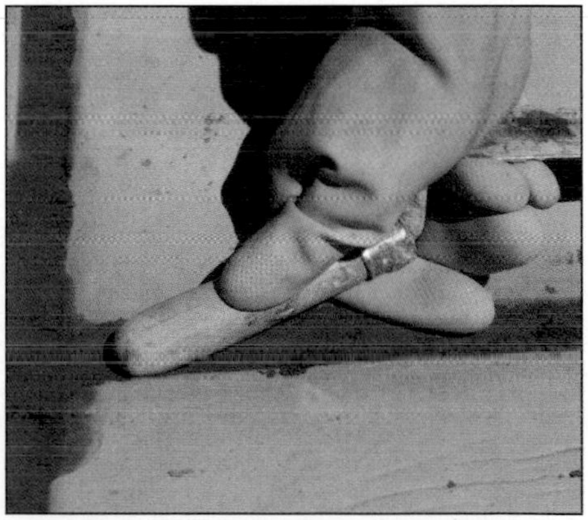

Some styles of tile look better with wide grout joints. Saltillo tiles and other hand-made materials look best with grout joints of at least ⅜ inch. At this width a grout float will pull the grout out of the joints as you apply it, so you'll have to use a grout bag for such installations. Squeeze the bag as you draw its nozzle along the length of the joint. Stop just short of filling the joint completely, then tool the joints smooth with the rounded end of a trowel handle.

TILING WITH FLAGSTONE

The term *flagstone* refers generally to rock fractured or cleft into flat slabs of various lengths, 2 inches thick or more. The type of flagstone most commonly used for patios includes bluestone, limestone, redstone, sandstone, granite, and slate. Its irregular shapes suit it to both casual free-form and formal geometric design schemes.

Cut stone is flagstone finished with straight edges and square corners. It ranges in size from about 1 foot to 4 feet across and comes in different thicknesses.

Whatever type of stone you're choosing, get paving at least 2 inches thick to avoid breakage. Figure about a ton of stone for 120 square feet and order 5 percent more for breakage. Large stones will cover a surface more quickly than smaller units but may prove harder to move, cut, and design.

Unlike ceramic tile, flagstone can be set in a sand base, but a properly installed mortared installation will give you years of maintenance-free service. A mortared patio requires a slab to provide a solid base. Cleft stone installations require an exterior mortar, generally Type-M (which has high compressive strength) or Type-S (high lateral strength).

PRESTART CHECKLIST

☐ **TIME**
About 16 to 20 hours for a 10×10-foot patio, not counting slab installation

☐ **TOOLS**
Hammer, small sledge, brick set, carpenter's pencil, mason's trowel, rubber mallet, mortar box, sponge, shovel, mortar bag, height gauge

☐ **SKILLS**
Troweling mortar and setting flagstone, using mortar bag, cutting stone

☐ **PREP**
Install new slab or repair an existing one

☐ **MATERIALS**
Flagstone, mortar, 2× lumber

Setting the stone

1 After you've finalized your pattern, take a trial run: lift the stones off in 3×3-foot sections—the size of an area you can finish in 10 to 15 minutes. Lay them next to the site in the same pattern. Mix enough mortar for the section and trowel a 1-inch thickness on the slab.

2 Set the large stones in the mortar first, keeping them in the pattern and using a height gauge to set them at the same height. Push the stones down; don't slide them. When the large stones are set, fill voids with smaller stones, cutting the stones to fit and leveling them with a rubber mallet.

STANLEY PRO TIP: Take a trial run

Variety is one of flagstone's design strengths, but it's also a weakness. Because flagstones range tremendously in size, shape, and color, you need to plan your pattern carefully. The best way to arrange your pattern is on-site, after you've poured the slab.

Set the stones on the surrounding grass so you can see their shapes and sizes. Starting with the largest stones, lay them on the slab, then fill in to the center with stones of approximately the same size. Match the contours of neighboring stones as closely as you can, but don't worry about matching them exactly; you can cut flagstones to fit and use small stones to fill the voids.

- Don't treat the stones as individual pieces; see how they look in pairs and threes. Visualize sections, not puzzle pieces.
- Vary the size, shape, and color as you go. Variety can add spice to the "life" of your patio too.
- Keep the spacing as uniform as possible: ½ to ¾ inch.
- Once you've laid the basic pattern, stand back and look at it from different angles. You can rearrange it if you don't like it.

3 Pull out low stones, add mortar, and reset them. Tap down the high stones, but if tapping them down won't level them, lift them and scoop out just enough mortar to make them level.

Clean off any mortar spills with a wet broom before you set succeeding sections. Don't wait until you've set the entire patio—the mortar will set on the first sections and you won't be able to get it off. Let the mortar cure three to four days, then mortar the joints.

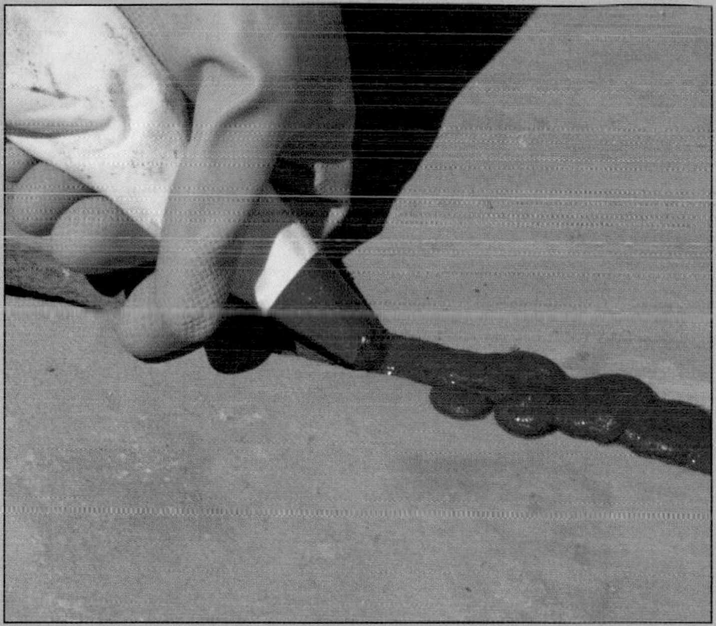

4 Mix mortar in a mortar box and fill the joints using a pointed trowel or mortar bag. The bag has a spout through which the mortar is squeezed into the joints—it's less messy and will reduce cleanup chores. Clean spilled mortar right away with a wet sponge. When the mortar holds a thumbprint, finish the joints with a jointing tool. Cover the surface with plastic or burlap (you'll need to keep it wet) and let it cure for three to four days.

Cutting the stones

1 Mark a cut line on the stone you want to cut. You can "eyeball" the line or set an adjoining stone on top of the stone you want to cut. Score the line with a set. Tap and move the brick set a bit at a time along the line.

2 Set the stone on a pipe or another stone, then break the stone with a single strong blow. Remove any excess stone along the contours of the cut line, shaping it with the sharp end of a mason's hammer.

Make a height gauge

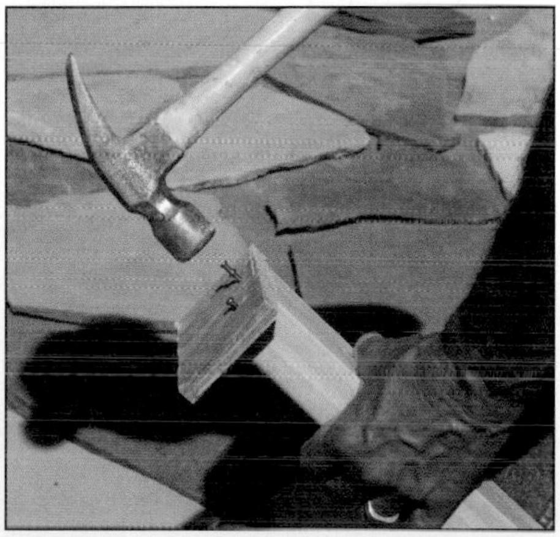

The thickest stone sets the height of the entire patio. If you set the large stones first, a height gauge will help you level each stone as you go. Make the gauge long enough to span the widest stone and augment your leveling efforts with a 4-foot level.

TILING OUTDOOR STEPS

Concrete steps are good candidates for tile, especially if the steps are an integral part of a tiled patio design. Even if they're not, tiled steps can improve the look of any outdoor entrance. The concrete has to be in good repair, however, in order to provide a solid substrate for the tile.

Take an inventory of the steps, using the methods shown here. Then repair cracks, level the surfaces (especially the treads), and clean off any oily stains that would interfere with the adhesive bond. Install an isolation membrane, if necessary, and roughen the surface.

The edges of concrete stairs will most likely be chipped or otherwise damaged, and if left unrepaired, the tile you set on them will chip also. Repair the edges with the methods shown on these pages, using a sand-mix mortar, not patching compound.

Use nonslip tiles with radius caps over the tread nosing. If you can't get radius caps in the style you want, some V-cap styles will make a good substitute. If neither is available, use standard field tile and round the edges *(page 109)*.

PRESTART CHECKLIST

☐ **TIME**
About 8 to 10 hours for a four-step entry, not counting prep time

☐ **TOOLS**
Tape measure, wet saw, drill, trowels, roller, grout bag, brick set or cold chisel, small sledge

☐ **SKILLS**
Repairing tile, installing tile, cutting tile

☐ **PREP**
Repair existing concrete surface, install backerboard on wood-frame stairs

☐ **MATERIALS**
Mortar, 2×8 form, brick or concrete block, isolation membrane, backerboard, felt paper, mesh tape, tile, spacers, joint compound, grout, exterior plywood, caulk

Preparing the steps

1 Repair the damaged edges of concrete steps by chipping away loose concrete with a brickset and small sledgehammer. If you don't have a brickset, use a cold chisel, but proceed with caution to avoid removing too much concrete.

2 Sweep away dust and loose material with a small hand brush, then wet the area with fine spray from a garden hose. Set a 2×8 against the front of the damaged step and keep it in place with bricks or blocks. Fill the recess with concrete and smooth it along the top of the form.

TILING A WOOD STAIR

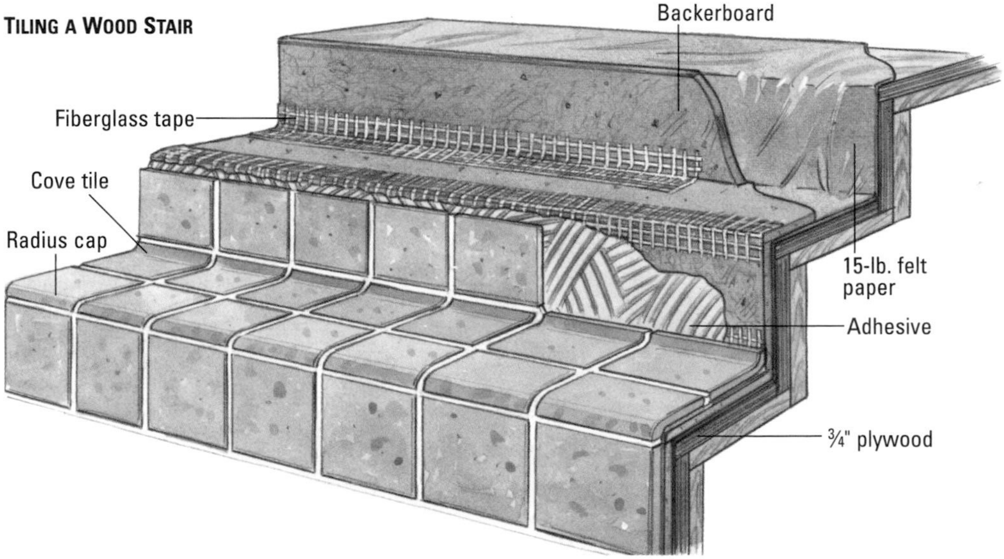

To keep the tiles on a wood stair from cracking, make sure the structure is solid and will not flex when walked on. Strengthen the stairs by adding a third stringer in the middle if necessary. Cover the treads, risers, and landings with ¾-inch exterior-grade plywood and waterproofing membrane. Then install backerboard over the entire surface of the stairs, taping the joints with backerboard tape and compound. Trowel on mortar and set the tile *(pages 182–183)*. Finish the edges with bullnose tile.

3 As an added precaution, install an isolation membrane over patched cracks. Roll on the material with a roller or spread a trowel-applied membrane with the smooth edge of a trowel. Work it to a consistent thickness with the notches, then even it out with the straightedge.

4 Dry-lay the tiles, including the radius cap and coves, to make sure everything fits correctly. Use a wet saw to cut all the tiles. Then use the same techniques used for tiling a patio *(pages 182–183)*. Spread type-M mortar over the bottom riser and comb it with the notched edges of the trowel. Set spacers along the bottom of the riser and rest the tiles on the spacers as you set them. Push the tiles into the mortar with a slight twist. Then set the radius cap tiles along the edge. Tile each riser and tread in the same fashion. When the mortar has cured, grout the tiles with a grout bag *(page 187)*.

Use nonslip tiles

Glazed tiles dress up the appearance of any stairs, indoors or out, but their slick surface makes them unsafe and unsuitable for use on stair treads. Even most unglazed tiles are slick when wet.

Your best choice for tread tiles is slip-resistant units made for use on stairs. For extra safety, install slip-resistant inserts in the tread edges. Typically these metal channels slip under the tread and feature a replaceable plastic or rubber insert that covers the nosing.

As a last resort, or to make an existing tiled surface more slip resistant, you can use self-stick abrasive strips that are manufactured for this purpose. These strips wear off in time, however, and require periodic replacement.

WHAT IF...
You want to tile only the risers?

Tiled risers provide a dramatic complement to hardwood treads. Choose a color that harmonizes with the color of the treads—patterns with earth tones or shades of blue go well with most wood stains. Use wall tiles or stone tiles. Install backerboard on risers that show signs of damage. Otherwise sand the finish lightly. Spread and comb thinset, set the tiles with spacers (on the bottom and the sides), and seal the top and bottom joints with caulk instead of grout.

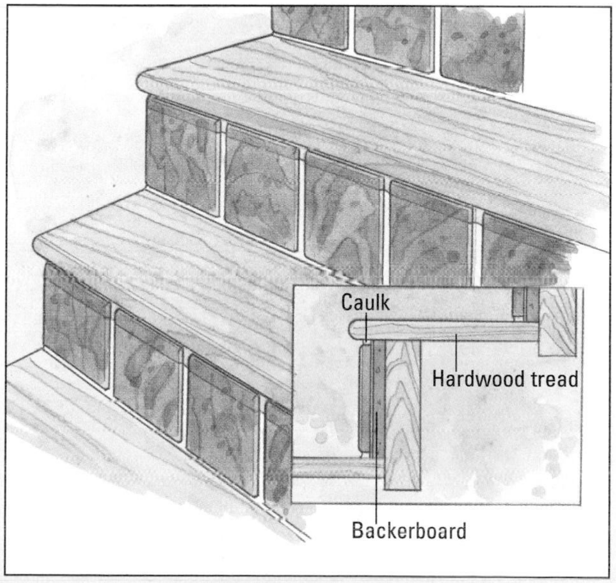

TILING AN OUTDOOR KITCHEN

Outdoor barbecuing became a popular pastime in the 1950s, and since then the technology of grills and accessories has improved dramatically. If you've always been part of the outdoor cooking craze or are joining it for the first time, an outdoor kitchen is something you can use.

Like any landscaping project, the scope of an outdoor cooking area is best determined by answering the question,"How do you want to use it?" For full-scale outdoor dining? For intimate gatherings with family or a few guests? Or merely for occasional weekend get-togethers?

At a minimum an outdoor kitchen requires a structure to house a grill. The unit illustrated here does just that, with little cost and effort. You can add a prep sink, under-the-counter fridge, rotisserie, and any number of storage areas. This design accommodates those features with the installation of additional bays.

PRESTART CHECKLIST

☐ **TIME**
About 24 to 30 hours

☐ **TOOLS**
Tape measure, shovel, hammer, rake, power tamper, cordless drill, hacksaw, concrete finishing tools, chalkline, mason's trowel, wire cutters, notched trowel, circular saw with masonry blade

☐ **SKILLS**
Installing a concrete slab, laying out and building with concrete block, setting tile

☐ **PREP**
Lay out, excavate, and pour concrete slab

☐ **MATERIALS**
Two-by stock for forms, decking screws, ready-mix concrete, mortar, concrete block, backerboard, metal lath, line blocks, ¾-inch exterior-grade plywood, thinset mortar, tile, grout, brick veneer

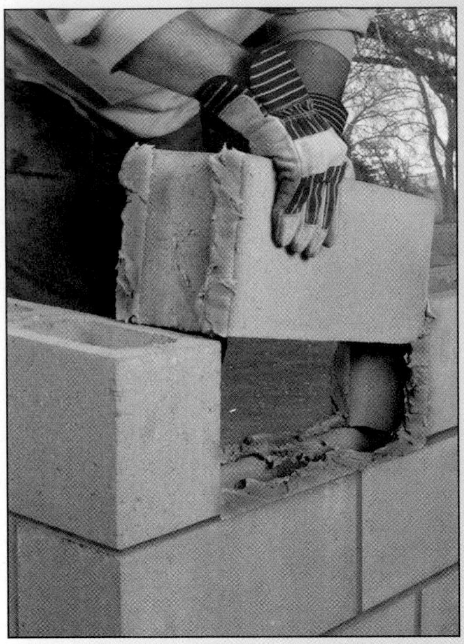

1 Lay out and pour the slab and footings as local codes require *(pages 176–181).* Snap chalklines to mark the location of the block walls. Using your dimensional plan, build the block walls, making sure the bay for the grill meets the manufacturer's specifications.

2 Cut ¾-inch exterior-grade plywood, metal lath, and backerboard to fit each section of the countertop. Fasten the plywood to the block webs with concrete screws (not anchors). Mortar the plywood, set the first piece of backerboard in the mortar, then install metal lath and the second backerboard.

OUTDOOR KITCHEN BASE

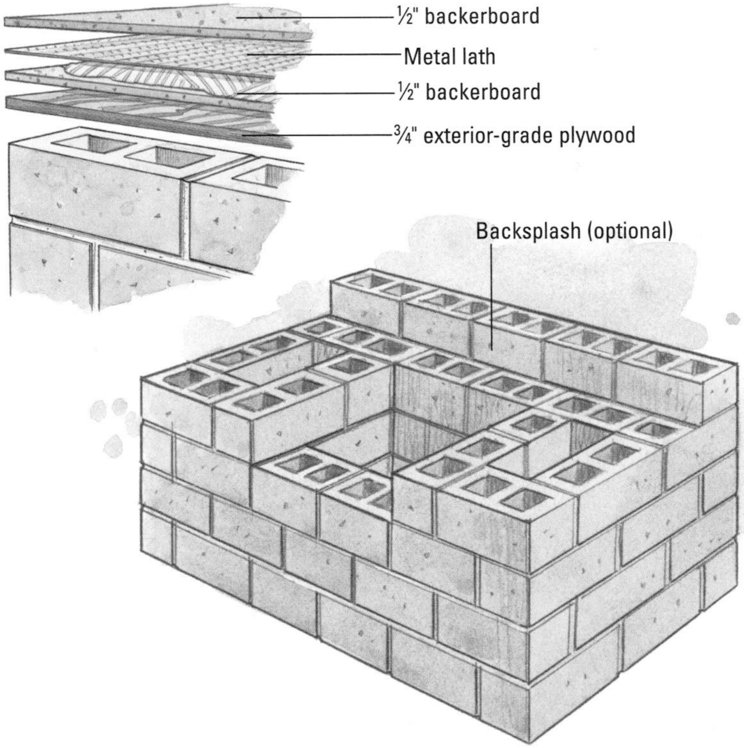

3 Starting at the bottom, spread and comb thinset on a section of the block wall. Set each piece of brick veneer in the mortar with a slight twist. Level the veneer and keep it straight with a straightedge.

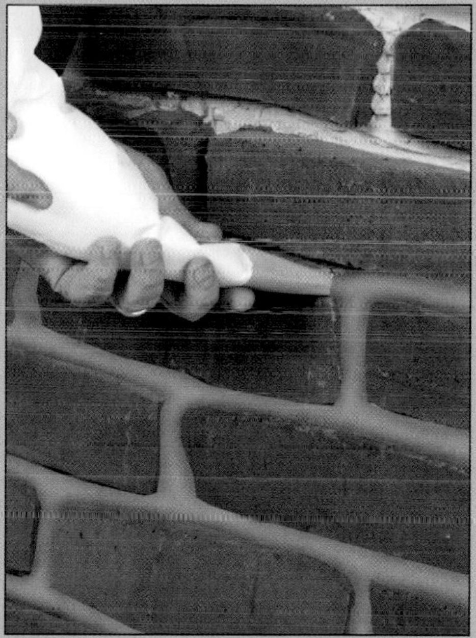

4 When the thinset has cured, fill a mortar bag with the mortar recommended by the manufacturer and squeeze the mortar into the joints. Let the mortar set up slightly, then tool it with a jointing tool.

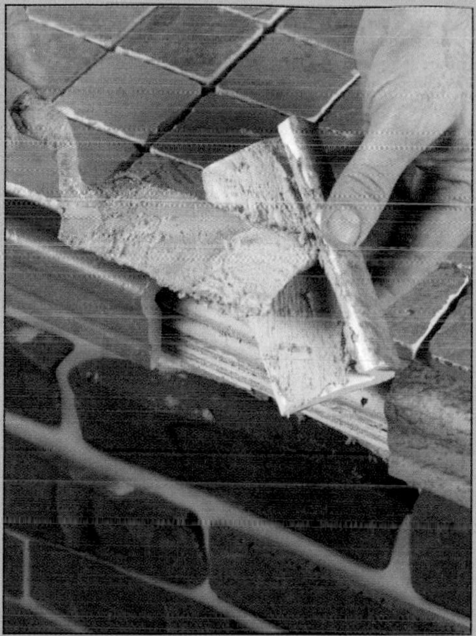

5 Dry-lay the countertop tile to make sure everything fits. Then spread and comb a level coat of thinset on the backerboard and set the countertop field tile. Make sure all the joints line up, then set the edge tile. When the mortar cures, grout and clean the tile and install the grill.

Installing a concrete countertop

Nothing beats concrete as a substrate for tile. It's flat, stable, and won't bend under compressive loads. Concrete countertops are also ideal for outdoor kitchen installations, but for large cooking bases you may find their expense prohibitive. On small kitchens, however, there's a ready-made alternative—precast concrete stepping stones.

Poured in a 3-inch thickness and in 3×3-foot squares, these units are available at most home centers and certain internet retailers (be careful of shipping costs, however). Besides providing an excellent base for tile, they offer an additional benefit—their 3-inch height makes it easy to set your countertop at exactly 36 inches.

To install this unit, use a circular saw with a masonry blade to cut it to 24 inches (the usual front-to-back depth of a counter surface). Apply mortar to the webs of the block walls and set the slab in place. For additional stability, fill the block cores with concrete and drill the slab to accommodate ½ inch rebar.

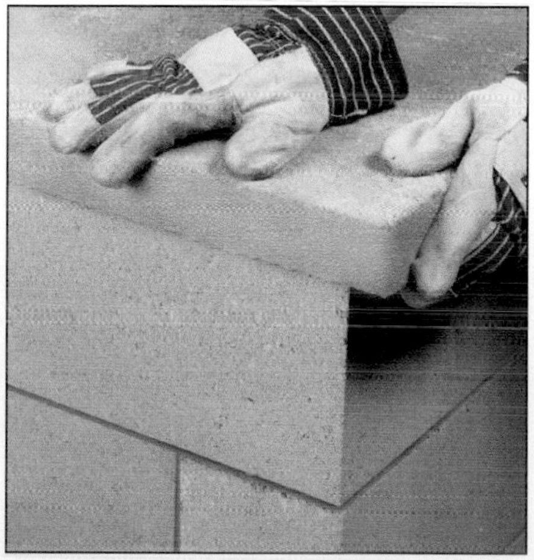

Installing undercounter storage

Installing an undercounter storage bay or recess for a refrigerator or other accessory means supporting the block above the bay. Lintels are made for this purpose. Using a hacksaw, cut the steel lintel to a length that extends over the opening by half a block on each side. Mortar the lintel in place and cover it with lintel blocks as shown.

INSTALLING RESILIENT & PARQUET TILE

Both resilient tile and wood parquet offer a wider choice of design styles than you might assume. Though they require different applications and offer different styles, both come in dry-backed and self-stick forms.

Resilient tile

Resilient tiles have always included designs that mimic other materials, such as granite, marble, brick, ceramic tile, and even wood parquet. Thanks to computer technology, today's patterns are much more realistic and attractive than they used to be.

Colors range from simple and subdued (perfect for an understated background) to bold and dramatic (ideal for a contemporary design scheme). Solid-color tiles are generally less expensive than their fancier counterparts. Combine them, as you would ceramic tile, to create dramatic effects. Resilient tile can handle most any flooring job—and at a fraction of the cost of other materials. It's among the easiest of materials to install.

Parquet

Parquet owes its exotic look to the arrangement of its individual fillets. Once hand-cut, individually glued, and expensive, today's tiles are machine-made and much more affordable.

The predominance of standard parallel-fillet patterns may lead you to believe design choices are limited. But step into any quality flooring shop (or any of several retailers' Internet websites) and you'll find triangular patterns, rhomboid shapes, interlocking triangles, and three-dimensional geometries set within each tile in the same and alternating woods. From a design standpoint, wood parquet offers almost as many opportunities as vinyl tile.

Limitations

Both vinyl and parquet tile, however, come with limitations. They cannot withstand outdoor conditions. Parquet will not last below grade or in wet locations. While you can install parquet in kitchens, it will not hold up well in bathroom installations. Vinyl can go almost anywhere, but it requires a waterproofing membrane when installed on concrete slabs below grade.

Resilient tile and wood parquet are easy to install and provide years of good-looking service.

CHAPTER PREVIEW

Laying out a resilient floor
page 194

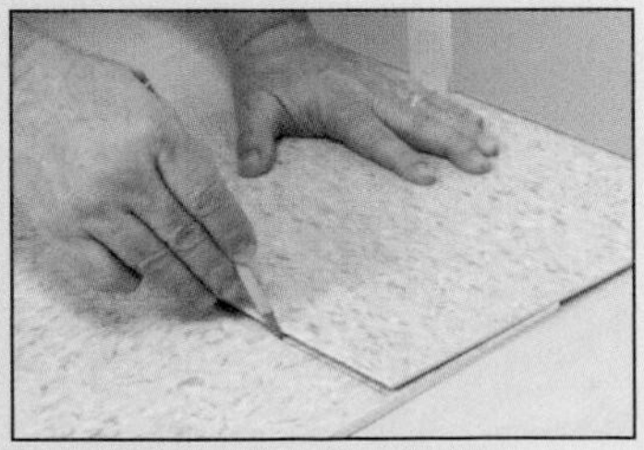

Installing dry-backed resilient tiles
page 196

Laying out a room and setting resilient tile in quadrants works best. Starting in the center of the room allows the focal point of the tile pattern to correspond to the focal point of the floor area. Snap a chalkline at the midpoint axis of two opposite walls, then the other two walls, and check for square. Dry-lay and adjust the tiles to come up with evenly sized edge tiles.

Installing self-stick vinyl tile
page 198

Installing parquet tile
page 200

STANLEY PRO TIP

Acclimate the tiles

Both resilient and parquet tiles need to acclimate (from 4 to 24 hours) to the humidity and temperature of the room in which you will install them.

Bring them in and open the cartons. Let them sit in the room for the period of time recommended by the manufacturer.

LAYING OUT A RESILIENT FLOOR

In most situations laying out the room and setting resilient tile in quadrants works best. Starting in the center of the room allows the focal point of the tile pattern to correspond to the focal point of the floor area. More important, laying out the installation in quadrants results in edge tiles that are the same width on all four sides.

The quadrant method, however, requires both patience and experimentation. To get evenly spaced edge tiles, you'll have to lay a row of tiles on one chalkline axis at a time and push the row back and forth until the spaces at the ends are the same size.

Bear in mind that edges look better if they are at least a half-tile wide. If your first trials end up with narrow slivers, take a tile out of the row and recenter the row on the layout line. Repeat the procedure for the other axis.

Because carpentry is an inexact science, almost no room is perfectly square. In older homes especially, you may find the out-of-square condition so severe that it results in one wall of radically tapered tiles. Try to "fix" your layout so tapered tiles fall in the least conspicuous part of the room; for example, on a wall opposite a doorway, in indirect light, or hidden underneath furniture.

PRESTART CHECKLIST

☐ **TIME**
Two hours for an 8×10-foot area, not counting preparation

☐ **TOOLS**
Tape measure, chalkline, carpenter's pencil, masking tape

☐ **SKILLS**
Measuring, marking

☐ **PREP**
Remove furniture, appliances, and inappropriate finished flooring

1 Prepare the subfloor and mark the center of the room by snapping chalklines between the midpoints of opposite walls. If the shape of the room is irregular or features protrusions that cover the center of a wall, snap the lines on the largest rectangular portion of the floor.

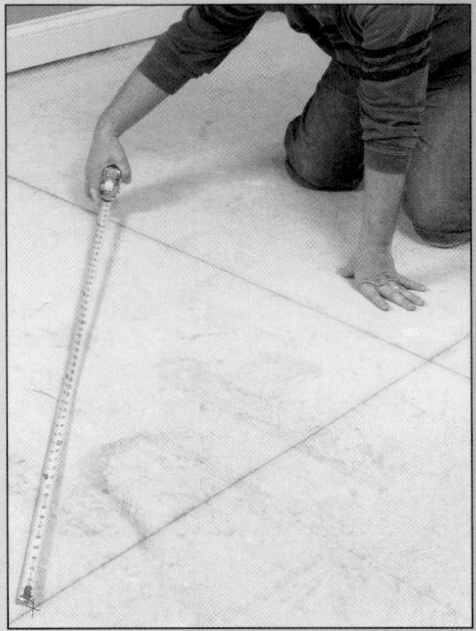

2 Check the lines for square using a 3-4-5 triangle *(page 195)*. Measure and mark 3 feet on one line and 4 feet on the other. If the distance between the two marks is 5 feet, your lines are square. If not you'll have to adjust the lines—use a long 2×4 to mark the diagonal on the floor.

Prepare the subfloor

Applying resilient tile to an improperly prepared subfloor is almost worse than not applying the tile in the first place. As its name implies, resilient tile conforms to every imperfection in the surface of the material upon which it's laid. Any light that reflects from that surface will magnify the imperfection and ruin the appearance despite all your hard work.

Wood. In new construction install $\frac{3}{4}$-inch plywood and $\frac{1}{4}$- or $\frac{1}{2}$-inch lauan or OSB for a smooth surface. On existing wood floors, install lauan plywood or OSB, staggering the joints and leaving a $\frac{1}{32}$-inch gap between them. Fill and sand all nail holes and gaps with a filler that's compatible with your tile adhesive.

Concrete. You can apply vinyl tile to concrete below, at, and above grade. Clean and smooth the surface *(pages 174–175)*. Grind off any protruding imperfections. Check for moisture by taping plastic sheets every 2 feet. If moisture beads under plastic after a couple of days, do not install tile. Remedy the moisture problem first, if possible. If moisture persists, choose another finished flooring material.

Vinyl tile or sheet goods. If existing material is cushioned, remove and prepare subfloor as above. If tile is installed on a wood floor and is loose, waxed, or glossy, cover with lauan plywood. On a concrete slab remove gloss and level embossed surface with an embossing leveler.

Ceramic tile. Remove tile and repair wood and concrete subfloors or level the tiled surface with self-leveling compound. Install lauan over plywood subfloor.

Carpet. Remove carpet and repair wood or concrete subfloor as above. Install lauan plywood over plywood subfloor.

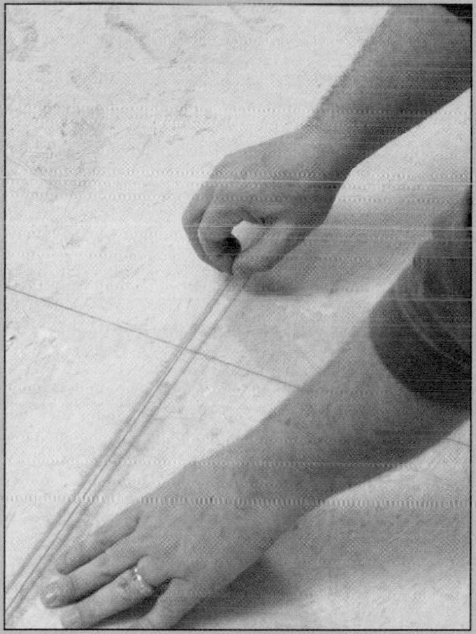

3 Adjust the lines until they are square by moving the chalkline slightly and resnapping the lines. If the diagonal measured more than 5 feet, move the line slightly clockwise with reference to the center point. If it was less than 5 feet, move it counterclockwise.

4 Dry-lay a row of tiles along both axes—from wall to wall. Measure the space for the tiles that will abut the wall. Adjust the line of tiles until the edge tiles are the same width and at least a half-tile wide. Repeat the adjustment on the other axis until you have even borders.

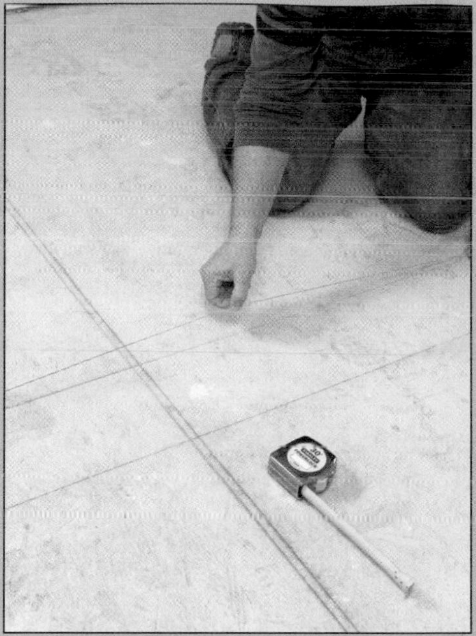

5 Mark the floor where the adjusted lines will fall and pull up the tiles. Resnap a new chalkline on these marks. This will give you a revised "center" point from which you will begin laying the floor. Make sure the adjusted lines are square.

LAYING OUT A RESILIENT FLOOR

Standard layout

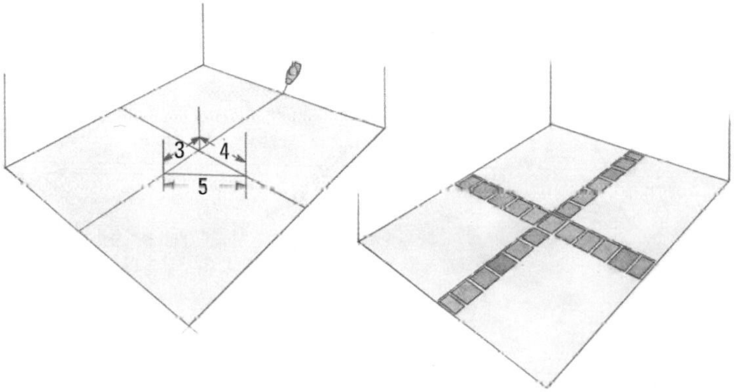
3
4
5

Snap perpendicular lines at the midpoints of the walls and square them. Dry-lay tile in both directions to center the layout and leave tiles of equal width at both edges.

Diagonal layout

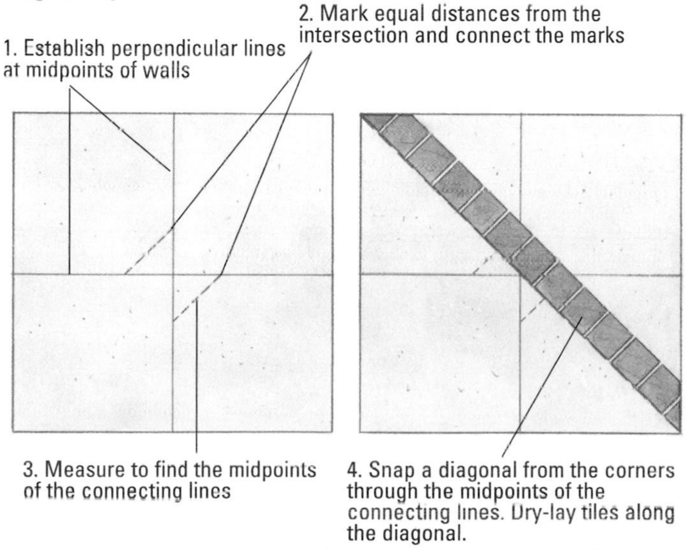
1. Establish perpendicular lines at midpoints of walls
2. Mark equal distances from the intersection and connect the marks
3. Measure to find the midpoints of the connecting lines
4. Snap a diagonal from the corners through the midpoints of the connecting lines. Dry-lay tiles along the diagonal.

INSTALLING DRY-BACKED RESILIENT TILES

When choosing an adhesive for dry-backed tile, be sure to read labels carefully. Picking an adhesive requires a bit of science—you'll find latex-based solutions, asphalt emulsions, alcohol resins, rubber cements, and epoxies. Ask your supplier to match the qualities of the adhesive to your job site.

Most vinyl adhesives are solvent-based, and that means they don't handle like thinset and other cement-based mortars. They tend to "grab" the trowel and are difficult to spread evenly. If you need to, practice spreading adhesive on a piece of scrap plywood before applying it to the floor. When you work with solvent-based adhesives, you must properly ventilate the room: Open the windows and exhaust the fumes with a window fan. Wear a respirator for full protection.

Work as much as possible from the untiled subfloor. To keep from tiling yourself into a corner, kneel on 2×2 squares of plywood at the last rows. Cut two pieces so you can move them alternately as you work across the floor.

PRESTART CHECKLIST

☐ **TIME**
About four hours for an 8×10-foot floor

☐ **TOOLS**
Trowel, utility knife, hair dryer, chalkline, straightedge, carpenter's pencil, 100-pound floor roller

☐ **SKILLS**
Setting and cutting tile

☐ **PREP**
Repair subfloor and snap layout lines

☐ **MATERIALS**
Tiles, adhesive

1 Starting at an intersection of lines, spread adhesive with the smooth edge of a notched trowel. Lay the adhesive right up to—but not over—the layout lines. Then comb the adhesive with the notched edge of the trowel. Let the adhesive become tacky.

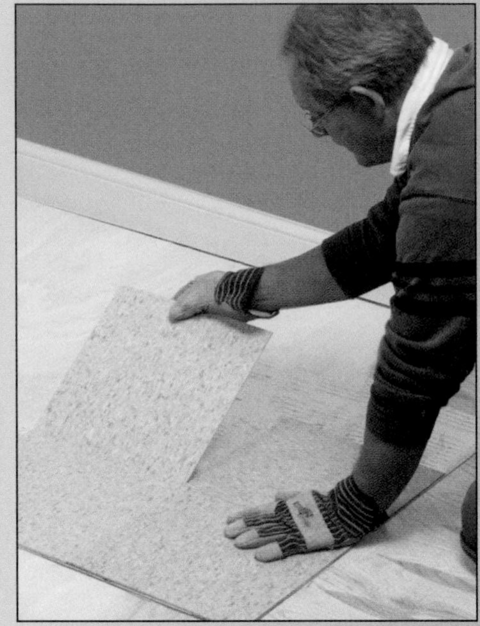

2 Line up the first tile with the intersection of the layout lines and set it on the adhesive. Then set the second tile against the first one and lower it in place. Don't slide the tiles—you'll push mastic up between the joints. Check the grain direction and set the rest of the quadrant.

SETTING SEQUENCES (PERPENDICULAR LAYOUTS)

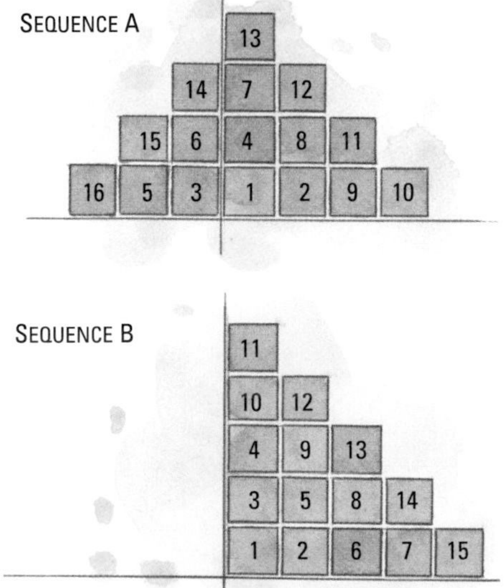

Use Sequence A when the adhesive has a long open time, which allows you to work more quickly because you don't have to stop as often to spread mastic. Use Sequence B when using a mastic with a short open time. For diagonal setting sequences, see *page 203*.

Check the grain direction

Most resilient tiles have a grain that results from the manufacturing process. The grain itself is virtually invisible but it does affect the color and perception of the pattern, depending on the angle of the light falling on the tile. Other tiles, both with and without grain, have a pattern that is directional.

Both grained and patterned tile must be laid in a certain order to achieve the ideal appearance. Look on the back of each tile before you lay it. If it has arrows imprinted on it, use the arrows as a guide. Dry-lay the tile with the arrows going in one direction, then experiment with the pattern, installing the arrows differently. Once you discover a result you like, use it consistently as you set the tile.

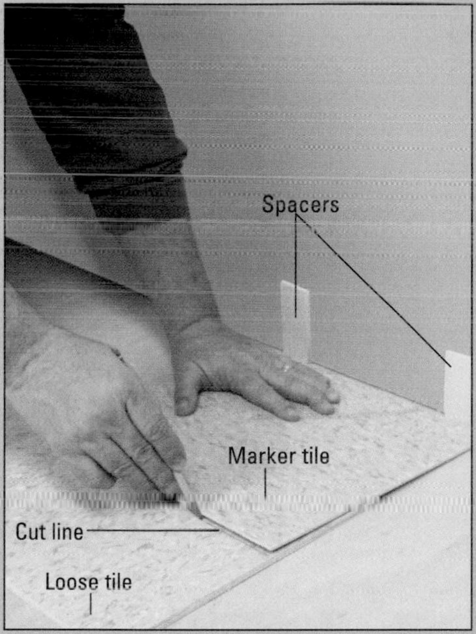

3 To mark the edge tiles for cutting, set a loose tile exactly on top of the last tile in a row. Then set a marker tile on top of that one, positioning it against ¼-inch spacers at the wall (resilient tile won't expand much, but the subfloor will). Run a pencil along the edge of the marker tile to mark the cut line.

4 At outside corners position a loose tile and a marker tile as if you were cutting an edge tile. Mark the loose tile as you did in Step 3, and reposition the loose tile and marker tile to the other corner. Mark the loose tile for the corner cutout.

5 When you have set one quadrant, clean off excess or spilled adhesive with the solvent recommended by the manufacturer (usually detergent and water). Don't wet the floor—excess liquid weakens the adhesive. Set the remaining quadrants. Roll the floor when finished.

Cutting vinyl tile

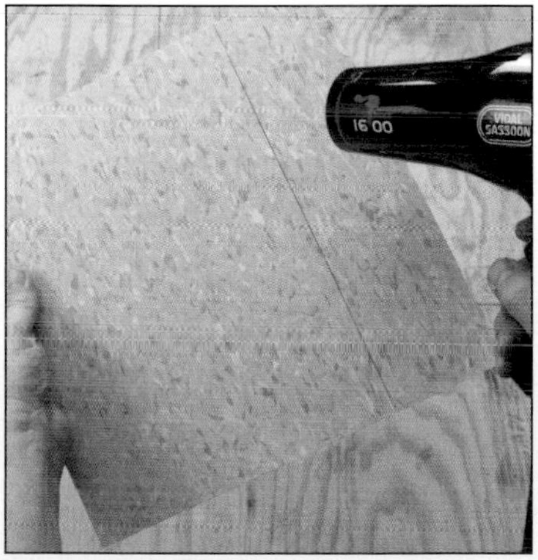

Brittle resilient tiles cut more easily if you warm the cut line slightly with a hair dryer.
Use a carpenter's pencil to mark the cut line and a utility knife to make the cut.

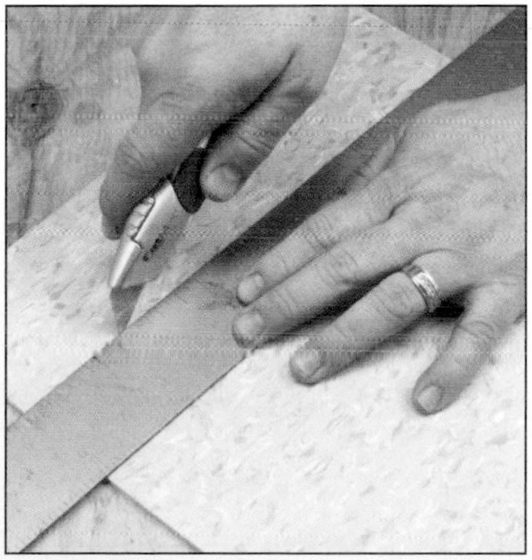

Score the surface of the tile with the knife, then make repeated passes until you have cut through the tile. If the cut edge will not be visible, snap the tile after a few passes with the knife instead.

STANLEY PRO TIP

Mix the lots

Tiles are manufactured in groups called "lots," and the color of the tile may vary from lot to lot. When you're purchasing tile, ask the dealer to supply you with tiles from the same lot. If you can't get the entire order from a single lot, mix the tiles from different cartons as you lay them. Doing so will spread any color variations randomly throughout the floor.

The easiest way to mix the tiles is to open three cartons and reassemble the tiles from each in a single batch.

INSTALLING SELF-STICK VINYL TILE

Self-stick vinyl tile (also called peel-and-stick tile) is a do-it-yourselfer's dream material. It requires only basic skills, minimal time, and a few tools. It also requires the same patience necessary for laying out any tile job and a precise eye when setting the first tile and those in the first row adjoining it. How straight the remaining installation looks depends in large part on the accuracy of the first row.

The steps shown here include the application of a primer. Some manufacturers don't recommend a primer. Others do, but only on porous surfaces such as plywood.

Once the tile comes into contact with the floor, the adhesive is unforgiving—you won't be able to slide the tile or adjust its position. If you misalign a tile, you'll probably have to pull it up and replace it. The tile will be damaged, but you might be able to find a place for it as a cut tile in a corner.

The paper backings on self-stick tile are surprisingly slippery underfoot. Keep the job site safe by placing a wastebasket at your side as you lay the tiles. Don't remove the tile backing until you're ready to set the tile. Dispose of the backing immediately.

PRESTART CHECKLIST

☐ **TIME**
About two hours for an 8×10-foot floor

☐ **TOOLS**
Long-handled roller, tape measure, heavy-duty scissors, putty knife, utility knife, chalkline, straightedge, square

☐ **SKILLS**
Laying tile accurately, cutting tile

☐ **PREP**
Repair, lay out, and clean floor

☐ **MATERIALS**
Self-stick tile, cove molding

1 Prime the subfloor, if necessary, with the product recommended by the manufacturer. Most primed surfaces benefit from two applications—the first one thinned and the second full strength. Both coats will go on easily with a long-handled roller.

2 Snap chalklines from the midpoints of opposite walls to locate the center of the room. Square the lines with a 3-4-5 triangle *(page 195)* and dry-lay the tiles along each axis. Move the layout until you have even tiles at the edges, then resnap the lines.

Cutting self-stick tile

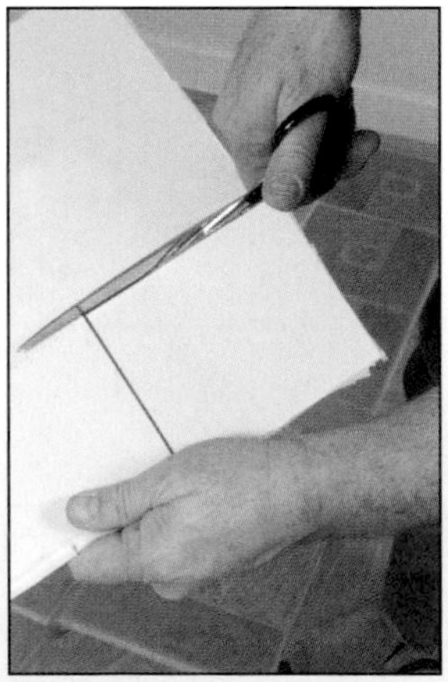

1 Mark the tile for cuts around obstructions but leave the backing on before cutting it. Using heavy-duty household scissors, cut the tile along the lines.

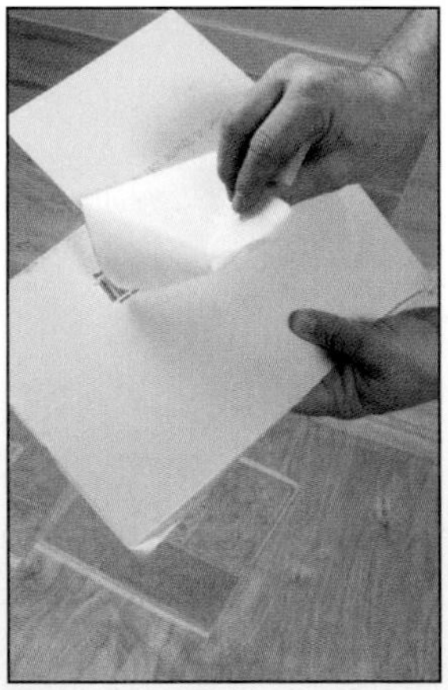

2 Peel off the backing and dispose of it immediately. The backings are very slick, and if you step on one, you might fall.

3 Position the tile carefully, placing the leading corner or edge against the neighboring tiles or the obstruction before you press it in place.

3 Arrange the tiles loosely along the layout lines with the arrows (grain) facing in the same or opposite directions (depending on the look you want). Starting at a corner of the tile and working slowly, peel away the paper backing. Don't pull fast—you might tear the backing, and a fresh edge is difficult to raise from the center of the tile. Set the corner of the tile at the intersection of the lines and press it down. Then roll it with a small roller.

4 Using the layout sequence of your choice *(page 196)*, continue setting the tiles, making sure each one butts squarely against its neighbors on two sides. Don't forget to maintain the arrows consistently. If you mistakenly lay a tile with the wrong orientation, warm the tile with a hair dryer to soften the adhesive and pry it up immediately with a wide putty knife. The tile isn't likely to survive removal without damage.

Installing vinyl cove molding

1 To fit an inside corner, score the back of the molding with a utility knife and cut a V-notch in the coved base. If you can't get the molding tightly in the corner, cut the material on your score marks. Cut and install all corners first, then cut and install straight runs to fit between them.

2 To fit an outside corner, warm the molding with a hair dryer before adhering it to the wall. You can increase the flexibility of the molding by paring away a thin layer from the back. Don't cut through the material.

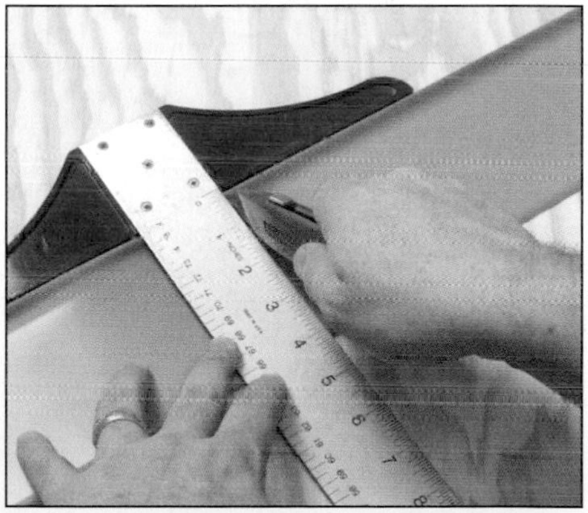

3 Cut all butt joints using a square to guide the knife. After applying the adhesive, roll the molding with a J-roller and press the flange against the floor and wall with a piece of 1× scrap.

INSTALLING PARQUET TILE

Most parquet tiles are cut with tongues and grooves, which makes installation easy. In the long run it pays to purchase the highest quality tile you can afford. A higher quality finish offers greater longevity and quicker installation time. The tongues and grooves of less expensive tiles don't always fit together smoothly.

To seat the tiles against each other, tap them with a hammer and a block of wood. Avoid sliding the tiles and kneel on sheets of plywood as you get deeper into the project. Be sure there is no adhesive between the knee boards and the tiles. Otherwise you'll take the tile up when you move the board.

Take special care in laying your first 10 to 12 tiles—these determine how well the joints on the rest of the floor line up. If any adhesive gets on the tiles, clean it immediately with a rag soaked in solvent. Never apply the solvent directly to the tiles—it could mar their finish. Don't forget to leave a ½-inch gap between the edge tiles and the walls.

1 Prepare the subfloor, then snap chalklines between the midpoints of opposite walls. If the shape of the room is irregular or features protrusions, snap the lines on the largest rectangular portion of the floor. That way your installation will be "centered" on the primary focal point of the floor. Square the lines with a 3-4-5 triangle *(page 195)* and adjust the lines if necessary. Dry-lay the tiles so you have edge tiles of the same width, and adjust the lines again if necessary. Don't forget to set a cork expansion strip along the wall when you're dry-laying the tile.

PRESTART CHECKLIST

☐ **TIME**
About 12 to 15 hours for an 8×10-foot floor

☐ **TOOLS**
Carpenter's pencil, hammer, extension cord, shop vacuum, fan(s), jigsaw or circular saw, chalkline, tape measure, notched trowel, carpenter's square, 100-pound floor roller, trim saw

☐ **SKILLS**
Measuring and cutting, setting and cutting wood tile

☐ **PREP**
Repair floor as necessary

☐ **MATERIALS**
Mastic or adhesive, cork strips, parquet tiles, adhesive solvent, rags

Prepare the subfloor

You can apply parquet over several different subfloors. Each calls for slightly different preparation.

Wood: In new construction install ¾-inch plywood. On an existing wood floor, remove the finish and repair. On planks wider than 4 inches, install ⅜-inch underlayment. Fill all nail holes and depressions and sand smooth.
Concrete: You can lay parquet on concrete at and above grade. Check for moisture by taping plastic sheets to the slab every 2 feet. If moisture beads under plastic after a couple of days, don't install tile. Remedy the moisture problem first, if possible. If moisture is still present, choose another finished flooring material. Clean and roughen the surface slightly to aid the adhesive bond.
Vinyl tile or sheet goods: If existing material is cushioned, remove and prepare subfloor. If tile is installed on a wood floor and is loose, waxed, or glossy, sand or strip the finish and repair.
Ceramic tile: Level the tiled surface with self-leveling compound. Remove damaged tile and repair.
Carpet: Remove carpet and repair wood or concrete subfloor. Install lauan plywood over plywood subfloor.

Spreading the adhesive
Spreading the right amount of adhesive takes practice. Try to comb out the adhesive so the ridges are about ⅛ inch tall.

2 Scoop a small amount of adhesive onto the floor. Holding the trowel at a 45-degree angle, comb out the adhesive with the notched side of a trowel. Spread the adhesive up to but not on top of the chalklines. Let the adhesive become tacky according to manufacturer recommendations.

3 Set the first tile in the adhesive exactly at the intersection of the layout lines. Use the edge of the tile, not the edge of the tongue or inside surface of the groove, to line it up. Position the tile with some precision; avoid sliding the tile, as this will push up the adhesive.

4 Hold the second tile at a slight angle to the first. With the tongue engaged in the groove of the first tile, push the tile simultaneously down and toward the first tile. Continue in a pyramid pattern. Tap the tiles together with a rubber mallet.

REFRESHER COURSE
Removing baseboards

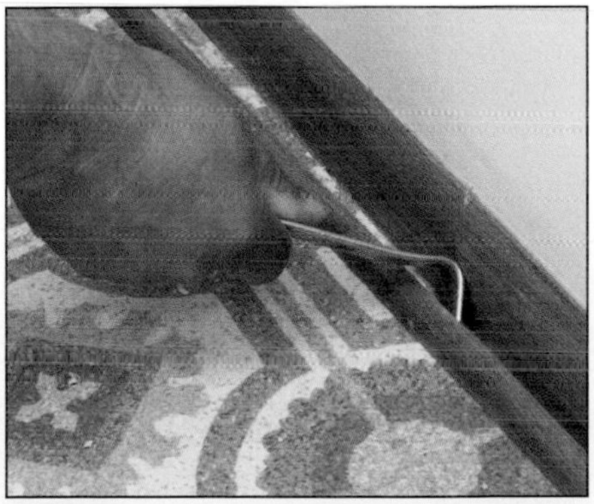

1 Starting at a corner, slide a small pry bar behind the shoe. Loosen the shoe until you can insert the pry bar next to a nail. Pry the nail out a little at a time. To avoid splits, loosen at least two nails before pulling the molding completely off the wall.

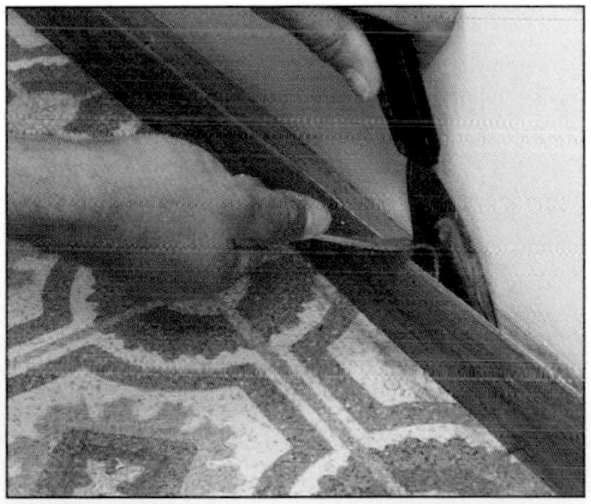

2 Begin at a corner or a mitered joint, working a wide putty knife behind the baseboard. Loosen each nail with a pry bar. Keep the putty knife behind the bar or use a thin piece of scrap as a shim to avoid marring the wall. Loosen all nails before removing baseboard sections.

Undercut the door casing

After installing underlayment, set a tile on the subfloor at a doorway and use a trim saw to undercut the door jambs and molding by the thickness of the tile. This way you won't have to make intricate cuts to fit tile pieces around the trim; you can just slip them under the trim.

Installing parquet tile *(continued)*

5 Using the same techniques, continue laying the parquet in the remainder of the first quadrant. When you reach a point where you have to work from the surface of the newly laid tile, spread your weight evenly over a 2×2-foot plywood sheet. When you reach the walls, mark the tile for cutting the border or edge tiles. Mark and cut each tile individually—don't cut them all to the same width unless you're absolutely sure the room is square.

6 Once you've completed the first quadrant, use the same methods to install the tiles in the remaining quadrants. Always start at the intersection of the layout lines. If you're installing the parquet in sections, roll each section with a rented 100-pound floor roller to set the tiles firmly in the adhesive. You must roll the floor within four hours of the application of the adhesive. Install cork expansion strips, usually provided by the manufacturer, along the edges.

SAFETY FIRST
Ventilate the work space

Many adhesives used in the installation of parquet are petroleum based and contain chemicals that evaporate rapidly. These chemicals and others, called "driers," are volatile and sometimes toxic.

When installing a parquet floor, be sure to provide plenty of ventilation—open windows to create cross drafts, exhaust the fumes to the outside with a window fan, and extinguish any pilot lights on gas-fired appliances. Wear a respirator and gloves.

Cutting the border or edge tiles

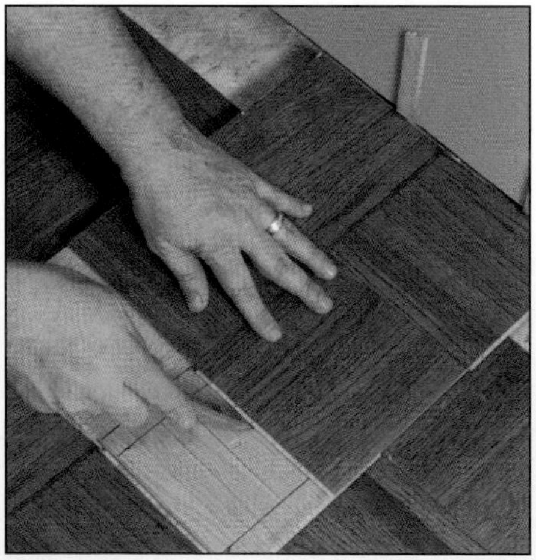

1 To mark tiles for cutting, set a loose tile bottom side up exactly on top of the last tile, then a marker tile on top of that one. Run a pencil down the edge of the marker tile to mark the cut.

2 Clamp the tile to a supporting surface and cut it with a jigsaw equipped with a fine-tooth blade. Cut the tile face down if using a regular blade or circular saw, face up with a reverse-cutting blade.

Installing parquet on the diagonal

1 Begin your diagonal layout in the same fashion as a perpendicular installation—snap chalklines at the midpoints of opposite walls and square the lines with a 3-4-5 triangle. From the center point, mark an equal distance on all four lines and connect the marks. Snap chalklines from the corners through the midpoints on the connecting lines (below). Dry-lay the tiles along the diagonal so you'll achieve edge tiles of equal width.

2 Starting at the intersection of the layout lines, spread and comb mortar along one of the diagonal quadrants. Lay the first tile square against the intersection of the lines, using the edge of the tile (not the tongue or groove) as your reference plane. With the second tile slightly raised, engage the tongue in the groove of the first and press it down and in. Continue setting tiles in this fashion, one quadrant at a time, making diagonal cuts at the walls.

SETTING SEQUENCES FOR DIAGONAL LAYOUTS

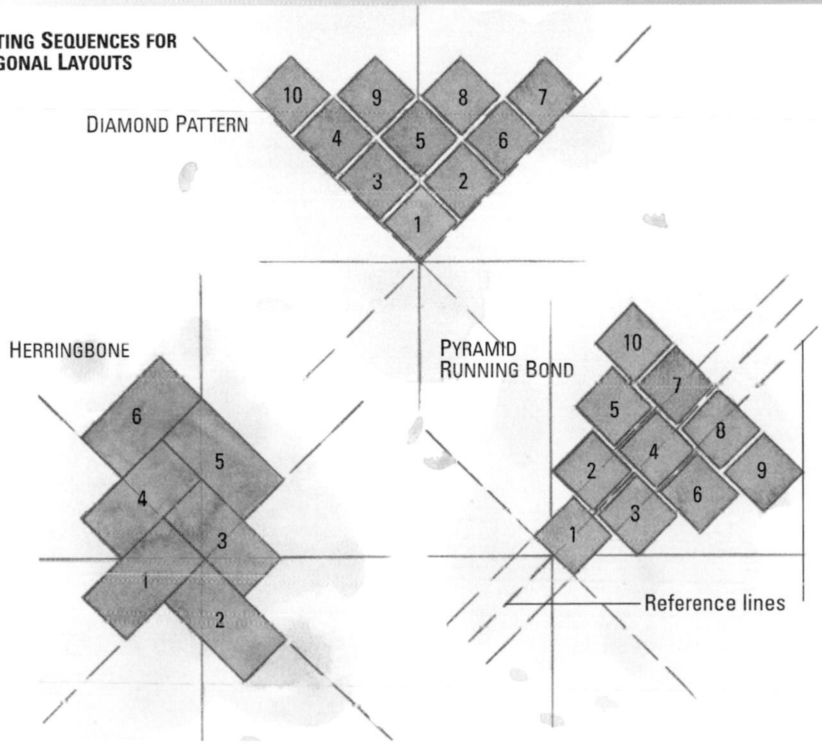

Making diagonal cuts

Lay a loose tile face down exactly on the last tile set in the adhesive. Position a marker tile on the loose tile and up against ½-inch spacers at the wall. Draw a pencil line along the bottom edge of the marker tile and cut the tile with a circular saw or jigsaw.

INSTALLING LAMINATE, CORK & CARPET TILE

Laminates, cork, and carpet tile offer many choices of alternative floor coverings, and although they vary considerably in cost, each combines appearance and durability with ease of installation.

Laminates

Laminates provide exceptional durability at a moderate cost—only slightly more than resilient tile. A tough melamine wear coat gives them their staying power. This top layer borrows technology from the manufacture of laminate countertops. It resists the impact of high-heeled shoes and damage from burns and stains.

Where a beautiful visual effect is paramount and practicality is important, laminate flooring fits the bill. Many single-tile patterns are made to look like wood, but you'll find an increasing number of granite, marble, and stone look-alikes, as well as abstract designs and ceramic patterns. You'll have your choice of individual laminate tiles or planks with tile "visuals"—individual tiles printed on a plank, complete with grout lines.

Carpet tile

Not long ago you might have considered carpet tile a less than first-rate floor covering. New materials and methods of manufacture, however, have improved its quality, environmental safety, and durability.

One aspect of carpet tile that makes it desirable is the ease with which you can cut and install it. This adds up to reduced installation costs and time. It also means you can customize your floor scheme with stunning effects. If you like, you can install carpet tile to mimic broadloom carpet. It offers an amazing array of design options at far less expense than a wall-to-wall installation.

Cork tile

Because cork is a natural product, each tile displays a unique color, pattern, and texture. All are comfortable underfoot, thanks to millions of tiny air cells in their surface, an attribute which also makes cork an excellent choice where sound deadening is important. Naturally resilient, it recovers quickly from denting, and its air insulating cells help keep the floor warm in the winter and cool in the summer.

Laminates, cork, and carpet tile offer a range of design and installation options that fit most budgets and skill levels.

CHAPTER PREVIEW

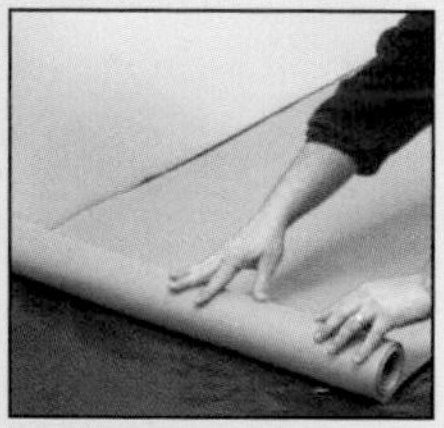

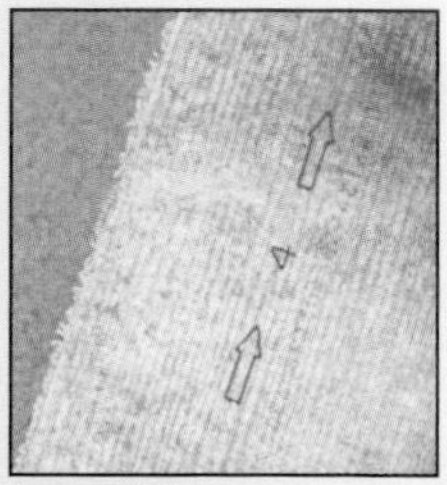

To create an offset pattern, snap the center layout lines (blue), then measure over half the width of a tile. Mark each end of the room and snap a new line with different colored chalk (red).

To create an offset pattern, snap the center layout lines (blue), then measure over half the width of a tile. Mark each end of the room and snap a new line with different colored chalk (red). You may need to adjust the lines so the layout has edge tiles of the same width. Always dry-lay the tiles to check the layout.

INSTALLING GLUELESS LAMINATE TILE

Locking laminate planks snap together, and like their glued counterparts, they float on a plastic foam underlayment. The underlayment allows the flooring to expand and contract as a unit and makes the floor feel more comfortable underfoot.

How you assemble the planks will vary with the manufacturer. Some styles use a tongue-and-groove configuration. Others employ metal locking strips. Some brands require that you angle the units as you engage the tongue and groove. Others snap together flat on the floor with the aid of a tapping block and hammer.

The "tilt-and-engage" style is the most common. Installing the first three rows of planks works best if you pull them toward you. That means you will install the first three rows about 3 feet from the wall and slide them to the wall as a unit after you've put it together. Then you can work on top of the tile you've installed.

Acclimate the planks to the room in which you'll install them for 48 hours. If you will be using laminate baseboards in the room, extend the underlayment about 2 inches up each wall.

PRESTART CHECKLIST

☐ **TIME**
Abotu 5 to 6 hours for an 8×10-foot floor, not including subfloor preparation

☐ **TOOLS**
Tape measure, metal straightedge, jigsaw, circular saw or table saw, trim saw, utility knife, hammer, tapping block, pull bar, pencil

☐ **SKILLS**
Measuring, setting, and cutting laminate

☐ **PREP**
Repair, replace subfloor

☐ **MATERIALS**
Underlayment, laminate planks, caulk

A. Preparing the layout

1 Roll out the underlayment, butting or overlapping the joints as instructed by the manufacturer. Tape the joints as instructed. Measure the room and divide the result by the width of the planks. Add the remainder to the width of a plank and divide by 2. This is the width of your first and last border row.

2 Open three cartons and mix the planks so color variations spread throughout the room. Use your computations from Step 1 to mark the width of the tile plank for the border row. Rip enough border planks for your starting wall. When using a circular saw, place the finish side down.

Preparing the subfloor

Wood: In new construction install ¾-inch plywood. On an existing floor, remove the finish and repair. Install ⅜-inch underlayment on planks wider than 4 inches. Fill all depressions and sand.
Concrete: Check for moisture by taping plastic sheets to the slab every 2 feet. If moisture beads under plastic after a couple of days, don't install planks. Remedy the moisture problem first, if possible. Clean and roughen the surface slightly to give it a "tooth" for the adhesive.
Vinyl tile or sheet goods: If existing material is cushioned, remove it and repair subfloor. If resilient material is installed on a wood floor and is loose, waxed, or glossy, sand or strip.
Ceramic tile: Level the surface with self-leveling compound. Remove damaged tile.
Carpet: Remove carpet and repair wood or concrete subfloor as above.

Choosing single laminate tiles

Laminate flooring is also available in individual square tiles, which offer more design options than planks. However, you may have a hard time finding them, and because production costs are higher for individual pieces, these tiles are slightly more expensive than their plank equivalents. On the other hand, using planked products results in increased waste because they require more end cuts to fit, so the cost difference may even out in the long run.

3 Starting in the center of the wall, snap the border planks together. When you no longer have space for a full plank, center the row, leaving an equal space at each end. Measure from the edge of the plank face (not the tongue) to the wall and subtract ¼ inch (to allow for spacers).

4 Mark the top of a full border plank, using the length from Step 3 and measuring from the edge of the face. Transfer the mark to the back of the plank with a combination square; cut the plank with a circular saw. Cut the left and right ends from separate planks to maintain the pattern.

5 Lock the left and right ends of the border row in place. Then push the border row against the wall, inserting ¼-inch spacers every foot or so. Number the order of the planks on small pieces of masking tape.

Laying out the grout lines

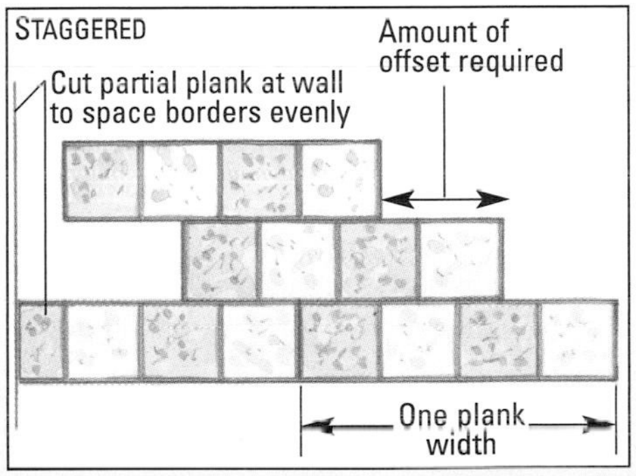

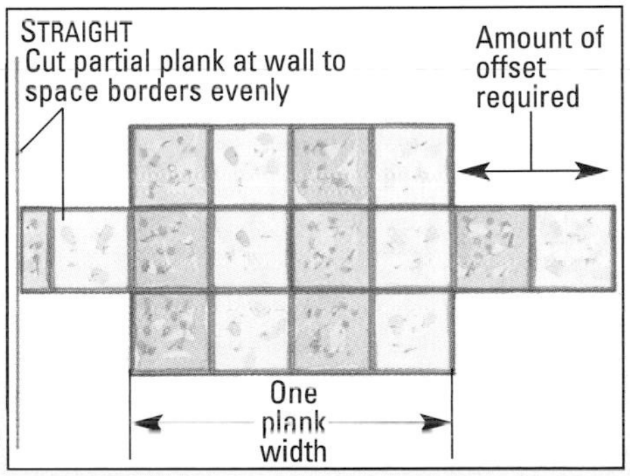

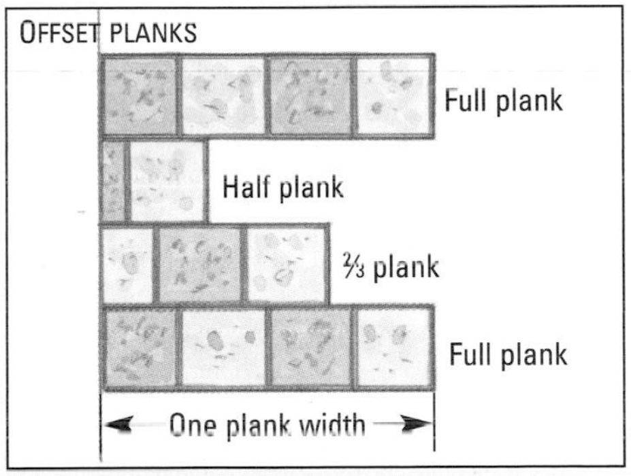

How you design the pattern formed by the grout lines of planked tile depends on the size of the visual and how much the manufacturer requires the joints between the planks to be offset. Some planks can only be laid in a straight grout pattern. Others are sized with visuals that may permit more flexibility. Each will require some experimentation in planning the borders.

Both staggered and straight patterns will produce evenly spaced tiles at the walls, but require cutting partial planks and result in more waste than an offset plank pattern. An offset plank pattern produces grout joints spaced randomly from row to row. Some manufacturers recommend the offset shown here. Others specify different lengths for each starting plank.

Because different grout patterns create dramatic differences in the appearance of a room, decide on the pattern in the planning stage and purchase a product that will produce the look you want. Bring your design to a tile retailer to get help in choosing the style that will meet your needs and be sure to get detailed instructions on how to lay the tile in the pattern of your choice.

B. Marking and cutting contours

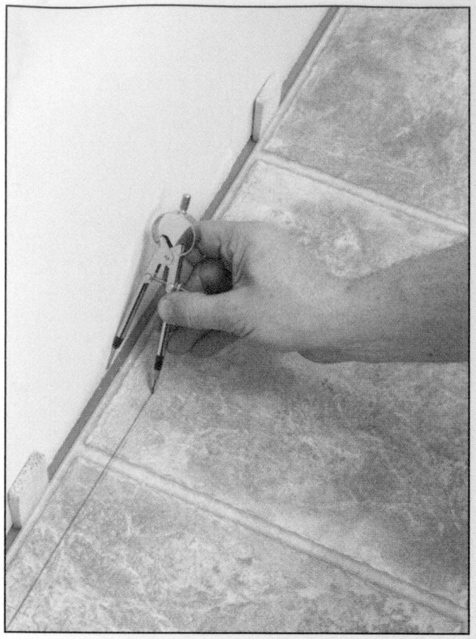

1 Variations in the wall can affect the layout, so the first row must follow the contour of the wall. Draw a compass along the planks, skipping the spacers. (Read the instructions; some recommend doing this after laying three rows.) Snap the second row together and cut the end planks.

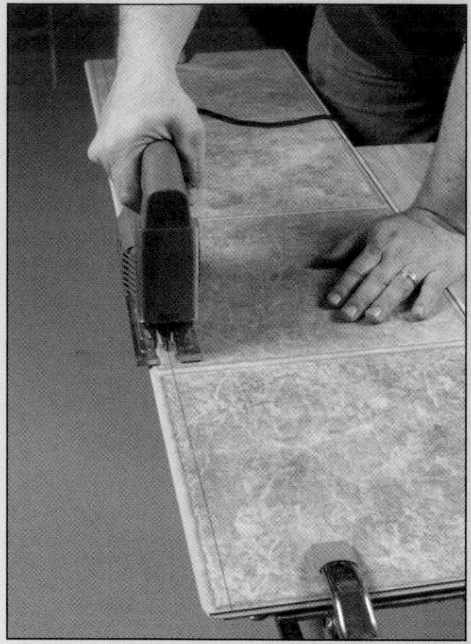

2 Disassemble the border planks and use a jigsaw with a fine-tooth blade to cut the scribed line. With a reverse cutting blade, set the good side up to avoid chipping the plank. If using a regular blade, keep the good side down.

C. Installing the planks

1 Working away from the starting wall, reassemble the border row planks in their original order. Maintain the offset directed by the manufacturer and snap the end plank of the second row to the first row. Tilt the plank and pull the tongue into the groove. Prop the plank on a piece of scrap.

STANLEY PRO TIP

Moisture-proof concrete slabs

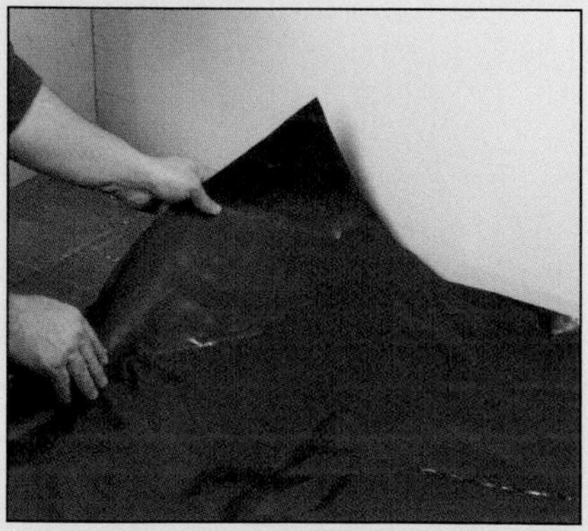

Most laminate products require a moisture barrier when laid on a concrete slab. Polyethylene sheets usually serve this purpose, but check with your retailer if the manufacturer's instructions don't address this aspect of installation.

Using a pull bar

When you reach the end of a row, you won't be able to lift the tile to snap it in place. In this case use a pull bar to assemble the units. Slide one end of the bar over the far end of the tile and tap the other end until the tile snaps into place.

Closing up the gaps

From time to time, even your best efforts will leave a gap between tiles that don't fit just exactly right. Close up these gaps as you go, using a tapping block and a hammer.

2 Tilt the second plank and push the tongue into the groove of the first one. Depending on the instructions, you can either pull each plank toward you and into the first row as you go or wait until you have assembled the entire row. Regardless of the method, lower the plank until it snaps into place.

3 Continue using the same methods to fit the planks together. When you have completed the first three rows, slide the assembly toward the starting wall, stopping short by a little more than the thickness of the spacers. Insert the spacers against the wall and snug the rows against them.

4 Continue snapping the planks together, working toward the other wall, closing up gaps as necessary with a tapping block and trimming the final row to fit. Tilt the final row and pull it into place, using a pull bar to snug the planks together. Trim underlayment flush with the planks as necessary.

Undercut the door trim

Like any other tile, laminate units raise the height of the floor. To avoid notching tiles around the door trim, set a tile on the subfloor at a doorway and use a trim saw to undercut the door jambs by the thickness of the tile. If it's necessary to trim the doors as well, use a circular saw to cut the some off the bottom.

Sealing the edges

Most manufacturers recommend sealing all exposed edges of laminate tile. This is especially important in bathroom and kitchen installations because it's imperative that water (or moisture) doesn't get under the tiles.

Some manufacturers recommend painting the edges with glue. But the safest way to protect an installation is to caulk the edges with mildew-resistant silicone caulk.
In bathrooms caulk around the toilet, tub, and vanity. In kitchens caulk in front of the dishwasher, icemaker, exterior doorways, and opening to the
laundry room.

Trimming the final row

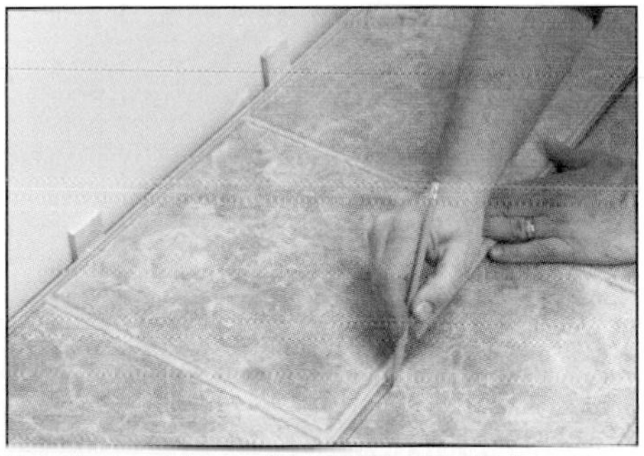

Despite your best efforts to make the last row of tiles come out exactly the same width as the beginning row, it won't—and that is why you don't cut all the edge tiles at once. Cut each tile in the last row separately, setting in the spacers first and marking loose tiles with a guide tile. Set the cut tiles in place, snapping them to each other and to the field tiles with the pull bar and tapping block.

INSTALLING GLUED LAMINATE TILE PLANKS

When you're shopping for glued laminate tiles or tiled planks, you'll find as many varieties of edge construction as you would for a glueless floor. Some manufacturers sell planks that you can install with or without glue, leaving the decision completely up to you. How to decide? Glued joints are stronger than most unglued installations and stand up to harder use. Use them in rec rooms, children's playrooms, in any environment where activity might disrupt the joints, and in bathrooms and kitchens where the glue will keep moisture out of the joints. If you're considering tiled laminate planks for a bathroom or kitchen, however, make sure the manufacturer's warranties apply to installation of the material in these rooms.

The joints of some products swell for a couple of months after the installation. Such swelling is normal and disappears when the glue cures.

Before installing the tiles, mix three boxes together to distribute color variations evenly, then acclimate the tile to the room for 48 hours.

PRESTART CHECKLIST

☐ **TIME**
Abotu 10 to 12 hours for an 8×10-foot floor, not including subfloor prep

☐ **TOOLS**
Tape measure, metal straightedge, jigsaw, circular saw or table saw, trim saw, compass, hammer, tapping block, pull bar, utility knife, pencil

☐ **SKILLS**
Measuring, setting, and cutting laminate

☐ **PREP**
Repair, replace subfloor

☐ **MATERIALS**
Foam underlayment, 6-mil polyethylene, laminate planks, caulk, masking tape

A. Setting up the rows

1 If you're installing the planks on a slab, lay down a 6-mil sheet of polyethylene as a waterproofing membrane. Then roll out the manufacturer's underlayment, following the directions for seaming. Some makers recommend butt joints, others suggest overlapping seams. Some say to tape their seams, some don't. If you're installing laminate baseboards or putting the planks in a bathroom or kitchen, extend the underlayment 2 to 3 inches up the wall and tape the seams with clear waterproof tape (available from a laminate retailer).

How much do you need?

Estimating the amount of materials you'll need for a laminate floor starts with the coverage in a carton. Some tiles are 15½ inches square, others are a foot square. Some planks are just under 4 feet long and a foot wide, others are larger.

Find out the carton coverage from the manufacturer or retailer—most large companies now maintain thorough Internet websites, complete with colors, patterns, and specifications.

When you order tiles, add 5 percent to the amount you think you need. When ordering tiled planks, add 15 percent. The extra accounts for mistakes and any damaged units.

Generally you can expect one roll of underlayment to cover about 100 square feet of floor. For a room of this size, you'll need two bottles of glue.

Orient the first tile

When you are ready to start laying laminates, make sure you start the first unit with the proper orientation. Most—but not all—laminates are installed by engaging the tongue of the new unit into the groove of the one already in place. Don't assume this is true for your product. Read the manufacturer's instructions before starting. Some laminates require you to remove the tongue from the first row.

2 Follow the directions for laying out a locking tile border *(pages 206–207)*, ripping the border planks in even widths. Then dry-fit the border row, adjusting and cutting the end planks to equal lengths. Dry-lay the border row, working from left to right. Do not apply glue yet.

3 With the border row in place, dry-fit the second row of planks, starting with the end pieces (as required by your layout pattern) and working from left to right. Tilt and engage the tongues into the grooves (or use whatever installation method is required by the manufacturer's instructions).

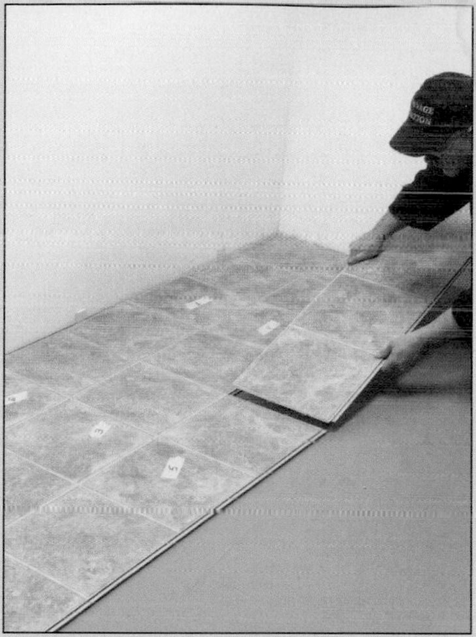

4 Dry-fit the third row of planks. Then stand back and inspect the installation to make sure the joints run parallel to the starting wall. If they don't, you may have to trim the edge planks to straighten the installation. Mark the order of the tiles on pieces of masking tape and disassemble the planks.

WHAT IF...
You're laying single tiles?

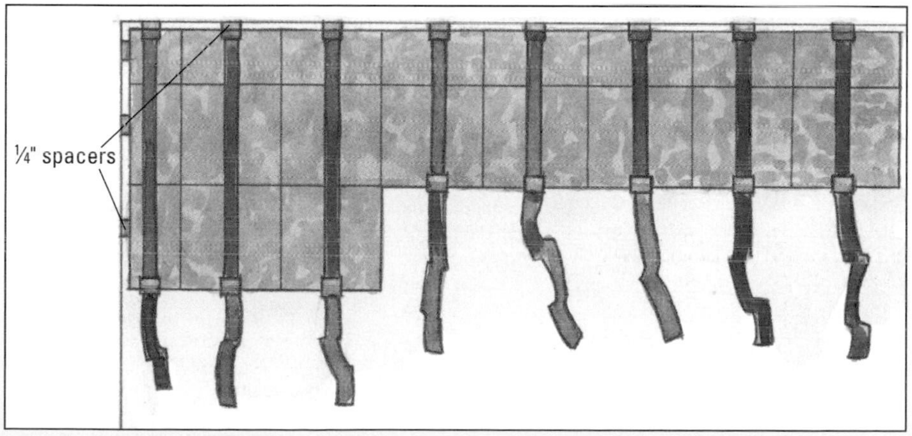

Some brands of glued laminate tile require clamping with ratcheting strap clamps. Some manufacturers recommend clamping every two tiles, others, every three tiles. Follow the recommendations and ratchet the tiles just enough to make the glue seep from the joints. Too much pressure will cause the joints to buckle. Wipe the glue immediately with the solvent recommended by the manufacturer (usually a light detergent-and-water solution).

The larger the floor, the wider the gap

All laminate flooring requires a gap around the edges of the room to give the flooring a space to expand and contract with changes in the humidity. Manufacturers' instructions generally call for about ¼ inch; this measurement is the minimum gap required.

Because wood fibers expand in relation to the amount of wood in the floor, the larger the floor area, the wider the gap has to be. In fact, the ¼-inch standard holds true for floors only from 100 to 1,000 square feet. From 1,000 to 1,800 square feet, you'll need to expand the gap to ⅜ inch, and for a 3,000 square-foot area, to as much as ⅝ inch. Large installations, generally over 40 linear feet in either direction, require a T-molding between sections *(see page 113)*.

B. Installing the planks

1 Replace the spacers along the wall if necessary. Set the end plank in the corner, and using the method recommended by the manufacturer, apply glue to the second plank—either the tongue, the groove, or both. Engage the planks with the method recommended by the manufacturer and pull them together. Properly applied glue seeps from the joint in a thin line. Wipe it up immediately with a damp rag, then wipe the residue again.

2 At this point, you can proceed across the wall, gluing and locking the entire first row of border planks, or you can set the planks in a stair-step pattern as recommended by the manufacturer. If clamping is required the clamps should cross the installation every 3 to 4 feet. Pull the clamps moderately tight and let the glue set for 15 to 30 minutes before releasing and resetting the clamps. For products not requiring clamps, tape the joints if required.

STANLEY PRO TIP

Start tile under toe-kick

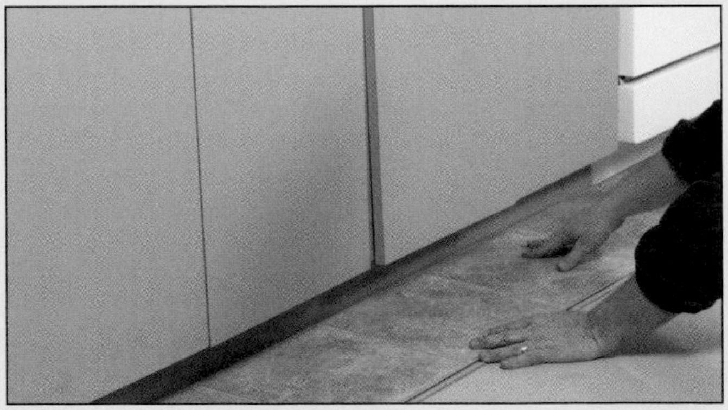

Before you choose a starting wall, consider any obstacles in the room, especially those that would interfere with putting down the first row. For example, a vanity or kitchen cabinet toe-kick will make it difficult to tilt the planks, especially if you install the last row there. Start the installation under the toe-kick and work toward the opposite wall.

Close the gaps

As you research laminate products, you may notice that each manufacturer configures the tongues and grooves differently. Most, however, require the use of a tapping block. When you snug tiles together with a tapping block, be careful not to damage the geometry of those edges. You might think you can get by with a scrap tile for a tapping block, but it's better to purchase the one made by the manufacturer. Tap gently to avoid damaging the edges of the tiles.

3 When you reach walls or other obstructions, you may not be able to tilt or tap the planks together. Make sure you have cut the end plank long enough to fill the space. Insert the short end of a pull bar over the end of the plank and tap the planks together with a hammer.

4 Continue assembling the planks, snugging the clamps every row or two and giving the glue ample time to dry before setting the next row.

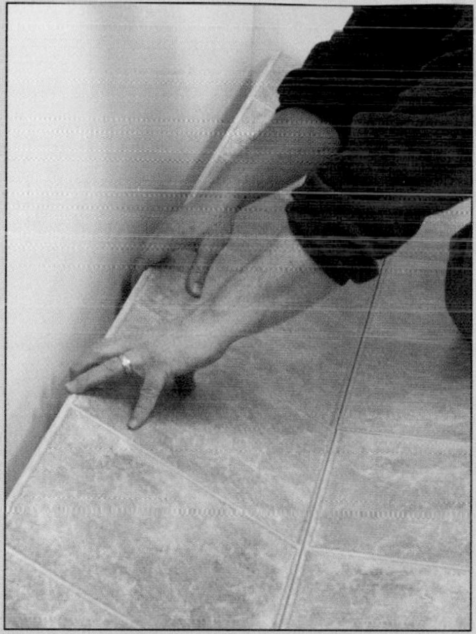

5 When you reach the last row, scribe the planks to conform to the surface of the wall. Be sure to include the spacer when you mark the tile for cutting. After cutting remove the spacer so it's easier to fit the tiles together. Use a pull bar to snug the planks.

Apply the right amount of glue in the right places

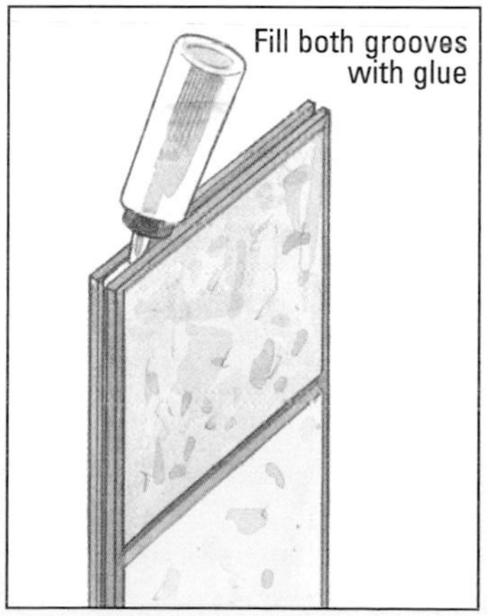

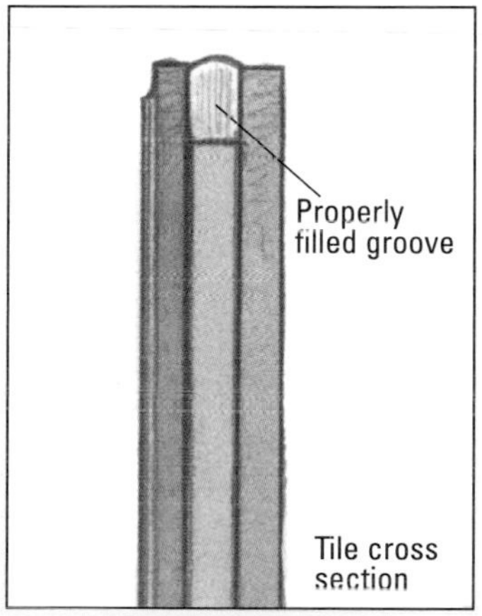

Different brands of laminate planks require different gluing methods. Some manufacturers recommend gluing the tongue of the plank, others the groove, and still others, both the tongue and groove.

One style of plank does not use glue at all—the edges come preglued and require the application of an activator.

One requirement that is consistent among all the products is the amount of glue you need to apply—and getting it right may take some experimenting. Properly applied glue just barely seeps from between fully closed joints. If you apply too little, the boards won't stay together; too much, and the boards won't stay together tightly.

Be sure to clean the excess off the surface immediately. Dried laminate glue proves very difficult to remove.

INSTALLING CARPET TILE

When it comes to installing floor covering material, carpet tile is the easiest and you can achieve some surprising design patterns with it. It's lightweight, cuts with ease, wears well, and goes on quickly. Furthermore it's less expensive than laminate products, it doesn't telegraph subfloor defects into the finished surface as dramatically as resilients, and it's softer and warmer underfoot than ceramic tile. When it gets worn in one place (as any flooring tends to do), you can pull up a tile or two and put down fresh ones.

Aside from quality differences, carpet tile falls into two general categories: self-stick and dry-backed. The application of self-stick tiles is more or less self-explanatory (right). Installing dry-backed tiles (which are usually a little thicker) means laying down a mastic or using doubled-faced carpet tape. Mastic applications usually leave a little more time to fine-tune the layout and keep the joints straight. Double-faced tape won't gum up the entire floor, a factor to consider if there's a chance you'll one day remove the tile from a solid wood floor. In either case acclimate the tile to the room for 48 hours before you install it.

PRESTART CHECKLIST

☐ **TIME**
About 15 minutes per square yard, not including subfloor preparation

☐ **TOOLS**
Utility knife, tape measure, metal straightedge, chalkline, 100-pound roller

☐ **SKILLS**
Measuring, laying, and cutting tile

☐ **PREP**
Repair and level subfloor

☐ **MATERIALS**
Carpet tile, mastic or double-faced tape for dry-backed installation

1 Prepare the subfloor, then snap chalklines from the midpoints of opposite walls. Square the lines with a 3-4-5 triangle *(page 195)* and dry-lay the tile on both axes. Move the rows back and forth until you have edge tiles that are at least a half-tile wide and equal at each end.

2 Carpet tiles are made with a certain "lay" to the pile, indicated by arrows on the back. Most manufacturers recommend setting the tiles at 90 degrees to each other to minimize wear appearance. With arrows in the same direction, the carpet will look more like a broadloom weave.

Prepare the subfloor

Wood: In new construction install ¾-inch plywood. On an existing wood floor, remove the finish and repair. On planks wider than 4 inches, install ⅜-inch underlayment. Fill depressions and sand smooth.
Concrete: Check for moisture by taping plastic sheets to the slab every 2 feet. If moisture beads under plastic, don't install tile. Remedy the moisture problem first. Clean and roughen the surface slightly to give it a "tooth." Don't install carpet tile below grade.
Vinyl tile or sheet goods: If existing material is cushioned, remove it and repair subfloor. If tile is installed on a wood floor and is loose, waxed, or glossy, sand or strip finish and repair.
Ceramic tile: Level the surface with self-leveling compound. Remove damaged tile.
Carpet: Remove carpet and repair wood or concrete subfloor as above.

Layout tips

Check the dye lot numbers on your carpet tile cartons. If you have different dye lots, install them in separate rooms to avoid a color transition in the same room.

Laying tiles with the arrows at 90 degrees will create a checkerboard pattern that greatly reduces the appearance of wear. Laying the arrows in the same direction helps the carpet look more like a broadloom weave. Laying tiles with arrows in a random pattern is not recommended,

To get the best visual effect, place the starting arrow so it points away from the largest source of sunlight.

Install each tile securely against the others but don't compress the edges. When cutting cut-pile tiles, brush back the pile at the edges to avoid trapping the piles in the joint.

3 Peel off the backing from self-stick tiles and set the tile squarely on the intersection of the layout lines. From this point you can set the tiles in repeated concentric squares around the center or in quadrants. Dispose of the backing. It's very slick and can cause a bad fall.

4 Lay the subsequent tiles in the same fashion, setting the tile with its leading edges against the previous tiles. Lay the tile down, keeping the pressure against those in place. Don't slide the tiles. Set the tiles in a stair-step pattern so you have two points of reference for the next tile.

5 When you reach the edges, you will have to cut the tiles individually. Make sure you cut the tiles from the back. When you have installed all the edge tiles, roll the floor with a rented 100-pound roller.

Cut the tiles

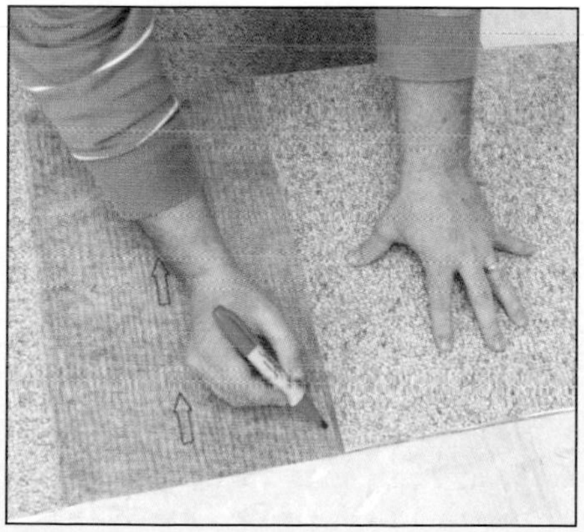

1 To mark a carpet tile for cutting, lay a loose tile upside down exactly on the last full tile already installed. Then lay a guide tile on this one and push it against the wall. Draw a line down the edge of the marker tile.

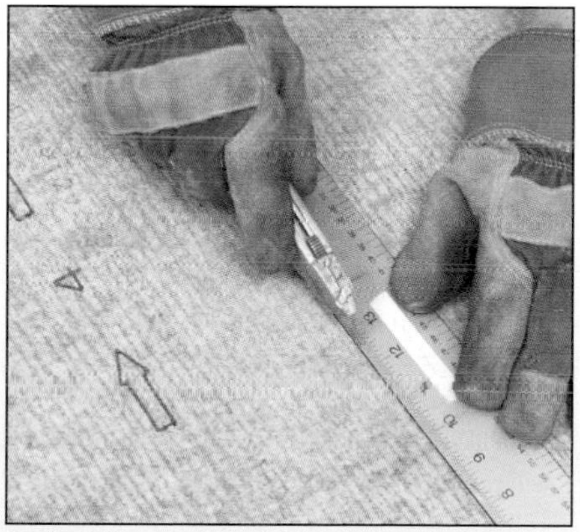

2 Remove the two tiles and, keeping the marked tile back side up, set a steel straightedge along the marker line. Make several light passes along the line with a sharp utility knife. When you have cut through the backing, bend the tile slightly and cut through it completely.

Applying mastic-set tiles

Dry-backed tiles are set in mastic or adhered with double-sided carpet tape. Some tiles are suited to both applications. Check the manufacturer's directions before deciding on a method.

In either case you must snap layout lines in the center of the room and start the installation at the intersection of the lines. If you're laying mastic, you'll use the quadrant method.

Apply the adhesive with a paint roller. Let the mastic become tacky, if necessary, then line up your first tile on the lines. Push the tile into place or pull it up and reposition it. Most tacky mastics allow plenty of working time. Continue setting the tile in one quadrant, making sure the edges of the tiles are butted securely against each other.

INSTALLING CORK TILE

Because cork tile is so porous, it requires a longer acclimation period (three to four days) than many man-made materials. That means if you normally run the air-conditioner in the summer and you're setting the tile in July, you should turn the air-conditioner on during the acclimation period. The same goes for the furnace in cooler seasons.

Like vinyl tile, the resilience of cork tile reveals subfloor defects dramatically. Some manufacturers require that you prime the subfloor (no matter what kind it is) before applying one part of a two-part adhesive (the second part is already on the cork tile). Other brands don't require a primer.

One thing is consistent throughout the industry: The mastic used is a reciprocal adhesive. That means it's a contact cement and sticks only to itself. Although it allows you some minor movement to line up the tiles, once you apply pressure with your hand, a roller, or a mallet, you will not be able to move the tile. If you've misaligned a tile, you will have to cut it out and replace it.

Mix up the tiles from several boxes before you lay them to spread any variations randomly across the floor.

PRESTART CHECKLIST

☐ **TIME**
About 20 minutes per square yard, not including subfloor preparation

☐ **TOOLS**
Fans, utility knife, tape measure, metal straightedge, chalkline, roller, pan, putty knife, mallet, beater block

☐ **SKILLS**
Measuring, laying, and cutting tile

☐ **PREP**
Repair and level subfloor

☐ **MATERIALS**
Cork tile, primer (required by some manufacturers), adhesive

1 Locate the center of the room or its largest rectangular surface by snapping chalklines at the midpoints of opposite walls. Don't worry that the adhesive will obscure the lines; it will dry clear. Adjust the lines so the layout has edge tiles of even width.

2 Using a brush so you don't splash adhesive on the wall, start applying adhesive along the walls of one quadrant only. Then work from this line back toward the center of the room, applying the adhesive with a paint roller. Let the adhesive become tacky (45 minutes to an hour).

Preparing the subfloor

Wood. In new construction install $\frac{3}{4}$-inch plywood. On an existing wood floor, remove the finish and repair. On planks wider than 4 inches, install $\frac{3}{8}$-inch underlayment. Fill depressions and sand smooth.
Concrete. Check for moisture by taping plastic sheets to the slab every 2 feet. If moisture beads under plastic, don't install tile. Remedy the moisture problem first, if possible. Clean and roughen the surface slightly to give the adhesive a "tooth." Don't install cork tile below grade.
Vinyl tile or sheet goods. Remove material and repair subfloor.
Ceramic tile. Level the surface with self-leveling compound. Remove damaged tile and repair.
Carpet. Remove carpet and prepare/repair wood or concrete subfloor as above.

STANLEY PRO TIP

Alternate colors of layout lines

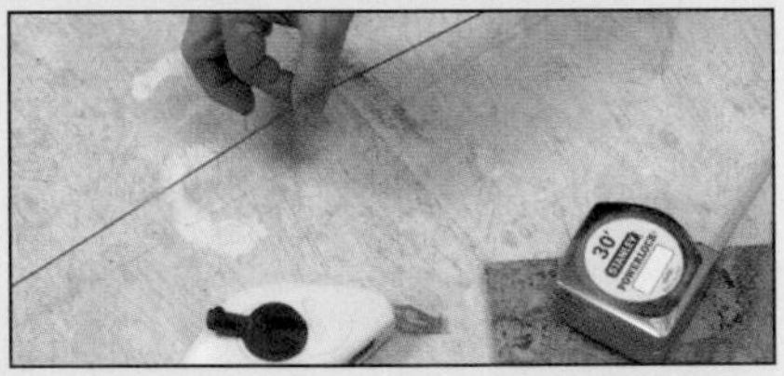

Cork tile is one of the few materials that looks better when its joints are offset from row to row. Getting the offset tiles on the same plane isn't possible without an offset layout line.

Once you've snapped your center layout lines, measure to their right (not their left—you won't have adhesive there) a distance equal to half the width of a tile. Mark each end of the room, then snap a new line with different colored chalk. Then spread the adhesive in that quadrant as above.

3 Set the first tile with its edges lined up with the intersecting layout lines. Hold the second tile with its edges next to the first and lower it into place, keeping the bottom edge on the layout line. Tap the entire surface of the tiles with a rubber mallet to secure them in the adhesive.

4 Using the same techniques, apply the remaining tiles in the row, tapping them with a mallet and a carpet-covered beater block *(page 106)*. Start the next row on the offset lines and proceed across the quadrant. Always work from installed tile to the corner—don't worry about kneeling on the tile—you won't dislodge it. However, kneeling or placing anything on the bare adhesive will weaken its bond. After you've laid the field tile, mark, cut, and install the edges.

WHAT IF...
A tile is misaligned when setting?

Every now and then you'll probably set a tile imprecisely on the layout lines. To remove a mislaid tile, use a wide putty knife inserted under a fresh corner. Slice the adhesive by moving the putty knife from side to side and prying it up at the same time. Reapply the adhesive to the floor and to the tile if it survives the removal process.

Protect the floor

Cork tile is not a "set and forget" product. Most tiles require the application of a finish after you have laid them. Before you apply the finish, vacuum the surface thoroughly and remove the residual dust with a very dry damp mop. Let the tile dry and apply the finish with a roller. Wait two weeks before washing the floor.

If adhesive gets on the walls

Adhesive made for most cork products is water soluble. If you happen to get adhesive on the wall, wipe it away with a disposable moist towel or rag.

If the adhesive dries on any surface it's not supposed to be on, you can rub it off with a dry rag.

MAINTAINING & REPAIRING

Today's tile products—from ceramic to cork to carpet—are some of the lowest maintenance flooring materials you can install. Regular vacuuming and/or damp-mopping with a mild cleanser keeps them in top condition. Wet installations, like showers and baths, however, require more attention.

Cleaning routines

Shower enclosures and tub surrounds require you to remove the accumulation of soap scum and water deposits and to take measures to keep mildew from forming.

Commercial products are effective cleaners, but household products you probably already have on hand provide less expensive alternatives.

Remove thin soap deposits and water spots with a vinegar solution (1 cup of vinegar to 1 gallon of warm water). Weekly cleaning will keep the tile shining and prevent mildew.

Dip an old toothbrush into full-strength bleach and scrub to clean the grout joints. Check colored grout in an inconspicuous place first to make sure the bleach won't remove the color. Then rinse everything with clear water to remove residue. Make sure the room has sufficient ventilation and be sure to wear eye protection, old clothing, and rubber gloves when using bleach or other cleaning agents. Never mix bleach with other chemicals; such mixtures can release toxic chlorine gas.

Polish metal glazed tiles with a metal polish recommended by the manufacturer, and if you have to scrub a tile surface, use a nylon scrubber. Metal scrubbers leave marks that are difficult to remove, and steel wool can scratch surfaces and leave behind metal fragments that will rust in the grout.

Assess the damage

Damaged tiles, cracked grout joints, water spots, and other forms of damage may be superficial troubles or may indicate more serious problems with the structure or the substrate. Try to assess the cause of the damage before making repairs.

You may be able to live with a few cracked tiles in an old tiled surface. In fact the cracks may add to its decorative charm. Matching an old tile pattern will likely prove difficult. Even if you can find the pattern, the tile may have developed a patina with age, and the new tiles will be more noticeable.

Water problems

If you suspect water damage, check the obvious sources first: damaged caulk or sealant, exposed joints at fixtures, deficient gaskets, or packing material around faucets. If the surface seems spongy, pull up a tile and check for the presence of a waterproofing membrane. If there isn't one, you'll have to take up the entire surface, repair or replace the subfloor, and reinstall a membrane, substrate, and new tile.

Regular cleaning keeps most tile in top condition. If cracks appear, look for underlying problems.

CHAPTER PREVIEW

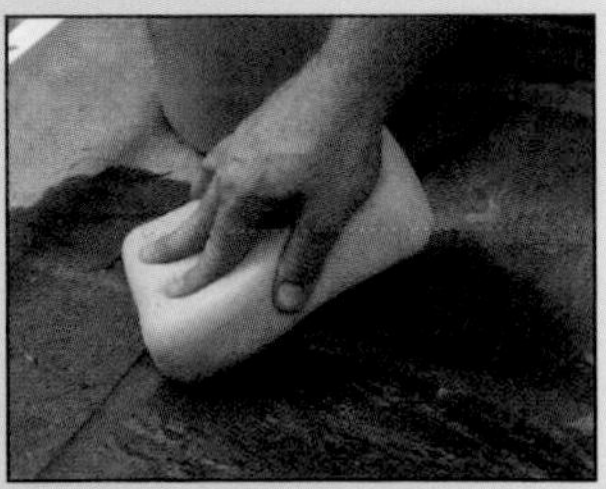

Cleaning and sealing tiles
page 220

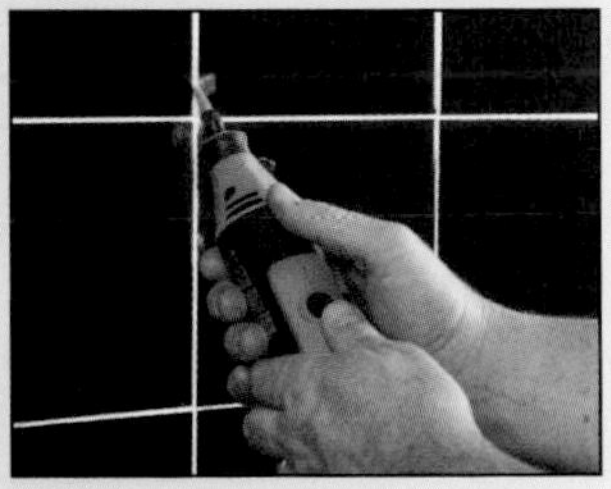

Replacing grout
page 222

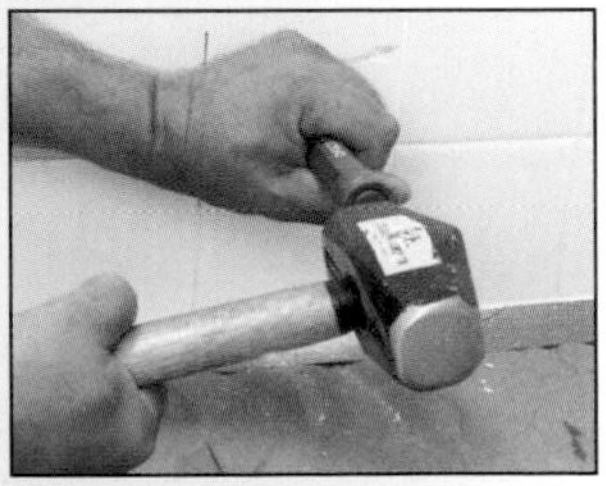

Repairing damaged ceramic tile
page 224

Wall tile stands up to a lot of rough treatment. Sometimes, however, a tile that suffers a sharp blow may crack. To repair a damaged wall tile, remove the tile, scrape out the excess, and replace it with a new tile, adding mortar to the recess and the back of the replacement. When any tile needs replacing, make sure the damage wasn't caused by underlying problems in the substrate.

Maintaining resilient tile
page 226

Caring for laminate tile
page 228

Caring for parquet
page 230

Maintaining carpet and cork tile
page 232

CLEANING AND SEALING TILES

Although regular cleaning will keep your ceramic tile in good condition, some surfaces, especially in kitchens and family rooms, may require stain removal.

When you need to remove a stain, start with the procedures outlined in the chart at right. If these solutions don't work, ask a tile supplier for a commercial stain-removal agent made for your tile. Stubborn stains often come out with a cleaning agent mixed with baking soda, plaster of paris, or refined clay. Deodorant-free cat litter works well. Mix the ingredients into a wet paste and apply it to the stain. Tape a plastic bag over the paste and let it sit for a couple of days. Then brush off the paste.

Unglazed tile almost always requires a sealer, and even presealed tile may need periodic stripping and resealing. Penetrating sealers soak into the tile bisque and preserve the natural color of the tile. Topical sealers lie on the surface of the tile and may lighten or darken the tile colors or change its sheen. Topical sealers wear off and sometimes require yearly reapplication. When tiles look dull it is probably time to strip and reseal them.

PRESTART CHECKLIST

☐ **TIME**
About 45 minutes to vacuum and damp mop a 15×20-foot kitchen, 90 minutes to strip it, about the same time to seal it

☐ **TOOLS**
Stripping: scrub brush and mop or scrubbing machine, vacuum
Sealing: vacuum, applicator, buffer

☐ **PREP**
Vacuum and clean surface

☐ **MATERIALS**
Stripper, sponge, sealer, bucket, rags

Stripping tiles

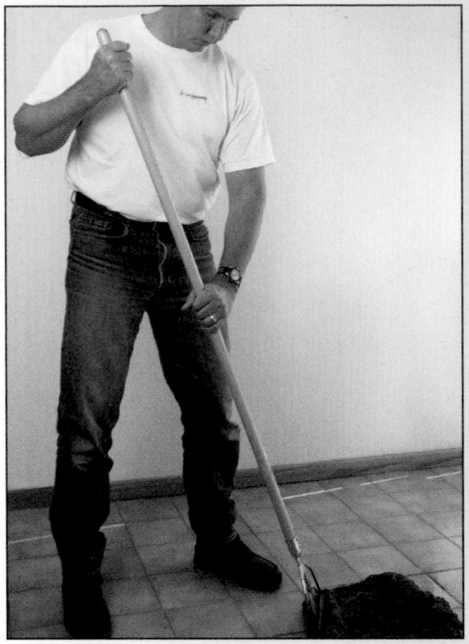

1 To remove old sealer, flow stripper on surface with a sponge or mop in an area that you can clean before the liquid dries (about 25 square feet). Scrub the area with a brush or with a floor-scrubbing machine. Do not let the stripper dry on the surface.

2 Remove residue with a sponge or rags. Some water-based strippers allow removal with a wet-dry vacuum. Rinse with clean water and wipe dry.

REMOVING STAINS FROM TILE

Stain	Cleaner and method
Ink, coffee, blood	Start with a 3 percent hydrogen peroxide solution; if that doesn't work try a nonbleach cleaner
Oil-based products	Use a mild solvent, such as charcoal lighter fluid or mineral spirits, then household cleaner in a poultice. For dried paint, scrape with a plastic (not metal) scraper.
Grease, fats	Clean with a commercial spot lifter
Rust	Use commercial rust removers, then try household cleaner
Nail polish	Remove with nail polish remover

Always rinse the stained area with clear water to remove residue.

Applying sealers

1 On newly tiled floors wait 48 hours before sealing. On existing floors vacuum the surface thoroughly to keep dirt and dust from becoming embedded in the new sealer.

2 Clean the tile with a commercial tile cleaning product following the manufacturer's directions. Rinse with clear water.

3 Apply sealer with a sponge applicator, paint pad, brush, or mop, as required by the manufacturer. Do not let sealer puddle or run on walls. Some sealers can't be overlapped. Some may require wiping with a clean rag. Allow time to dry between coats. Reapply one or two additional coats.

SAFETY FIRST

Floor care products can be toxic

Many strippers and sealers are solvent-based and highly caustic. Even water-based products contain harmful chemicals. All floor care products are potentially dangerous—observe the manufacturer's safety precautions.

Wear rubber gloves, old long-sleeve clothing, pants, and eye protection. Wear a respirator to avoid breathing toxic fumes and put a fan in the window to provide adequate ventilation. Perform tile maintenance tasks when the children are out of the house.

Working with waxes

Many unglazed tile surfaces lend themselves to waxed finishes. Some waxes contain pigments that enhance the color of the tile.

To properly renew a waxed floor, strip the old wax and wash the surface thoroughly with a mild detergent. Rinse with clear water and let it dry completely. Wax the surface in successive thin coats with the applicator recommended by the manufacturer. Allow each coat to dry and buff in between. Repeated thin coats leave a brighter shine than one thick coat; they also reduce wax buildup.

A dull shine doesn't necessarily call for rewaxing. Clean the floor with a soap-free cleaner and buff with a cloth or rented machine. When using a buffer start in the middle of the floor with the brush level. Tilt the handle up or down slightly to move it from side to side. Don't push the machine. Buff across the surface.

REPLACING GROUT

Replacing grout on an entire wall or floor is a monumental job, but if you've inherited an installation that is crumbling and generally falling apart, you probably have no other choice. Make the task easier by using a rotary hand tool.

Don't be deceived by grout—it is a remarkably hard material. If you need to cover a large section and don't own a rotary hand tool, buy one. Kits that come complete with bits are moderately priced, have an assortment of do-it-yourself applications, and are well worth the investment when removing large areas of grout. Once you own this tool, you'll find a host of around-the-house applications for it.

If the grout is stained, discolored, or mildewed, don't replace it—clean it. Most large home centers carry cleaning solutions formulated especially for grout. Many of these products contain bleaches and other caustic chemicals, so wear eye protection, gloves, and old clothes (long-sleeve shirts) when using them. Provide adequate ventilation in the room.

Before you tackle even small repairs, find out what caused the grout to deteriorate. A few small areas may not indicate a problem, but large cracks may not only have been caused by a structural problem, they may have let water behind the tile. In this case you're better off removing the tile and starting over.

PRESTART CHECKLIST

☐ **TIME**
About 30 minutes per square foot

☐ **TOOLS**
Rotary hand tool, grout saw (for small repairs), margin trowel, mixing paddle, bucket, grout float, sponge

☐ **SKILLS**
Using power tools, floating and cleaning grout

☐ **MATERIALS**
Grout, bucket, sponge, rag, water

1 Use a rotary hand tool with a diamond grinding burr to remove large amounts of damaged grout. Choose a bit that is slightly smaller than an empty grout joint and work the tool with two hands. Take care to keep the shank of the bit in line with the joint so you don't snap the bit or chip the tile.

2 Brush the joints with a hand brush and wash them out with clear water. Let the joints dry overnight, then mix up the amount of grout you can apply before it sets up. Apply the grout with a grout float, forcing it into the joints at a 45-degree angle and working diagonally *(pages 104–105)*.

WHAT IF…
You're removing only a small amount of grout?

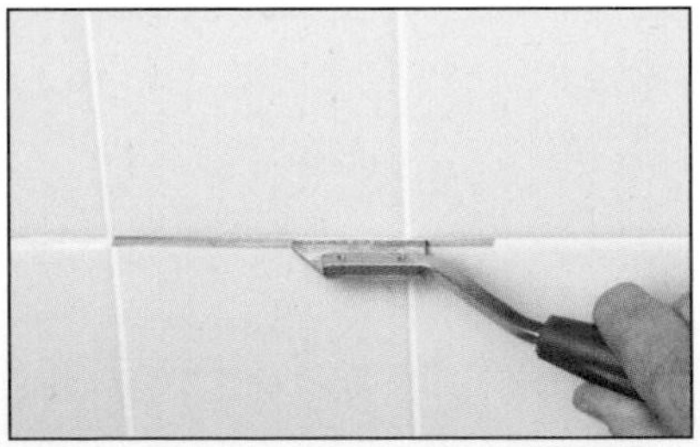

If you have only one or two small sections that need repair, you may be able to get by with a grout saw—a small, handheld tool available at local hardware stores.

To get the grout out of the joint, hold the tool so the blade is flat against the joint. Work the tool up and down (or back and forth) in the joint until you have removed about half the grout. For wide grout lines, use a rotary hand tool. Chip out mortared joints with a cold chisel.

STANLEY PRO TIP
Handle grout easier and faster

Although it's important to follow the manufacturer's directions when mixing up a batch of grout, there's one item you might not find printed on the bag—the size of the mixing container. The task will go much faster if you can scoop the grout out of the container and onto the wall with the grout float. Mix the grout in a medium-size plastic dishpan or similar container that makes its removal easy.

3 When you have completed one section of the installation, scrape off the excess grout with the grout float, holding the float just short of a 90-degree angle. Don't press too hard or you will draw the grout out of the joints. Let the grout set up, then dampen a sponge and clean the grout residue from the surface. When the first section is clean, grout and clean the remaining sections with the same methods.

4 Once you have grouted and cleaned the entire installation, let the grout set up. Using a soft rag, wipe the haze from the surface. Some grouts leave a haze that requires a good deal of elbow grease to remove. Use pressure and a scrubbing motion if necessary. Seal the grout (and the tile if necessary) with the product recommended by the manufacturer.

Matching the color

Generally you will want to replace the grout with one of the same color. If you're replacing an entire installation, that's not too much of a problem. The new grout can be slightly "off hue" from the original and no one will notice.

If you're replacing the grout in only a few joints, try to remove a chip (not dust) from a damaged section to take with you when you purchase the new grout. Use a utility knife or small screwdriver, taking care not to damage the tile.

If necessary mix two grouts of a similar hue to get a good match.

REFRESHER COURSE
Letting the grout set up

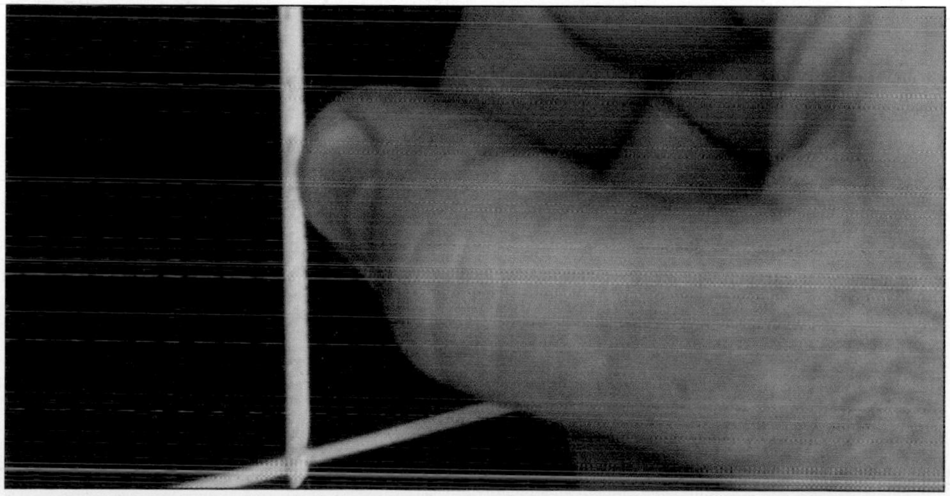

To avoid pulling the grout out of the joints while you clean them, wait until it sets up. To find out if the grout is hard enough to withstand a cleaning, push your thumbnail into it. When your thumbnail makes no impression, you can start cleaning.

REPAIRING DAMAGED CERAMIC TILE

Tile is the most durable wall and floor covering, but it is not impervious to damage. Improper installation, poor adhesive bonds, and falling objects can cause it to crack or chip.

Repairing the problem begins with removing the grout and tile. Before replacing the grout and tile, diagnose the problem to see if you need to make a structural repair.

Cracked joints are most often caused by an improper grout mix or the absence of expansion joints. If the grout is soft and powdery, remove it and regrout. If the cracked grout is hard, remove it and fill the joint with a matching colored caulk.

Cracked tiles on a long length of floor are caused either by a faulty adhesive bond or an underlying crack. Before you remove the tiles, tap them lightly with a metal object, such as a wrench. If you hear a hollow sound, the bond is probably at fault and a thorough cleaning and new mortar will fix the problem. If the wrench "rings," the bond is probably solid; you may need to isolate the crack with a membrane.

PRESTART CHECKLIST

☐ **TIME**
About an hour and a half to remove and replace grout and tile, at least a day to regrout a large area

☐ **TOOLS**
Grout saw or utility knife, hammer and cold chisel, putty knife or margin trowel

☐ **SKILLS**
Breaking tile with a hammer and cold chisel, driving fasteners, troweling

☐ **MATERIALS**
Replacement tiles, thinset, grout, tape

Removing and replacing damaged tile

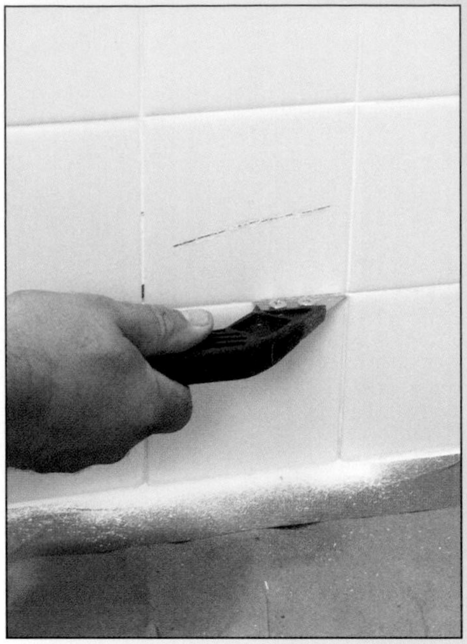

1 Score the grout around the damaged tile with a carbide grout saw or utility knife. Scoring reduces the tendency of other tiles to crack when you remove the damaged area. Protect the tub or area below with heavy paper.

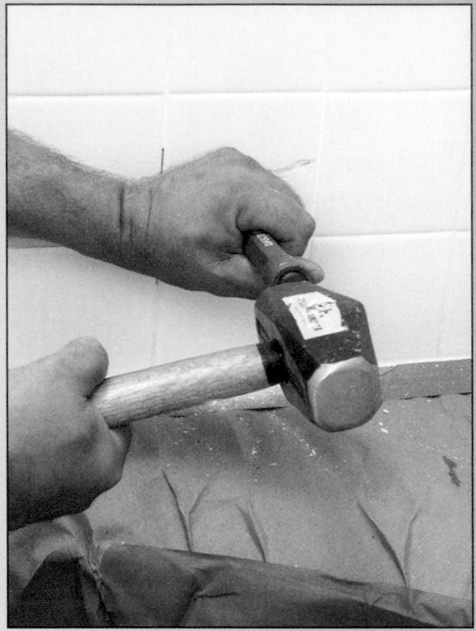

2 Break the damaged tile with a small sledge and cold chisel, starting from the center of the tile and working to the edges.

Adding a towel bar to a tile wall

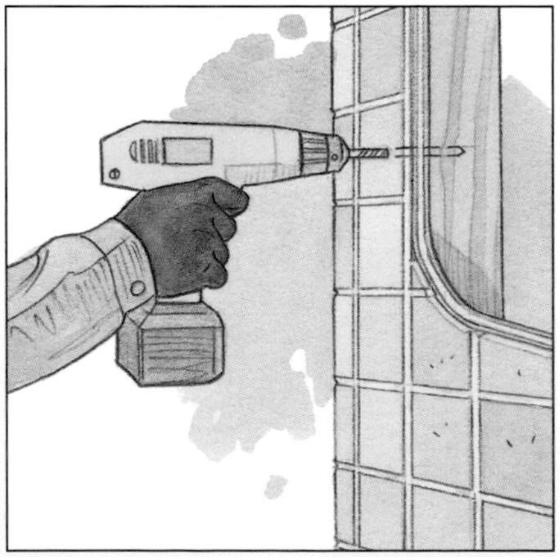

1 Mark the location of the accessory on the wall, level and centered on the studs if possible. Nick the glaze at the mark with a sharp awl and hammer. Use a masonry drill bit to drill through the tile. Anchor the hangers to the studs with wood screws.

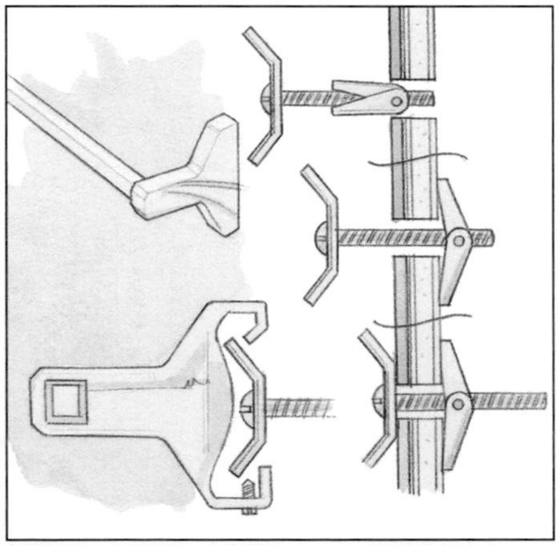

2 If you can't center the accessory on the studs, drill through the tile and the wall. Insert a toggle bolt screw into the hanger and refasten the toggles. Push the toggles through the hole until they expand. Tighten the screw until the fixture is secure.

3 Remove the broken pieces, prying them out with a putty knife or margin trowel if necessary. Scrape off the old adhesive from the wall.

4 Back-butter the new tile with a sufficiently thick coat of mortar. If possible use the same adhesive or mortar used on the old tile. Use thinset if you don't know what mortar was originally used.

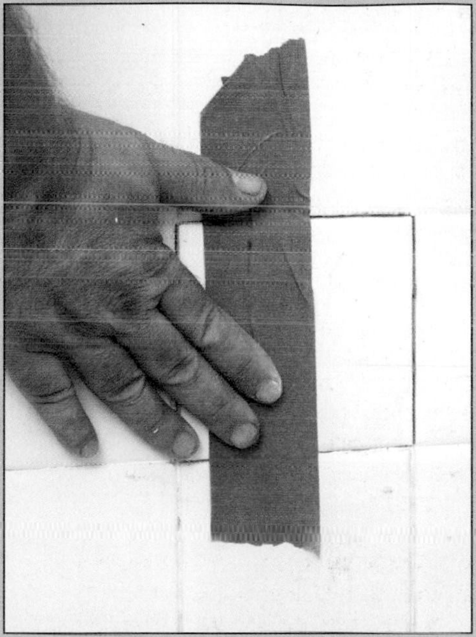

5 Press the new tile in place with firm pressure. Make sure it's level with the rest of the surface. Remove the tile and adjust the layer of mortar if necessary. Center the tile in the recess. Use nails or spacers to keep it aligned. Tape the tile until the mortar cures, then apply grout.

Repairing tile on a cracked slab

1 Remove grout from the joints along the entire length of the crack, including at least one tile beyond those damaged. Following the manufacturer's directions, apply adhesive and an isolation membrane.

2 Trowel thinset into the recess and back-butter each tile. Replace the tiles and level them. Grout and clean when the mortar is dry.

APPLY GROUT

Regrouting a small area

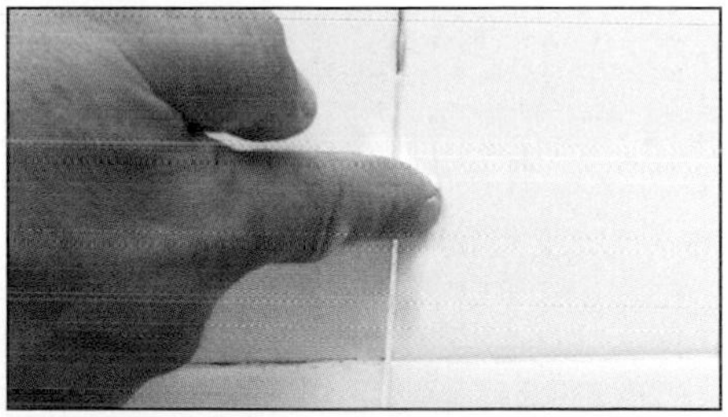

When regrouting a small area or a single replacement tile, take out the old grout with a utility knife or grout knife. Unless you are replacing the entire area of grout, try to match the color of the existing grout. Mix a small batch and let it dry; then compare it with the existing grout.

If grouting a large area, apply the grout with a float. On a small area or a single tile, use your finger to press the grout into the joint. Shape the grout with a wet sponge.

MAINTAINING RESILIENT TILE

Modern resilient tile is so easy to maintain that the biggest problem you're likely to experience is the tendency to overdo it. Doing too much causes premature wear and dulling.

The first rule of resilient tile maintenance is "keep it clean." A regular schedule of vacuuming (not with an upright model or beater bar attachment) and damp-mopping does more than anything else to keep a resilient floor in tip-top shape. If you need to address an unusually soiled spot with a cleaning solution, use a product recommended by the manufacturer. Steer clear of generic products made for all floors.

The chemicals in vinyl tile are prone to interact with the chemicals in other synthetic products, especially the rubber backings of area rugs. Many rubber backings stain vinyl. Don't use a rubber-backed rug unless the manufacturer or retailer gives the OK.

Be wary of felt or fiber scratch guards that self-stick to the bottom of furniture legs. They work initially, but gradually accumulate grit and scratch the floor. Check them periodically and replace them when they fill up with dirt.

You can remove some minor scuffing with a tile cleaner and #0000 steel wool. Rub gently.

PRESTART CHECKLIST

☐ **TIME**
About 45 minutes to vacuum and damp-mop a 15×20-foot kitchen; about 30 minutes to remove and replace a damaged tile

☐ **TOOLS**
Cleaning: vacuum, sponge mop, bucket
Repairing: hair dryer, putty knife, notched trowel or plastic scraper, rolling pin

☐ **MATERIALS**
Cleaning: manufacturer's cleaning solution
Repairing: adhesive, replacement tile

1 To remove a damaged resilient tile, set a hair dryer on high heat and concentrate the heat for a minute or so on one edge of the tile. Insert the blade of your putty knife and work it back and forth, pushing forward to break the adhesive bond.

2 Don't expect the tile to come up in one piece. It will tear and leave small pieces stuck in the adhesive. Warm and scrape each piece until you have removed all of them.

Maintaining no-wax floors

No-wax floors are manufactured with a vinyl or polyurethane coating applied to their surface. Of the two, the urethane is tougher, but for both, no wax means no wax. If you start waxing one of these materials, you'll dull the finish, make it dangerously slick, increase its tendency to collect dust and dirt, or all three. To maintain the shine of a no-wax floor, just keep it clean.

Once a week, vacuum the floor and damp-mop it with a mild detergent solution—even if the floor doesn't look dirty, it is, and those microscopic dust particles will wear away the sheen. Make sure you rinse the floor thoroughly. Occasional buffing will also bring back the shine. If you have to "refinish" a no-wax floor, use a product made by the manufacturer especially for this purpose.

3 Using a notched trowel, spread adhesive into the recess left by the damaged tile. If a regular trowel proves unwieldy, notch the end of a plastic scraper and use it to comb the mastic. Make sure the adhesive covers the floor at the edges.

4 Before you set the replacement tile, make sure its orientation conforms to pattern if necessary. The arrow won't help because you can't see the other tiles' arrows; instead, eyeball the pattern. Set the tile at an angle with one edge tight against the other and lower the tile into place.

5 Make sure the new tile adheres tightly to the adhesive by rolling it with a rolling pin. Warm the surface slightly before you roll it. The heat will soften the adhesive and help bond the tile.

REMOVING STAINS FROM VINYL TILE

Stain	Remove with
Asphalt, shoe polish	Citrus-based cleaner or mineral spirits
Candle wax	Scrape carefully with plastic spatula
Crayon	Mineral spirits or manufacturer's cleaner
Grape juice, wine, mustard	Full-strength bleach or manufacturer's cleaner
Heel marks	Nonabrasive household cleaner; if stain remains, use rubbing alcohol
Lipstick	Rubbing alcohol or mineral spirits
Nail polish	Nail polish remover
Paint or varnish	Wipe with water or mineral spirits while still wet. If dry, scrape carefully with a thin plastic spatula. If stain still shows, rub with rubbing alcohol.
Pen ink	Citrus-based cleaner, rubbing alcohol, or mineral spirits
Permanent marker	Mineral spirits, nail polish remover, or rubbing alcohol
Rust	Oxalic acid and water (1 part acid to 10 parts water); extremely caustic; follow all directions

After removing the stain, wipe the area with a damp cloth to remove residue.

Preventing dents and scratches

Resilient flooring is more prone to dents, scuffs, and scratches than other flooring. Unlike spots, you can't remove them. Here are some ways to prevent dents:

■ Protect the floor when moving appliances. Lay plywood panels on the floor and "walk" the appliance across the panels.

■ Use floor protectors to keep furniture legs from denting the floors; the heavier the furniture, the wider the protector should be.

■ Avoid furniture with rolling casters. If you must have casters, use double rollers.

■ Keep dust and dirt outside the house—use mats or rugs at entrances but avoid rubber-backed rugs. They can discolor resilient flooring.

■ Keep the floor clean with regular sweeping or vacuuming but don't use vacuums with beater bars.

CARING FOR LAMINATE TILE

As durable as laminate tile is, laminate products are not indestructible. Laminates (especially the thicker, more expensive products) are more subject to denting than scratching, and you won't be able to get the dents out.

To keep the surface from scratching in the first place, take the precautions listed in "Preventive Maintenance for Laminate Tile," *(page 22)*. In addition don't drag heavy appliances or furniture across a laminate floor. Use an appliance dolly or air pad when resetting the refrigerator, and ask friends to help move sofas, dressers, and other large pieces of furniture.

Plastic furniture casters are deceptively harmful to laminate floors. Small pieces of grit embedded in the roller over time abrade the surface of the floor. If you have plastic furniture rollers, replace them with rubber rollers.

Humidity plays a role in laminate maintenance also. Keeping the room humidity at 50 percent will ensure the joints stay closed, thus preventing an accumulation of dirt between tiles.

PRESTART CHECKLIST

☐ **TIME**
About 45 minutes to vacuum and damp-mop a 15×20-foot floor; about 20 minutes to repair a tile and 30 minutes to remove and replace a damaged tile

☐ **TOOLS**
Cleaning: vacuum, sponge mop, bucket
Repairing: utility knife, plastic spatula, circular saw, chisel, hammer

☐ **MATERIALS**
Cleaning: manufacturer's cleaning solution
Repairing: masking tape, patching compound, replacement tile

Repairing a damaged tile

1 If the damaged area lies in a wood-grain or other straight pattern, square the damaged area with a sharp utility knife. If the pattern is irregular, you may want to leave the outlines of the patch slightly irregular. The wear layer on laminate tile is extremely hard—use a sharp blade. Don't cut clear through the layers of tile. Only remove the top layer. Vacuum up the chips and dust from the area to be patched.

Preventive maintenance for laminate tile

Sweeping will do for daily cleaning, but vacuuming is necessary before you damp-mop a laminate floor. Don't wax the floor. Wax leaves a film that deadens the shine.

Laminate tile is among the easiest of floor materials to care for, but no material maintains itself. The best thing you can do to keep its surface shiny is to use area rugs or mats at home entrances to trap as much loose dirt as possible. Use felt pads on furniture legs and check them periodically—you will have to change them regularly because they pick up dirt and can act like small circles of sandpaper.

Sweep or vacuum the floor daily to remove loose dirt and grit. If something gets spilled, wipe it up immediately and clean the residue with a spray cleaner recommended by the manufacturer.

Damp-mop the floor once a week with a mild cleaning solution and a string mop. Don't flood the floor; wring the mop until it's just damp.

2 To make cleanup easier, apply tape around the damaged area. Squeeze a small amount of the manufacturer's repair compound into the damaged area and press it into the recess with the edge of a plastic spatula. Smooth the compound level with the tape. If the compound comes out of the area when you smooth it, lower the angle of the spatula. Let the repair dry thoroughly.

3 When the repair compound has dried thoroughly, remove the tape carefully. Most compounds are made to shrink as they dry, so the repair should now be level with the surface of the surrounding tile. If some stray putty got on the floor, wipe it with a damp cloth.

REMOVING STAINS FROM LAMINATE TILE

Stain	Remove with
Candle wax	Scrape carefully with plastic spatula
Crayon, rubber heel marks	Rub out with a dry cloth or acetone if needed
Grape juice or wine	Rub with a dry cloth or concentrated cleaner
Lipstick	Paint thinner or acetone
Nail polish	Acetone-based nail polish remover
Paint or varnish	Wipe with water or mineral spirits while still wet. If dry, scrape carefully with a thin plastic spatula. If the stain still shows, rub with rubbing alcohol.
Pen ink	Acetone or paint thinner
Shoe polish	Acetone or paint thinner
Tar	Acetone
Others	Start with concentrated cleaner, then acetone

After removing the stain, wipe the area with a damp cloth to remove residue.

Removing a tile

In the unlikely event that the damage to a laminate tile is so severe that it warrants removal, you have two options.

If the floor is a glueless installation, you may be able to unsnap the tiles up to and surrounding the damaged tile.Then replace the tile and reassemble the floor.

If disassembly is not possible, or if the edges of the tile are glued, you'll have to cut the tile out.

Mark the perimeter of the damaged tile with masking tape (blue tape provides a more visible line). Set a circular saw to the thickness of the tile and equip it with a fine-tooth blade. Cut the tile along the taped line. Chisel out the corners and remove any pieces of tongue or groove. Using a sharp utility knife, cut the tongue and protruding groove edges from the replacement tile and glue it in place.

CARING FOR PARQUET

You're sure to get good results if you treat your parquet floor as you would a piece of fine furniture. Use the cleaner that is made or recommended by the manufacturer. Never clean the floor with water or water-based products.

Wipe up spills immediately with a damp cloth and dry the area with a dry cloth. Old T-shirts are excellent for this purpose. Do not use cleaners that contain abrasives, caustic chemicals, bleach, or ammonia. For routine cleaning, it is best to use a solvent-based cleaner or a one-step cleaner/polish combination.

Most prefinished parquet tile comes with a durable acrylic or polyurethane finish. Some finishes are no-wax, others benefit from waxing. Check the manufacturer's directions before you purchase cleaning products. Acrylic waxes are not generally recommended for wood floors, and some polyurethane finishes must never be waxed.

Almost all wood finishes change color over time. You can slow this process somewhat by keeping the drapes closed. Areas covered with rugs won't be subject to color changes and the color difference will be revealed if you decide to move the rugs later.

PRESTART CHECKLIST

☐ **TIME**
About an hour to vacuum and clean a 15×20-foot floor; about an hour to remove and replace a damaged tile

☐ **TOOLS**
Cleaning: vacuum, cleaning product applicator
Repairing: circular saw, chisel, hammer, notched plastic scraper, trowel, putty knife, utility knife, backsaw

☐ **MATERIALS**
Cleaning: manufacturer's cleaning solution
Repairing: mastic, replacement tile

1 To remove a damaged parquet tile, set your circular saw to the thickness of the tile and equip the saw with a fine-toothed blade. Make a series of parallel plunge cuts about 2 inches apart, stopping just short of the adjacent tiles.

2 Using a ¾-inch or 1-inch chisel with the bevel down, cut out the sections of parquet between the lines. Keep the chisel as flat as possible—you may have to remove the first section one layer at a time. Clean out any wood scraps and scrape off the old adhesive with a putty knife.

Refinishing a parquet floor

Parquet tile, especially tile with a thick veneer, is an excellent candidate for refinishing. Using a pad sander and a medium-grit sandpaper, start sanding along the diagonal of the room. Work the sander from one side of the room to the other. Then shift directions and sand along the other diagonal length of the room. Make a final pass parallel to and along the longest wall of the room. Repeat this three-pass process with succeedingly finer grits of sandpaper.

Stain and varnish the floor with the product of your choice, either a penetrating or surface finish. Penetrants sink into the wood pores; they won't wear out unless the wood does. Surface finishes don't soak into the pores of the wood; they stay on top and generally are less durable.

STANLEY PRO TIP

Cut the tongue

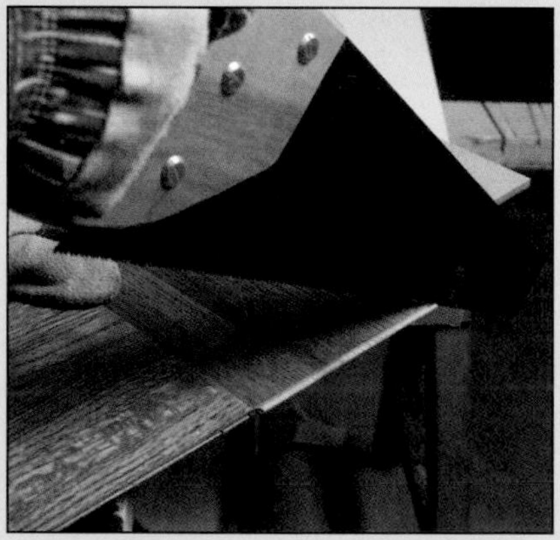

To remove the tongues so a new parquet tile can replace a damaged unit, clamp the tile to a work surface and cut the tongues with a backsaw. Use two hands and keep the saw vertical and lined up on the edge of the tile.

3 If the parquet is tongue-and-groove (and most quality tiles are), the tongues will get in the way when you replace the tile. When you cut out the damaged tile, cut the tongues on the surrounding tiles. Now you have to cut the tongue from the replacement tile and press it into freshly laid adhesive. Use a notched plastic scraper to spread the adhesive and make sure the new tile is pressed flush with the old tile.

4 Clean off any excess adhesive that seeped through the joints, and weight down the tile with heavy books or exercise weights. Let the adhesive dry overnight. If the replacement tile is prefinished, it might look more glossy than the originals. You can reduce the new-tile gloss a little with a light burnishing with #0000 steel wool. If the tile is unfinished, stain and finish it to match the surrounding floor.

Preventive maintenance

Regular vacuuming is parquet's best friend. It helps keep tracked-in grit from scratching the floor and dirt from being ground into the joints.

To keep the grit to a minimum, place slip-resistant nonstaining mats at entrances, use casters or felt pads under furniture legs, and avoid walking with any kind of spiked shoes (athletic or heels).

Floor mats in front of stoves, refrigerators, and sinks help prevent stains. Use them in the bathroom too.

Always use the cleaner that the manufacturer recommends. Generally these are solvent-based solutions, but several new environmentally friendly cleaners are showing up on the market.

MAINTAINING PARQUET

Problem	Remedy
Bubbles in finish	For light damage, sand and recoat; if heavy, sand, stain, and refinish
Chewing gum, crayon, candle wax	Freeze with ice in a bag, scrape with plastic scraper
Cigarette burns	Burnish with fine steel wool or scrape charred area; wax, or sand, stain, and refinish
Dents	Cover with dampened cloth and press with an electric iron
Scratches	Wax the area or hide the scratch with a thin coat of dusting spray rubbed into scratch
Seasonal cracks	Increase humidity in dry season—install humidifier, boil water, open dishwasher after rinse
Surface stains	Remove with sandpaper or steel wool, feathering edges; or clean with one of the following solutions:
Heel marks	Wood cleaner or wax
Oil and grease	Try wood cleaner first. On waxed floor, use TSP or soap with high lye content. On surface finish, use TSP.
Pet stains	Wood cleaner, followed by mild bleach or household vinegar for up to an hour. A remaining spot is not likely to sand out. Cover damage with rug or remove, replace, and refinish.
Ink	Use procedure for pet stains
Water spots	Buff lightly with #0000 steel wool, then wax. If necessary sand with fine paper, stain, and recoat.

MAINTAINING CARPET AND CORK TILE

Carpet tile requires periodic deep cleaning because no matter how frequently you vacuum it, dirt and grime eventually works its way down into the fibers.

Most cork products are finished with a varnish that requires periodic reapplication and keeps the cork from soaking up the dirt.

Both materials benefit more from routine preventive maintenance than the occasional deep cleaning. Regular vacuuming helps keep tracked-in grit out of the fibers and joints.

Nonstaining (primarily for cork) mats at entrances further control dirt, and casters or cups under furniture legs minimize dents. Floor mats in front of stoves, refrigerators, and sinks help prevent stains.

When deep-cleaning carpet tile, vacuum first to remove as much loose soil as possible and apply a spot removal agent to heavily soiled sections. Remove all the furniture you can and put plastic bags around the legs of everything you can't move. Ventilate the room with fans to speed drying.

Although these pages feature a cleaning powder, some carpet tile can stand up to steam and water-based cleaning methods. Ask your supplier which cleaning methods are compatible with your carpet tile's weave and adhesive.

PRESTART CHECKLIST

☐ **TIME**
About 2 hours for an 8×10 floor

☐ **TOOLS**
Vacuum cleaner, floor brush or carpet machine, sponge mop, utility knife and putty knife (for tile removal), scissors for carpet repair

☐ **MATERIALS**
Manufacturer's cleaning agents, varnish for cork tiles, sponge or applicator

Deep cleaning carpet tiles

1 Use the manufacturer's or retailer's recommendation before purchasing a carpet cleaning solution. Sprinkle the cleaning powder evenly across the surface of the floor. Properly applied it should appear as a thin layer on the carpet.

2 Using a short-bristled floor brush or rented carpet machine, work the powder into the fibers of the carpet. To avoid the possibility of premature wear, do not brush too heavily in any one area. Leave the powder in the fibers for the recommended time.

WHAT IF...
The carpet has sprouts or dents?

From time to time even the best carpet tiles will have a fiber or two that come loose from their backing. If your carpet tile shows "sprouts" of this kind, don't pull them—you'll create holes in the fabric. Gently pull the sprouted fibers up and trim them flush with the others.

Dents in carpet are more difficult to remedy than other maladies. Start by using the back of a tablespoon to work the fibers up in the area of the dent. If this doesn't work try wetting the area first or warming it slightly with a hair dryer. If the dent won't come up and the carpet is in a visible area of the room, it's better to replace the tile.

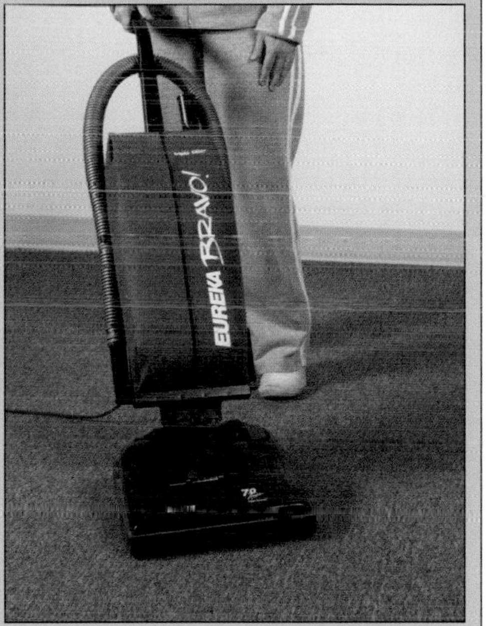

3 Vacuum the cleaned area thoroughly using a high-quality vacuum with beater bars. Go over each section both with and against the grain in order to ensure removal of all the cleaning powder and soil.

Cleaning cork tiles

1 Vacuum a cork floor with a high-quality canister vacuum. Don't use an upright vacuum or canister attachment with beater bars—doing so risks tearing up the surface of the tile.

2 Using either a cotton string mop or a synthetic sponge mop, damp-mop the floor. Don't overwet or flood the surface—you'll warp the tile and weaken the adhesive bond. Because it is a wood product, don't use commercial cleaners. Purchase a cleaner made by the manufacturer.

WHAT IF...
You have to replace a carpet tile?

The procedure illustrated below works equally well for both carpet tiles and cork tiles. The removal of cork tiles is more difficult because of the reciprocating glue. Always work from the center of the tile outward. Working from the edges will damage them.

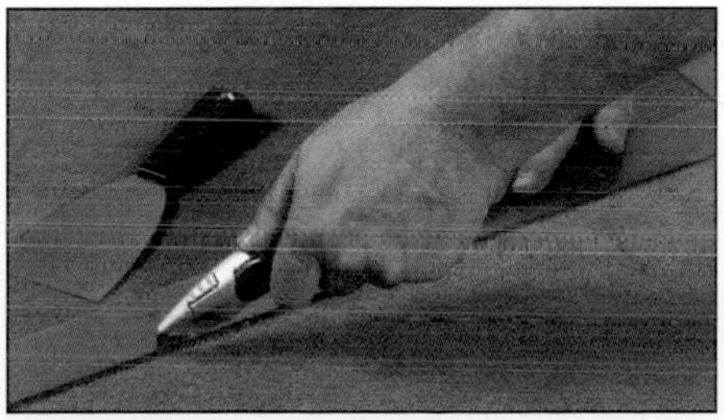

1 Using a metal straightedge (optional) and a sharp utility knife, make several passes in the center of the tile until you have cut through to the subfloor.

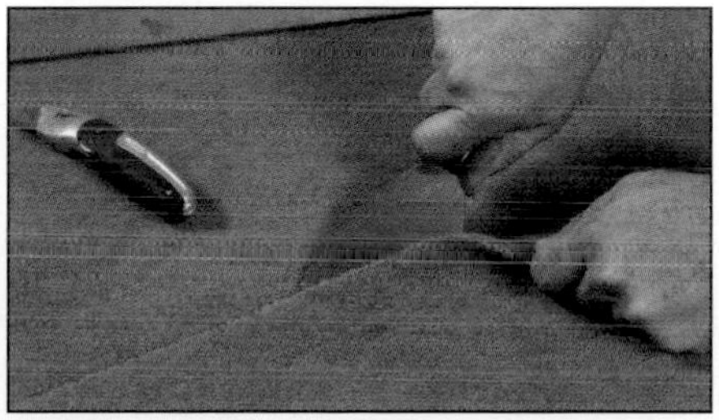

2 Insert a 3-inch putty knife under the cut you've made and remove one-half of the tile by prying and seesawing the putty knife back and forth to break the adhesive bond. Repeat the procedure on the other half of the tile. Replace the adhesive, press in the tile, and roll it.

Refinishing cork tiles

Although a wear-layer varnish protects modern cork products, you must periodically renew the cork's surface. Clean the floor as described above and let it dry. Then use a sponge or lamb's wool applicator to reapply the varnish. Never use a generic product—always use the solution made especially for cork.

Glossary

Actual dimensions: The actual size of a tile. as measured with a tape or ruler. *See nominal dimensions.*

Additive: Any of several chemicals or compounds added to fresh concrete to make it more workable.

Agglomerate: A mixture of stone byproducts, chips, and grains mixed with resins and formed into tiles that resemble stone.

ANSI: (American national Standards institute). Organization which sets standards and provides information on design and engineering safety.

Back-butter: To apply mortar or adhesive to the rear face of a tile before setting it.

Backerboard: Any of several cement or gypsum-based sheets used as substrate for setting tile. *See cement board.*

Back-mounted: process by which groups of tiles are held together to facilitate uniform spacing.

Backsplash: Surface that abuts or is attached to the rear of a countertop along its entire length, typically 3 to 4 inches high.

Beater block: Manufactured or home-made tool covered with soft surface. Used to set tiles level on surface.

Bisque: The clay-and-liquid mixture that forms the body of the tile.

Bond strength: The measure of an adhesive's ability to resist separating from tile and setting bed when cured.

Brick veneer: Any of several products in various thicknesses made of clay or other materials and additives whose appearance resembles brick.

Building codes: Ordinances established by local communities to govern quality and construction methods used in building a home or other structure.

Bullnose tiles: Flat tile with at least one rounded edge. Used to trim the edges of a tiled installation. Also called caps.

Butt joint: A joint formed when two surfaces meet exactly on their edges, ends or faces.

Casing: Wood or other material around the perimeter of a door, window, or other opening in a wall.

Caulk: Any of several compounds used to seal surface gaps or joints. Applied in semi-liquid form from tubes or a caulking gun, it dries to flexible bead that keeps out liquids. Available in a wide range of colors and in sanded or unsanded mixtures.

Cement board: A type of backerboard made from a cement base and coated or impregnated with fiberglass mesh.

Cement-bodied tile: Tile whose bisque is formed of mortar as opposed to clay.

Ceramic tile: A type of tile composed of refined clay usually mixed with additives and water and hardened by firing in a kiln to a minimum of 1800°F. Can be glazed or unglazed.

Chlorinated polyethylene (CPE): Synthetic plastic used as a membrane to make tiled substrates waterproof.

Cleft: Describes process of forming stone paving pieces by splitting smaller pieces from larger rock.

Coefficient of friction: The force required to move an object across a horizontal surface—used as a measure of slip resistance.

Control joint: An intentional gap cut or formed in a concrete surface to control where the surface cracks.

Cove molding: Describes a type of floor trim tile whose base is curved inward.

CTI: Ceramic Tile Institute of America.

Darby: A long-bladed wood float used to smooth the surface of fresh concrete.

Dot-mounted: Process by which groups of tiles are held together by plastic dots to facilitate uniform spacing.

Down angle: A trim tile with two rounded edges used to finish off an outside corner.

Drywall: A gypsum-based sheet product covered on both sides with paper and used to finish interior wall surfaces.

Efflorescence: A powdery white substance that forms on the surface of masonry walls, caused by the evaporation of water from dissolved salts.

Expansion joint: An intended space or gap built into materials subject to cracking. Allows materials to expand and contract with temperature changes without damage to the remainder of the surface.

Extruded: Describes the process of shaping a tile by pressing it into a die.

Field tiles: Flat tiles with unrounded edges used within the edges of a tiled installation.

Float: A flat, rectangular wood or metal hand tool used for smoothing mortared surfaces

Flush: Having the same surface or plane as an adjoining surface.

Frost resistance: One of six ratings applied to ceramic tile and appearing on cartons in the form of a snowflake, indicating that the tile is suitable for exterior applications subject to freezing.

Gauged stone: Stone tile cut to uniform dimensions.

Glaze: A hard, most often colored layer of lead silicates and other materials fired to the surface of a tile. Used to protect and decorate the tile surface.

Grade: one of six ratings applied to ceramic tile, indicating its suitability for use in certain applications.

Granite: A naturally occurring stone composed of quartz and other minerals. Generally found in reds or browns.

Green bisque: clay that has not been fired (not a reference to its color).

Greenboard: A moisture-resistant drywall product made for wet installations, such as baths and showers. Greenboard is not waterproof.

Grit: An indication of the size of an abrasive particle, as in sandpaper. A 100-grit particle will pass through a grid with 1⁄100-inch holes.

Grout: A mortar mix used to fill the joints between set tiles. Available in many colors and in sanded or unsanded mixtures.

Grout float: A float with a soft rubber surface used to press grout into tile joints.

Hang: Describes the ability of an adhesive to hold a tile on a vertical surface while the adhesive is still wet.

Impervious tile: Tiles whose density resists completely the absorption of liquids. Generally used in hospitals, restaurants, and other commercial locations.

Inside corner: The plane on which walls or other surfaces form an internal angle.

Isolation membrane: A flexible sheet or liquid product applied to subsurface of a tile installation to allow cracks to expand under the tile without telegraphing into the surface.

Jamb: The surface of wood or other material on the immediate side or top and bottom of a door or window frame.

Joint compound: A plaster-like product used with paper or fiberglass mesh tape to conceal joints between drywall panels.

Latex-modified thinset: Thinset mortar mixed with latex additive to increase its flexibility, resistance to water, and adhesion.

Layout lines: Chalklines snapped to guide the placement of tile.

Level: Having all surfaces exactly on the same plane. Also describes a hand tool used to determine level.

Listello: Narrow tile formed for use in borders.

Marble: A naturally occurring hard variation of limestone marked with varied color and vein patterns.

Margin trowel: a narrow rectangular trowel used for mixing mortar and applying it in narrow spaces.

Masonry cement: A powdered mixture of portland cement and hydrated lime used for preparing mortar. Used to bind sand or other aggregate materials together.

Membrane: A sheet of protective material, such as felt paper or polyethelene applied to the substrate of a tiled surface, used either to waterproof it or contain cracks, or both.

Mexican paver: A handmade tile, generally low-fired or sun-dried and unglazed, characterized by blemishes, imperfections and irregular edges.

Mil: A measurement of thickness equal to one one-thousandth of an inch

Mortar: Any mixture of masonry cement, sand, water, and other additives. Also describes the action of applying mortar to surfaces or joints.

Mosaic tile: Any tile less than 2 inches, generally vitreous and made in squares or hexagons. Generally mounted on sheets or joined with adhesive strips.

Mud: Trade jargon for cement-based mortars, usually applied to installations where it is applied in a thick layer, as in shower stalls or in the brown and scratch coats of stucco.

Nippers: *See tile nippers.*

Nominal dimensions: The stated size of a tile, representing the ratio of one side to the other and usually including the width of its normal grout joint. Not necessarily the actual dimensions of the material. *See actual dimensions.*

Nonvitreous tile: Low density tile whose pores absorb liquids readily. Generally used indoors in dry locations.

Open time: The amount of time a mixed mortar can be used before it starts to set up.

Organic mastic: One of several petroleum or latex-based adhesives for setting tiles. Exhibits less strength, flexibility, and resistance to water than thinset adhesives.

Outside corner: The plane on which walls or other surfaces form an angle.

Particleboard: A sheet product made from compressed wood chips and glue. Not as durable and exhibits less screw-holding power than plywood of similar thicknesses.

Pavers: Any of several unglazed vitreous clay, shale, porcelain, or cement-bodied floor tiles, from ½- to 2-inches thick.

Penetrating sealer: A sealer that penetrates the pores of tile and grout to form a water- and stain-repellent layer.

Perimeter joint: An expansion joint around the edge of a surface, used to allow the material space in which to expand.

Permeability: A measure of the ability of a substance to transmit moisture.

Plumb: A surface that lies on a true vertical plane.

Plumb bob: A weight, typically pointed, suspended on a line or string, used to determine is a surface is truly vertical.

Poly: Industry jargon, short for polyethylene.

GLOSSARY *(continued)*

Polymer-modified: A substance like grout or mortar to which an acrylic or latex solution has been added to increase its strength and workability.

Porcelain: Any of several hard-bodied vitreous tiles fired from purified clay at very high temperatures.

Quarry tile: Unglazed, vitreous or semi-vitreous tiles, usually ¼- to ½-inch thick, most often used on floors.

Radius trim: A trim tile whose edge turns down to form a smooth, glazed border.

Retardant: A chemical added to grout or mortar to slow its curing process.

Ridge-backed tile: Tile with ridges on the back, made to increase the strength of the adhesive bond.

Rod saw: A tungsten-carbide blade with a rounded surface set in a standard hacksaw frame and used for cutting curves in tile.

Saltillo tile: A soft hand made tile dried in the sun instead of being fired.

Sanded grout: Grout containing sand, which increases the strength and decreases the contraction of the joint.

Screed: A long board, 2x 4 or 2x6, used to level a masonry surface.

Sealer: Any of several topical or penetrating products used as a protective coating on grout and unglazed tile surfaces.

Semi-vitreous tile: Tile of moderate density that exhibits only a partial resistance to water and other liquids.

Setting bed: Any mortared surface on which tile is set.

Set-up time: The amount of time an adhesive can be used before its chemicals reactions cause it to harden.

Shower Pan: The floor of a shower stall, which houses the drain. Can be a prefabricated unit or one poured and formed from mortar.

Slake: To allow a masonry mixture additional time after initial mixing. Allows the liquid to thoroughly penetrate the solids.

Slate: A naturally occurring stone composed of compressed shale deposits, generally rough-surfaced and grey or black.

Snap cutter: A bench-mounted tool consisting of a carbide scribing wheel and a pressure plate that cut straight cuts in tile by snapping it along a scribed line.

Spacers: Small plastic pieces, usually x-shaped, used to ensure consistent grout-joint width between tiles.

Square: Surfaces exactly perpendicular or at 90 degrees to another. Also describes a hand tool used to determine square.

Stone tile: Naturally occurring materials that are cut from quarries and sliced or hand split into thin sections for use as tile. Generally marble, granite, flagstone, and slate.

Straightedge: A length of metal or wood with a perfectly straight surface. Used to mark a straight line on material or to determine if edges or surfaces are on the same plane.

Subfloor: A layer of wood sheet material, generally plywood, used to provide a stable foundation for other flooring materials.

Substrate: Any of several layers, including the subfloor, beneath a tile surface.

Taping: Describes the process of applying paper or mesh tape to drywall joints in preparation for application of joint compound.

Terra cotta: A low-density tile made of unrefined natural clay and fired at low temperatures.

Terrazzo: Small pieces of granite or marble set in mortar often in a pictorial pattern, then polished.

Thin-set mortar: Generic term used to describe a wide range of mortar-based tile adhesives.

Tile nippers: A hand tool similar to a pliers but with levered jaws of hardened steel. Used for cutting small notches and curves in tile.

Toenail: Act of driving a nail at an angle to a surface when joining two pieces attached on dissimilar planes.

Trim tile: Tiles with at least one rounded or otherwise configured edge, used at corners or to define the edges of an installation. Common examples are cove trim, bullnose, V-cap, quarter-round, inside corners, and outside corners.

Trowel: Any of several flat and rectangular or pointed metal hand tools used for applying and smoothing adhesives and mortars.

Up angle: Describes a trim tile with one rounded edge used to finish an inside corner.

V-cap: V-shaped trim, often with a rounded upper corner, used to edge countertops.

Vitreous tile: An extremely dense ceramic tile with a high resistance to water absorption. Used indoors or outdoors, in wet or dry locations.

Waterproofing membrane: Any of several synthetic sheet materials used with or without adhesives to make a surface waterproof. Polyethylene and 15-pound. felt paper are common examples.

Wet saw: A high-speed power saw equipped with a water-cooled carbide blade used for making straight cuts in tile.

INDEX

Metric Conversions

U.S. Units to Metric Equivalents			**Metric Units to U.S. Equivalents**		
To convert from	**Multiply by**	**To get**	**To convert from**	**Multiply by**	**To get**
Inches	25.4	Millimeters	Millimeters	0.0394	Inches
Inches	2.54	Centimeters	Centimeters	0.3937	Inches
Feet	30.48	Centimeters	Centimeters	0.0328	Feet
Feet	0.3048	Meters	Meters	3.2808	Feet
Yards	0.9144	Meters	Meters	1.0936	Yards
Square inches	6.4516	Square centimeters	Square centimeters	0.1550	Square inches
Square feet	0.0929	Square meters	Square meters	10.764	Square feet
Square yards	0.8361	Square meters	Square meters	1.1960	Square yards
Acres	0.4047	Hectares	Hectares	2.4711	Acres
Cubic inches	16.387	Cubic centimeters	Cubic centimeters	0.0610	Cubic inches
Cubic feet	0.0283	Cubic meters	Cubic meters	35.315	Cubic feet
Cubic feet	28.316	Liters	Liters	0.0353	Cubic feet
Cubic yards	0.7646	Cubic meters	Cubic meters	1.308	Cubic yards
Cubic yards	764.55	Liters	Liters	0.0013	Cubic yards

To convert from degrees Fahrenheit (F) to degrees Celsius (C), first subtract 32, then multiply by 5⁄9.

To convert from degrees Celsius to degrees Fahrenheit, multiply by 9⁄5, then add 32.